Frank L. McVey and
the University of Kentucky

The Thomas D. Clark Studies in Education, Public Policy, and Social Change

SERIES EDITOR: Richard Angelo

This series is dedicated to the memory and example of Thomas D. Clark (1903–2004). The breadth and variety of Dr. Clark's contributions to historical understanding in the Commonwealth are unmatched, and he was a tireless advocate for the improvement of public education.

Sponsored by the University of Kentucky's College of Education in cooperation with the University Press of Kentucky, the series puts research on the Commonwealth in the spotlight, research that augments the understanding of national or regional developments or emphasizes the relevance of those same developments to the pace and direction of change here at home. While remaining open to a variety of methodological approaches, the overall aim of the series is to encourage an imaginative engagement with the tasks and opportunities that define the present.

Frank L. McVey
and the
University of Kentucky

———◆—◆———

A Progressive President and the Modernization of a Southern University

Eric A. Moyen

THE UNIVERSITY PRESS OF KENTUCKY

Editorial and Sales Offices: The University Press of Kentucky
663 South Limestone Street, Lexington, Kentucky 40508-4008
www.kentuckypress.com

15 14 13 12 11   5 4 3 2 1

Library of Congress Cataloging-in-Publication Data

Moyen, Eric Anthony, 1974–
  Frank L. McVey and the University of Kentucky : a progressive president and the
modernization of a southern university / Eric A. Moyen.
      p.   cm. — (Thomas D. Clark studies in education)
  Includes bibliographical references and index.
  ISBN 978-0-8131-2983-9 (hardcover : alk. paper) — ISBN 978-0-8131-2993-8 (ebook)
  1. McVey, Frank LeRond, 1869–1953. 2. University of Kentucky—Presidents—
Biography. 3. University of Kentucky—History—20th century. I. Title.
  LD2772.7.M38M69 2011
  378.769'47—dc22
  [B]

                          2010044907

This book is printed on acid-free recycled paper meeting
the requirements of the American National Standard
for Permanence in Paper for Printed Library Materials.

Manufactured in the United States of America.

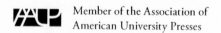

Member of the Association of
American University Presses

To President Lee Todd,
for a decade of leadership and service
to the University of Kentucky
and the commonwealth

Contents

Illustrations follow page 186

Series Editor's Foreword

If anyone opposed the nomination of Frank L. McVey as the University of Kentucky's new president in the summer of 1917, it has gone unrecorded. The Board of Trustees, like the search committee, was unanimous in its enthusiasm. And as Eric Moyen notes in this long-awaited and meticulously researched biography, once the offer was made official, the "normally prudent" McVey accepted "with uncharacteristic haste." At forty-seven, he was already well-known in reform circles, his impressive credentials capped most recently by a successful six-year stint as president of the University of North Dakota. But the ambitious McVey had also been scouting opportunities to leave Grand Forks for months—unfavorable changes in the state's political climate had seen to that—and Lexington proved to be just the ticket.

The selection of McVey's predecessor, Henry Stites Barker, had an altogether different character. Contention and delay marked the proceedings from the start. James K. Patterson, the outgoing president in 1909, had served the school with distinction since its founding as an A&M college forty years earlier and was vocal in his opposition. Against those who favored the appointment, the revered but imperious patriarch insisted that Barker was unqualified. Henry S. Pritchett, the influential first president of the Carnegie Foundation for the Advancement of Teaching, took the same view. And as if all this weren't enough, Barker, a widely respected lawyer and circuit court judge from Louisville, a longtime friend to Patterson, and a prominent member of the board since 1900, had reasons of his own to be reluctant. Finally, in June 1910, after five months of public silence and some backstage maneuvering, the stalemate ended. Convinced now that any one of the other potential candidates would make for an even worse choice, Patterson reluctantly swung his support to Barker. That was enough for the judge to accept the presidency, but only on the condition that his duties be postponed until the following January when his term on the appellate bench expired.

What began so inauspiciously came to a sad conclusion a few years later. In December of 1916, a special committee of the board was appointed to make a recommendation on a pending but controversial proposal to merge what were then two separate colleges—mechanical and civil engineering. However, that same committee was also charged with a more general responsibility: "to investigate . . . conditions causing or tending to produce discontent among the alumni and student body and general public toward the existing administration."

The result, a detailed report submitted to the board in early June, concluded with sixty-nine recommendations, the first of which read in part, "We are convinced that the welfare of the university and the State which it serves demand [Judge Barker's] retirement at an early date to make way for a professional educational administrator." Softening the blow only slightly, the report was quick to add that Barker "had been grievously sinned against in this matter," placed in the "impossible situation of being a captain of a ship without ever having studied navigation." The report's second recommendation was as hard-hitting as the first. In order "to prevent the annoying and thwarting of another president as President Barker had been annoyed and thwarted," it called for Patterson to vacate the seat on the Board of Trustees that he had continued to occupy since his retirement.[1]

McVey was an economist, a Yale PhD, better prepared than most to be "the captain of the ship." By the time he retired, he had engineered or supervised most of the reforms envisioned in the report that had paved the way for his arrival twenty-three years earlier. Bureaucratic procedures were firmly in place, campus facilities had been expanded and improved, and the colleges of education and agriculture now enjoyed new prominence in what had become a more highly diversified curricular environment. Academic professionalism—a commitment to graduate education and specialized research—had taken root in the ranks of a much larger faculty, and thanks in part to steady and dramatic increases in the annual number of graduates, the institution's reputation statewide was better than ever. Moyen salutes McVey as the University of Kentucky's founder, but he also makes it clear that it was not smooth sailing by any means. Even before the downturn brought on by the Great Depression, for example, McVey had to contend with repercussions at once political and budgetary resulting from the nation's first full-scale confrontation over the teaching of evolution. In the years that followed, he was regularly bested in the struggle for resources by the presidents of the other state-supported institutions. And while his difficulties in capturing the imagination of political leaders in Frankfort persisted, McVey also had to cope with students and alumni who saw athletics and social life as their only priorities, along with the often yawning indifference of the public itself.[2]

One finds solid institutional history here, to be sure, but there is more awaiting the reader than that. Moyen succeeds brilliantly as a biographer in bringing McVey to life, a task made all the more challenging by the man's temperament. He was devoted to a liberal-progressive politics; he worked tirelessly on behalf of the ideals of the university. He was committed to school reform as a means to social reform; to research and publication; to art, when he could find the time, because he loved to paint. But for all of his energy and imagination, McVey was notably self-contained, understated, emotionally reserved, even in childhood—not solemn by any means, but serious, businesslike. No one would ever call him colorful.

The dynamic and often surprising interplay between public and private unfolds across the span of McVey's long life in these pages, but never more poignantly, it seems to me, than in the episode centered on the death of his first wife, Mabel, and his subsequent marriage to Lexington native Frances Jewell. Mabel died in the spring of 1922. Had she lived, the evidence suggests the couple would have moved on, leaving Lexington just as they had left Grand Forks. But when Frank McVey fell in love again, this time with a woman twenty years his junior, he began to see his professional aspirations in a new light. Soon after the couple exchanged vows in November of 1923, it became apparent that he had also committed himself "for better or for worse" to the university and the state of Kentucky itself. Offers from other state universities would continue to come his way—from Missouri, from Ohio, from North Carolina—but he never expressed interest. In effect, Moyen concludes, he had torn up his résumé.[3] Decades later, in 1949, looking back from the vantage point of his retirement, McVey published *The Gates Open Slowly: A History of Education in Kentucky,* one more token of what had turned out to be his deep and lasting dedication to the future of the commonwealth and the prosperity of its people.

RICHARD ANGELO

Notes

1. For more on these episodes, see Hopkins, *University of Kentucky: Origins and Early Years* (1951), chapter 12, "The Close of Patterson's Reign"; Talbert, *University of Kentucky* (1965), chapter 4, "Sixty-Nine Recommendations." For the Investigating Committee report, see *Bulletin of the University of Kentucky* 9, no. 5 (1917): 18, 19 (quotations).

2. Student life had an altogether different silhouette, style, and tone in the decades before World War 1, however. See Morelock, *Taking the Town.*

3. Cf. Birdwhistell, "Educated Difference," especially chapter 2, "Our University Too: Frances Jewell and the Refinement of a Women's Sphere."

Acknowledgments

Long before my academic interest in Frank McVey and his role at the University of Kentucky, I had developed a personal affinity for the institution on an entirely different level. I grew up in a neighborhood bordering the southern edge of UK's campus, and my boyhood summers were spent traipsing across the rolling hills and through the woodlands that comprised part of the university's experiment station (now the arboretum). On Saturdays in the fall I peddled lemonade or hot chocolate (depending on the weather) to football fans as they walked to Commonwealth Stadium. As a teenager I spent countless summer nights playing basketball on the "blue courts" and wandered around campus observing "college life." These and other experiences engendered in me an understanding of something special about colleges in general and the University of Kentucky in particular.

This book is the result of a conversation between University of Kentucky president Lee Todd and Terry Birdwhistell, dean of the University of Kentucky Libraries. After they discussed the pivotal role Frank McVey played at the University of Kentucky and why a biography detailing his influence had not been written, both individuals approached me to see if I would be interested in such a project. Given my background in Lexington and my training in the history of higher education, I jumped at the chance to write this biography and to gain a deeper appreciation for the development of the University of Kentucky. I want to thank both of them for entrusting me with this task.

Despite my enthusiasm, it is fair to say that without the help of a small army of people, this book would not have come to fruition. Chief among these individuals is a small group of mentors under whom I had the privilege of studying during my time in graduate school. At the University of Kentucky, Richard Angelo, Terry Birdwhistell, and John Thelin all read copies of the manuscript and offered invaluable insights, questions, and constructive criticism. My advisor while I earned my master's degree at the University of Alabama, Forrest McDonald, and his wife, Ellen, also took time to read the manuscript and offer their own constructive criticism. The willingness of these individuals to go beyond any reasonable expectation of assistance is greatly appreciated.

Members of the Lee University faculty and staff also aided me in the process. Everyone from President Paul Conn to our office's student workers offered their support in numerous ways. I am particularly thankful to Dean Debbie Murray, who helped provide me with a secluded desk to work on the manuscript; Dean Matthew Melton, from the College of Arts and Sciences, who read a draft of the manuscript; and my department chair Bill Estes who has been a wonderful friend and mentor. It is fair to say that I have never come across a more collegial group of faculty members than those who constitute the teaching staff in Lee University's Helen DeVos College of Education. They have provided invaluable guidance and support, and I am so fortunate to work with such a group of colleagues.

I would be remiss if I did not take time to acknowledge the unusual "research assistant" who helped me on this book. The late UK historian Charles G. Talbert actually planned to write a biography of Frank McVey in the early 1970s. He passed away before ever beginning the manuscript, but the extensive notes that he took while researching were donated to University of Kentucky Special Collections. Talbert's notes gave me a substantial head start on this project. I am certain that he would have written a vastly different biography had he been afforded that opportunity. Many times during the past years I have wished that he and I would have had a chance to discuss our perspectives on McVey.

The staff members at the University Press of Kentucky have been wonderful partners in this process. I can't imagine an academic press being more helpful, supportive, and willing to aid a rookie historian on his first book project. Specifically, press director Stephen Wrinn graciously offered insight and advice at key points in the process. I am thankful to him for being more than just a professional colleague but a friend as well. Allison Webster, Ila McEntire, and Carol Sickman-Garner have helped guide this manuscript into book form, and I appreciate their efforts on my behalf.

Far more people helped in various ways. My mother, Mary Lu Moyen, an English grammarian extraordinaire, helped me with questions of syntax and footnote alignment. Many members of University of Kentucky Special Collections have used their expertise to help me with this project. Deirdre Scaggs, Doug Boyd, Frank Stanger, Nancy Demarcus, Matt Harris, Gordon Hogg, Ester Edwards, Mark V. Wetherington, and Anthony Day all offered me assistance during the past five years. I have also benefited from the labors of archivists whom I have never met in person. Curt Hanson at the University of North Dakota, Emily Haddaway at Ohio Wesleyan University, and Erin George at the University of Minnesota saved me hundreds of miles and many days by copying, scanning, e-mailing, and mailing me important information and documents for this project.

I owe my greatest debt of gratitude to my family, who sacrificed weeks of time together during what would have been much more leisurely faculty summers over the past half decade. My two daughters, Emmy and Anna Grace, don't even realize this yet, but they waited too long to learn how to ride a bike without training wheels and swim in the deep end of the pool without help because of my time away from them. My wife, Missy, graciously allowed "Frank" to become part of our family, and she took up far more than her fair share of responsibilities to provide me with the time and encouragement necessary to complete this book. As has been the case for our entire life together, she once again adopted my dreams as her own, and I am grateful beyond measure for her love, selflessness, and companionship.

Introduction

A Northern Progressive and
a Southern University

As the years go on the state university will become more and more
important to the people of the commonwealth because the people
will need the interpretations of social movements, the knowledge
and understanding of scientific investigation and discoveries, and the
benefit of trained personnel to carry out the purposes of the state.
—Frank LeRond McVey, 1936

Once a prominent figure in American higher education, Frank LeRond
McVey has become a rarely remembered former president of an aspiring
state university. At the University of Kentucky (UK) he is most often remembered as the husband of Frances Jewell McVey or as the president
who guided the university through the Great Depression. McVey has
largely been ignored by historians of American higher education. McVey's
relative obscurity, however, is not justified considering his significant influence among university leaders between the World Wars I and II.

As a university president from 1909 to 1940, McVey increased the
academic stature of two institutions. His seven years at the University of
North Dakota provided excellent preparation for McVey's tenure at UK.
He utilized his academic training, his government experience, and his
knowledge of higher education to lead a sometimes uninspired southern
state university to reach for higher goals. It was often a long, arduous, and
seemingly thankless task. His tireless efforts placed him among leading
university administrators, whom historian Frederick Rudolph character-

ized as possessing a "presidents' club psychology," in the sense that they "recognized one another as being caught up in a web of problems and purposes that was characteristic of all of them."[1]

Writing at the same time McVey assumed university leadership, Thorstein Veblen labeled this ubiquitous group of administrators "Captains of Erudition." These individuals attempted to combine the leadership of the academic enterprise with a model taken from captains of industry. Much of Frank McVey's leadership style resembled Veblen's characterization. Like most university presidents, McVey took a "businesslike" approach to campus administration. He became a "strong man" that the UK Board of Trustees allowed to have a "free hand" in organizing and managing the bureaucracy of an increasingly complex institution. Veblen disliked much of the competitive nature of this new business model, and his "captain" was in no way a term of endearment. However, he accepted the fact that "some such administrative machinery is a necessity in any large school that is to be managed on a centralized plan." Like McVey, the very best presidents demonstrated "scrupulous integrity," as they regularly found themselves in the spotlight, speaking not only to the academy but to the larger populace as they attempted to impart their vision of how higher education could better serve society.[2]

Veblen listed other, largely negative traits common to university presidencies that did not apply to McVey. First, McVey did not, as Veblen suggested of most presidents, "fall short of the average of their academic staff in scholarly or scientific attainments." Veblen also asserted that the captains of erudition had adopted an unfortunate frame of mind that was "solicitous of appearances, and peculiarly heedless of the substance of their performance." Unlike McVey, many presidents were far more interested in the perception of success than they were in building "substance" into academic programs. As such, they tended to "overstate their facilities for meeting all needs . . . [and] the measure of success which they actually enjoy[ed]." All of this, according to Veblen, was intended to gain them a competitive advantage over perceived rival institutions.[3]

Veblen conceded that a few individuals "with ingrained scholarly ideals and a consistent aim to serve the ends of learning will still occasionally be drawn into the executive office by force of circumstances." McVey was one such leader, which often placed him in stark contrast to the baser elements evident among many typical "captains of erudition." Upon McVey's arrival in Lexington, his scholarly record of research and publication far surpassed that of the average UK faculty member. The young president was also far more interested in actual academic improvement than he was in the false appearance of excellence. Because of this, he was far more likely to highlight UK's inadequacies than he was to tout its successes. He was the antithesis of certain presidents whom Veblen characterized as synonymous with "minor politicians who make a living by keeping well in the public eye and avoiding blame." Ironically, McVey's insistence on remaining above the political fray probably hindered his efforts. Certainly, the presidents of some of Kentucky's regional colleges wielded far more political clout than did McVey.[4]

As Veblen argued, the prestige for which many presidents fought was recognized among the "laity rather than with the scholarly classes." For McVey, this translated into a professional life of renown among leaders in the academy, but little formal acclaim among Kentuckians. Although McVey transformed UK from a struggling state college into a modern university, he received his greatest accolades outside of the commonwealth. During his tenure at UK, he was elected president of both the National Association of State Universities and the National Association of State Land-Grant Colleges and Universities. As president of the Southern Association of Colleges and Schools, he played a pivotal role in reforming that agency. He served as the first president of the Southeastern Conference and held numerous other significant posts in the field of higher education. Despite his prominent place among university executives of the era and his long list of successes, McVey's life and accomplishments have largely drifted into obscurity.[5]

To understand how and why this happened, McVey's life and career must be placed within the historiography of higher education. In his landmark study *The American University,* Laurence Veysey depicted an epic struggle of competing visions for the nature and structure of American higher education at the turn of the twentieth century. By 1910, however, this competition had ended as the vast majority of universities and their leaders adopted a generally agreed-upon vision of the research university and its role in American society. As such, academic architects were no longer needed to build great universities, only contractors to implement their blueprint. Frank McVey embraced the role of academic contractor. Imbued with a progressive vision of how state university research and expertise could aid home states, his goals were self-evident.[6]

However, architectural renderings rarely foresee, and often fail to understand, the untold challenges existing on the landscape being transformed. As historian David O. Levine suggested, the structure of higher education's future may have been established at a number of wealthy institutions, but "their contemporary influence remained limited." The "so-called elite universities [and their leaders] had less impact than historians, educators, and the public have assumed." Roger Geiger bolstered this argument by asserting that during the years of McVey's professional career, no more than two dozen universities were "seriously committed to research as an institutional goal." While these elite few turned from "parochial interests and clienteles into bureaucratic organizations integrated with national communications networks," hundreds of other institutions had not yet evolved in this manner.[7]

McVey came to realize this about Kentucky. Instead of finding a commonwealth poised to embrace a modern state university with an enhanced public mission, McVey found a rural, agriculture-based society suspicious of centralization. Deeply held loyalties to localism, traditionalism, and anti-intellectualism provided inherent opposition to reform by Kentuckians who seemed hell-bent on refusing McVey's vision for their university.

In this way, McVey's story partially fits with Clyde Barrow's neo-Marxist critique of higher education in that era, Barrow asserting that "there were bitter political contests over how modern universities would fulfill their changing historical mission by responding to the needs of an industrial democracy." Barrow lamented the way in which administrators succumbed to a dominant "corporate liberalism" that sought to "control the means of mental production" by censoring more radical elements of the academy who criticized the evils of capitalism. Barrow actually identi-

fied McVey and the way in which he sought to ameliorate powerful capitalist interests in North Dakota by refusing to defend the political actions
of a left-leaning faculty member. He also noted McVey's comment that
wise university presidents would avoid hiring radical faculty members
who might offend board members and harm a university's relationship
with a state legislature.[8]

In many other ways, McVey's story remains at the periphery of Barrow's history. Barrow highlighted the power exerted by private funding
agencies (the Carnegie Foundation for the Advancement of Teaching and
the General Education Board), as they subsidized research at leading U.S.
universities by requiring such institutions to match, or even double, grant
allocations. Like most universities, UK was not one of the fortunate institutions. Of the more than $300 million distributed by private funding
agencies during the first three decades of the twentieth century, nearly
three-quarters of it went to only twenty institutions. Those left out of the
funding largess, like McVey and UK, found that supporting "competitive
research" was so costly that most schools "simply could not compete in
scholarship or graduate education." McVey's struggles at the University of
Kentucky are representative of the struggles at hundreds of similar institutions that comprised the "proletariat" of higher education—an example of
how the other 90 percent survived. As a whole, they possessed the lion's
share of college students in the United States, even though they did not
receive the financial support offered to the wealthier institutions.[9]

Roger Geiger elaborated on this, noting that private funding agencies
implemented an elitist agenda to make the strong universities even stronger. He highlighted the General Education Board's plan to "make the
peaks higher," which created immense challenges for the less prestigious
but aspiring institutions. The national powerbrokers in higher education
knew McVey and liked him, often recommending him for various executive posts in higher education. Nevertheless, he remained the president of
an institution that found itself on the outside looking in. McVey desperately wanted support from national foundations, and he desired their approval. This was illustrated by his attempts to have UK invited to become
a member of the American Association of Universities. Instead, it was not

the foundations that controlled UK, but the people, who were suspicious of a liberal president and his policies.[10]

A quintessential progressive administrator in a conservative state, McVey faced his challenges directly. He sought to create a university that not only trained Kentucky's leaders but also worked to solve the commonwealth's social and economic problems. Constantly pushing for greater efficiency, he believed that UK faculty could materially improve the lives of Kentuckians if given sufficient resources. McVey's Kentucky experience mirrored what historian William Link identified as the "paradox of southern progressivism." According to Link, southern progressives faced challenges from "traditionalists" who held a competing vision of the nature and aims of democracy, the role of government and public education, and reform efforts generally. Like other progressives in the South whom Link described, McVey "believed in, even revered, majoritarian democracy." Yet he felt compelled to "persuade an otherwise contented, largely rural population of the urgency of reform and of the need to end the traditional means of governance." McVey would declare, "The modified social state that is upon us requires a conversion of the citizen from his old view founded on the let alone procedure to one from which he looks at the state as constituted of all of us. Some of us carry out the will of all of us for the common good."[11]

As McVey attempted to carry out the common good, he faced a unique challenge. He was an outsider—a Yankee progressive in a southern state. McVey had earned his PhD in economics at Yale under the direction of Arthur Hadley, who would eventually become president of that institution. As a young professor at the University of Minnesota, he became a productive scholar, writing books and articles on industrialization, government, and economic systems. As director of Minnesota's tax commission he sought to modernize the state's tax codes. He returned to the academy as president of the University of North Dakota. In 1917, however, his ambition would lead him south to Kentucky, where he sought to implement his modern vision of higher education.

Kentucky's entrenched conservatism delayed the hiring of a progressive administrator for its flagship university until much later than many other southern states. In his study of southern state universities, Michael Dennis concluded that after World War I, southern state universities remained poorly financed and "academically undistinguished," but they had become "institutions closely connected to an emergent bureaucratic state and deeply involved in the social life of the South." Kentucky proved to be an exception. Upon arriving in 1917, McVey found an institution stifled under the continuing influence of an aging president emeritus who still stressed "liberal culture and mental discipline," concepts that had long before succumbed to more modern visions of the university not only in the North but in the South as well.[12]

It was the struggle between traditional education and progressive reform that made McVey's story so intensely local. The national trends that so influenced McVey's worldview held little currency in the Bluegrass. His life's work became providing a foundation for Kentuckians to appreciate more fully the modern state and the university's place in the present and future of the commonwealth. While McVey never turned away from the national stage, he came to understand that Kentucky was his life's work. After nearly twenty years on the job in Kentucky, he wrote, "I hope somebody will be interested in this diary, but I am afraid it will be too local and too personal. Local in the sense that the doings are confined pretty much to the University and the state and personal because I am a part of the university."[13]

More than seven decades later, it is apparent that McVey's focus was not a weakness, but a strength. Despite McVey's role in various national organizations, the story of his leadership is, in large measure, inextricably tied to the story of the University of Kentucky. For historians, it serves to highlight how a struggling land-grant institution fared in its endeavor to replicate the accepted pattern of university development. In reality, most state institutions experienced the same growing pains as UK, rather than simple emulation of elite universities. Similarly, the vast majority of students who attended state schools found themselves at institutions like UK, not at the nation's elite universities. As Geiger noted, by the mid-1920s only 8 percent of American college students attended universities that possessed the resources to qualify for grants from the General Education Board, an agency that distributed millions of dollars to help expand higher education. Hence, the value of McVey's story is in the fact that it helps further an understanding of the diversity and complexity of American higher education during the first half of the twentieth century.[14]

McVey's biography remains relevant to higher-education officials across the nation as well as policymakers in Kentucky today as they strive to implement the commonwealth's own mandate to make UK a top-twenty state research university. Frank McVey's presidency reveals that themes from the past are still linked to present-day challenges. In reviewing UK's historic challenges, one might be reminded of William Faulkner and his oft-quoted remark that "the past is never dead, it isn't even the past." McVey's struggles in the first half of the twentieth century still exist today. His story remains the story of the University of Kentucky. His vision has never been fully attained, and the outcome still remains in doubt. It remains up to Kentucky's leaders and the citizens of the commonwealth to determine whether McVey's hopes and aspirations for the University of Kentucky will finally be realized nearly a century after his arrival in Lexington.

Chapter 1

The Making of a Progressive President

1869–1917

It is time to recognize the fact that a university is a great latent force that can be utilized in many directions. It ought to be closely related to every department of the state. It should be the medium through which statistics are gathered, information collected, advice given, problems solved, in fact a real part of the state government.
—Frank LeRond McVey, 1910

Education is the creation of an attitude of mind which is characterized by fairness, openness, and willingness both to receive, and to undertake the search for, the truth.
—Frank LeRond McVey, 1915

Frank LeRond McVey was an Ohio Buckeye by birth. His lengthy career as president of a southern state university and a nationally prominent figure in higher education would prove far more noteworthy than his birthplace and the events of his youth. However, his upbringing in a progressive Republican family in the Midwest left indelible marks upon his worldview. Furthermore, the personalities of both of his parents imprinted distinguishing characteristics on his disposition for the remainder of his personal life and professional career.

Alfred Henry McVey and Priscilla Ann Holmes (Anna) of Ohio were married in January 1869, and the following November Anna gave birth to their first son, Harry McVey. After a short while Anna decided she disliked the name Harry, and the couple changed the baby's name to Frank LeRond McVey. Frank McVey and his four younger siblings lived a generation removed from the farm or manual labor, a trend that would become increasingly common but was still relatively rare in the nineteenth-century Midwest.[1]

At home Frank benefited from the advantage of well-educated parents. Alfred McVey had graduated from Ohio Wesleyan University and opened a law practice in Wilmington, Ohio, where he became increasingly involved in corporate law. His entrance into the legal affairs of railroads placed him squarely in the midst of the greatest transportation revolution the nation had seen. Alfred's work required a move from Wilmington to Toledo, where the family remained for a decade. Hard times, however, forced them to sell their house on the outskirts of town and move into an area of Toledo populated primarily by working-class immigrant families. Although Frank had the good fortune of growing up in a well-educated family, the McVeys did not lead an overwhelmingly elite or privileged lifestyle. In 1883, the McVeys moved to Des Moines, where Alfred built a successful law practice, arguing cases at different levels of the federal court system. The McVeys made Des Moines their home, and Frank spent the remainder of his childhood in Iowa.[2]

Alfred McVey's personality, education, and career certainly influenced young Frank, as his scholarly interests later revealed. Alfred McVey's granddaughters described him as a sweet individual possessing great charm. Frank's brother Edmund McVey remembered their father as being rather reserved. Certainly, Alfred loved learning and attempted to instill the same love in his children. After dinner, he spent many nights around the table reading books to them. During the family's more difficult financial times, Alfred worked hard to purchase books and hide them from his more practical and disapproving wife.[3]

Frank's mother stood in stark contrast to Alfred. The daughter of a successful Ohio farmer and part-time preacher, Anna Holmes McVey had graduated from Xenia Female College before getting married. Edmund described his mother as a serious woman who had no sense of humor. Even her granddaughters remembered her as humorless and strict. Others who knew her gave virtually the same description, using terms like "Quakerish" and "Puritanical" to portray her. Everyone feared her because "she was very tart." A devoutly religious woman, Anna had the family read from the Bible each evening before bedtime. The McVeys attended a Methodist church wherever they lived, and two of Frank's brothers became ministers.[4]

The differing personalities of Frank's parents greatly affected his personality and the way in which the future leader would interact with those around him. He adopted his father's work ethic and love of books, but his mother had molded his temperament. One of McVey's nieces later commented that Frank's parents' contrasting personalities had produced a "very austere" individual "of whom everybody was pretty much afraid." Frank exhibited a no-nonsense personality and temperament, displaying a pensive disposition even as a young boy. As his brother noted, "Frank was older, seemingly older than his years justified."[5]

Despite his stern disposition, Frank experienced the joys and frustrations of an average midwestern boyhood. Frank's younger brothers worked for an individual who provided soap and towels to local businesses in the Des Moines manufacturing district. Each day they stopped by their patrons' establishments to sell more soap and pick up old towels. The family horse, Exeter, became so accustomed to the route that he automatically stopped there even when it was not necessary, causing Frank to suffer significant embarrassment while on dates with his girlfriend. The horse's behavior frustrated Frank's attempts to hide the fact that his brothers worked at such a job to earn extra cash, revealing the extent to which he aspired to a different lifestyle.[6]

Frank and his siblings spent a great deal of time outdoors. After moving to Toledo, they often returned to Wilmington for extended periods of time. Their vacations frequently included family hunting trips and camping excursions. These experiences in nature set a precedent for young Frank, and later in his life he would continue to take weeks at a time to wander in the outdoors. Summers allowed for such recreation; the rest of the year revolved around education.[7]

Frank attended public schools in both Toledo and Des Moines—

primary school in the former and high school in the latter. His brother Edmund intimated that the McVey brothers struggled socially when they were in school in Toledo. The immigrant children at their school were, according to Edmund, older and bigger, and "consequently we had rough times at school." At the same time that Frank and his brother were struggling socially, they also faced trying times in the classroom. One of Frank's few journal entries concerning school, which he penned later in his life, offered a melancholy remembrance, Frank recalling that he "stood in line to recite and [was] punished with the ruler for small offenses." [8]

Frank's school experiences, however, did not stifle his love of learning. His father took every opportunity to instill his love of books in his children. Besides reading to them around the table at night, he spent time with his children outside reading poetry about nature. Alfred's efforts proved successful. At an early age Frank read dime novels, which had been forbidden, and fell in love with Coffin's *Boys of 76, Robinson Crusoe,* and *Swiss Family Robinson,* as well as numerous history texts. Frank later recalled that his father's library was rather extensive for the time, and he also took advantage of the Des Moines public library. [9]

After graduating from high school, Frank remained in Iowa and took classes for a year at Des Moines College. He then decided to leave home and follow in his father's footsteps at Ohio Wesleyan University (OWU) in Delaware, Ohio. Frank noted that he attended college primarily because "my father was a college man and had in mind a professional training for his son." Despite McVey's previous postsecondary coursework, Ohio Wesleyan still classified him as a freshman. This apparent setback proved advantageous to Frank, providing him with a younger cohort with whom he would spend the next years forging lasting relationships. [10]

During his first year at Ohio Wesleyan, McVey immersed himself in collegiate life, living as a typical nineteenth-century "college man." His myriad pursuits included intramurals, active membership in the Phi Gamma Delta fraternity, and participation in a literary society, among other things. This traditional collegiate experience also included regular visits to the chapel, along with morning devotionals. Since the curriculum stressed the classics and included Greek and Latin, other course options were limited. With such a relatively prescribed curriculum, it would not be until later in his collegiate career that McVey actually chose a profession to pursue.[11]

Outwardly, Frank appeared to be living the life of the privileged college man of the day, but his family was not, as his brother put it, "over possessed with money." In fact, Edmund McVey had dropped out of high school to work, and his parents demanded nearly his entire paycheck for family expenditures. Although the details are not entirely clear, Frank was not able to continue at Ohio Wesleyan for his sophomore year. His brother stated that "he hadn't behaved himself at college. . . . He was spending too much money, or so my dad thought." Janet McVey Hall concurred, noting that he originally dropped out of college because of family financial problems. However, she did not suggest that poor behavior had anything to do with Frank's leaving the institution.[12]

In order to make ends meet, Frank began looking for teaching positions. The small town of Orient in western Iowa (Adair County), with a population of about three hundred, was looking for both a teacher and a principal for its local high school. Frank sought the position, and the board agreed to hire him. Frank enjoyed immediate success, and by the end of the semester the county superintendent of schools had granted him a teaching certificate. The school attempted to renew his contract after his first year, but Frank declined the offer and eventually returned to OWU.[13]

During this second tenure McVey became a much more focused student. Deeply inspired by a series of symposia concerning labor problems and political economy, he decided upon an academic field to pursue. Regarding these lectures, McVey later wrote, "I gathered some very clear views relative to many problems that had been exceedingly vague in my mind." Having chosen economics, McVey began devouring texts on the subject. Thus, within a matter of two years, he had answered two essential questions concerning the life that lay ahead of him: "One, as to my calling [education], and the other as to the specific thing that I should undertake to teach [economics]."[14]

In addition to his coursework and extracurricular activities, Frank discovered romance. He proposed to Helen Irwin near the end of his se-

nior year but apparently did not inform his family of their engagement. It
was only when his brother decided to visit Frank that Edmund learned of
his plans to marry. Helen then invited both Edmund and Frank McVey
to visit her family during the following Christmas break at her family's
vacation home near Jacksonville, Florida.[15]

Frank's first priority, however, was to find a teaching job for the next
year. He secured letters of recommendation from professors at Ohio Wesleyan, as well as from the university's president, J. W. Bashford, who described Frank as "a young man of fine abilities and fine mental training.
. . . He is a young man of superior Christian character and will succeed
admirably as a teacher." Despite such letters of recommendation, Frank
had not found a job by commencement. This was due in part to the severe
economic depression of the 1890s. The resultant job market led many college graduates, including McVey, into graduate school.[16]

The financial crisis also began to accentuate political distinctions,
which had been latent for decades. Frank's parents were staunch Republicans. However, Frank's political views had developed in the heart of the
Gilded Age, when party affiliation was more important for patronage
than for policy. Differences on issues such as the tariff existed, but national candidates tended to evade questions that would alienate constituents. During the Gilded Age leadership came not from Washington, but
from business giants in the rapidly expanding cities of the industrial
Northeast. The lack of federal regulation resulted in uneasy economic
times for laborers and farmers, and in 1893 the bubble burst, giving greater momentum to the Populist Party.

In the midst of this fiscal and political turmoil, McVey moved to New
Haven, Connecticut, to pursue a PhD in economics at Yale. One could
hardly imagine a more significant time in the nineteenth century to be
involved in the study of the nation's political economy. Less than a decade
earlier, in 1885, economists had first organized into a national professional association. By the mid-1890s, economic issues were paramount for
those inside and outside the academy. National debate raged concerning
the role of government in the regulation of big business and supplying a
steady currency for the public. McVey immersed himself in his studies at

Yale. Unlike he had during his undergraduate years, he concentrated almost entirely on his academic pursuits. He took full advantage of the opportunity to study with influential individuals in the academy, including Charles Schwab, an editor of the *Yale Review,* and noted scholar William Graham Sumner. Arthur Hadley, professor of political economy and the future president of Yale, directed his dissertation.

After Frank's first semester the McVey brothers traveled to Florida to visit Frank's fiancée, Helen. Having little money, they paid about fifteen dollars each to ride a fruit boat to Jacksonville. Hoping for warm weather, they arrived during an unprecedented cold spell. Apparently, Frank's visit with Helen did not go as planned either. Sometime shortly after the holidays Helen broke off their engagement. Upon reading of Helen's death a half century later, Frank wrote in his diary, "As I look back over this engagement it seems to me to have been just as well. Miss Irwin was a fine woman, but our backgrounds and interests were rather wide apart." In actuality their interests were not especially disparate. After graduating from Ohio Wesleyan, Helen Irwin went on to work with Jane Addams before moving to Cleveland, where she focused on early childhood education. Whatever the details of their breakup, the stoic McVey pressed on with his graduate studies and succeeded with distinction.[17]

After a year of classes at Yale, McVey focused on his dissertation. In 1894 Arthur Hadley suggested that McVey examine the Populist movement, noting, "You could connect it with your studies in money, or with my course on corporations." McVey followed Hadley's advice and managed to complete his PhD in two years. Frank wrote *The Populist Movement* in the spring of 1895, and the following year the Macmillan Company published it for the American Economic Association. This work was one of the first major academic studies of the third party, published at a point when the nascent movement's fate was not yet clear. The Populists had celebrated successful gains in the 1892 presidential election and the midterm elections of 1894, but they had not yet suffered the disappointing defeats coming in 1896.[18]

Although McVey's political and economic views would evolve over the decades, this early study, like the research of many graduate students, mirrored the intellectual ideas of his more conservative professors at Yale. McVey criticized the Populist platform, arguing that state ownership of the railroads was a move for political power, rather than a reform meant to aid Americans. He found the party's platform to be based on discontentment, an emotion leading to "absurdity" in policy, and void of a larger constitutional philosophy. Rather than state control, discontented citizens needed to advance the cause of government regulation. If they did not, McVey correctly predicted, the party would fail, as the two-party system would incorporate a moderate version of the proposed reforms.[19]

McVey's work impressed his professors, and the faculty members who knew Frank and his work best endorsed him without reservation. Arthur Hadley noted, "His work has been unusually good. I am confident that any institution which secures his services as an instructor will add at once to the efficiency of its teaching work as well as to its outside reputation." William Graham Sumner, in an almost prophetic tone, stated, "I think he is qualified to fill an important position in any college. . . . His personal traits are all such as to qualify him for great success in this kind of work."[20]

For a time it appeared that his professors were so impressed that they might keep him on at Yale. While completing his dissertation in the spring of 1895, he thought he had secured a position at Yale, but it was snatched away from him. Arthur Hadley then attempted to keep McVey in New Haven with a modest salary as an assistant professor. McVey agreed to stay, but before the year was out, mathematics professor Irving Fisher expressed his desire to transfer to the Economics Department, and the university allowed him to do so. With Fisher's salary as an experienced professor, Hadley was out of departmental money, and McVey was out of a job. Frank later opined in his diary, "If I had stayed on in New Haven life would have been very different and probably not so pleasant. Who can tell?"[21]

Without a faculty position waiting, the twenty-six-year-old PhD moved to New York City and began freelance writing and research for the Reform Club. During the fall of 1895 he traveled thousands of miles throughout the Northeast, interviewing more than three hundred individuals in sixty-one towns. His labors resulted in a pamphlet for the Committee on Sound Currency, entitled "Quality of Money and Wages." McVey, however, did not view this job as a viable long-term option, and he continued searching for a teaching position.[22]

Within a year, McVey had accepted a nonfaculty position in the Teachers College at Columbia University, beginning as an instructor of history in the Horace Mann School. When he learned that this laboratory school had a vacancy for the spring term in 1896, McVey originally balked, noting, "Two reasons keep me from accepting it, a preference for the West to New York City, and the fact that it is not college work." McVey's dissertation director, however, viewed the post as a means to secure a faculty position in the near future. He wrote McVey to congratulate him on receiving the position and added, "I . . . trust that it may only be the stepping stone toward a better one." McVey eventually accepted the post and was invited back for another year at the end of his term of service. However, other opportunities had developed, and McVey pursued them. Still, his brief tenure had provided gainful employment, and in the future he would add his stint at the Teachers College of Columbia University to his résumé.[23]

In the fall of 1895, while he was working for the Reform Club, McVey had applied for a position at the University of Minnesota. William Graham Sumner and Arthur Hadley wrote letters of recommendation to William Fowell, then a professor of political science at Minnesota, each providing some insight into McVey's personality. Sumner stated that McVey gave great satisfaction by his "zeal and industry," adding, "He is a man of very sound character and grave manners." Hadley commented upon McVey's capacity in "setting others at work." Fowell remained interested in McVey, and the two corresponded occasionally while McVey worked in New York.[24]

This correspondence between McVey and Fowell revealed the way McVey's views on economics were becoming more progressive. In one letter to Fowell, McVey stated, "My association with Professor Sumner had given a wrong idea of my views on the tariff." After stating that he had arrived at Yale as a "protectionist," he added, "I left Yale with a better idea of the theories of free trade, but also with a recognition of the practical side of protection. . . . I am not an extremist." McVey wrote that as an economics professor dealing with controversial issues, he would "endeavor to bring the merits of each before the student without bringing in the personal equation. By that I mean an honest effort to present the merits of both sides without urging the acceptance of either one." Of course, McVey would not actually be so altruistic. Two years later he expressed his frustrations with the economic views held by many in the business community when he commented that he found businessmen "bright and prosperous but with wrong economic ideas." He added, "The men were a study to me. I got a good deal out of it, but I was impressed with the great tasks professors of economics have on their hands to get the right ideas in the minds of the people."[25]

McVey finally received a telegraphed offer from Fowell in the spring of 1896. He accepted the professorship in economics, although he complained about the one-thousand-dollar salary, noting that his teaching position at the Horace Mann School paid about 20 percent more. "Two hundred dollars," he wrote, "is quite an item to me and not such a large one to the university." Still, he thanked Fowell for the offer and added that he looked forward to hearing from him soon.[26]

After accepting the professorship, McVey returned to Des Moines for the summer to spend time with his family. His correspondence with Fowell during the summer demonstrated McVey's rather forceful personality. In May, he again noted his frustration with the salary that he had accepted, hoping that the Board of Regents would reconsider. He was also concerned with the classes he would be assigned and their sizes. He argued for smaller sections, commenting that they provided opportunity for discussion rather than simple dissemination of facts. He suggested textbooks, as well as curricular changes in the economics sequence. In later letters he continued along these same lines and asked if he would be made chair of the Economics Department. By the time the young professor arrived in Minneapolis, Fowell was well-informed concerning McVey's opinions.[27]

McVey moved to the University of Minnesota at a time when it was growing in prestige and stature. Under President Cyrus Northrup's leadership, the university had expanded course offerings, increased student enrollment, and attracted highly qualified professors. McVey was one of many promising faculty members hired by Northrup as he sought to build a first-rate university. He and Fowell served as the only two members of the Economics Department, and the new professor made an immediate impact by implementing progressive teaching methods in the classroom. He also worked with the Political Science Department, which offered classes in politics and economics.[28]

McVey's progressivism extended beyond the classroom. By his second year he had begun delivering lectures to local social service organizations. In 1898 he became the president of Minneapolis Associated Charities. In this position he helped organize various charities and the services they offered, gave lectures addressing ways to improve social conditions, and linked town and gown by getting students involved in service work in Minneapolis. He published numerous articles in professional journals and wrote a text entitled *The Government of Minnesota,* which served as a handbook explaining the functions of government at various levels within the state and helped solidify McVey's growing influence.[29]

Beyond McVey's professional and civic activities, he again found time for romance. Mabel Sawyer was a student at Minnesota who lived a few doors down from McVey's residence. (Mabel also became friends with Frank's sister Kate, who attended the university.) By Christmas 1897, Mabel was collecting McVey's mail while he was away for the holidays, and McVey's first hints of affection appeared when he wrote that he hoped to see her before she left for a brief vacation at the beginning of 1898. As events unfolded, McVey apparently adopted the advice of his former roommate and lifelong friend Fred Rector, who suggested, after learning of McVey's original broken engagement, that "if you ever fall in love again, close matters up without much delay."[30]

When McVey returned for the spring semester in 1898, the courtship began in earnest. He frequently asked Mabel to spend time visiting with him, reading weighty academic texts. In one letter McVey stated, "It will be nine or a little after before I come down. I will bring a heavy book called *Distribution of Wealth* for us to read. I think you will enjoy it, dearie." Frank's more romantic suggestions included riding bicycles and taking walks, but his work often took time away from the courtship. He lamented, "The boys wish me to criticize a debate for them this evening so that I will not get down to the house until about 9:20. It is my duty dearie."[31]

In June 1898 Mabel Sawyer graduated with a degree in literature, and immediately the couple began planning their wedding. As they settled on a date, their letters took on a sensual tone. Mabel began calling Frank her "naughty boy" and recalled the more romantic moments from their previous months together. In one letter she teased, "I have missed you already as much as if you had been gone the full month my nice old naughty-boy! Don't you wish you could see how well I am looking after a full night's sleep and an afternoon nap too? . . . Oh how I wish I were in Des Moines now and sitting beside Frank in the very same hammock where he did something so very daring." The usually reserved Frank reciprocated in kind: "I am getting accustomed to our exile but there is constantly present the old longing to hold you in my arms and to kiss you Mabel, to look possibly at the pretty legs, to see you again." Frank addressed the sexual aspects of a relationship in a rather professorial tone: "Custom and ways of thinking these days have made us all prudes and when any attempt is made to talk of ourselves people act foolishly. . . . When we come to talk of these things my Mabel I don't want you to shrink from them."[32]

After getting married in September 1898, McVey became more involved in church affairs. As with his views on economics, higher education, and government regulation, McVey's views on religion had evolved from his rather conservative background to become those of a liberal reformer. For example, he wrote Mabel, upset that ministers were wasting their opportunities to speak on crucial issues such as ethics and justice, noting, "The people are anxious for light and leadership. As I see it the pulpit has not given it to them." He concluded, "There is a sort of struggle between what I would term the old and new Christianity that is Christianity with and without science."[33]

Viewing himself as a reformer in this church struggle, McVey broke

with his parents' Methodism and joined a Presbyterian church in Minneapolis. One semester he led the congregation's college-age Sunday-
school class, adopting the theme "Modern Apostles of Social Reform."
The class examined the views of such progressives as Jean Rousseau, Robert Owen, Karl Marx, William Lloyd Garrison, and Arnold Toynbee.
McVey also gave many of the Sunday-evening sermons at Andrews Church
and served as a visiting preacher for other congregations. His Sunday-
evening sermon titles included "Organized Charity," "Can the Church
Do Anything for the Laboring Man?" "The Church and City Life," and
"Economic Functions of the Church."[34]

Despite his involvement in local religious affairs, McVey was not satisfied with the surrounding religious landscape. Attending a service in Phil-
adelphia, McVey remarked, "I received yesterday . . . a spiritual awakening.
No grander service or more inspiring sermon have I ever heard than that
yesterday afternoon. It was in the Episcopal Church. The music was more
than grand, it was actually religious." He continued, "It affected me greatly and I am sure toned me up spiritually, something I needed dreadfully."
At home he continued to face frustrations.[35]

McVey's progressive views extended beyond religion and into his academic studies as well. As would be expected of a forward-looking social
scientist at the beginning of the twentieth century, McVey looked for ways
to apply his area of expertise to social-improvement efforts. He traveled
widely in conjunction with his research. His hard work resulted in greater
recognition at the university, as well as in the larger academy. At Minnesota he was promoted to full professor in 1900. The following year David
Starr Jordan, the president of Stanford, wrote to inform him of his nomination for a professorship in economics at the young but well-endowed
institution, but the position fell through. He was elected to the Council of
the American Economic Association the same year, and he continued to
expand his service involvement in the Twin Cities.[36]

The good fortune McVey experienced professionally at the turn of the
century did not always extend to his personal life. In April 1901 Mabel
gave birth to a son who died during his first week of life. Frank's father,
Alfred, offered his condolences and wisdom: "Such bereavements are hard

to bear but much easier than if the little fellow had lived a year or more and had entwined himself permanently in our lives and affections." In addition, he offered advice: "I hope you and Mabel will bravely bear up under this your first trial. . . . Lay the little one away as quietly and as quickly as possible and disturb Mabel as little as possible." All recorded evidence (or lack thereof) suggests that both Frank and Mabel did just that. No correspondence between the two discussing the loss exists, nor does any discussion in McVey's journal. Fortunately, Mabel gave birth to a healthy child, Virginia, on 23 February 1903. Less than two years later son Frank Jr. was born. Mabel then gave birth to their third and final child, Janet, in 1906.[37]

The McVeys' growing family did not deter Frank from expanding his professional endeavors. Apart from the numerous articles McVey had been publishing for scholarly journals, he remained active in local civic affairs. His research, along with his civic activism, resulted in his acceptance of a position as the director of the "Twin City Municipal Exhibit" for the 1904 World's Fair in St. Louis, which required a great deal of his time and energy. Preparations for the World's Fair exhibit seemed to be going well until McVey faced a minor fracas with civic leaders from St. Paul's Commercial Club. Their frustrations did not result from the exhibit itself, but from errors in an entry McVey had penned for the *Encyclopedia Britannica*. The article contained omissions and factual errors, including the statement that Minneapolis was the state's capital, which incited protests from some St. Paul residents. In response, the club requested that McVey be removed not only from his post as director of the World's Fair exhibit but from the university as well because of his "scandalous falsehoods" and "willful misrepresentations."[38]

Such vitriol suggested the serious tension between the Twin Cities, which existed long before McVey's entry in the encyclopedia. Publicly, McVey defended himself in the local papers by arguing that the errors and deletions were the result of the editing process and no fault of his own. The encyclopedia agreed to make changes to the entry in its next edition. Privately, McVey pleaded with one of his friends on the other side of the Mississippi River to help "quiet some of the animosity" from St. Paul.[39]

While McVey worked feverishly on the World's Fair exhibit, he also entertained thoughts of leaving the Twin Cities for the South. A position opened when Charles Dabney announced his resignation as president of the University of Tennessee in Knoxville in order to take the helm at the University of Cincinnati. McVey immediately solicited the assistance of others in recommending him for Dabney's job. Cyrus Northrup obliged, writing that McVey possessed "much experience in dealing with men and although he is not probably much more than thirty years of age he is remarkably mature in appearance and manner." Northrup added that the young professor possessed "executive force [and] would do credit to your institution and make its work a success." This letter showed the extent to which McVey had made a favorable impression at Minnesota.[40]

McVey also asked his friend Martin Hardy, serving as a minister in Charlotte, North Carolina, to pass along transcripts of speeches that McVey had made, as well as an advance copy of his book *Modern Industrialism*.[41] While Hardy subsequently attempted to use his connections with individuals at Tennessee, Frank tried to use his influence to help Hardy return north to a church in Chicago. Although McVey was not offered the post at Tennessee, one of his letters on behalf of Hardy to an individual in Chicago revealed McVey's views of the South and the work he desired to accomplish there. Discussing Hardy, McVey commented that "the backwardness" of the region had "rather affected his point of view and perhaps given him a sense of the great difficulty that he must be confronted with . . . in the South."[42]

In 1904 D. Appleton Co. published McVey's most influential work to that point, *Modern Industrialism*. Although McVey had been a prolific author of journal articles, this book brought him acclaim as an economist with a national reputation in his field. Just as important, in an era of great debate over the relationship between industry and government, this work placed McVey squarely in the progressive camp. *Modern Industrialism* surveyed the history of industrial growth in England, Germany, and the United States, and the final section of the text examined the current levels of government regulation of private business. McVey concluded that in the United States problems surrounding industrialization required that the government renounce its historically laissez-faire stance and take a more active regulatory role. He recognized, however, that "it is clearly demonstrated that we must have stronger political institutions . . . and a more enlightened public opinion, before we can talk about the enlargement of duties and functions of the state in the management and conduct of industry." This revealed a continued evolution in McVey's liberal leanings and placed him squarely in the progressive camp, which desired greater state intervention in the nation's economic and social affairs.[43]

Although the University of Tennessee did not offer him the presidency, McVey continued to labor for promotion to an administrative position. In 1906 it appeared that the University of South Dakota might offer him its presidency, but this opportunity too fell through. McVey was ready for his tireless efforts to yield tangible results, but nothing had yet solidified. Even his students opined about his workaholic tendencies in a tongue-in-cheek tribute poem: "An industrious man is McVey, / He labors so hard night and day— / Writing books, meeting classes, / Uplifting the Masses, / That we fear he will soon pass away." McVey's efforts would finally pay off with an executive position, but it would not be in higher education, as he had expected.[44]

----·----

Through his research on Minnesota government and the state tax laws, McVey had become known to politicians across the state. In 1907 the state passed a law creating a tax commission composed of three members. The act required that the three members of the commission be assigned within ten days of the bill's passage. Governor John Johnson signed the legislation and appointed McVey and two others to the commission that very day. McVey was a prime candidate for the position for numerous reasons. He had studied tax commissions in the South, he understood the basic agencies that existed within Minnesota's government, and his volunteer efforts had made him a visible leader in the state's capital. Furthermore, his *Modern Industrialism* addressed government's regulatory responsibilities with regard to industry.

McVey did not accept the post without trepidation. Just a few months prior to his appointment he had briefly entertained the idea of moving to California as an entrepreneurial businessman. But, as he wrote, "A second thought, however, brings to one's mind the delights of scholastic life with its freedom of thought and of the time to live." Years later, he recalled his anxiety about leaving his stable occupation for one fraught with politics. His father, Alfred, certainly did not console Frank when the elder wrote expressing his doubts "as to the wisdom of acceptance in view of the near prospect of your being made head of your department at an advance in salary." Alfred warned that a Democratic governor was appointing Frank but that Johnson would likely be succeeded by a Republican, who might want to appoint his own commission.[45]

Although McVey had been considering an executive position in higher education, his appointment as chair of the tax commission was a product of chance. The three members drew straws, and McVey picked the shortest one. Each member received a salary of $4,500, an increase in pay for McVey. He resigned his professorship at the university to begin helping the state modernize its system of taxation and raise greater revenue.[46]

The tax commission sought to address inequities in property assessment—especially at large iron ore mines. In order to remedy this, the commission focused its efforts on reforming the tax scheme for the mining industry. Armed with statistics, the commission set out to traverse the state and gather firsthand knowledge of how Minnesota's iron ore mines operated. In 1907 the members of the commission boarded a horse-drawn wagon and visited some of the largest iron ore mines in the world. After visiting eight to ten mines a day on the fact-gathering tour, the commission returned to the Twin Cities and met with representatives from the mining industry. They had determined that smaller mines actually bore the brunt of the tax burden and that larger ones paid less than their fair share. The commission then began the task of processing the information to make suggestions for tax reform.[47]

Under McVey's leadership, the commission divided the active mines into five different categories and recommended new tax codes based on the ease or difficulty of extracting the metal from the earth. Frank was a Republican and Governor Johnson a Democrat, but all public indications suggested that the two remained on cordial terms. However, in December 1908, shortly before the legislative session began, an auditor wrote McVey and attached an unidentified newspaper article that stated, "Owing to the heavy increase in assessed valuation of the iron mines ordered by the commission last year . . . there have been rumors of a coming change on [the] commission." The governor decided to retain McVey, but such rumors alone provided a stark contrast to the security of a full professorship. In the following legislative session, however, Johnson vetoed a bill to reform the tax on iron ore, arguing that it would have imposed too great a tax on one section of the state.[48]

This setback, along with other personal and professional factors, eventually led McVey back into higher education. Although McVey's salary with the commission exceeded his prior earnings, he and Mabel had trouble managing their money. While Frank was busy traversing the state gathering data on tax issues and meeting county assessors, Mabel and the three children traveled south to avoid the harsh Minnesota winter. Frank wrote Mabel on 19 February to apologize for having forgotten Valentine's Day. He told Mabel that he had been examining their financial situation and said, "I find we shall be pinched to get out under present conditions." After listing their current expenses, Frank noted that he had "just $45 to pay on the $300 I owe the banks, get you home and reduce the bills which . . . amount to $150 or thereabouts." He concluded by asking Mabel to skimp whenever possible.[49]

Mabel responded by sending a short letter, along with five dollars. When Frank replied to her matter-of-fact missive, he took on a quarrelsome tone, grumbling that her letter did not contain "a word of sympathy for the feeling of loneliness that knaws [sic] at my heart all the time." Then he became more combative, suggesting that she might be "one of those foolish women who never learn that love is a plant that thrives when nourished, but rapidly fades when neglected"—a peculiar statement considering his own time away from home, his rather businesslike writing, and the recently forgotten Valentine's Day. He continued venting his frustrations: "There is such a wealth of power, feeling and beautiful capacity in you, as

I know from time to time, that I refuse to be robbed of. I want something more than just the place of provider."[50]

Mabel penned her scornful response: "I only keep comprehensible things in my collection." She quipped, "I should hate to have you think I have fallen below grade or grown so old that I can no longer appreciate a love letter. No decent woman does that and I think I am still that." Doing a bit of venting of her own, Mabel added, "All my life when such good times have come my way there has always been someone to apparently begrudge me what little joy I was getting, but I never expected to see any of this from you Frank, and this horror looks suspiciously like something of the sort." Touching on the root of the argument, she noted, "It certainly is the curse of life that the most desirable thing, love, and the most contemptible means, money—should have any such relationship." She concluded, "I will not write again until I feel just like it. Maybe tomorrow—perhaps for days." Money problems were certainly creating tension. The McVeys had two options: curb their spending or increase their income. Both Frank and Mabel desired the "finer things," and like many others Frank desired a larger salary. This desire, fueled by immediate need, was definitely a factor in his decision to leave the tax commission.[51]

On the professional side, McVey had not given up his scholarly endeavors while working in state government, and he did not burn his bridges. While working full-time with the tax commission, McVey had remained active in academic and professional associations, always keeping his eyes open for an administrative position in higher education. Even in 1907, the year he assumed his role with the tax commission, he unsuccessfully sought consideration for the presidency at the University of Missouri.[52]

In the end, McVey felt called to the academic life. In 1908 he informed Mabel that a former colleague at the University of Minnesota, Frederick Jones, had accepted a position at Yale and predicted (incorrectly) that when Cyrus Northrup retired, Jones would be offered the presidency. Then, in an extremely rare instance of transparency and indecision, he asked Mabel, "What move ought we to make? It may be that I am unduly anxious about the political job that I now hold, but the next six months are full of uncertainties, and I feel that when the final end comes I want to be in educational work."[53]

———••———

By the time McVey learned that he was a candidate for the presidency of the University of North Dakota (UND), he had developed an impressive résumé for someone not yet forty years old. Promoted to the rank of full professor at the University of Minnesota, he had served as president of the Minneapolis/St. Paul Associated Charities for a decade and directed the Twin Cities exhibit at the St. Louis World's Fair, all the while remaining active in numerous professional and academic associations. Having published his dissertation, "The Populist Movement," he had then completed two more books, *The Government of Minnesota* and *Modern Industrialism.* Most important, his success as chair of the Minnesota tax commission had highlighted his administrative abilities.[54]

The University of North Dakota, founded less than a quarter century earlier, needed someone with McVey's academic credentials and administrative acumen, not to mention his seemingly boundless energy. Though financially stable in 1908, when its president, Webster Merrifield, announced his intention to retire, the nascent institution competed with the normal schools and the agricultural college for the state's meager number of college-bound students. By the beginning of 1909 McVey remained on the short list of three possible candidates for the position.[55]

When the Board of Trustees formally offered McVey the presidency on 12 January 1909, he found himself in a favorable position. Although his appointment with the tax commission expired in May, Governor Johnson had recently offered him a reappointment for a six-year term at an annual salary of $4,500. The university offered him a better financial package, with a starting salary of $5,000 and complimentary use of the twenty-two-room president's mansion, built just five years earlier. In spite of McVey's personal financial troubles he kept the institution waiting for an answer, thanking them for the offer but requesting an on-campus visit before he would make a decision.[56]

McVey's timing seemed impeccable. He had previously agreed to speak to the North Dakota legislature in Bismarck, and two days before his scheduled address the board had voted him as its choice. McVey addressed the assembly by outlining the five primary challenges facing state legislatures in the new century. His speech revealed the markings of a staunch progressive. He argued for the wise use and protection of natural resources, the development of a strong public health system, modernization of the tax codes, and a commitment to constructing a highway system. Not surprisingly, he called for increased funding for and commitment to an educational system that would meet the social and industrial demands of a modern society.[57]

Following the address, Frank and Mabel visited the campus, which consisted of fourteen buildings. Its total income for the 1908–1909 academic year was less than $200,000, and of the fifty-one faculty members just nine held PhDs. Seventy-five students planned on graduating that spring. Despite these modest numbers, UND had recently established a number of professional schools. Along with colleges of law, mines, education, and engineering, the institution had opened a medical school in 1905. These programs, however, were poorly staffed. The law school, for example, had only three faculty members. In sum, McVey found UND on better footing than other colleges in the state, but not on par with the organization, faculty, and prestige of other state flagship universities in the Midwest.[58]

Still, in 1909 the personality and political climate of North Dakota provided a good fit for McVey. Like McVey, the majority of North Dakota's citizens were Republicans. They had opposed the policies and platform of the Populists, just as McVey had done in his dissertation. However, the progressive impulse had successfully made inroads in the Great Plains and led to calls for cooperative practices to help struggling farmers on the frontier. These developments paralleled McVey's evolving political philosophy, as well as his growing interest in state intervention and aid for education and agricultural and economic development. McVey's upbringing and academic training gave him a clear understanding of the railroad practices and policies that dominated North Dakota politics. At the time, in fact, he was conducting research for a book on railroad transportation. Finally, McVey would be moving west from Minnesota, like thousands of North Dakota settlers. In short, in 1909 the state provided a political environment in which McVey could successfully lobby for the interests of the university.[59]

Returning to Minneapolis after his campus visit, McVey found himself in an advantageous position. He finally possessed a measure of job security in his current governmental post, and he had delivered a successful speech before the North Dakota legislature. Always the opportunist, McVey responded to the Board of Trustees by stating that, after examining the cost of living in Grand Forks, he did not see how "in justice to myself and my family I can accept the position on the terms set forth in [board member] Mr. Gunderson's letter." McVey then asked for a salary of $6,000—double the salary of his predecessor. The board agreed to his stipulation, and he accepted the presidency, beginning a tenure of more than thirty years in higher-education administration.[60]

With the opportunity to make his personal imprint on an institution, the thirty-nine-year-old president-elect promptly began lobbying political leaders to help advance the work of the university. He appeared before a joint session of the state legislature and delivered a speech on the value and operation of a state tax commission. Described as a "masterly presentation of the subject," McVey's speech won him the personal approval of the state's policymakers and led to the creation of North Dakota's tax commission. He also addressed the Joint Committee of Appropriations in February to discuss the needs of the university.[61]

McVey arrived in Grand Forks with little fanfare. It would be more than a year until his official inauguration, affording him time to carry out initiatives to increase the university's visibility within the state and beyond. However, his lofty goals could be accomplished only through reforms implemented on campus. He exhibited his progressive impulses as he spoke of greater efficiency, reorganization, consolidation, and better management and began by restructuring various colleges and departments while creating numerous committees to help implement other changes. He sought recognition or accreditation by national higher-education agencies and associations. Some academic fields, such as engineering, would take a longer time to reorganize; other programs underwent minor changes that brought the publicity that McVey desired. Many faculty committees were modified, and some were created. One committee's sole responsibility was to work toward earning the university a Phi Beta Kappa chapter, a goal that it accomplished in 1914. McVey worked with another group of professors to create an official remuneration scale for the teaching staff. Assistant professors earned between $1,500 and $2,000, associates made between $2,000 and $2,500, and full professors earned $2,500 to $3,000. Deans earned between $3,000 and $3,500.[62]

Along with increased salaries came increased expectations. McVey's greatest emphasis for faculty reform involved scholarly productivity among faculty members. As he noted to the Board of Trustees, "A university should be constantly engaged in presenting printed matter on important subjects to the public." McVey successfully lobbied for appropriations to create a scholarly periodical, the *Quarterly Journal,* published by the university. Faculty could receive modest funds to do research and travel to professional meetings. Others were encouraged to complete their doctorates. McVey kept a file on each professor's scholarly accomplishments and rewarded productive members with promotions and public recognition.[63]

McVey also sought to improve graduate education deliberately to ensure its high quality and its prestige. As the university expanded its graduate course offerings, it sought to increase graduate enrollment. When McVey arrived, the school had two graduate students. By 1910 McVey had convinced the board to provide limited financial assistance for its most promising students, and five scholarships were offered to encourage graduate research. The number of graduate students for the following year increased to seven, and by 1912 graduate enrollment had expanded to twelve. At the same time McVey convinced the University Council to resist the premature attempt to offer doctoral work and to focus instead on master's degree programs.[64]

In order to support the work of these students as well as the efforts of the faculty, McVey emphasized upgrading the library. At convocations he stressed the importance of reading good books, and his attempts to expand holdings suggested his sincerity. During his first year the library added in excess of ten thousand volumes to its collection, an increase of nearly 25 percent. Library books were reorganized and policies for patrons formalized. To better serve the university, McVey lobbied for an expansion of the library program, including an increased number of student assistants working for the librarian.[65]

McVey raised expectations for undergraduate academic work and instituted reforms to encourage an organized, intellectual climate. In 1910, for the first time, the university provided students with a formal schedule, listing the time and location of each class. The university began keeping careful records of students' academic performance. Those seeking a diploma were expected to maintain a C average, finish incomplete work, and meet other administrative requirements. Students failing 60 percent of their work were subject to dismissal.[66]

The convocations required for freshmen and recommended for everyone else symbolized a fresh era for president-student relations at the university. Rather than getting to know the students by name, a practice common to old-time presidents, including his predecessor, Webster Merrifield, McVey began speaking at assemblies and convocations—what he called "Between Us Days." He took these opportunities to address issues of interest to the students, while promoting his agenda of increased scholarship, high ideals, and Christian character. In one convocation entitled "Why Are We Here?" McVey emphasized sound character and the acquisition of a "cosmopolitan disposition." The president asserted that college was the proper place to train students for careers in business because it provided an opportunity to work on punctuality, honest dealings with colleagues, and intellectual development through "systematic mental labor."[67]

McVey's lectures to the students, as well as his "Paragraphs from the President," which appeared regularly in the student newspaper, carried moralistic themes common among progressive reformers and liberal Protestants of the time. He cautioned against keeping company with the lazy and idle, as well as wasting time playing cards. He warned that though students' mothers had taught them the importance of keeping a clean room, "if we make our minds the lodging place for mental filth no act of housekeeping can make them clean." After postulating that one could surmise a great deal about a person by examining his or her library, he urged students to procure a good dictionary and a modern Bible. The latter was of special value because of the "immense amount of wisdom" it contained, as well as its high-quality writing.[68]

McVey took a different approach to student discipline. One former student noted that it was not uncommon for former president Merrifield to "tiptoe the corridors of Budge Hall and sniff at the several doors to see if any of 'his' boys were smoking." McVey moved away from such a strict in loco parentis approach, but he could not avoid being immersed in student behavioral problems. Increasing numbers of students sought housing in Grand Forks, and the typical problems of pranks, hazing, drinking, and breeches of moral conduct continued to consume his time—especially during his first years.[69]

Through various means, however, McVey gradually moved away from the old style of discipline. Rather than snooping around the dormitories looking for trouble, the McVeys regularly opened their house to students so that they could visit in a formal setting. In 1913 McVey established a faculty committee of discipline that addressed all but the most egregious offenses. This type of intervention allowed a quicker resolution to problems, as McVey was often out of town, while providing McVey time to focus on other reforms. Finally, the president informed students that he favored a student court where punishments could be decided by students' peers, with the right to appeal the decisions to the administration. However, a student court was never established during McVey's tenure.[70]

The relational change between the students and the president resulted from McVey's vision of the modern university president combined with his personality and temperament, which was not particularly warm or inviting but somewhat detached. McVey maintained a degree of separation between himself and the undergraduates that had not previously existed. As one student recalled, "He was a rather aloof man and not particularly close to or popular with the students." He added that the students did not disdain him, but a typical undergraduate "would not engage in conversation [with him] on the campus without being given considerable encouragement." George Geiger noted, "McVey tended to be remote and impersonal," and Elwyn Robinson, a historian of the state, described him as "somewhat standoffish." More important, as a progressive president, McVey turned his efforts and energy outward rather than inward. That is, he sought greater support from the state and recognition from the academy. McVey's relationship with the students was a product of this modernized vision.[71]

Like other progressive administrators, McVey wanted increased offerings that would "prepare [students] for fields of usefulness." For women, this usually meant creating or expanding programs designated for females within the already existing academic structure. By doing this, the university could increase its enrollment and claim to serve the state better with minimal added expense. The university already accepted women into its education program, but it was the Teachers College that controlled courses in "Household Economics." By 1911, following national trends, these classes were organized into a formal Department of Domestic Science. The president encouraged the expansion of this program, noting, "It is not the purpose of the University . . . to train young women in domestic science alone, but it is desirable that a much wider preparation should be given them through associated work in the departments of bacteriology, chemistry, physics and biology." McVey also sought expanded offerings in library science: "The demands for young women well educated and well trained in library work are very great, and the university should provide an opportunity for such training, especially when the facilities are already at hand."[72]

McVey initiated and publicized the creation of a nursing degree. He coordinated his efforts with those of the dean of the Medical College to develop a course consisting of both collegiate classes and practical experience in local hospitals. McVey was particularly proud of his nursing initiative and touted it as evidence of the type of courses designed to benefit both the students on campus and the state's residents. He boasted in the local papers that the nursing program was one example of North Dakota being "in advance of Minnesota."[73]

Many of McVey's reforms took years to implement. Other proposals failed to materialize. By the beginning of his second year, however, the incipient transformation of the institution's outlook and image was evident. As historian George Geiger noted, "In the eighteen months that elapsed between his assumption of office in June, 1909, and his formal inauguration in September, 1910, the University experienced the most thorough-going and rapid revolution in its history."[74]

--- • ---

As the fall semester began in 1910, the university utilized McVey's formal inauguration as a time to invite the leaders of American higher education to Grand Forks to see the changes. As news of his accomplishments spread throughout academia, McVey hoped the occasion would provide public affirmation of his reforms by notable university executives. The inauguration ceremonies included the dedication of two new buildings and a celebration of the university's twenty-fifth anniversary. Among those in attendance were all the presidents of the state's other colleges, as well as North Dakota politicians and businessmen—including railroad magnates James Hill and Howard Elliot. The disparate crowd was symbolic in that members of the local community, state government, big business, and higher education now gathered together. These individuals represented various constituencies that McVey hoped to unite in his quest to create a true university in the "West," as it was still often called. To that end, his inaugural speech was broadly inclusive.[75]

McVey concluded the weekend of events with his address "The University and Its Relations." His speech embodied the progressive spirit of higher education, in which he had been immersed as a graduate student at Yale, as a faculty member at the University of Minnesota, as a civil servant in state government, and as a professional economist. It served as a foundation for the policies that he would continue to implement throughout his career as a university administrator. After briefly touching on the history of the institution, he delineated the common characteristics of a true university. In order to carry out its mission properly, he declared, the university needed to understand and cultivate its varied relationships.[76]

McVey reminded his audience that the University of North Dakota was the state's flagship institution in a system that included an agricul-

tural college, two normal schools, and separate schools for science, industrial training, and forestry. He focused on the "difficult problem of
cooperation and coordination" inherent to the system. While McVey
spoke of good feelings among the schools, he clearly laid out areas where
other institutions needed to acquiesce to the state flagship. After arguing
that the university had no intention of creating an agriculture program,
he warned, "Nor do I believe the Agricultural College wishes to engage in
the professional training of engineers." Concerning the preparation of
teachers, he asserted, "It is well accepted by most educators that the place
for a teachers college is at a university . . . [and] the university should delegate the short course training of teachers to the normal schools." After
claiming that "efficiency is the thing we seek," he argued against a proposal to establish a single governing board for all the state's institutions of
higher education.[77]

He also addressed the role of religion at a state university. UND
would honor the separation of church and state by abstaining from sectarian theological instruction, while continuing to emphasize the "faith set
forth by the founder of Christianity 'in love of God and the service of
man.'" While arguing that religion was "essential to good citizenship . . .
and the movement of events to the constant betterment of political and
social activities," he recommended that religious instruction and ministry
be maintained by local churches and by allied student groups such as the
YMCA and the YWCA. McVey welcomed churches to "establish themselves around the university, where the work of educating young people
can be carried on to the very best purpose."[78]

McVey emphasized the most salient points of his administrative philosophy. He delineated the larger trends in higher education of which
UND needed to be a part. The nation, he argued, had moved from an
individualistic orientation to a social one, and with this came an increased
need for universities to address this transformation. Faculty needed training in up-to-date "scientific" methods of instruction and problem solving.
The university needed to respond to modern society with an expanded
curriculum that complemented the liberal arts with flourishing professional schools. He encouraged the state "to move steadily forward as rap-

idly as the needs of its people demand," and he challenged UND to strive
for increased efficiency in its academic programs. The words *efficiency* and
efficient appeared more than a half dozen times in his speech, the word
scientific almost as many. McVey commended recent efforts to expand the
university's role, while emphasizing the importance of state government's
assistance in the reforms that needed attention.[79]

Finally, highlighting the vital relationship between the university and
the state, McVey concluded:

> It is not beyond the truth to say that a university is a beacon light to the
> people of the commonwealth, pointing out to them, not only where ad-
> vances are to be made in the realms of commerce and trade, but in the
> fields of morals, general knowledge, and better living. . . . We may say
> that there is no clearer indication of the advances a people have made
> than that set by their university. Once free from political control, and
> truly of the people in the larger democratic sense, it means that the peo-
> ple of a commonwealth where such an institution exists are truly turned
> toward real progress and the light of the lamp of civilization.[80]

In an open letter to the residents of Grand Forks, published in the local
paper during the inaugural weekend, McVey reiterated the importance of
a cooperative relationship between the university and the state's citizens.
He outlined his plan to provide liberal arts education and applied coursework "until every man and woman who desires it, whether at home or on
the campus," had the opportunity to benefit from the university. The institution would aid industry by supplying leaders in the business world
and by developing more efficient methods for those leaders to utilize. Finally, he argued that UND would implement practical programs to serve
as "the right arm of the state."[81]

Although McVey avoided using the exact terminology, he proposed
that UND enact its own version of the "Wisconsin Idea." Developed by
Charles Van Hise, president of Wisconsin's state university in Madison,
the Wisconsin Idea sought to make the university an asset to state government. Professors who were specialists in their fields provided expert advice
and research on the numerous challenges facing the state. By addressing

issues such as taxation, public health, agriculture, and engineering, the University of Wisconsin worked closely with government officials and representatives in Madison to better the state. McVey essentially proposed duplicating this program in North Dakota.[82]

McVey called for the faculty to focus on applied research. He emphasized the role of service in the university's relationship to the state, another integral component of the Wisconsin Idea. Working with and for the people of the state and its government could take on many forms. In Wisconsin it entailed everything from professors aiding local farmers by conducting experiments with cattle, to the Wisconsin faculty's drafting legislation to curb the excesses of unrestrained capitalism. The program developed by Van Hise sought, like most progressive reforms of the time, to make the state government function efficiently to meet the needs of the larger population. The great irony was that operating a university as the people's institution, although couched in terms of expanding democracy, often removed tasks and decision-making authority from the common citizen to the trained expert.[83]

The early reforms accomplished by McVey and detailed in his inaugural address revealed that he, like other administrators, adopted reforms based on scientific principles of management. In this way all segments of society, from farmers and blue-collar employees to industrial leaders and government officials, could participate in and benefit from the state flagship university. In turn, the university could gain the trust of the people and generate greater support through increased enrollment and funding. However, the "Wisconsin Idea" would be hard to replicate in North Dakota. It did not boast the same population, history, or resources. Lying beyond the original Northwest Territory, the state had existed for less than a quarter century. Most importantly, although the university served as the state's flagship institution, it did not include the agricultural and mechanical arts programs provided by the Morrill Land-Grant Act. Hence, the implementation of an ambitious vision would require not only administrative acumen but a successful public relations program.

McVey benefited from a North Dakota faculty apparently eager to adopt his strategy. Even before McVey's arrival, the faculty council had passed a resolution to "endeavor to make the university a larger factor in the life of this state." During the preceding academic year faculty meetings had twice included lectures entitled "The University and the State," as well as an address entitled "The University and the Alumni." Many professors realized that UND needed to connect with people outside Grand Forks, and McVey's arrival provided an agent ready to enact policies that would help the faculty accomplish this goal.[84]

In McVey's first year as president he organized the Extension Department, which became the logical way to implement programs that would provide services to North Dakota and increase the university's visibility throughout the state. Initially, the extension program focused on one-time lectures and correspondence courses. In 1910 McVey sought to expand its work by creating a position for a director of extension. He argued that the value of extension work could not be overestimated, but the greatest problem was securing funds to operate the program.[85]

Although the amount was far less than what McVey desired, the state appropriated $3,500 in 1911 to be used for extension services over a two-year period. With these funds, McVey managed to hire N. C. Abbott away from the Agricultural College to serve as field organizer for the newly created Bureau of Educational Cooperation. Four general programs were placed under the bureau's purview: information services, university lectures, correspondence courses, and public speaking. McVey noted, "There is no reason why the people of the state should not use to the full the information that is available at the University."[86]

McVey became a tireless speaker, modeling for the faculty his own vision of extension lectures by traversing the state and offering expert advice in layman's terms. His 1910 speeches encompassed many topics, including "Changes in Standards in Philanthropic Work," "The College Man in Business," "City Planning," "The New Moral Code," and "The Making of a Town." Through his lecture tours McVey sought to bring the university to the people and to persuade individuals of the value of extension programs.[87]

McVey served as a model for the type of applied research he hoped to see the university's faculty members conduct as a part of the outreach effort. His *Railroad Transportation*, published in the fall of 1910, exemplified the type of publication that he believed would be useful to academics and state policymakers. The work traced the history of the railroad industry in the United States and then examined the current organization and operation of the booming business. Along with historic and economic accounts, however, McVey also included a final section, "The Relation of Railways to the Public," which addressed policy and regulation issues.[88]

While the faculty council appeared enthusiastic about introducing progressive policies at the university, most of its members lacked the educational training and credentials McVey desired. Of the handful of PhDs, only historian Orin Libby and sociologist John Gillette possessed substantial academic reputations. Libby had studied under the direction of Frederick Jackson Turner at the University of Wisconsin, and Gillette had studied with Albion Small and John Dewey at the University of Chicago. Both would eventually have immensely successful careers in Grand Forks, and McVey now sought to bring more individuals with their training and academic outlook to campus.

In his first few years, McVey hired a number of PhDs as he attempted to upgrade the faculty and create an atmosphere that emphasized scholarship along with teaching. Although these faculty recruits helped transform the outlook and temperament of the university, they also created some problems for the president. The younger and better-educated faculty, those who had been trained in science and efficiency, occasionally displayed contempt for senior faculty members: the deans of the various colleges, despite their decades of service, usually lacked the credentials of even the assistant professors who had just arrived on campus.[89]

McVey's efficiency model also created problems. His reliance on the "PhD Club" when seeking "advice and ideas" was "too obvious not to be noticed and resented by the older faculty who had not completed their graduate studies." This created awkwardness when the president skipped the "chain of command" in seeking to implement policies, instead discussing matters with those he regarded as capable of enacting them—who rarely happened to be the deans. This approach created advancement opportunities for younger scholars but frustrated those in administrative positions. For example, from the time McVey arrived until 1914, the deanship of the College of Arts and Sciences, where the greatest number of PhDs served, changed hands four times before Vernon Squires accepted the position.[90]

Nevertheless, by the end of McVey's third year he had set in place a foundation on which he could build. By the fall of 1911 enrollment in the college exceeded five hundred students for the first time, despite tight budgetary constraints. McVey's continued popularity as a speaker in North Dakota and the Upper Midwest revealed the extent to which people in the state supported the president and his programs at the university. During the 1911 legislative session in Bismarck both houses invited McVey to address elected officials on the topic of "Conflict in Government." He accepted invitations from dozens of different professional associations, including agricultural groups, press associations, teachers unions, and tax officials. McVey consistently used his position to model for citizens the ways in which the university's intellectual resources could aid the state. At the same time, he exemplified for the faculty the type of professor who would most benefit the institution.[91]

With the university on firm footing, McVey petitioned the Board of Trustees to allow him to travel to Europe during the summer of 1912. The board agreed to fund McVey's travels and granted him a leave of absence from mid-June until late September. On June 14 he left his family in Minnesota for the summer and traveled to Europe. McVey, who had been a prolific writer up to that point, now found himself without a clear research and writing project. He hoped that European travel would provide him with inspiration. Mabel McVey wrote to him, "I am candidly glad you are having this trip for I think it is exactly what you need, family or no family. I hope it will mean much in the way of inspiration and revelation to you." She added, "For while I [am] most satisfied with your work in North Dakota I am very anxious for you to do some piece of work that will be a real original contribution."[92]

Without a topic in mind, he went abroad to conduct qualitative research on town planning and educational reform, as well as agricultural and industrial development. In England and Norway, McVey focused on higher education. After attending the Imperial Congress of British Universities and listening to the speakers focus on higher education's role in preparing men for the Empire's civil service, McVey opined, "It is clear indeed that Great Britain has lagged a long way behind the United States and Germany in her educational development. . . . Oxford has just established a chair of agriculture." At the University of Christiana in Norway, McVey presented two lectures concerning social and industrial development in the United States.[93]

McVey spent the majority of his time in Germany, examining agricultural and industrial development. He surmised that Germany's success in developing a modern industrial and agricultural economy with little poverty was the result of a people educated in the habits of industry, an honest and efficient government, the government's growing role as an employer, and farmers' success in achieving high yields with relatively small acreage. However, he found other trends less encouraging, noting, "There is also an undercurrent of moral decline that crops out in the risqué literature to be found everywhere." In his journal he stated, "The government here regulates nearly everything, but it evidently does not regulate the sale and exposure of obscene literature and pictures. . . . One may see photography in so called high class stores that should be repressed." He argued that low wages and the increased cost of living had led to delayed marriages and "resultant immorality." McVey's conclusion regarding the situation in Germany was insightful, considering the decades of tumult that lay ahead: "Today Germany has a benevolent despotism which has accomplished remarkable results under the shrewd leadership of the present emperor, but there is without question a time of reconstruction to come."[94]

McVey's European visit was intended to serve him both personally and professionally. On both accounts, however, it failed. The scattered thoughts he penned in his journal revealed his attempts to find a topic worth examining at length, but the number of issues he tried to explore kept him from focusing on any topic long enough to devise a clear research project. McVey had predicted this lack of success when he opened his journal: "I sit down with premeditation to write everything that occurs from the time of leaving to the return of the traveler from foreign lands[, which] fills me with fear at the labor involved and probably use-lessness of the whole performance." In the end he failed to produce a major publication based on his European travels.[95]

The voyage created personal problems as well. Both Mabel and Frank planned on his hiring a German maid and cook during his summer visit. As Mabel wrote him, "Do not forget that you are going to bring home some good German maids for the house. The more I think of it the surer I am it is the best scheme." McVey conducted interviews with different women and eventually settled on two individuals. After receiving the news of Frank's attempts to hire help, Mabel wrote, "If it is a success I will have another reason for being undyingly grateful to you." Unfortunately, the "scheme" that the McVeys were attempting to implement was illegal. Mabel wrote her husband to make sure that he instructed the women to tell immigration officers that they did not have any definite engagement for employment in the United States. Finally, she warned Frank to meet the women away from the docks, where trade unions placed agents look-ing for contract-labor-law violators.[96]

Both women managed to make their way through immigration with-out problems, but after six months of working under Mabel's direction they abandoned the McVeys. One of the workers reimbursed McVey for having paid her way to the United States, but the other left indebted to him. Accordingly, he kept her trunk, despite pleas from various individu-als in Minneapolis, where the young woman had fled, to return her be-longings. McVey argued, "It is not a question of the money so much as a question of being done by you as you should be done by." McVey did not release the trunk until the young woman's new employer in Minnesota finally wrote him a check for $51.25.[97]

Despite these challenges, McVey's growing status among national or-ganizations and his work on behalf of the university were impressive. He presented papers at national conferences and continued to gain visibility. He served as vice president of the American Economics Association and as a member of the National Education Association's committee to lobby Congress on pending vocational education legislation. He also accepted committee assignments for the National Association of State Universities, which studied reorganization issues in education and the economy of time in education.[98]

University enrollment remained strong, and the faculty expanded its research and course offerings, despite receiving less state aid than McVey had hoped for. In addition, McVey hired John J. Pettijohn from the University of Wisconsin to serve as director of extension services. During the first year of Pettijohn's leadership the faculty delivered more than fifty lectures throughout the state. Pettijohn himself, who truly believed in the value of extension services and made it his life's work, issued upward of forty addresses.[99]

Three other professors, all in the social sciences, also enjoyed a special relationship with McVey as he tried to emulate the Wisconsin Idea. Wisconsin PhD Orin Libby focused on North Dakota history, collecting archival materials and delivering extension lectures. He was a social activist who lobbied for state parks and a nationally recognized historian who managed to secure UND as the site for the 1914 annual meeting of the Mississippi Valley Historical Association. Sociologist John Gillette had earned his PhD at Chicago and campaigned for reform of the state's prisons and mental institutions. He called for the creation of "social centers" throughout the state to organize citizens and find solutions to common social problems. In addition, he held a national position with the Child Conservation League of America. Finally, James E. Boyle, another Wisconsin PhD, worked in McVey's field of political economy, writing books about North Dakota's government and working on issues involving farm marketing and farm credits. These three young professors symbolized McVey's transformational leadership at UND and became close confidants of the president.[100]

McVey's successes during the first half of his tenure as president were tempered by a series of challenges that dominated the last years of his administration. Limited resources and lack of state support, trouble with faculty retention, political turmoil, and related issues of academic freedom all took a toll on McVey and his initiatives. At the same time, his busy travel schedule placed pressure on his personal as well as his professional life. The challenges and controversies that began in 1913 and continued for the remainder of his tenure at UND would play no small role in his decision to leave the university in 1917.[101]

When the legislature convened in 1913, it appeared that the university would be supported with greater resources. At the end of the session, however, McVey was blindsided by the governor's veto of the $3,500 appropriation for the extension program he had fought so hard to initiate. Despite these cuts to the program's funding, McVey still managed to lure John J. Pettijohn to UND. After one year, however, the young scholar left for Indiana University, where he would develop a model extension program and eventually move on to become a leading advocate of extension work throughout the nation.[102]

This slash to funding for the extension program signaled the beginning of a series of developments that limited the success of McVey's broad program. Of the $300,000 McVey had requested for improvements, the university only received $84,000. Then the state ruled that the millage tax rate, of which the university was a major benefactor, was unconstitutional. These cuts resulted in a major deficit of more than $50,000. McVey and the university were accused of mismanaging funds. The president responded by writing letters explaining why the institution found itself in dire straits and defending it against charges of poor bookkeeping. Regardless, by December 1914 he faced a potential crisis. McVey had to speak to UND students before the Christmas holiday—a time usually reserved for topics of interest on campus—concerning rumors that the university would have to close its doors. He stated that while the university was in crisis, its credit was good, and the students did not have to worry about the school closing.[103]

Nevertheless, many high-caliber professors began to leave. In 1914 alone McVey lost a sizable contingent of his leading scholars. Pettijohn's decision to leave was not isolated: Melvin Brannon, dean of the College of Liberal Arts and director of the State Biological Survey, became president of the University of Idaho. Gustave Ruediger, who had been a leader in public health initiatives, resigned his professorship to become director of a new public health institute in Illinois. Among other promising faculty to leave was Robert Henry, who resigned his post as dean of the law school during the summer of 1914.

Adding to the adversity McVey faced with regard to the budget and faculty retention were controversies surrounding the academic freedom of professors. The challenges McVey faced in Grand Forks existed as part of a larger trend in higher education. Although issues concerning professors' rights had been debated for centuries, the last decade of the nineteenth century through World War I was an era in which academic freedom was challenged, abridged, fought for, and (to some extent) established on a formal level. At UND, however, McVey's desire to keep the university in good standing with the political left and right would diminish the academic freedom of the faculty he had so diligently attempted to build.

McVey's most controversial (and public) academic-freedom case originated with the activities of law professor Joseph Lewinsohn (JD, University of Chicago). The first trial developed in 1912, when Lewinsohn campaigned for third-party candidate Theodore Roosevelt and recruited two faculty members to help him in the cause. His activities upset N. C. Young, the conservative chair of the Board of Trustees. Young insisted that professors—in this case Lewinsohn—either cease their political activity or resign their posts. McVey met with Lewinsohn, arguing that faculty positions at the university precluded activity in national and state politics, even though he felt it reasonable to be a public participant in local political affairs. Lewinsohn offered his resignation, but McVey asked him to stay on. The law professor agreed, believing that while he and McVey disagreed concerning the political activity of professors, the president would leave such actions up to each individual.[104]

The following year Lewinsohn attended an organizational meeting for the state's progressives in Fargo. McVey and Young discussed Lewinsohn's participation, and Young reiterated his position that faculty members either abandon political causes or leave the university. McVey then spoke with law school dean Robert Henry, voicing his objection to Lewinsohn's participation in the meeting. Henry subsequently met with Lewinsohn, who tendered his resignation again, stating, "If I were to remain here I should be compelled either to engage in an unseemly and distasteful wrangle with the administration or to sacrifice the rights and be recreant to the duties of citizenship. Neither course commends itself to me." He added, "It will be a sorry day for American education if the policy of suppression adopted here ever becomes general." He concluded by noting that he held no personal vendetta against the president and trusted that they would maintain a friendly relationship.[105]

This time McVey did not ask Lewinsohn to reconsider. Instead he agreed to present his resignation to the Board of Trustees. The president then took issue with the professor's argument that he or the board was impinging on Lewinsohn's academic freedom. McVey compared the position of a faculty member to that of a judge who must remain nonpartisan despite being involved in the political process. McVey told Lewinsohn, "As soon as a professor enters politics he makes the university an object of political purpose. . . . You cannot escape their [political] consequence, and to develop a theory about academic freedom that you can escape them and still take part in them, is entirely beside the mark." He continued by arguing that academic freedom entailed the right to speak on social and economic questions as long as professors refrained from allying themselves with a political party, adding, "The life of the universities in this state and elsewhere depends upon their being able to keep above this kind of politics, the kind you want to engage in." McVey concluded, "I do not acquiesce at all in your view that the educational life of the university and of the state is endangered by this attitude. To my mind, it is good sense and good policy."[106]

Although the Board of Trustees accepted the professor's resignation in February 1914, the issue did not subside. Rather, it became a matter of public debate. Lewinsohn, McVey, and Dean Henry debated the issue in the local papers. Henry spoke out publicly against McVey's views, stating, "I radically disagree with his view of the matter. I do not believe that participation in politics by individual members of the faculty within moderation will do serious harm to the university." He apologized for any role he might have played in perpetuating the belief that Lewinsohn's political activity would jeopardize his chances of reappointment. He then reiterated

his displeasure at McVey's stance on academic freedom. In private correspondence with McVey, however, Henry stated that Lewinsohn was un-
popular with the law students, fellow professors, and the local community.[107]

Lewinsohn responded in the paper by arguing that the primary issue
involved was academic freedom. He cited portions of McVey's letter to
him and added that, according to UND trustee N. C. Young, "The Republican Party must be preserved in North Dakota and we cannot have
professors going around trying to break it up." The professor stated that he
had not been informed about any limitations on his employment and that
prior to his second year he had been promoted to full professor. He asked,
"If there was a question as to my retention; why raise either my salary or
my rank?" Apparently aware of the private remarks regarding his unpopu-
larity, Lewinsohn also included a letter signed by all but three of the law
students, expressing "our appreciation of your services and our regret over
the announcement of your resignation as a member of the law school faculty. . . . You have won the esteem and respect of the entire student body
of this law school." The students asked the professor to reconsider and
wished him well if he did not return. The student newspaper editorialized,
"There is little chance for argument when we state that he is one of the
ablest and most learned professors that ever stepped inside of our class
room. He is a master of every subject that he teaches."[108]

News of Lewinsohn's departure was not confined to the local press.
An editorial in the *Los Angeles Tribune* argued that the professor had been
ousted from his post because he was a progressive. McVey responded in an
article reprinted in the *Grand Forks Daily Herald,* stating that Lewinsohn
had not been forced to leave. Instead he had resigned voluntarily and was
continuing his services through the semester. McVey concluded, "The
evident purpose of this whole matter is to make political capital and to
establish a reputation as a martyr, in order that later on it may be used for
the purpose of securing political advertising."[109]

The Lewinsohn controversy continued through the summer. Law
professor Charles Carpenter criticized the Board of Trustees' handling of
Lewinsohn, and the board responded by firing him. After Carpenter's
removal Dean Henry resigned in protest, accepting a position at the Uni-

versity of Illinois. Later that year the controversy ran its course when N. C. Young resigned from the Board of Trustees.[110]

The entire incident placed McVey on the defensive. He discussed the Lewinsohn case at great length in his 1914 biennial report. He also prepared an article entitled "Academic Freedom and Political Activity," in which he made a distinction between academic freedom and individual political liberty. Academic freedom, he argued, involved the right to "teach and to publish the results of scholarship without let or hindrance." Political liberty, on the other hand, involved opportunities in partisan politics. The former, he reasoned, was essential to the integrity of a university, but the latter was an entirely different issue. In essence, McVey viewed his own position as one that upheld the traditional principle of *Lehrfreiheit,* a professor's right to teach and do research without political interference. When a professor abandoned the scholarly pursuit of truth and engaged in the political realm from which he sought protection, the principle of academic freedom no longer applied. This, asserted McVey, was exactly what Lewinsohn had done.[111]

With such a distinction, McVey believed, the Lewinsohn case did not involve academic freedom. He added that state universities were to be free from politics and that participation by faculty members in such politics "at once makes the University a subject of attack for the purposes of securing control of it, in order to reap any advantages that might come from the use of members of faculties as political speakers or as a means of awarding political plums." He determined that involvement in politics allowed marginal professors the opportunity to declare their removal from a position as a violation of academic freedom. The university professor, he concluded, needed to be a "gentleman" who refrained from politics in order to conduct his research and teaching in a manner that allowed for true academic freedom. Reaction to the recent events in Grand Forks made it clear that McVey's support from the faculty was indeed limited. As historian Louis Geiger noted, the president "could be arbitrary and at times high-handed"; one dean recalled, "He thought he was very democratic, but he was an aristocrat at heart."[112]

McVey's entanglement with academic freedom in North Dakota was part of a much larger national movement to define "academic freedom" and institutionalize the concept. As such, McVey found himself in concert with university executives across the nation. For example, Ohio State's president, W. O. Thompson, emphasized a professor's role as a "gentleman" in "the search for truth." This required that "the orderly progress of research and scholarship" not lower itself into "unnecessary offenses." In McVey's view, Lewinsohn's actions constituted such an offense. Historian Christopher Lucas summarized the matter faced by McVey and other university presidents: "Questions of academic freedom were about public relations, about . . . voicing sentiments calculated to arouse the ire of those upon whom the university necessarily depended for support."[113]

As McVey and other university presidents offered their own "managerial concept" of academic freedom, which drew a distinction between "academic freedom" and academic license," American professors were creating a separate interpretation of their rights. In 1913 a joint resolution among the American Economic Association, the American Sociological Society, and the American Political Science Association enumerated a more liberal interpretation concerning "liberty of thought, freedom of speech, and security of tenure for teachers." These ideas were adopted and expanded by the American Association of University Professors in 1915.[114]

McVey found himself on the front lines of the battle to define academic freedom because of North Dakota's political situation, which had grown increasingly intense during his tenure as president. The state's agricultural economy relied heavily on financing from the East (usually the Twin Cities), and that often pitted farmers against bankers. Moreover, the Populist Movement and Eugene Debs's success in the Upper Midwest had created a hotbed for radical politics and reactionary responses. The political posturing faced by university presidents was even more intense for McVey during his last years in office, as the left-leaning Nonpartisan League began gaining considerable political momentum. McVey was attempting not only to secure funding from the state but to keep the university from becoming a political weapon in the hands of hostile camps.

As the state slid into political turmoil and McVey continued to feel the pressure, the legislature decided to create a Board of Regents to coordinate the activities of North Dakota's public colleges. McVey had chaired a committee to study the feasibility of such a board in 1910, but the committee had opposed the idea. Nothing further happened until conservative governor Louis Hanna backed the creation of the board in January 1915. The legislature formed a committee to study the problems of North Dakota's colleges and universities, which condemned the state's schools for creating institutional rivalry that had led to the duplication of programs and financial waste. After criticizing requests for increased faculty salaries, the study added that the state's educational leaders (including McVey) believed "that the final aim and obligation of statehood is higher education."[115]

McVey had reason to oppose the creation of an overarching board. As the leader of the state's flagship university and someone who understood the financial complexities of state support, his university held an advantage over other institutions. The agricultural college's ability to procure federal funds—especially after the passage of the Smith-Lever Act in 1914—was the one exception. McVey was in a position to create almost any type of academic program at his institution, while encouraging the other colleges to focus on specific primary purposes such as education, science, agriculture, and forest management. In many respects, then, the new board was another loss for McVey. He had opposed its creation, and he had maintained a good relationship with his own university's board. However, in the final days before its inception he became far less vocal in his opposition. This may have been due to the unusually intense criticism of his institution's use of funds and the realization that such a board held the possibility of assisting the state's flagship in becoming North Dakota's educational cornerstone.[116]

McVey's concerns about academic freedom, as well as his successes in keeping the university relatively free from political interference, are best understood by examining his views within the context of higher education in North Dakota. For example, the agricultural college in Fargo and its president, John Worst, faced a much more challenging scenario. The college had begun publicizing the ways in which various owners and businessmen were taking advantage of the state's farmers. The state's newly created Board of Regents eventually fired Worst and replaced him with an administration more sympathetic to the conservative interests in the state. During his tenure, McVey faced no such scrutiny or direct attacks.[117]

For McVey, an expanding economy eased some of the university's financial difficulties. At the same time, McVey's political acumen protected him from the political battles to which others would fall prey. In 1915, when the governor supported the formation of the Board of Regents, the legislature's $185,000 appropriation for the university was the highest amount received to that time. Still, McVey and the university had not received funding for building new structures on campus since his first year in office. That came during the 1917 legislative session, when the Nonpartisan League, which controlled the governor's office and the state's House of Representatives, appropriated $90,000 for campus construction. McVey confided in Mabel that "if matters stand and get thru clear to the end as they now stand the university will be fairly well off for the next two years."[118]

Despite an improved outlook in 1917 (not including World War I, which affected institutions across the nation), events at the university and the capitol, starting as early as 1912, had frustrated McVey, and he had been seeking presidential positions elsewhere. Both Colorado and Idaho had expressed interest in him, and even when these two possibilities did not result in a job offer, he told Mabel, "I am coming to think that I could have a real record that shouldn't be thrown away." Clearly, he was beginning to look elsewhere for a position where he could exercise his leadership.[119]

McVey had been flirting with the idea of a move as early as 1913, when the state's growing political tension and his own ambition resulted in ever-increasing frustrations. He had expressed interest in the presidencies of both the University of Washington and City College in New York, but both opportunities fell through. He wrote Mabel, "We will continue to rule over gentiles. So the text seems to be remain where we are, do our duty and be as happy as possible." When he received official news of his rejection, he again confided in his wife: "The thing seems pretty well shaped up . . . with your man out in the cold and left to the Red River Valley."[120]

By 1915 McVey was getting desperate, sending letters to search committees across the country and even looking for potential professorships. When M. P. Shawkey, a trustee at West Virginia University, wrote McVey to tell him that their search was well advanced and that the board was considering two or three candidates seriously, McVey responded with a letter detailing his accomplishments and admonishing Shawkey to keep a "matter of this kind open for the consideration of everybody who might be eligible so long as the question has not been decided." Despite his pleas, he was not considered a serious candidate. At nearly the same time that McVey expressed interest in the West Virginia job, he wrote Professor Edwin Seligman at Columbia University, opening his letter by saying, "I find myself looking back to my teaching days with increased interest and longing. . . . The grief a man has to go thru as a college executive raises many queries and among them is the one whether teaching is not the larger field." McVey then asked if anything was available: "I am writing you as the dean of economists whether there are any calls for a man with such experience as I have had."[121]

Mabel, who rarely had much positive to say about the University of North Dakota or Grand Forks, became even more frustrated in 1916, when the Board of Regents did not approve the purchase of a car for the president and his family. Instead it appropriated funds for a horse. Mabel wrote Frank, "Well, if the regents can do nothing on maintenance of anything else, so be it. . . . I am very much impressed by the fact that people in general think we are old fogies. And I begin to believe that you are fundamentally a duffer." She took the opportunity to state, "The children are too disgusted for words that it isn't an auto. . . . Frank [Jr.] told me today that he thought Grand Forks was a rotten place." Mabel's general tone suggested that she concurred with her son.[122]

Although the financial situation at the university appeared to be on the upswing and many of the controversies concerning political freedom had passed, McVey continued to look for other employment during the remainder of his time in Grand Forks. Rumors of openings kept circulating, and Frank spoke with his wife about positions at Purdue, the University of Texas, New Hampshire State College, and most notably the

University of Minnesota. None of these, however, came to fruition. In 1917 McVey was targeted by the University of Wyoming, but he declined the invitation.[123]

When the right job offer finally arrived, McVey was quick to take it. At almost the same time that Wyoming approached McVey, he received a telegram asking if he would be interested in the presidency of the University of Kentucky. McVey did not conceal his excitement when he wrote Mabel, "Here are two university positions in one week. . . . It never rains but it pours, that was well illustrated today. . . . Ho! How it did rain!" McVey met with members of the search committee later that week, and at its next meeting, the Board of Trustees at the University of Kentucky unanimously voted to offer him the presidency. McVey accepted less than a month after the initial contact, and his family began preparing to move south.[124]

When news of his pending departure arrived in Grand Forks, many students, faculty members, and others involved in higher education expressed sadness. Lewis Crawford, the president of the North Dakota Board of Regents, wrote McVey to express his regret on behalf of the board and added, "We have felt for some time that your standing in the world of scholarship and educational administration would soon draw you to a more ancient and honorable seat of learning." The *Quarterly Journal,* which McVey had assisted in creating, recalled that when McVey arrived, the university "lacked organization; it lacked fixt [*sic*] standards of scholarship. . . . Its broad function as a State University had not yet been grasped." All this had changed, however, because of McVey's efforts.[125]

The *Student* lamented McVey's departure and summarized his administrative reforms during the previous eight years. McVey, it opined, had arrived at the university "when its educational standing was not secure. . . . President McVey has placed the University on a sound foundation and is leaving it in the best of working order." The paper cited McVey's accomplishments: The institution had been classified as one of seventy universities by the U.S. Bureau of Education. The law school was one of forty members of the American Law School Association. The medical school had earned an A classification by the American Council for the Advancement of Medical Education. UND was one of eighty-six institutions with a Phi Beta Kappa chapter, and its "entrance requirements" were "now the same as those of Minnesota, Wisconsin and Chicago." In sum, McVey had created a university where before a college had existed.[126]

Two of McVey's final speeches in Grand Forks best represented the philosophy of higher education that he had developed during his lifetime and refined while at the helm in Grand Forks. Speaking to students a final time, McVey read passages from the Old and New Testaments before addressing the ways in which World War I would forever change American society:

> There is a new viewpoint in the matter of the individual as he is being subordinated to the good of the whole . . . In America since we have entered the war we are getting a new viewpoint of the functions of the state, and the government has extended its functions in the regulation of the affairs of the nation . . . The progress is toward the greater care of the happiness of the individual and the protection of his life by the state . . . With this new state must come the new citizenship. We have too long taken the state for granted. Now it must occupy a larger place in the life of the citizen, and there must be a new sense of responsibility, a new realization of what the state has done for us and is doing. . . .
>
> A new theology will grow out of the present crisis. Again and again one hears the statement that there has been a general breakdown in religious ideals, and that the people have lost touch with the religious spirit. The reason for this is that the present theology will be founded on the New Testament and the teachings of Christ as they really are, not as they have been interpreted. The new theology must be based too upon the facts of science which have been firmly established.
>
> The relationship of all this to the university is that it is our business to put ourselves in accord with these new things. During his four years the student should formulate his ideals on these things and be ready to face the world with strength. Above all it is important that he should establish deep religious convictions, for these are the mainstay through life.
>
> To you I commend the university. . . . Its influence has been for the good of the state, and for the winning of high honor in the nation. It is for you to maintain its honor and its high standing.[127]

The content of his farewell speech to the citizens of Grand Forks differed greatly from his speech to the students, but his conclusion remained the same. He argued that the residents of the town needed to view the university as more than an economic asset. It served, in fact, as an essential component of the well-being of the state, and in that position it needed to be free to seek the truth. In a messianic tone, McVey concluded that what "will save this nation after the war are the universities."[128]

McVey's speeches exemplified his inclusion within a much larger group of university presidents, for whom, as David Levine stated, "education was increasingly viewed as the salvation of progress and democracy." His work at UND epitomized the progressive academic imbued with a sense of administrative efficiency and unbounded faith in the scientific method. McVey integrated these qualities with a liberal Protestantism guided by science and focused on service. This combination of traits resulted in an emphasis on liberal arts along with professional studies to help prepare students to become future leaders who could meet the growing needs of a modern society. McVey's childhood, education, and professional experience had helped create a quintessential modern man ready to address the problems of the modern world. However, at UND McVey met a general public and state government skeptical of the increased funding required for such an ambitious vision. The state's inability to fully support McVey led to his decision to leave the northern plains.[129]

In a broader sense, McVey's time at the University of North Dakota provided a clear example of the challenges faced by administrators attempting to raise the standards of their institutions to the caliber of elite colleges. In his classic study *Great American Universities,* published in 1910, Edwin Slosson not only listed a coterie of impressive institutions but discussed the development of the "Standard American University." In many respects, McVey's work in Grand Forks was a success, even though UND had not become a "great American university." Rather, McVey managed to develop a "standard" university in a state that did not have the population or the resources to implement a program that would rival the universities of Minnesota, Michigan, or Wisconsin.[130]

The challenges McVey met at the University of North Dakota were similar to those faced by scores of "standard" institutions throughout the country, but the "great" universities, with their superior resources and impressive reforms, garnered most of the nation's attention. His administrative style had been tested at UND, and he would bring the same work ethic and temperament to his next position. McVey's progressive vision and the frustrations he met in trying to implement it led him to a southern college struggling to reach even the level of a "standard" university. In many ways, the young president's experiences in structural reform, faculty development, limited budgets, extension work, academic work, and state politics would serve him well. In other ways, however, nothing could prepare a Yankee progressive for the challenges of building a university in the Bluegrass.

Chapter 2

A Southern University and a Northern Progressive

1917–1920

The university is a vital force and not merely an abiding place . . . I look to you for sympathy, for support, and for substantial help. With these generously given, the University can do its part in the building of the Commonwealth of Kentucky.
—Frank LeRond McVey, 1918

The normally prudent Frank McVey accepted the presidency of the University of Kentucky with uncharacteristic haste, suggesting desperation on his part to extricate himself from an increasingly tense situation in North Dakota. On 25 July 1917 McVey received a telegram from Abraham Flexner, a Kentucky native serving as secretary of the General Education Board in New York. Flexner, who had gained prominence through his research and writing about higher education, had learned of the opening in his home state, recommended McVey to the presidential search committee, and personally contacted McVey in order to set up an interview.[1]

McVey was on the East Coast for work, but the search committee managed to contact him within the week. They set up a meeting at the LaSalle Hotel in Chicago, where McVey could stop on his return to Grand Forks. The president arrived late at the meeting and, according to university legend, excused himself to take a quick shower. He emerged from the bathroom without a shirt, and as Thomas Clark recounted, the search committee was impressed with the hair on his chest. McVey's son, Frank

Jr., however, recalled that it was the hair on his back that made the impression. Folklore aside, the search committee immediately sought to secure McVey for the position. Judge Richard Stoll, a leading member of the Board of Trustees who chaired the search committee, assured McVey that he was confident the committee would grant their unanimous support in recommending him for the presidency. He added, "I have met no man yet to whom I would rather entrust the future of the University."[2]

The search committee unanimously recommended McVey, and the Board of Trustees supported the choice. McVey immediately found himself in the driver's seat, asking questions about the quality of the president's housing and requesting time off to conduct a research project. The Carnegie Endowment for International Peace had offered McVey a grant to write a report concerning the economic impact of the World War I in England, but it would take much of the fall semester to research and write the study. Stoll saw no reason why McVey could not stay in Washington, D.C., until mid-October (a period that McVey would manage to extend through the rest of the fall semester), adding that the board was willing to help McVey in any way it could. Stoll also noted that one newly acquired property (eventually called Maxwell Place) needed repairs, but that the renovations would make it an attractive residence for the incoming president.[3]

While the McVeys were considering the post, both of Frank's parents offered unsolicited advice. Frank's mother wrote first, noting that despite the proximity of Kentucky to Ohio, Indiana, and Illinois, the commonwealth was far different from its neighbors on the northern side of the Ohio River. She then argued that the competition from other institutions within Kentucky made this post no more desirable than the situation he had in Grand Forks. His father, however, took a different view later in the week. He cautioned that the job would "require a great deal of labor, and . . . is not free from some difficulty," and wrote, "Kentucky has not arrived at the enthusiastic state of mind which has prevailed in Minnesota, Wisconsin, [and] Michigan . . . with reference to their State Universities." However, Alfred thought his son should take the job to avoid any more political trouble with the Nonpartisan League in North Dakota.[4]

In August the Board of Trustees offered McVey the presidency at a salary of $8,500. News of the board's vote reached him at Cass Lake in Minnesota, where he was vacationing. He accepted the post without delay and devoted the remainder of the summer to concluding his work in Grand Forks and spending time with his family. Remembering the family's enthusiasm at the prospect of moving, Virginia McVey recalled that her father would sleep on the porch of the president's house in Grand Forks with his children, telling them stories about the South and Kentucky, generating anticipation for their upcoming relocation. She noted that all the siblings were excited about the move.[5]

When the McVeys first considered moving to Lexington, Frank confided in Mabel that although the University of Kentucky was poised for significant change, North Dakota still stood "much in advance of it [UK] in many ways." These were generous words, considering the depths to which the institution had fallen. For one thing, a leadership struggle had dominated university affairs. In addition, the University of Kentucky lacked financial stability, clear academic organization, an adequate physical plant, plans for growth, and sufficient faculty resources. A comprehensive survey of alumni revealed that high levels of concern about nepotism, a lack of academic standards, and political infighting further harmed the university's reputation."[6]

Many of these problems resulted from the actions of President Emeritus James K. Patterson. The Scotch-born executive began as president in 1869, the same year that McVey was born, and continued in his post for more than forty years. In that capacity he had saved the university from regional, political, and religious factionalism that threatened to destroy the institution. However, he governed the university in stereotypical "old-time" college president's fashion, which is to say that he ruled with an iron fist. From finances, fund-raising, and faculty issues to student discipline, campus construction, and alumni relations, the tough-minded administrator shaped the university to his liking.

When Patterson spoke of retiring, it was on his terms only. His conditions included the title "President Emeritus," an active role on the Board of Trustees, a full-fledged faculty post (save the teaching and research), and a position as the university's representative at state and national association meetings and conferences. In the end, the board agreed to Patterson's stipulations for retirement, including an annual retirement stipend of nearly $3,000, as well as continued residency on campus.[7]

When Patterson retired, a small group of men on the Board of Trustees suggested that Henry Stites Barker, a native of Christian County and a judge on the Kentucky Court of Appeals, serve as the next president. Barker himself originally scoffed at the suggestion. Although he had served on the Board of Trustees for nearly a decade and had attended the Agricultural and Mechanical College, he did not hold a college degree and had no experience in teaching or administration at the college level. Patterson voiced his opposition to Barker for the same reasons. Even Henry Pritchett, the famed president of the Carnegie Foundation for the Advancement of Teaching, wrote Barker to encourage him to reject the offer. Kentucky already lagged behind other states and needed a trained expert to lead the university in its necessary reforms.[8]

Despite Barker's lack of experience, the Board of Trustees offered him the presidency in February 1910. After a short time even Patterson, concerned about the other potential candidates, had changed his mind and decided to support the nomination. Finally, after nearly four months of deliberation, evidence of his own misgivings regarding his suitability for the post, Barker accepted. He would later argue that he took the position solely because of Patterson's strong encouragement. Regardless, the board had chosen the wrong man, and he had accepted.[9]

Foreshadowing the future struggles between the president emeritus and the acting executive, Barker and his wife moved onto campus, not into the president's house (which Patterson still occupied) but into a wing of Patterson Hall, a women's dormitory. Barker's hands-off presidential style was immediately evident. He expected department chairs to serve as administrators in their various fields. He emphasized the agricultural and mechanical engineering programs, while giving those professors greater freedom in the work they conducted. As registrar Ezra Gillis, who served under Patterson, Barker, and McVey, would later note, "The atmosphere of freedom for ideas and initiative which developed in Barker's first days was like opening the window of a stuffy room to a fresh breeze." Unfortunately, such freedom without central direction led to greater duplication and waste.[10]

When the acting president attempted to initiate his policies, he met with stiff resistance from the former executive. Patterson first charged Barker with breaking state law concerning the number of scholarships given to each county. After Barker successfully defended himself against this claim, the president emeritus followed with another legislative investigation concerning Barker's misuse of state funds. Barker fired back that he had been misappropriating funds because state law did not allow for Patterson's large pension. Eventually acquitted of these charges as well, he continued to meet resistance from Patterson at every turn. In sum, the university had two presidents, and their policies and personalities could not have been more divergent.[11]

When Barker suggested a merger of the College of Mechanical Engineering with the College of Civil Engineering in 1916, existing tensions between the two exploded. This led the board to recommend a thorough investigation of the merger proposal, as well as "other conditions causing or tending to produce discontent among the alumni and the student body and the general public toward the existing administration." The university's "investigating committee" interviewed more than 150 individuals affiliated with the school concerning its current problems and sent out sixteen hundred questionnaires to alumni. The board took the opportunity to hire outside educational experts to serve as the "survey commission" that would study the state of the university and make recommendations to the investigating committee and to the Board of Trustees.[12]

Not surprisingly, both the committee and the commission found Patterson's actions detrimental to the university. A transcript of a panel interview with Patterson and Barker revealed the extent to which the former friends had become enemies. Patterson claimed that his actions stemmed from his hope that the university would become a leading educational institution not merely in the state, but in the South, rather than a "mossback institution" with a "questionable reputation." The president emeritus further argued that under Barker's administration the morality of the student body had fallen into serious decline.[13]

Barker retaliated that Patterson had a talent for lying "by mingling truth and falsehood together." The new president added that no one man could take the disparate groups of young Kentuckians who found their way to the university and "fill them up on discipline and make Presbyterian preachers out of them in less than four years." He compared his relationship with Patterson to the "proverbial drop of water dripping on him for five years" and added that accepting the presidency was "one of the biggest mistakes of his life." When asked about the kind accolades that Barker had bestowed upon Patterson when he retired, Barker responded, "Oh yes, I was a big fool in those days." [14]

The survey commission's first recommendation was that Barker resign from the presidency—a recommendation with which he gladly complied. However, the report also stated that Barker had been "grievously sinned against" as he attempted to lead the university. The current president served in "an impossible situation" and had displayed "a largeness of soul, a devotion to duty[,] a loyalty to his friends and a charity to his enemies which are beyond praise." The report chided Patterson's actions and admonished the board to prevent "the annoying and thwarting" of the next president's administration, something they had failed to accomplish during Barker's tenure. Concluding that Patterson, "notwithstanding his anxiety for the welfare of the institution which formerly he had served so notably, wrought serious injury to it," the report proposed specific suggestions to curtail the actions of Patterson when the next president arrived—one of the few recommendations the board did not fully adopt. [15]

The survey commission expanded its investigation to include the university's structure, developing a series of sixty-nine policy recommendations for the Board of Trustees to consider. The commission argued that "the lack of an adequate conception of the presidency has been the most important single cause of the difficulties in which the university has become involved." The next president, the report recommended, needed to have expertise in administration and act as an advisor to the board. In this role the leader needed to formulate university policy relating to finances, the physical plant, faculty, and other disparate issues and instruct the board as to what needed to be done. This precise delineation of the president's role clearly fit McVey's personality and profile and helped make his first years in the office easier.[16]

The report made dozens of additional recommendations to be implemented in the years ahead. While many were minor, others, if enacted, would greatly change the structure of the university and help define its mission for the commonwealth in the twentieth century. The commission recommended that the Board of Trustees reduce its size from thirty-two members to fifteen, allow no county to be represented by more than one member, hold quarterly meetings, and publish the minutes of these sessions. Furthermore, the board needed to adopt an antinepotism policy and avoid appointments based on considerations other than merit.[17]

The Board of Trustees, argued the report, needed to recognize the faculty (including assistant professors) as the legislative arm for the teaching staff. It called for the revival of a faculty council, consisting of the various campus deans, to serve as the administrative arm of the faculty as it practiced its legislative functions. Along with this, professors needed more equitable teaching loads, funding for conference presentations, and a more uniform salary scale.[18]

These faculty improvements were to be coupled with higher academic standards. The report noted that of the 105 professors at the university, only 10 held doctorates. The faculty had a combined total of 176 degrees, but only 25 had been earned at "Class I" institutions. Related to this, almost 40 percent of the degrees earned by the faculty were from the University of Kentucky. The College of Mechanical and Electrical Engineering was criticized for serving as an example of "inbreeding" that had "few parallels." Noting the lack of research and publication, the report argued that scholarly productivity needed to be encouraged and rewarded. Related to this, it noted that the financially strapped university usually rewarded faculty members not with an increase in pay, but with an increase in title. Because of this practice, approximately half the faculty served as full professors. The report argued that when a young faculty member deserved an increase in pay and title, the university should either pay the individual more money or allow the professor to move to another institution that could properly accommodate such talent.[19]

The report recommended more stringent entrance requirements and encouraged a greater role for faculty in enforcing academic standards. It also advocated the adoption of an "honor points" system like the one McVey had instituted at the University of North Dakota. Under this plan students would be awarded points for passing a class, as well as additional points for earning As or Bs. Finally, all requirements were to be strictly enforced for athletes on campus. Furthermore, the president was not to be tied down with petty discipline problems: the university needed a committee designated to address such issues. The commission argued that this group be large enough to safeguard individual professors from undue pressure placed on them by influential families who might encourage ignoring a particular student's behavior problems.[20]

Additionally, the survey commission argued that the university lacked a central authority. It recommended a clear leadership role for the president, while emphasizing the importance of a solid internal structure responsible for delegating duties and transmitting details to each functioning level of the institution. Along with a strong administrator, the commission stressed the need for a proper protocol that would send problems through the appropriate immediate administrative superior. This was to be balanced by a faculty member's right to appeal to the Board of Trustees on controversial or contested issues. Concerning finances, the president would present the budget to the board, and a newly created central business office would be operated by a chief business agent. In essence, the president's office would be stronger, as would the general bureaucracy of the institution—a clear example of the progressive impulse in higher education.[21]

Regarding the campus, the report lamented the deplorable conditions of many of the university's buildings and encouraged more efficient use of structures. The men's dormitories, for example, were "bare, ugly, dilapidated, untidy, unsanitary, [and] ill smelling." The report recommended that the university shut down these structures as soon as they had the resources to do so, because they "would be condemned as a public nuisance in any decent residence district of any American municipality." Many buildings needed repairs, other buildings needed to be constructed, and some satisfactory structures were not operating at efficient levels. The commission highlighted that the classroom facilities were not being used nearly enough during the workweek hours and noted that when classes were in session, the number of students in most classes did not come close to capacity. Finally, the study encouraged the president and the board to develop a clear plan for campus growth and to hire two individuals to oversee the necessary changes, one for the physical plant and another for the university grounds.[22]

The survey commission addressed a number of ways the next administration could encourage academic excellence. It urged the adoption of policies limiting the number of undergraduate classes with low enrollments. More than 50 percent of the classes offered had fewer than ten students, and the meager university budget could not afford to finance such marginal classes. To remedy this problem, the report suggested that faculty loads be evaluated by examining the number of classes taught (recommending that it be lower) and the number of students per class (arguing that it should be higher). Aligning classes and increasing enrollment would provide more funding for priorities such as lab equipment and library holdings, which stood at a modest fifteen thousand volumes.[23]

Making the necessary bureaucratic changes would be a challenging task. The university's academic structure as well as the scope and sequence of courses required reorganization. The report cited duplication of classes as the individual colleges failed to work together within a clear university-wide system. The reforms for the graduate program, the teachers' program, and the Department of Home Economics were less controversial than those dealing with the colleges of agriculture and engineering, but coordination among all programs was essential to the improvement of the university.[24]

The concerns in agriculture centered on the relationship between the college itself and the affiliated experiment station and Extension Department. These divisions operated in isolation from one another, and this prevented a central administrator from coordinating their activities. The university had already attempted to resolve these problems, but they persisted. In the years prior to McVey's arrival, Fred Mutchler, superintendent of the Department of Agricultural Extension, and Joseph Kastle, dean of the College of Agriculture, had struggled to work together. Kastle resigned his post, and George Roberts succeeded him. Under Roberts's administration Mutchler continued to operate with brazen independence. He made personnel and financial decisions either without the consent of the dean or in defiance of him. The survey commission stated that his actions could be construed as nothing less than insubordination to the Board of Trustees, and the continuance of autonomous behavior should result in dismissal.[25]

Beyond personality and personnel issues, the commission called for a strong dean to coordinate the research conducted at the experiment station, the classes offered at the college, and the demonstrations provided across the state through the Extension Department. Not only would this reform emulate immensely successful agricultural colleges such as the universities of Illinois and Wisconsin, but it would also ensure Kentucky's compliance with the Smith-Lever Act, which Congress had passed to increase aid to agricultural extension work in individual states. McVey's job would be made easier because he had the support of a majority of the faculty members in agriculture. These faculty members had notified the board through a formal report that they wished to see closer coordination among the programs within each branch of the College of Agriculture.[26]

Reorganizing the various colleges of engineering presented an even greater hurdle. The separate colleges consisted of Mechanical and Electrical Engineering, Civil Engineering, and Mining Engineering. Each program exhibited fierce loyalty to its particular field and to its students and faculty members. In 1911, for example, when the Executive Committee of the board called for a merger of the Civil Engineering and Mechanical and Electrical Engineering colleges, the outcry was so great that the full Board of Trustees promptly voted the measure down despite its obvious benefits. In 1916 President Barker again encouraged the Board of Trustees to unite two of the three colleges of engineering while creating a separate College of Mines. During this attempt the dean of the College of Civil Engineering, Walter Rowe, publicly opposed the plan and challenged Barker's support of Dean F. Paul Anderson—the successful and flamboyant head of the College of Mechanical and Electrical Engineering. Rowe added that he would bow his knee to no one and insisted that the board reject the "peanut politics" that had resulted in the proposal. After Rowe's article appeared, a flier was distributed throughout the campus further condemning the action, as well as the university administration. This resulted in the board's call for a thorough study of Barker's proposed merger, his administration in general, and the state of the university.[27]

In the end, Rowe's actions jeopardized his career at the University of Kentucky and increased the board's resolve to support McVey's merger of the engineering colleges. The survey report found Rowe "guilty of serious lapses in right relations to his colleagues and to the administration." Although the committee could not prove the dean's involvement in orchestrating the dissemination of the derogatory letter on campus, the impropriety of Rowe's actions was "too obvious to need comment." The fiasco also led to a closer examination of Rowe's credentials, and it was discovered that he had lied about earning a master's degree. This revelation led the investigation committee to call for his retirement.[28]

The survey commission recommended the immediate consolidation of the engineering schools into a larger College of Engineering. It encouraged the Board of Trustees to hire a dean from outside the university who had experience at coordinating a larger college. The investigating committee agreed on merging the schools, but the board postponed the merger for a year to allow McVey time to assess the situation, observe Anderson's work in the existing program, and provide Anderson an opportunity to make his own case for the deanship of the consolidated colleges. Although Anderson had been the subject of much criticism from Rowe and other members of the university and local community, the board found his work admirable and the accusations against him unjustified. Therefore, he deserved consideration for the new post.[29]

The extensive list of recommendations presented by the survey commission and largely accepted by the Board of Trustees proved to be a godsend for McVey. As he initiated the much-needed reforms as president, he could point to the work of both the committee and the commission as justification for his actions. At the same time, however, the report revealed the university's precarious position and the monumental task that McVey

faced. It noted that no administrator had managed to capture "the imagination" of the commonwealth's citizens concerning the role that the university could play in the life and well-being of the state. One of McVey's
primary tasks would be the "stimulation of the interest of the whole commonwealth in higher education as embodied in the University and the
quickening of its efforts to bring the U of K into the front rank of institutions which serve with high effectiveness." This standard would measure
McVey's success. The commission argued that Kentucky could "reasonably expect to reap some of the advantages of unity which have operated
so remarkably in the last twenty years to develop great institutions like
Minnesota, Wisconsin, Illinois, and California." Each of these universities had incorporated a land-grant college as a part of the flagship university, but none operated below the Mason-Dixon Line.[30]

Despite the existing challenges, the presidency offered McVey an opportunity to implement progressive reforms that would stabilize the struggling university, serve the commonwealth, and eventually bring the
institution recognition and prestige. The extent of the university's failure
in the years prior to McVey's arrival had engendered a sense of desperation
that would aid McVey in his early years. The commonwealth's historic
failure to adequately fund the school now helped to align many of the
state's concerned citizens, its politicians, and the board members as advocates for the university, if just for a while.

Not only did those associated with UK promise to secure the support
of many across the state, but they pledged their allegiance to McVey and
his plan for the university—even before he had formulated one. McVey
already had the confidence of the governing board, and he successfully
wooed the commonwealth's press. The *Lexington Leader* editorialized,
"McVey will bring to the University of Kentucky those qualities of scholarship, executive ability, tact and progressive leadership without which
this university cannot realize the ambitions of its founders or . . . see Kentucky take her rightful place in the sisterhood of states." McVey was also
pleased to receive a welcome from University of Alabama president George
H. Denny, who (knowing the mood of the South toward northerners) assured McVey that at least one university president would welcome him to

the region. McVey responded that he looked forward to seeing Denny regularly since he had decided to "cast my lot with the southern group of universities." Even President Emeritus Patterson, after voting for McVey, stated, "I believe that we have eminent reason to congratulate ourselves."[31]

Although the Board of Trustees was eager to move forward, McVey had other responsibilities to address. At the beginning of September McVey and his family traveled south to Washington, D.C., bypassing Lexington altogether. McVey was eager to begin his research on war finance in England, and the family used the opportunity to enroll their children in elite private schools in the nation's capital for the entire academic year. McVey's work in Washington epitomized what many progressives in the Bluegrass had hoped to find in a president: a leader who embraced the growing relationships among the federal government, philanthropic foundations, and higher education. Before McVey's hiring, the *Lexington Leader* noted that the university had "failed itself" and the cause of education throughout the state. The institution, it argued, needed an individual who understood finances and one who would not view federal aid as "the price of an alliance," but as an integral part of a modern university.[32]

After spending a few weeks in Washington, McVey finally visited the campus in mid-September. While in Lexington he managed to deliver a number of speeches at various welcoming gatherings. He offered a short address on Friday, during a reception in his honor at the Buell Armory. In his first formal speech to the student body he addressed the university's integral role in preserving representative government, calling it the "richest fruition and highest expression of democracy." After noting that the condition of a state university was representative of its people's progress (a remark that could have been construed as rather condescending, considering the troubles at Kentucky), he added that the current war demonstrated the value of education and highlighted the role modern public universities could play in addressing the challenges facing a democracy.[33]

Writing Mabel, McVey was upbeat about everything at UK except the current state of the president's home. Otherwise, he appreciated the kind welcome and explained that many of the existing troubles were "wholly unnecessary" and that he could bring the situation under control. In sum, he maintained that the state of the institution was not nearly as bad as he had assumed. The picture he painted may have been accurate, but it was probably shaded in order to encourage his wife about the move: McVey failed to note what others close to him would later recall. Years later, for example, he laughed as he described a rather unimpressive reception held not in a formal assembly hall, but in the building used to house the university's weapons. Lemonade was the single refreshment offered, and it was served out of a washtub sitting on the floor. Kentucky indeed was far different from its neighbors to the north.[34]

McVey left again for Washington but returned a month later to speak to the student body and to present his first report to the board. In both instances, the emboldened president challenged the status quo at Kentucky. He held his first "Between Us" day with the underclassmen, explaining that he would speak to them twice a semester to address issues directly relating to the student body. In his first speech he focused almost entirely on student behavior. Declaring that the war imposed an emphasis on the "serious" aspects of student life, he urged them to end hazing and asked them to refrain from "being a thorn in the flesh of the community." Destructive or juvenile behavior, he asserted, would raise the ire of local residents and prevent the legislature from properly supporting the institution. Instead students needed to focus on their academic affairs. He explained that he had chosen not to embarrass the students by quizzing them on the U.S. Constitution, but he wanted to emphasize that a clear understanding of American history and government was essential to serving as good citizens, particularly during a time of war.[35]

The president's first report to the board echoed many of the recommendations made by the survey commission. McVey highlighted the reforms he thought crucial to improving the university and argued that the areas most in need of change could be organized into two basic categories. The first was a lack of administrative coordination on the campus, which he asserted could be properly handled in due time. Essential to this process was the merging of the engineering colleges. This was, he contended, "in line with modern educational organization and thought" and would increase "efficiency" in the engineering program. Along with coordinating the various branches of agricultural work, the university needed to focus on campus planning and reorganizing the Board of Trustees.[36]

The second crisis facing the university was its lack of funding. Salaries remained woefully inadequate, and increases were needed to recruit and retain a faculty of highly qualified scholars and teachers. Poor funding for the library had made proper instruction in the humanities and social sciences "impossible." In the broader scheme, the university was unable to meet its obligations to the state. The agricultural and natural resources of the state could be vastly improved with the assistance of "scientific study," but the university required more money to carry out its work. Finally, the commonwealth needed to expand the curriculum with more diverse offerings in order to meet the demands of the New South, most notably a business program. Business majors had become increasingly common elsewhere, but the University of Kentucky had not received the funds to make this important addition to its offerings.[37]

McVey concluded his report with a progressive's faith in the commonwealth's eventual support of the university. He argued that when the institution received the funding it required to serve the state well, the people in turn would become more liberal in their support. The president expressed faith in his abilities, in the university's potential to serve Kentucky, and in the commonwealth's reciprocal support of the institution. These views epitomized the progressive hopes prevalent among university administrators across the country, but they would be challenged during his tenure as president. Such ideals had proven successful in many wealthier states, but in the South a different scenario prevailed.[38]

McVey continued his monthly visits to Lexington, and in late November, while still dealing with institutional problems, he turned his attention to some personal affairs. Renovation of the president's home was under way, but it would not be completed by the time his family arrived, so McVey needed to find a place for them to live. He secured a house to rent on Ashland Avenue, a few blocks from campus, and purchased the family's first car. Mabel had wanted one for years, but they had not settled on the type. Taking his wife's advice, Frank purchased a battery-powered

Franklin. Pleased with his choice, he wrote Mabel bragging about its "high speed" and expressing confidence that she too would like it. He confided in her, though, that learning how to drive was more difficult than he had imagined. (Both he and Mabel had car accidents during their first years in Lexington.)[39]

McVey demonstrated greater skill at running the university and its governing body. His second report to the board at the December meeting revealed that, though largely absent during the fall semester, he had managed to create a foundation for future change. He had held meetings with the Executive Committee of the board, the faculty, the University Council, and other key committees. He had met with the governor twice and attended a vocational education conference in Frankfort to discuss curriculum formation to meet the standards of the Smith-Hughes Bill. The president boasted that twenty-four of the sixty-nine recommendations presented at the beginning of the summer had been accomplished (at least on paper) before he moved to Lexington: "There has been some change in the spirit of the University in the last few months."[40]

A December meeting revealed the extent to which the board was ready to follow McVey's lead. The president, with the approval of a faculty committee, had developed a constitution to govern the procedures of the university, which he presented to the board. McVey also discussed the rules and regulations that would govern the Board of Trustees in the future. The president clarified details of the proposed organizational structure. Included were the responsibilities of the faculty, the faculty senate, the University Council, the various colleges and their deans, and the Executive Committee of the Board of Trustees. Although the board had the opportunity to amend the constitution, it chose instead to adopt it in its entirety by a unanimous vote.[41]

McVey's other reforms were also under way. Accounting procedures were reorganized and a stenographic bureau created. McVey appointed a committee to create an infirmary staffed by a nurse to deal with the threat of "possible epidemics" (an insightful precaution, considering the influenza breakout the following year). Steps toward academic reorganization were taken as McVey pushed for expanded academic offerings, as well as funding for campus repairs and construction. McVey had been preparing information for the state legislature, which would begin its biennial session in early 1918. He had not yet determined, however, "just how far the university should go in asking for these things in the coming legislature."[42]

The president made numerous public appearances to advertise the progress of the university. He spoke to the Kentucky Press Association, the Eastern Kentucky Association, the state conference of the YMCA, and the Lexington Rotary Club. He sought assistance from the Journalism Department, requesting that it publicize the university's accomplishments. He recommended that the institution begin sending press releases about its work to the smaller county and town papers, as well as the dailies in the larger cities. McVey's emphasis on public relations seemed to work. Concerning his speech on the financial problems created by the war, the *Lexington Herald* stated that the members of the Rotary Club probably had not ever listened to "a more interesting or a more illuminating discussion of any topic." The article added that Kentucky was lucky to have a man like McVey and noted that the state could take pride in itself for having as president of the commonwealth's flagship university "a man who is a real force and a real leader in the educational affairs of the nation."[43]

During the spring of 1918, McVey's family remained in Washington, D.C., while the children completed their schooling and the president's house remained under renovation. Frank, on the other hand, moved to Lexington to meet the most important challenge of his early administration. Although his speeches to the public and in meetings at the university had laid a proper foundation, none of his proposed reforms or administrative acumen would matter if he could not convince the state legislature to increase its financial support. The General Assembly met biannually in Frankfort, and a successful legislative session would set the tone for reform on the campus for years to come.

As McVey geared up for the battle in Frankfort, he hoped that the Executive Committee of the Board of Trustees would assist him in navigating Kentucky's unique political waters. In a letter to Judge Richard

Stoll, McVey listed the primary goals of the university and discussed their political implications. One goal remained "administrative" in nature: re-organizing the university's governing structure. The other pressing issue centered on funding. McVey hoped to lobby for a bill that would increase the university's general operating revenue, as well as legislation that would bolster the federal government's support of particular university activities through matching state funds. The 1914 Smith-Lever Act, which provid-ed matching funds for agricultural extension work, needed reauthoriza-tion at the state level, and the Smith-Hughes Act (passed by Congress in 1917) would provide federal dollars for teacher training in agriculture, domestic science, and industrial instruction if Frankfort complied.[44]

Although a novice in Kentucky politics, McVey certainly understood the standard approaches necessary for success, and he outlined a plan for the university to secure all it could from the state government. He hoped that the state superintendent of public instruction would find a legislator to sponsor a bill for the Smith-Hughes appropriation, presumably to make it look as if the university was not asking for too much. McVey directed the College of Agriculture to write a bill for Smith-Lever funding and asked Fred Mutchler's legislative contacts to introduce the bill.[45]

McVey himself took the initiative for an increase of general appro-priations. He began by delivering a report to the governor and the state legislature. The report offered facts and figures and addressed the larger issues of why the state university existed and what benefits it could bring the state if it were properly supported. In comparing Kentucky to other schools, he looked entirely to the North, suggesting that what had been accomplished in Ohio, Indiana, Illinois, Michigan, and Wisconsin could be replicated in the Bluegrass. He noted that the state university "stands today waiting for the word to go ahead. Limited funds, limited equip-ment, and limited staff hold it back." He went on to discuss various reve-nue schemes that would benefit the university and, in turn, the state.[46]

He then backed up his written suggestions with personal appearances at the capital. Speaking to the House Committee on Revenue and Taxa-tion, McVey pleaded for an increase in appropriations through a specific taxable equation. He noted how far behind Kentucky lagged when compared with its northern neighbors and shared pictures of the dilapidated structures on campus. His pleading worked, and the committee adopted McVey's suggestions with little controversy, sending a bill to the floor for passage.[47]

McVey did all he could outside the capitol building to guarantee success. He pleaded his case personally with the governor. He skipped a meeting in Washington, D.C., concerning national war efforts, to be available in case he was needed. He even wrote a thank you letter to a student who had helped pull some wagons out of the pond near campus after other students had pushed them into the water. He remarked that when he worked with politicians from around the commonwealth, he found them quick to highlight poor behavior as justification for withholding financial support. "When students of the university endanger its good name," he asserted, "they are making it more difficult for the university to do its work in the state."[48]

As the session came to a close, McVey had reason to celebrate. His request for a specific tax formula for higher education had resulted in an act that provided the university with 1¾ cents for every $100 of assessed property. This amount was estimated at $350,000, which greatly expanded the state's previous appropriations. The bill contained similar provisions for the state's normal colleges. Furthermore, the state appropriated the necessary matching funds required for both the Smith-Hughes and the Smith-Lever acts. Publicly, McVey made few comments and continued to point out that the state's support of the university still lagged behind that of many of the states bordering the commonwealth. However, writing Stoll in a personal letter near the end of the legislative session, McVey noted that the university had four main legislative goals and that all were being met with virtually no modifications. He concluded, "As legislation goes . . . such a result can be looked upon as distinctly satisfactory and creditable."[49]

Even before McVey successfully lobbied the state for increased funding, he went about finding the best ways to spend money. After the session in Frankfort the implementation of reforms became aggressive. During his first years at the University of Kentucky, the president's interests and expenditures fell along two general lines: improvements to the physical plant and enhanced academics. The academic issues were complicated, involving not only the restructuring of programs, departments, and colleges but also the hiring of the best individuals to implement his agenda.

One of McVey's pressing problems was that of finding someone who would procure larger amounts of federal funding and successfully coordinate agricultural activities in the state. During the months prior to McVey's hiring, the College of Agriculture, the survey commission, and the Board of Trustees had agreed that the university needed an experienced scholar with a strong personality and administrative skills to fill such a role, but no obvious candidate emerged. The day after offering McVey the presidency, Richard Stoll wrote McVey concerning the urgent necessity of finding the right person to assume the deanship in agriculture as soon as possible.[50]

McVey agreed, and within a week of receiving Stoll's letter, he wrote Thomas Cooper at the Agricultural College in Bismarck, North Dakota, to see if he would be interested in moving south. McVey had known Cooper for many years and trusted his administrative abilities. Cooper had attended one of McVey's classes at the University of Minnesota and had gone on to do agricultural work in Minnesota before being hired by a group of wealthy capitalists in North Dakota to ensure that the state's agricultural college would not challenge their agenda. McVey certainly knew the political climate in North Dakota and realized that Cooper's previous affiliations would not make him the favorite "college man" among many in power in North Dakota. McVey added that the Kentucky position would pay $5,000 and requested that Cooper recommend some others he thought might be capable if he were not interested.[51]

The president then recommended Cooper to the board, stating that the young professor had overseen significant advances during his three years with the Better Farming Association before he became director of the experiment station at the North Dakota Agricultural College. McVey added that Bradford Knapp, chief of the Extension Division in the southern states, agreed that Cooper would be a valuable asset to the work of the university and the commonwealth. The president recommended that Cooper be offered the deanship at a salary of $6,000, as well as occupancy of the Scovell house, just off the campus. Despite some grandstanding from Patterson, who voiced his preference for a Kentuckian, the board, still in its honeymoon period with McVey, offered Cooper $6,200, with use of the Scovell house at a cost of $200 per annum. Just before the New Year Cooper sent McVey word that he would be coming within the week. McVey wrote his wife to tell her that he was relieved to have someone on whom he could depend "to look after the agricultural end of the University." Cooper had proven to be a shrewd and forceful administrator in North Dakota, and McVey trusted that the same would be true in Kentucky.[52]

Not only did Cooper's arrival mark the beginning of the career of a highly celebrated professor at the university, but it signaled the demise of Mutchler's position as he continued to resist the leadership under which he had been placed. After one semester with Cooper as dean, Mutchler phoned McVey and asked for a meeting. In that session, Mutchler asked the president to specify what political activity he had engaged in that aroused the administration's criticism. McVey responded that political activity, in the way of supporting one party over another, was not to blame, but that Mutchler was guilty of "engineering the appointments in the Department for the purpose of developing a machine" in order to advance his own agenda and protect his position. Mutchler remained on staff through the fall of 1918, but when Cooper arrived as dean, the professor's days were numbered. The new dean succeeded in driving him out by the end of the year.[53]

From all indications in the report, the survey commission expected the merger of the engineering colleges to be far more difficult than the coordination of activities in agriculture. However, McVey combined the schools with minimal backlash from the faculty and staff. Unlike the situation in agriculture, which the president attempted to solve immediately, in engineering he waited for more than a year to begin the merger. By then all involved understood that it was coming, and little resistance remained. McVey's recommendation for the dean of engineering, however, did create a minor stir that resolved itself in a matter of months. The survey commission had argued that Paul Anderson was "not the man to be placed in charge of the proposed unified college of engineering." The report noted that "many charges against his methods of administration, his university ideals, his business practices and his personal habits are made in widespread fashion and by apparently well-informed persons." Anderson's "reputation for [im]morality" included accusations of drinking, gambling, and excessive indebtedness.[54]

Despite these concerns, McVey recommended Anderson for the deanship in June 1918. After certain board members expressed reservations, McVey removed his motion until he had an opportunity to study the earlier complaints, which were raised again at the board meeting. McVey did not find enough evidence of wrongdoing to change his mind, and the board acquiesced to McVey's repeated recommendation, beginning a successful career for Anderson as the dean of the College of Engineering. The successful engineering merger, a proposal that had cost Barker the presidency, occurred under McVey's guidance with relatively little controversy. He then turned his attention to other organizational problems.[55]

The College of Arts and Sciences did not need to be merged but did require expansion. To do this, McVey transferred a number of departments from other colleges and created new ones as needed. He placed the departments of botany, zoology, and bacteriology with arts and sciences rather than with agriculture, arguing that the College of Agriculture would address applied sciences rather than "fundamental" sciences. Latin and Greek were combined into the newly created Department of Ancient Languages, while modern languages were divided between romance languages and German. The joint department of history and economics was separated, and the History Department was broadened by the addition of political science. Similarly, economics was extended by the incorporation of sociology. Philosophy and psychology were divided into distinct programs. To meet the needs of all the new departments, the faculty increased from forty-two to fifty-four instructors in one year.[56]

With these departmental modifications came changes in the students' curriculum requirements. Two years of general work would be required before students could begin advanced work in their chosen fields. From the twenty-two departments six broad groupings were created, and students needed to take a number of electives from the different categories. Attempting to defend the structural and academic changes, McVey explained that he had "not abandoned the old position" of learning for broad and noble pursuits and noted that he resented the accusation that too many courses lacked useful applications. He argued that the aim was to render greater possibilities for service in the commonwealth and that the reorganized college now possessed the ability to do so.[57]

McVey also oversaw other academic restructuring. The law school set into motion reforms to elevate admissions requirements, and a nursing program was developed. Home economics was placed under the governance of the College of Agriculture, and programs such as music, as well as art and design, were added to the College of Arts and Sciences. McVey placed faculty hires funded in part by the Smith-Hughes Act in the education program. The same department initiated a lab school jointly operated with the city of Lexington. However, the superintendent of public schools, M. A. Cassidy, and McVey agreed that the aims of the university and the city schools were disparate, and the school was discontinued. McVey did not abandon the idea, however, and in the near future a university model school opened on Scovell Park, the property donated by the city of Lexington—a policy that benefited both town and gown.[58]

After World War I ended, McVey immediately sought to develop programs that he felt would benefit the university and the state. Many of his proposals resembled those he had initiated at the University of North Dakota, but others were entirely fresh endeavors. However, McVey clearly wanted to expand more rapidly than the budget would allow. Hence, he had mixed results with academic expansion and faculty development, primarily because of budget constraints.

One of McVey's successes was in general university extension work. Creating an effective outreach arm proved far easier in Kentucky than in North Dakota because agricultural extension work already existed, and he faced no competition from other institutions. In January 1919 John Pettijohn, who had worked with McVey in Grand Forks and had later become federal director of extension as part of the Bureau of Education, wrote McVey proposing a cooperative agreement between his extension service and the university. McVey agreed to the arrangement, and in 1919 the Board of Trustees included $3,700 for general extension work in the annual budget, only a fraction of the more than $200,000 expended on broader agricultural extension work.[59]

The newly created "university extension" program resembled the plan McVey had instituted in North Dakota. The president wrote that it would operate in four primary areas: "instruction by correspondence, instruction by letters, general welfare work, debates and public forum." The most successful of these endeavors was in correspondence work, which began during the fall semester of 1919. Lacking a director, McVey and his secretary, Wellington Patrick, helped organize courses in twenty-three subject areas, recruiting more than thirty professors to teach the classes. Within a few years McVey had expanded the program's budget to $25,000. The university now offered extension lectures, organized women's clubs, promoted debates at high schools, and shipped books throughout the state. Of course, this effort paled in comparison to the extension work in agriculture for which the university was primarily known throughout the commonwealth.[60]

McVey faced a tougher time instituting programs that did not receive financial support from the federal government. Some of his programs were tabled, and he chose not to propose others, already knowing their fate. For example, he suggested opening a school of pharmacy, arguing that the university would spend approximately $6,000 a year to operate the program, while it would generate another $3,000 on its own, leaving only a $3,000 balance. The board voted to defer the matter until it knew more definitely the role the university would play regarding statewide health care.[61]

At the beginning of 1919 McVey also began corresponding with Elwood Street, a social worker and director of the Welfare League of Louisville, who desired to create a school of social work there. Street suggested having students take courses in Lexington for either two or three years before transferring to Louisville, where they would engage in fieldwork and extra classes. McVey liked the idea but thought that the operation would require a director and an assistant, which the university could not afford. Street then approached the University of Louisville, and it agreed to meet the expenses. (More than a decade would pass before the University of Kentucky added a department of social work.)[62]

Along with changes in the university structure came higher expectations for faculty members. Despite the inordinate number of full professors at the university, few possessed the training and credentials that McVey desired. Only nine held PhDs, and one other had earned an MD. McVey immediately encouraged scholarly productivity from a faculty that had published little. His first challenge to the professors came while he was still in Washington, D.C., conducting research of his own. At that time, McVey sent out a form letter asking three questions: What books or articles have you published in recent years? What is your current research project? And, what plans do you have for research and publication in the years ahead? This must have been a disconcerting change in tone for the largely unproductive faculty.[63]

Integral to facilitating research was the recruitment of active scholars to the university. McVey had enlisted a handful of individuals even before his arrival in Lexington, including Thomas Cooper, and the legislature's increased appropriations allowed McVey to secure dozens more faculty members—thirty-seven professors and instructors for 1918–1919 alone. This was an astonishing number considering that the university had approximately one thousand full-time students that year. McVey's recruits more than doubled the number of PhDs and infused life into the university. However, the large number of outsiders arriving on campus caused concern among some.[64]

McVey regularly informed the board of faculty publications but argued that faculty research remained far from what it ought to be. To encourage scholarship, the president employed a variety of strategies. He had started the *Quarterly Journal* at the University of North Dakota to aid faculty publication. Wisely, he did not choose to replicate this approach exactly at Kentucky, but in 1919 he convinced the Board of Trustees to fund a monograph series for work done by university professors. Within a year, two works had been published in the series. McVey also created a research club for those engaged in publication after graduate school and recruited upward of twenty faculty members to join the group by 1920.[65]

McVey struggled to retain productive scholars with such a modest budget. The state's increased appropriations allowed the president to hire new scholars, but skyrocketing postwar inflation negated the increased salaries. Although Kentucky had substantially raised salaries, the university failed to retain many of its most promising professors. In October 1919 McVey informed the Executive Committee of the Board of Trustees that the institution had lost at least twenty-five faculty members who had left for better pay at other institutions or in the private sector. These included many of McVey's hires, as well as older professors who had engaged in scholarly work. The College of Agriculture alone had lost fifteen individuals.[66]

Despite the unprecedented legislative success in 1918, the university's income fell short of projections. Under the assessment plan, McVey hoped to receive $350,000, a $200,000 increase in state support. However, assessments did not match the estimates, and the university received approximately $265,000 from the state treasury. Although a substantial increase over past years, this was not enough to fund McVey's programs. McVey proposed that at some point in the future the university needed to receive a specific dollar appropriation from the commonwealth, but that did not help him in the short run, and the University of Kentucky continued to suffer the consequences.[67]

Not all productive professors left as a result of budgetary constraints. As was the case at the University of North Dakota, McVey let one well-trained professor leave because of his radical views. Arthur Calhoun had written McVey to apply for a sociology position for the fall of 1918. Although a native of Pennsylvania, the professor noted that he had spent years in the South and desired to return to "a state university with a future." McVey hired Calhoun, who proceeded to give a public address sympathizing with the Bolshevik Revolution in Russia. Immediately, a local paper defended the professor's right to present his views but questioned the administration's (presumably McVey's) prudence in allowing him so public a platform.[68]

At the end of Calhoun's first year McVey did not renew his contract. The Interstate Teachers' Agency and the *Chicago Tribune* both inquired about the professor's departure. Defending his decision, McVey argued that Calhoun was a good man but that he wanted "departmental viewpoints . . . to be somewhat similar." Calhoun did not fit the desired profile. Unlike Lewinsohn in North Dakota, Calhoun did not make a scene after his dismissal, but McVey again found himself letting a professor go in order to preserve public support. He explained that a university was not the appropriate place for propaganda and that professors needed to refrain from personal conjecture and stick with answers provided by research.[69]

Fortunately for McVey, Kentucky was a conservative southern state, far less interested in protecting radical views than North Dakota had been. However, many years later, McVey confided that his greatest regret in the early years was allowing Calhoun to leave. Although lacking documentary evidence, historian Thomas Clark stated that McVey let Calhoun go because of pressures extending beyond the speech itself. Clark believed that tobacco owners, prominent in and around Lexington, feared Calhoun's interest in the labor practices and treatment of families working in the tobacco industry in Kentucky and North Carolina. Whatever the case, McVey clearly felt pressure to hire "safe" faculty members. For example, when the possibility of a social work program existed, McVey asked one professor, "Can you give me some idea of his viewpoint on various matters, more particularly his attitude on the movement in Russia and whether he is in favor of maintaining a republican form of government in this country." He added, "It seems almost absurd to ask questions of this kind, but I find it necessary to do so."[70]

In Kentucky, McVey seemed to face more criticism for hiring "outsiders" than he did for letting radical faculty members go. Many of McVey's hires came from the Upper Midwest. Some were former students at the University of Minnesota who had gone on to complete their graduate studies, and others came from North Dakota, where McVey had become familiar with their work. After arriving in Kentucky, McVey hired Archie Whipple away from the university in Grand Forks, while Thomas Cooper and Carl Lampert were recruited from other institutions in North Dakota. Interestingly, in his report to the Board of Trustees in 1919, McVey did not divulge the source of his hires.[71]

Despite certain challenges, McVey had great success in restructuring academic affairs in just two years. His second general area of reform, improving the physical plant, proved more difficult. McVey's plans for campus development were divided along two lines. The first included specific plans to repair existing structures and strategies for construction projects (which would come later). These specific projects were to be a part of McVey's second initiative, which included devising a clear and coherent plan for campus growth. The president hoped to construct many modern buildings, which would require a long-range plan to organize a successful building campaign into a larger unified architectural scheme.

McVey first hired a superintendent for buildings and grounds. Even before McVey had permanently arrived on campus, he wrote the superintendent of grounds at UND, Archie Whipple, and solicited his services for the campus in Lexington. Arguing that Kentucky offered a better climate and a lower cost of living, he also added, "We have a big job here in the matter of repairs and later in the construction of new buildings which I am sure the legislature is going to let us have later on." Offering an opportunity for "a man to make a record for himself" and a salary of $1,800, McVey convinced Whipple to move south.[72]

As soon as Whipple arrived in Kentucky, McVey put him (and others) to the task of renovating the campus. He assigned a select group of faculty members to work with Whipple as part of a committee "to take care of all problems pertaining to the buildings and grounds." A day later he wrote Whipple to detail the most pressing campus problems and needs. McVey wanted the campus grounds properly manicured and the brush taken away. He ordered repairs of several sidewalks and the cleanup of unsightly entrances to various buildings. Finally, he requested that the committee make a survey of the repairs needed in the campus facilities.[73]

McVey's proclivity for micromanagement, however, would not allow him to relinquish such tasks. He continued to monitor Whipple's correspondence with the War Industries Board in order to secure federal funding for construction projects related to the war service training programs on campus. He oversaw Whipple's progress on renovation projects such as repairs to the floors in different buildings. While admitting, "You will know this better than I," he continued to badger Whipple about sidewalk repairs and the need for boardwalks on campus. In 1919 McVey was still writing to Whipple listing projects to be accomplished during the summer. The June list included renovations, repairs, paint jobs, and paving projects.[74]

While McVey dealt with improving the campus, he also set his sights on expanding it. In 1918 he directed business agent D. H. Peak to purchase four lots that were up for auction behind Patterson Hall (the women's dormitory), placing no limit on the bid needed to secure the land. He allowed Peak to buy other properties near the campus as well. After the university began its aggressive acquisitions policy, property prices spiked, and McVey had to exercise restraint. McVey had been purchasing lots for well under $1,000 in 1918, but such prices were unheard of in subsequent years. To counter this trend, McVey and Peak often acted coolly toward the sellers, while privately keeping a watchful eye. For example, an African American Baptist church off Winslow Street was originally "secured" at a price of $8,000 by a local realtor. Rather than enter into negotiations at the time, McVey simply waited a few months and then negotiated a price of $5,400.[75]

Although postwar inflation and campus growth plans proved to be a sore spot for town and gown relations in other communities, McVey's ambitions enlivened support for the university in the local community. In one instance, with McVey's leadership and encouragement, the city commissioners actually saved a crucial piece of property for the university. In early 1919 the Lexington city commissioners proposed the sale of Scovell Park, adjacent to the university, to a tobacco company for the construction of warehouses. Up to that time the property had been used as a dumping ground for the city, but it was becoming valuable because of its location. The commissioners agreed to hear views concerning the proposal. A public outcry ensued. Harry Giovannoli, editor of the *Lexington Leader,* opposed the sale publicly in his paper, indicating that his position was based entirely on McVey's opposition to the sale. McVey argued against the sale because of its detrimental impact on future plans for the campus. The paper noted that "one of the most distinguished educators in America" had come to Lexington because of the support pledged to him by the state and local community. The university's impact on the community, Giovannoli asserted, far outweighed any benefits a tobacco warehouse could provide.[76]

The city commissioners held a public meeting on Friday, 14 March, to hear from concerned citizens. The arguments presented dealt primarily with the economic impact the university had on Lexington, estimated at more than $1 million annually. This impact would likely grow should the university be given its due support. Unsubstantiated rumors that Lexington was in danger of losing the university to another town were also presented. One speaker claimed that a town had offered the institution more than five hundred acres and $1 million if it would move there, although the town was not named. In any event, public support for the university was evident, and the city commissioners agreed to give the property to UK as a gesture of Lexington's cooperation.[77]

McVey's larger purpose was to develop a clear and consistent campus plan. When the 1918 legislature appropriated additional funding, McVey quickly contacted the Olmsted Brothers to secure their firm's services to help accomplish this goal. John Olmsted and Frederick Olmsted Jr. carried on the work of their famed father and had advised dozens of universities. They informed McVey that John Olmsted would make a preliminary visit to Lexington and devise a plan for growth at a price of $1,000 plus $200 traveling expenses. McVey agreed.[78]

Olmsted asked McVey for a comprehensive university plan for the next fifty years. Apparently without consultation, McVey laid out a lofty vision. He maintained that the campus needed to be adequately prepared for a student body of six thousand, which would require new buildings for athletics (including a gymnasium), law and political science, agriculture, domestic science, administration, biological science, physical science, public health, and farm engineering. A "women's building," men's union, auditorium, library, museum, armory, and student commons would also be necessary, along with additions to the existing chemistry and engineering facilities. He added, "We shall need in time, I have no question, a building for medicine and for pharmacy."[79]

After a preliminary visit and the university's payment to the architectural firm, little else was done. Although John Olmsted provided a rough sketch in August 1918, McVey had hoped for a great deal more. Olmsted continued to ask for information from other individuals on campus, but McVey persisted in taking the responsibility largely upon himself. After a year of little progress, Olmsted wrote McVey, "I have been for a long time wondering whether you realized that we were waiting for more information to enable us to revise our preliminary plan for the university campus." McVey responded, "Evidently both of us have been doing the same thing because we have been wondering why we did not receive a more extensive plan and information from you than we have already had." McVey added that the university's buildings and grounds superintendent had sent him a map of Lexington and noted that while the university had paid $1,200, it had received only a plan that was "very general in character."[80]

For McVey the situation worsened. He took the plans, with which he was dissatisfied, and presented them to the Board of Trustees in December 1919. He then requested that the Olmsted Brothers supply copies for each board member to examine. Two months later, in February 1920, John Olmsted died, and his brother did little to improve the strained relationship between McVey and the firm. In March the firm sent three copies of the most recent plans, but they were still unsatisfactory. Correspondence between McVey and the firm ceased. In a letter written two years later McVey would declare, "We have no building program in hand at the present time."[81]

It was (and is) not clear whether McVey or the university adopted Olmsted's style, which shunned the quadrangles and symmetry so common to other universities in favor of free-standing structures "surrounded by open space, accentuated by landscaping." Olmsted favored a large park-style campus in which each building could in some way stand alone. Rather than imposing a "quad," Olmsted preferred to allow the local topography to play an important role in the development of a campus. In many respects, the buildings constructed during McVey's early years at the university adhered to this style. At the same time, evidence does not exist to suggest that the plan was either rejected or adopted. Furthermore, it is not certain whether adoption of such a program would have saved the university from its campus design struggles in decades to come.[82]

What remained clear was the failure to develop a long-range campus plan before the university experienced substantial growth. When McVey sent Olmsted's plan to William Halbert, another architect, Halbert criticized it as a "hodge podge" that lacked a coherent theme or organization. McVey had relied almost solely on his own ideas and those of the Olmsted Brothers, and the impact of this focus would be felt by the university well into the twenty-first century. As one student of the institution's architecture noted, "UK had but a single spokesman on the campus master plan—Frank McVey." His failure to include varied perspectives was coupled with his decision not to adopt a true campus plan for the next two decades. However, lack of consideration for the university's future expansion did not keep McVey from asserting himself when it came to campus construction.[83]

McVey oversaw a range of repairs that continued to improve the dilapidated campus. By the end of the fall term in 1918 the Administration Building boasted new offices for the president, the dean of men, the dean of the College of Arts and Sciences, the superintendent of buildings and grounds, the business agent, and the registrar. The building also housed the newly created stenographic bureau. The chapel had been remodeled, as had the Agricultural Building. The old dormitories that had been so deplorable were being renovated, and the heating plant had been modernized. An automobile shop, constructed for engineering, had been funded by the government because of its use by servicemen in training. In the spring of 1919 it cost $48,000 to restore the president's house alone. McVey noted the potential criticisms of this expense but argued that the renovated president's house would serve the university for the next fifty years.[84]

McVey projected that an additional $50,000 would be needed during the next year to keep the university functioning properly. He concluded, "Under existing conditions and circumstances the university cannot hope for any extended building program for some time." Although McVey understood the financial realities prohibiting construction, he continued to press the Board of Trustees for campus buildings. At nearly every opportunity he noted the need for more recitation rooms, offices, dormitories, and dining facilities. Defending his decision to renovate the older dorms into classroom buildings, he argued, "Between the housing of students and the development of a university along scientific and other lines, I consider the latter the more important." He reasoned that the city would not aid in the construction of classroom buildings, but it could assist in housing students. Until the university could do both, it was better served by meeting academic necessities. In 1920, McVey listed the building needs for the next decade: twenty new structures, including five dormitories, and improvements to existing facilities, at a cost exceeding $5 million. Finances, however, dictated that such expansion would have to wait until a later era in McVey's presidency.[85]

As McVey began his reform efforts on campus, America's entry into World War I created additional challenges. During his first year at the helm, the most notable impact was the drop in student enrollment and the absence of professors and staff members who had left for military service. McVey immediately sought to implement programs geared toward helping the war effort, despite the limited human resources at his disposal. He offered the university's cooperation in providing military training. In this respect Kentucky was fortunate to have McVey as its leader. He had spent a great deal of time in Washington, D.C., and understood the ways in which the university could serve the national government.[86]

The war added to McVey's off-campus responsibilities just as he was arriving on campus permanently. In January 1918 Edward Hines, chair of the Kentucky Council on National Defense, informed McVey of his nomination to the War Emergency Employment Service for the post of state director of the public service reserve. McVey's primary duty was to secure laborers for industrial service throughout the commonwealth. He began with an eighteen-day campaign across the state to find citizens who would serve as mechanics, electricians, carpenters, and drivers. After the initial campaign he enlisted agents throughout the state to register men to enlist at the university for job training in their assigned areas. His work continued for the year, and he received one dollar for his services.[87]

The most notable addition to campus was the Students' Army Training Corps (SATC). Similar programs had been instituted across the South and the nation, but McVey decided to place the SATC under the direction of the College of Arts and Sciences. In this way, McVey recruited men to campus for military service to compensate for the loss of students who had left to fight in the war. The program accommodated a wide range of students with its two sections, A and B. Those in section A took classes in "military science," as well as other collegiate courses. Those in section B were placed in vocational classes. By the completion of the fall semester of 1918, the university had trained more than six hundred men in the collegiate section of the SATC and approximately double that number in vocational work. In addition to those on campus in the fall, the university housed several hundred others during the summer months.[88]

The approximately two thousand SATC members proved to be both an asset and a liability to the work McVey was attempting to accomplish. McVey stated that the work of the university in the fall semester "so far has been largely given over to meeting the needs of the government. . . . Many of our plans for the college have been held in abeyance or only partially carried thru because of this more immediate need." For example, the College of Law, which remained part of the undergraduate program, lost approximately a third of its enrollment. Many of those who did attend also served in the SATC, and McVey concluded that the requirements of military training took away the necessary time and inclination students needed to succeed at their studies: "The effect of our national government experiment in mixing intensive military life and training with university work made the class training necessarily very poor."[89]

Not only were students having problems meeting their classroom obligations, but many of the faculty and staff members struggled to meet the demands of a campus short on professors. McVey lamented that twenty-nine members of the faculty and staff in the College of Agriculture (including the experiment station and the extension service program) had enlisted in some form of war service. Although attendance in the College of Agriculture had dropped 60 percent from the previous year, the courses needed for graduation remained the same, which greatly stretched the teaching staff. Speaking for staff not only in agriculture but across the entire university, McVey noted, "Teachers have volunteered cheerfully to teach extra hours and subjects out of their departments." To remedy this problem, McVey convinced the University Senate to shorten the academic term.[90]

McVey utilized the SATC to the benefit of the university in ways other than enrollment. Despite the fact that Germany would surrender before the year's end, he managed to negotiate a contract with the government for the maintenance of the collegiate section through June 1919. After the cessation of hostilities, the university quickly returned to its former operations but continued military education through the Reserve Officer Training Corps (ROTC). Considering all that the university had done for the war effort, McVey sought $95,000 from the government for its services during the conflict. Included in this was the construction of an automobile shop (for vocational training), as well as $10,000 for fixing the lawn where barracks had been constructed. The war department finally settled on a payment of $80,000.[91]

The hundreds of men on campus for military and educational training created a different set of challenges. McVey expressed his displeasure with rumors of gambling, dances being held on the Sabbath, and women loitering around the men's barracks. Far more serious was the influenza outbreak that spread across the nation. Because of the cramped quarters in dormitories and military barracks many universities were struck particularly hard by the "Spanish flu." As the number of cases on campus grew, McVey agreed to close the university from 11 October to 3 November. After the epidemic, he reported that four hundred cases of the flu or colds had been reported, along with fourteen cases of pneumonia. Of these, eight students died. These numbers, however, were relatively low compared with the losses experienced at other institutions of higher education, and McVey attributed this to the military personnel on campus.

The gymnasium and one dormitory were turned over to military authorities and the Red Cross, and two nurses from the Red Cross along with two military doctors oversaw the care of sick students. Their "good judgment" and "resourcefulness," argued McVey, had led to a situation that was handled "as well as it could possibly be handled under the circumstances."[92]

After the war had long passed, McVey recalled that "the university was greatly disturbed" by an altered curriculum designed to meet military demands and the relatively quick return to a standard course of study as demobilization occurred. All told, a thousand UK students and alumni served in World War I, and eight of them lost their lives. McVey's progressive leadership during the war demonstrated his ability to identify needs at both the state and the national levels and to determine ways in which higher education could help meet them. In so doing, he managed to place the university on firm footing despite the tumultuous times.[93]

Considering the demands made upon the university during the war, the accomplishments of McVey's first year and a half were all the more impressive. He reported to the Board of Trustees at the end of 1918 that of the sixty-nine recommendations submitted by the survey commission, only a handful remained undone. These dealt with nepotism, a university lab school, the role of the dean of women, the distribution of funds across the various colleges and departments, and improvements to the physical plant. A teaching-load reduction for the dean of women would be accomplished as soon as McVey hired one. The lab or model school had been started in conjunction with the city school system, and the university was moving toward forming its own school separate from the local system. Nepotism had been dealt with in most cases, and the few remaining personnel issues would be addressed if necessary. Future hires would follow guidelines created by the board. A more equitable distribution of funds throughout the various colleges and departments would be instituted for the upcoming academic year. And while improvements to the physical plant had been made, lack of funding limited what could be done. As soon as the funds were available, renovations would be conducted.[94]

By 1919 the first phase of McVey's presidency was coming to a close, and it had been a resounding success. America had entered the postwar era, and the university returned to its prewar activities. It did so, however, with a renewed vision and an upward trajectory, a distinct contrast to the distressed state of affairs existing prior to the war and to McVey's arrival. However, his time, effort, and energy were geared toward a limited number of plans that he deemed essential to building a modern university. He sought to expand appropriations, continue campus renovations before developing a building campaign, raise faculty standards and salaries, increase the expectations of a growing student body, and emphasize useful research that would benefit the commonwealth and, in turn, the university. As he implemented these reforms, he brought greater attention to both the university and his own abilities as president. During the years ahead he would have to build upon what he had set in motion.

In the spring of 1919, McVey's next step was to have the University of Kentucky's name placed on the Association of American Universities (AAU) list of officially sanctioned institutions. McVey was not yet seeking to have the institution actually admitted to the AAU, which consisted of approximately twenty elite institutions in the nation. He simply desired to have it listed as an approved institution. Centre College served as Kentucky's lone representative on the list, and McVey believed that the work being done at his university was of the same caliber as that being conducted in Danville. He argued, "I know something of the work done by the University of Tennessee, University of Texas, University of Alabama, and other southern institutions on the list, and in no respect is this work superior to that done here."[95]

McVey's petition was passed on to Dean Kendrick Babcock at the University of Illinois, who chaired the Committee on Classification for the AAU. Babcock was one of three experts who had come to Kentucky as a member of the 1917 survey commission. Babcock wrote McVey, "As you know, I have some fairly up-to-date and firsthand knowledge of the organization and work of the University of Kentucky." Therefore, he requested evidence of the progress made in the last two years with respect to the sixty-nine recommendations. He added that if good work had been accomplished in Kentucky, McVey "must have had an interesting and satisfying period of service, though no doubt there has been an abundance of hard work and frequent need for all your resources of firmness and diplomacy." [96]

McVey's response to Babcock provided a summary of the work he had accomplished in two years. He agreed that Babcock's concerns were "entirely fair" and defended his request for the AAU's recognition with a concise statement of the progress made under his leadership. The faculty now served under a "modern" constitution (which allowed the faculty a greater role in policymaking through the University Senate), and many "first class" people had been recruited. McVey had reduced many of the professors' course loads and, at the same time, had increased salaries, on average, between 20 and 25 percent. No professor was earning less than $2,000, and most were making between $2,500 and $3,000, a dramatic improvement. The university had hired a dean of men and created a committee on discipline. Thus, professors' academic work now took precedence over much of their old-time in loco parentis responsibilities. [97]

In addition, students were being held to a higher standard of work. Along with passing courses, students received "credit for quality," a policy McVey had instituted at the University of North Dakota and one that had been recommended by the survey commission. Under this scheme students needed not only to pass their classes but to earn a certain number of high marks in their major in order to graduate. McVey provided a list of recent alumni who had gone on to graduate studies at research universities and noted that procedures had been implemented to check on students who had fallen behind in their coursework. [98]

McVey also reported that major renovations had taken place on campus. He argued that it would take at least two years to bring the current physical plant up to par, but much had already been accomplished. Concerning the highly criticized dormitory situation, McVey noted that two of the dormitories had been reconstructed and no longer housed students. One had been transformed into classrooms, and the other was being renovated to house some of the arts and science departments. The library remained in the same building, but McVey had greatly expanded its holdings. To foster academic opportunities, the library's budget had grown by more than 100 percent to over $10,000 annually, not including custodial services, which had previously been part of the budget. In sum, significant improvements had been made in the quality of people on the campus and in the physical plant. McVey's efforts paid off, and by the end of the year the university had been placed on the AAU's list of approved institutions.[99]

Others in the South were taking note of McVey's accomplishments. In May 1919, the presidential search committee at the University of North Carolina at Chapel Hill requested an interview with McVey. McVey met with representatives in Cincinnati in May, and after the meeting the chair of the search committee, Victor S. Bryant, wrote McVey, stating, "Each member of the committee was delighted with the interview with you, and each personally expressed a desire to have you come to Chapel Hill." Bryant went on to say that the committee did not have the power to elect the next president and asked that McVey keep its praise confidential. He asked McVey to respond to his letter, apparently hoping McVey would agree to come.[100]

The University of North Carolina was well in advance of the University of Kentucky, particularly in the areas of faculty recruitment and the physical plant, McVey's two primary focal points in Lexington. North Carolina's progressives had offered generous support for higher education, and the University of North Carolina benefited from the philanthropy of Mary Lily Flagler Bingham. A native of the Tar Heel State, she had married Henry Morrison Flagler, who helped start Standard Oil. After his death she remarried Judge Robert Worth Bingham, who published the *Louisville Courier-Journal* and the *Louisville Times*. In 1917 she had willed the University of North Carolina an endowment for faculty salaries that generated $75,000 annually. Frederick Koch, a former member of McVey's faculty in North Dakota who had accepted a position in Chapel Hill, informed McVey that the university had been growing by "leaps and bounds" and reported that it had a half million dollars for the physical plant. In 1922 the Association of American Universities inducted the University of North Carolina as the second southern institution in the AAU.[101]

Despite the university's position and the favorable feedback he had received from the search committee, McVey responded cautiously to Bryant: "I trust that you will understand that I cannot write you to the effect that I will accept a position that has not been tendered to me, nor can I tell you in the same letter that any given salary would be acceptable." Despite his unwillingness to commit to North Carolina, he was still nominated for the position when its board met that June, but its members eventually elected Harry Woodburn Chase, who was chair of the faculty at Chapel Hill. In his celebratory history of the University of North Carolina, Louis Round Wilson wrote, "President McVey had made a fine impression upon the committee and his record as President of the Universities of North Dakota and Kentucky was notable, but it was not sufficient to outweigh the values exhibited by Chase." [102]

Had McVey expressed the same eagerness to go to North Carolina as he had toward Kentucky, he might have been elected. Months later, President George Denny at Alabama learned that McVey had turned down the opportunity to go to the University of North Carolina. He remarked that North Carolina was in his estimation the leading southern state university and asked if McVey had really turned them down. McVey responded that he "could have gone if I had been willing to say the word." Later Denny wrote that McVey was wise to stay in Lexington, noting, "Although for the time being Carolina is stronger than Kentucky, Chapel Hill has the handicap of Alabama and the nineteen others." Presumably, he was alluding to McVey's advantage in leading a state flagship university that housed the "A and M" college rather than competed against it. [103]

Recognition from the American Association of Universities demonstrated the influence of McVey's presidential leadership at the University of Kentucky. The University of North Carolina's interest in McVey and his unwillingness to respond to its advances revealed the extent of his commitment to carrying out the necessary reforms at UK and confirmed the support he was receiving from the Board of Trustees and from the commonwealth as a whole. Much of his success was due to the timing of his arrival. Despite the larger tragedy of World War I, McVey responded to the conflict in a way that also benefited the institution. During the war, the University of Kentucky modeled the ways in which civic interests could be met through higher education, and many in the state took note of the changes occurring at the university.

Wide-ranging support for McVey and the university developed. Owsley Stanley, governor from 1915 to 1919, was one of McVey's most crucial allies. Stanley was the son of a Confederate preacher but had become a progressive governor. Among other reforms, Stanley called a special session in 1917 to modernize the state's revenue system, which led to the creation of a state tax commission. In 1918, he signed the bill that increased appropriations to the University of Kentucky. In Lexington McVey had the support of both the Democratic and the Republican newspapers. The *Herald* likened McVey's inauguration to dreams coming true for the state. The *Leader* declared the beginning of a "golden epoch of usefulness and force for the state's greatest institution of learning." With this support McVey ushered in an unprecedented era of university growth and restoration.[104]

The sad state of affairs at the university before McVey's arrival helped mobilize support for reforms at the university as well. Despite Patterson's accomplishments during the nineteenth century, his continued presence on campus after his retirement had harmed the institution. As other southern universities began modernizing, Kentucky stood still. The University of Virginia and the University of North Carolina led the way, and Kentucky's closest counterparts hired progressive administrators years before McVey's arrival. Charles Dabney served the University of Tennessee during the late nineteenth and early twentieth centuries. George Denny brought change to the University of Alabama. Samuel Chiles Mitchell and Ward Barnard Hill initiated similar reform programs in South Carolina and Georgia. Kentucky, on the other hand, had chosen a well-intentioned yet inexperienced state judge to head its flagship university in 1910, and by 1917 the university found itself lagging far behind other southern institutions.[105]

Frank McVey entered this environment and ushered in an unprecedented era of growth. His reforms focused on creating a modern and efficient university that would emphasize useful research through extension programs and social service programs. The expanded role for the university would be supported by tax initiatives. Most early reforms focused inward, on internal changes, but McVey also attempted to forge strong links between the university and the state. The war effort provides the best example of what McVey hoped to do in Kentucky. Although tangible changes in the relationship between the university and the commonwealth were limited during McVey's first two years, an attitude of cooperation seemed to be forming. As McVey's administration moved out of its "honeymoon" period, the president would face personal and professional challenges that threatened his continuance at the university. The response of the state would determine whether his career in higher education would take place in the Bluegrass or somewhere else.

Chapter 3

McVey's Darkest Days
1920–1922

Unless the members of this Association [the National Association of State Universities] have had their heads in the sands of oblivion or contrawise extended into the clouds of fancy, of which no state university president has been accused, no one here can be ignorant of the increasing criticism of higher education that has arisen in the past five years.
—Frank LeRond McVey, 1923

As the new decade began, Frank McVey's influence was evident to concerned citizens in Kentucky and throughout American higher education. Nearly all his reforms, however, focused on internal renovations, restructuring, governance, faculty issues, and increased presence across the commonwealth. To be sure, the impact on the psyche of the state was apparent in the major newspapers. Enrollments continued to climb, yet not one significant structure had been built during McVey's tenure (the university had utilized federal funds to build a shop during World War I). In 1920 McVey reported that of the 1,629 students attending the university, 700 lived off campus, and 200 others did not enroll because they could not find lodging. Another nagging issue was low faculty salaries. McVey reiterated his mantra for increased funding: "The question of salaries is becoming more and more serious. . . . We often get people of less experience and the standards of the University are in danger of being lowered." Two months later he lamented that "men are leaving us all the time" and that filling positions was becoming more difficult. Faculty teaching loads rose, and graduate students increasingly assumed classroom responsibilities to meet the challenge.[1]

Along with the growing pressure to retain current faculty members and hire new ones came a second urgent demand: developing a physical plant to accommodate the growing student population. McVey warned the board that the challenges of the years ahead would be far different from those faced during the recent past. Construction and renovation of buildings became an integral part of McVey's plan to create a true research university. In December 1920 he presented the board with a list of construction needs for the decade ahead. He cited more than thirty construction projects, with an estimated cost exceeding $5 million. The price tag seemed astronomical for a state whose support had been less than wholehearted.[2]

Indicative of the state's unwillingness to support even modest growth of the university was the plight of the Memorial Building Fund. McVey initiated the idea in 1919 in an attempt to raise funds for the construction of a building that would serve as both a monument to Kentuckians who had lost their lives during the Great War and a facility for student activities and convocations. As the first circular sent out during the summer of 1919 to alumni and other citizens stated, it would "honor the dead" and "inspire the living." McVey's fund-raising goal was $300,000, but actual pledges resulted in just over half that amount. Collecting on the promises proved even more difficult, and the building campaign stalled.[3]

Struggling with private fund-raising, McVey needed a substantial increase in revenue from Frankfort to accomplish his ambitious plan. Earlier that year he had hosted both chambers of the legislature on campus. In his "Kentucky Tomorrow" speech he had emphasized the changes that were transforming Kentucky from an agricultural to an industrial state. The university could play an integral role in the process if it received the proper support. He offered his services to Governor Edwin Morrow in developing a taxation plan and stressed the need for an income tax. In the end, however, McVey concluded that Kentuckians were "not ready for an income tax." The legislature kept the same funding plan that it had adopted in 1918, providing less than half a million dollars for university operations. McVey's budget estimate of $630,000 would have to be seriously trimmed because of the state's limited income. This appropriation would barely keep the school functioning.[4]

By the spring of 1921 McVey took a more aggressive stance to promote increased revenue. The successful growth of Kentucky's public schools meant that the wave of students coming to Lexington would continue for the rest of the decade. He predicted (rather accurately) that by 1930 the student population would more than double, to approximately 3,500. The university, as it stood, would be unable to accommodate the growth. To procure the necessary support, McVey presented preliminary steps for a publicity campaign to force the state's politicians to expand funding of the university. First, a group of "prominent" men needed to tour the campuses of nearby public universities in the North to examine physical plants, operations, and the support given by other states. Next, the university needed to host a meeting with leading newspaper editors to discuss the university's predicament and secure their support. Then, a separate statewide committee, along with interested alumni, needed to be organized "to interest the people in the University and [its] educational problems." Finally, a "series of articles in the press running over a considerable period of time" would be necessary to bring the issue to the forefront of the next legislative session.[5]

The board agreed to pay $2,000 for a trip to the Midwest, and in mid-May McVey led a group of about twenty individuals to survey Ohio State University, Purdue University, the University of Wisconsin, and the University of Illinois. The discrepancies they found were immense. In a report issued to the people of Kentucky, they contrasted the levels of support at home with UK's midwestern peers. Taxes levied above the Mason-Dixon Line ranged from $2 million to $5 million, but Kentucky's remained at $400,000. Wisconsin, for example, possessed a population similar to that of Kentucky and provided $1.14 per capita for "university work." The Bluegrass state, in contrast, garnered only 14 cents from each of its residents. Illinois had invested $9 million in its physical plant, and Ohio State stood at $7 million. The University of Kentucky remained at $1.25

million for its campus. Furthermore, UK lagged behind in its funding for agricultural work, while the midwestern institutions had already appropriated millions of dollars for expansion of buildings and programs.[6]

The commission summarized the situation: "The development of Kentucky industrially, agriculturally and educationally depends in no small measure upon the maintenance of a high grade State University. . . . For years the University of Kentucky has been in the rear of the procession." To remedy the situation, the report challenged the legislature to appropriate $8 million over the next six years for the physical plant. It listed fifteen structures that the university "must have in the near future." UK also needed $300,000 added to its annual operating budget. The commission opined that the university "has the basis for a great institution" and that considering its limited resources, the work accomplished had been "extraordinarily high." Finally, it noted McVey's leadership and stated that with him at the helm Kentuckians could anticipate an era that would "place our University in a position second to none in its special field," but that such excellence demanded an expanded financial base.[7]

The commission's report stressed that despite Kentucky's greater natural resources, its support of higher education lagged well behind that of the other states visited. In the weeks following, statistics provided to McVey by the U.S. Department of the Interior further illuminated Kentucky's refusal to support its flagship institution properly. States such as Indiana, Missouri, and Minnesota had similar assessed valuations of property as the commonwealth. While Kentucky provided 19 cents for every $1,000 of assessed wealth, the states listed above appropriated 64 cents, 37 cents, and $1.54 respectively. Although Kentucky's expenditures seemed in line with other southern state universities, most of those states had far less total wealth and provided a far greater percentage of income for higher education. For example, Georgia gave 44 cents of every $1,000 of assessed wealth to higher education, Virginia 55 cents, and North Carolina 72 cents.[8]

Some data from the Department of the Interior contradicted its own reports as well as the commission's letter to the people of Kentucky. However, even the most favorable statistics highlighted the woeful support of higher education in the Bluegrass. One letter from the Department of the Interior stated that Kentucky gave 17¾ cents per capita, another that it provided 26 cents (a little better than the 14 cents asserted by the commission). Regardless, Kentucky did not even fare well when compared to southern states. North Carolina appeared slightly ahead in its support, Georgia and Alabama slightly behind. The report noted one more important factor to consider during the Jim Crow era: the states listed below Kentucky had much larger African American populations, making "the available funds for the higher education of whites [in those states] far above that of Kentucky." Hywel Davies of the Department of the Interior, ignoring the rights of black students in the South (while unintentionally highlighting the inequity), concluded, "Kentucky really stands at the very bottom of the list." [9]

McVey incorporated the statistical data into a larger historical context and linked his requests to the commonwealth's well-being: "The University has reached a very definite turning point in its history. It can not go on farther without increase in equipment and income. It will be necessary to determine within the next year just what policy is to be followed on the part of the State." McVey stated bluntly that two options existed. Either Kentucky could appropriate funds "for the enlargement of the plant and increase in equipment," or it could "frankly say that the State can not meet the situation." If the latter were the case, the university would need to limit its enrollment to approximately fifteen hundred, which would be tantamount to informing neighboring states that they would have to share in the higher education of Kentucky's children. To avoid that outcome, as McVey repeatedly warned, citizens needed to understand that the university's job was not only teaching but research that would help improve the "economic and social welfare of the state." [10]

Just as McVey's "Plan for the Larger Support for the University" began, McVey faced a crucial decision, and the university faced a potential crisis. During the summer of 1921 the University of Missouri offered McVey its presidency. McVey and George Denny at Alabama had casually corresponded about the position in March 1921, but little else was said for some time. McVey had a connection to Missouri as well: his brother-in-law John Park lived in Kansas City and apparently had ties to the University of Missouri's governing board. He wrote McVey later in the year noting that the institution wanted him because he had been president of both northern and southern schools and would best understand the problems faced by a border state.[11]

Missouri offered him the presidency during the summer of 1921, and unlike other job possibilities McVey had entertained while at Kentucky, he would seriously consider this post under the scrutiny of the public spotlight. News of the job offer shocked many in Kentucky, and they expressed their fears in the local papers as McVey contemplated a move to Columbia. A deluge of telegrams and letters, along with numerous editorials and resolutions, revealed the immense respect and popularity McVey had earned in less than four years in Lexington.

The state's leading newspapers were unanimous in their calls for McVey to stay in Kentucky. The *Lexington Herald* stated, "It would be nothing short of a disaster to Kentucky for this State to lose the services of Dr. McVey as president of the University." The *Courier-Journal* stressed that McVey's work had only just begun. One article claimed that "his loss would be lamentable any time. It is particularly unfortunate now." The *Louisville Times* highlighted McVey's accomplishments and explained what his retention would mean for the Bluegrass: "Under his hand the University has broadened and strengthened, and if he stands by his task it will some day be an institution which will be of more value to the state than all the fustian, outworn tommyrot about horses, women, manors and hospitality."[12]

McVey's popularity with the press was matched by the devotion of the university faculty. Dr. William Funkhouser argued that many faculty members had turned down job offers because of their belief in the work McVey was doing. After hearing the news of his possible departure, a meeting of professors was called, and they unanimously adopted a resolution encouraging the president to remain in Lexington. In their letter they begged McVey not to embarrass Kentucky by leaving and, in so doing, "interrupt the admirable program you have so auspiciously entered upon to bring this University to a realization of its full measure of usefulness." They praised the leadership McVey had exhibited during his short tenure, expressed their confidence in his abilities, and argued that they were "not unmindful of the sacrifices you have made in the face of deterrent forces that would long since have daunted a less courageous soul." Finally, the faculty pledged its "hearty support and cooperation" to see that McVey's plans for the University of Kentucky were realized.[13]

Individuals, civic clubs, and newspapers promised to support an increased appropriation for the university. T. W. Rainey of the Lexington Kiwanis Club said that Kentuckians could not blame McVey for making a move "unless we rally to his support, and help him to realize his plans for the institution." The Lexington Chamber of Commerce echoed this sentiment by calling "upon all of the business and civic organizations of Lexington to rally to the support of the University and to give assurance to the President of their readiness to give their aid to the utmost in securing financial resources for the University's development." Similar comments were issued in newspapers and telegrams by groups from all regions of the state.[14]

One insightful editorial came from John M. Atherton of Louisville. First printed in the *Louisville Evening Post* and then reprinted in the *Lexington Leader,* Atherton's piece called on the state's commercial and civic clubs to assure McVey that if he stayed he would "receive the support at the next session of the Kentucky Legislature to which he is entitled, because of the importance of the work he is doing, and the necessity of securing in our State a real State University." He argued that being "the real founder of a great university should be sufficient to satisfy the ambition of anyone," but citizens needed to promise to "do our part in the work he has begun." Moving from generalities to specifics, Atherton argued that the state needed to pass a flat tax designated specifically for the university. This money would be used to develop the physical plant. The state then needed to issue millions of dollars in bonds that would become part of an endowment that would secure UK's position alongside other "great State universities."[15]

McVey was actually leaning toward staying at Kentucky before news of the Missouri position leaked to the press. However, he was content to allow the possibility of a move to garner the public support for which he had been so desperately working. Frank wrote Mabel and expressed worries concerning the president's house in Columbia, a serious issue to her. She responded on July 7: "I shouldn't worry about Missouri if I were you— Certainly if they expect their president to live in a hole of a house the job is a hole of a job, which this isn't, complacent as Ky is in some respects." Publicly, McVey left both states hanging. Privately, McVey wrote John Pettijohn, who had worked for McVey in North Dakota, "Great pressure has been brought to bear upon me to remain here. While I know that the opportunities at Missouri are greater, yet, my inclination is to remain here until certain things are accomplished. This is more than I have said to anybody else up to this time." Concerning the $12,000 salary offered to him by Missouri, McVey added, "The University of Kentucky meets all of the loaves and fishes that are offered by the University of Missouri."[16]

In late July McVey informed Missouri of his intention to stay in Kentucky, a decision for which he received much praise. President Denny at Alabama expressed the common sentiment when he wrote McVey, "For our sake, I am glad to know that you are going to remain with us [in the South]. I confess I did not know that the missionary spirit was so well developed in you. Just how you could turn down the Missouri proposition, I am at a loss to understand. Certainly, I rejoice that Kentucky has won." The feeling was echoed throughout the Bluegrass.[17]

As the academic year began, McVey seemed to have positioned the University of Kentucky for great things. His tireless publicity efforts, the tour of state universities north of the Ohio River, and the groundswell of support for his decision to stay all seemed to foreshadow unprecedented legislative support. At the first board meeting after McVey's decision to remain in Kentucky, he presented his plan for the upcoming legislative session. It included $965,000 in appropriations for 1923 and $840,000 for 1924. The events of the preceding months provided hope that his requests might actually gain the necessary support.[18]

As the meeting of the General Assembly drew near, however, McVey faced an unexpected challenge. Kentucky became the first state in the union to have a full-fledged confrontation concerning the teaching of evolution in public schools. This particular issue of academic freedom brought derision from the North but found its most fertile soil in the South. The "monkey-law" controversy McVey faced in Kentucky, although far less spectacular than the judicial showdown in Dayton, Tennessee, a few years later, served as the nation's first important legislative battle concerning evolution and academic freedom. McVey, therefore, became a leader in the political struggle at the same time that he was seeking larger appropriations from the government.

The earliest signs of protest appeared as isolated incidents. However, the author of an editorial in the *Louisville Evening Post,* a "well known and justly respected man" from Elizabethtown, tied two potentially explosive issues together: funding and academic freedom. The article noted the growing media attention afforded McVey and his institution, and it surmised that there would soon be a move to fund the university at a level that would enable it to "rank with other institutions of like character in our sister states." Rumors had surfaced, however, accusing professors in Lexington of undermining the faith of young students by denying the divinity of Christ and the authority of Scripture through the promotion of Darwinian evolution. If this were true, the article's anonymous writer warned, he would oppose funding for the university. The paper responded by agreeing with the importance of the issue but concluded that a visit to the campus and a talk with President McVey would clear up any misunderstandings.[19]

In just two weeks, the move toward an organized campaign against teaching evolution gained momentum. Writing in the *Western Recorder,* a publication of Kentucky's Southern Baptists, M. P. Hunt took aim at the university. Noting the state's plans for greater financial support, he proclaimed, "Now is the time for Christians of Kentucky to call the university's hand." Hunt demanded an end to teaching that undermined faith in the Bible and argued that the issue "should be agitated in all of our district associations and that our coming General Association should make a deliverance calculated to arouse the Christian citizens to the peril of the situation."[20]

As one fundamentalist Southern Baptist attacked the university, a progressive within the denomination immediately came to its defense. O. O. Green, pastor of the First Baptist Church in Richmond, warned McVey and offered him unsolicited advice. He attached the article from the *Western Recorder,* writing across the top, "Can this be a shot across the bow of the university boat?" Green's letter answered in the affirmative, expressing dismay at the "spirit" of the publication and arguing that it served as a "bad omen" because of the number of people who supported the campaign. Green warned that J. W. Porter, pastor of Lexington's First Baptist Church, exerted great influence on the fundamentalist wing of the Southern Baptists and that he was eager for a fight. He encouraged McVey to assuage Porter in order to neutralize him. However, he added that if he could not succeed at the task, he might want to seek the support of E. Y. Mullins, president of the Southern Baptist Theological Seminary in Louisville. Mullins had written an editorial in a series entitled *The Fundamentals,* which sought to protect orthodox faith against the onslaught of modernity and in the process served as a focal point for the growth of the fundamentalist movement. However, Mullins was a progressive, who, in the words of Green, had "been dealing with that 'Crowd' [Porter's fundamentalist wing of the denomination] for a good many years." [21]

Despite the warning from Green, McVey did not appreciate the gravity of the coming battle. He thanked Green for his advice, adding, "I have great faith in the good sense of the people of the state and doubt if there is likely very much to come from this." McVey then penned a letter to Victor Masters of the *Western Recorder,* protesting the position and tone of Hunt's article. He failed to send the letter, however, apparently choosing to wait for the fight to come to him. The early fall came and went without fanfare.[22]

The debate returned with renewed vigor in December, shortly before the ensuing legislative session. In early December, J. W. Porter presented a resolution asking the Baptist State Board of Missions to create a committee to examine accusations that certain state schools were teaching

Darwinism. The resolution protested evolution generally and suggested that the committee should "look into funds" allocated to the University of Kentucky if it did not "conform to the requirements of the resolution." Porter's actions were reported in the paper, and McVey responded candidly that UK obviously taught organic evolution, as did all the leading universities in the world. McVey immediately secured the support of the *Courier-Journal*, which stated that the university did not advance or prohibit any specific faith. Denominations within the Christian faith, argued the editorial, varied on their opinions of evolution; therefore, the Baptist push to force its sectarian views on the state university violated the principle of separation between church and state. If the resolution actually resulted in the passage of legislation, it would discredit both the commonwealth and the university.[23]

By the end of the month the battle lines were being drawn, and the controversy in Kentucky began to attract national attention. The state's small-town papers were likely to support the attacks on the university, but the *Lexington Herald* and the Louisville papers offered unequivocal support to the university in their opposition to the anti-evolution efforts. On Christmas Sunday, the conservative *Lexington Leader* argued that teaching Darwinism should be permitted, provided that the content and the professors delivering it were not hostile to Christianity. A combative letter from William Jennings Bryan was read the same morning from the pulpit of the First Baptist Church. Bryan praised Reverend Porter for his stand against evolution, arguing that the movement afoot in Kentucky "will sweep the country and we will drive Darwinism from our schools."[24]

In January 1922 Bryan added the support needed for the fight by traveling to Kentucky, where he spoke to a joint session of the legislature before delivering his "Enemies of the Bible" speech in Lexington. Bryan's impassioned oratory sparked a nerve among fundamentalist Kentuckians, and shortly thereafter G. W. Ellis of Barren County introduced a bill in the House of Representatives prohibiting the teaching of evolution, atheism, agnosticism, and Darwinism. House Bill 191 carried a proposed penalty of up to $5,000, as well as a jail sentence from ten days to a year. The battle had been joined.[25]

Even as McVey remained out of the public fray, the local press fueled the controversy. The *Lexington Herald* asked, "Is it possible that in the year of our Lord nineteen hundred and twenty-two, here in Kentucky we are to witness another outbreak of medieval theological intolerance?" Adding scriptural imagery, the editors concluded that such legislation attempted to confine "the new wine of science within the old bottle of literal scriptural interpretation." The *Lexington Leader* answered editorially, arguing that the *Herald*'s editor misunderstood the concerns being raised in the General Assembly. It reasserted that teaching evolutionary theory was not a problem so long as it was presented by "men who are not hostile to the Christian religion."[26]

Despite the publicity of the proposed bill, McVey remained unsure of an appropriate and effective course of action. McVey was the first state university president in the nation to deal with such an organized campaign concerning evolution and academic freedom. The ramifications of the evolution controversy and its potential negative impact on UK and higher education generally were unprecedented. When asked about his position, McVey responded, "I am not certain just what course I shall pursue, but if I do issue a statement I will let you have a copy of it in advance." In a 23 January letter to the editor of the *Louisville Evening Post*, McVey wrote, "I shall be glad to know what you have to say about the proposed legislation introduced by Mr. Ellis." He added that some had suggested that he make a statement, and others had intimated that he should debate with Reverend Porter. He rejected the idea of a debate but was noncommittal about making a statement. He concluded, "I shall be glad to have your reaction on the matter."

The following day the *Post* printed an editorial quoting an unnamed but prominent theologian who stated that holding to the theory of evolution did not preclude belief in Christianity. Writing privately to McVey, Lewis Humphrey informed McVey that President E. Y. Mullins at the Baptist Seminary in Louisville had helped him with the editorial. McVey thanked Humphrey for the "very enlightening discussion of the evolution matter."[27]

McVey's ambivalence on the issue of open resistance to the antievolu-

tion movement and its attack on academic freedom ended with the introduction of a companion bill proposed in the Senate by J. R. Rash of
Madisonville. Although Senate Bill 136 proposed lesser punishments, it
still banned teaching evolution. The die cast, McVey decided to cross the
Rubicon, developing a strategy and executing it with energy and acumen.
McVey knew he needed to address the full legislature. First, however, he
made a list of prominent theologians, educators, and politicians and
penned a letter to them, seeking their opinions of the proposed legislation.
Running out of time, he chose instead to send a telegram or so-called
night letter to dozens of influential individuals. In the telegram McVey
simply stated that the legislature had proposed legislation to prohibit the
teaching of evolution in public schools and asked the recipients to "wire
collect your opinion as to such a legislative act to be used in opposing the
bill." [28]

McVey received almost fifty replies in four days. He organized them,
removed the two that were in favor of the proposed bills, and sent them to
the press for publication. Both Lexington papers published the comments,
as did the *Louisville Courier-Journal,* the *Louisville Evening Post,* and the
New York Times. Replies from many clergymen tended to be serious.
C. R. Hemphill, president of the Presbyterian Theological Seminary in
Louisville, proclaimed that the "bill against teaching of evolution [is] in
my opinion unwise." Another labeled the legislation "unAmerican and
contrary to the spirit of Jesus Christ." Letters from leading educators
across the nation tended to be more caustic. The former U.S. commissioner of education called the legislation "unwise, absurd, and ridiculous,"
adding, "Why not require schools to teach the stationary world as the
center of the universe." One dramatically referred to the bill as "intellectual suicide." Charles Eliot, president emeritus of Harvard, expressed his
disbelief and asked rhetorically, "Is not derision the best form of opposition to the bill." Yale president James Angell argued that passage of the
bill would "make Kentucky the laughing stock of the world." Nicholas
Murray Butler of Columbia University, adding sarcasm to his contempt,
noted that the bill was incomplete and needed amendments "to include in
its prohibition the use of any book in which the word evolution is . . . re-

ferred to in any way. It might even be desirable to include a prohibition of books that use any of the letters by which the word evolution could be spelled." He added that the bill's author must be "in close communion with the rulers of Soviet Russia, since he is faithfully reproducing one of their fundamental policies."[29]

The strategy embedded in McVey's telegram was clear: allow leading educators and ministers to say publicly what he could not. Afterward McVey could speak to politicians as a moderate voice, without risking the votes that he needed to defeat the legislation. The extent of this approach is revealed in McVey's letter to Woodrow Wilson. The former U.S. president responded in a telegram that he was not at liberty to express his views on the matter. McVey replied, "To say that I am disappointed is to put the matter mildly." He informed Wilson that his former secretary of state, William Jennings Bryan, had visited Kentucky, giving speeches "full of misstatements and untruths." He added, "As the foremost leader of America, I felt that I would secure from you an expression that would at least check Mr. Bryan's view." In a final plea for help from the former president, McVey stressed, "I trust that you will be willing to undertake to say something about this matter and to wire me again protesting against such legislation so that I may have your telegram to present to the committee before this coming Wednesday." President Wilson did not oblige.[30]

Some did not reply to McVey's telegram because they understood the nuanced cultural aspects of Kentucky. Charles Brown, dean of the Divinity School at Yale University, voiced his opposition to the bill in a letter to McVey and explained that he had chosen not to reply to the original telegraph because he believed "that for a northern man to undertake to influence legislation in a southern state would do more harm than good." A month later the University of Wisconsin president replied similarly: he had remained silent because he believed that his opinion "would prove to be a negative quantity under the conditions in Kentucky. . . . Personally I rather suspect that anything from me would be regarded as ipso facto heretical in Kentucky."[31]

The voices that did offer their views provided McVey with ammunition as he planned to meet with the commonwealth's political leadership.

The day after publication of the responses to McVey's telegram, he appeared before the Senate to speak against the legislation. As planned, McVey played the role of the level-headed moderate. First reading the responses to his "night letter," he then argued that those who proposed and supported the bills meant well. However, passage of such laws violated the principle of religious freedom by promoting one sectarian view. Dictating instruction in the commonwealth's public institutions and the university in particular created a grave situation by infringing upon the principle of academic freedom. President Mullins of Baptist Theological Seminary joined McVey in speaking against the bill. Their appearance in Frankfort led to two alternative bills and a temporary tabling of the original bill—moderate successes that bought McVey time to defend his position.[32]

McVey's appearance in Frankfort, though successful in leading to further debate and affording McVey time to formulate his next step, did not fully reassure those defending academic freedom. The superintendent of public instruction, George Colvin, for example, wrote McVey a day after his appeal, confiding, "There was a sense of unreality about the whole proceeding in the Senate Chamber. . . . I could hardly convince myself that the whole thing was not a hideous nightmare." He praised McVey for his determination not to "grow disgusted and quit." In a moment of hyperbole, he compared McVey's position with that of Christ on the cross, adding, "I am wondering if you are a big enough man to say and pray 'forgive them, they know not what they do.'"[33]

The press highlighted the despair of the progressive president, who had such faith in the will of the people, and challenged the movement against academic freedom. The *Lexington Herald* quipped that after listening to the antievolution forces in Kentucky, "we have decided to abandon the monkey-descent theory and hook up with the more convincing proof that perhaps some of us originated with the fish of the sucker variety." The *New York Times* opined that the fracas in Frankfort dispelled the notion that the success of the American school system was due in part to its close connection with the people themselves. The usually confident McVey understated the political situation by calling it "not very satisfactory."[34]

Following McVey's defense of academic freedom in the Senate, two alternative bills were offered. Baptist ministers drafted a bill stipulating that "the teaching of any theory that will weaken or undermine the religious beliefs of the pupils, shall be forbidden." Another bill, attributed to the Louisville minister E. L. Powell and McVey, prohibited "teaching detrimental to the belief in God as the creator of man and the universe." These compromises offered a conciliatory tone and revealed the extent to which those who opposed the original bill feared its passage. However, in a personal letter McVey denied that he had cosponsored a substitute bill. He wrote a letter to Mullins in mid-February commending him for his public stance against the legislation and noting that "the other little incident [presumably the alternate Senate bills] divided for the time our forces in this contest." Mullins replied to McVey's letter by stating, "What I did at Frankfort was to advocate a substitute bill in order to save what looked like an ugly situation. There was strong evidence that the original anti-Darwin bill might be pushed through." Mullins recounted that he had "labored hard for a number of hours the night before with a committee to convince them of the error of their way in pushing the original bill." Apparently, McVey opposed the amended bills in favor of a wholehearted fight against what had originally been proposed.[35]

McVey's next two public attacks against the antievolution legislation differed greatly in tone and content. A forceful and somewhat antagonistic approach came during one of his "Between Us" talks on campus, when he attributed much of the current trouble to "half baked statements by students in arguments with persons who have no background in modern science." McVey admonished the students to stop confusing religion with theology and challenged them to think for themselves. The second, however, was his conciliatory appeal "To the People of Kentucky." The letter, released to the press for publication on Sunday, 12 February 1922, became a defining moment in McVey's presidency.[36]

McVey wrote that he needed to address the current situation because of the "confusion and misunderstanding" surrounding the antievolution movement in Kentucky and its growing focus on the flagship university. Affirming his "abiding faith in the good sense and fairness of the people of the state," McVey stated "as emphatically as possible" that the university did not teach "atheism, agnosticism, and Darwinism (in the sense that a man is descended from baboons or gorillas)." Nor did UK attempt to damage, challenge, or instill specific religious doctrines in its students. He affirmed that the university did indeed teach evolution because failure to do so would isolate UK from the modern world by eliminating at least a half dozen of the subjects currently taught.[37]

McVey then sought to define evolution in a way that was not antithetical to faith in God. Evolution was "development and change . . . a great simple principle of growth." It included the assertion "that development goes on during long ages under varying influences. . . . It is the belief that the earth was formed ages ago and has evolved gradually and slowly." These ideas testified that "God works through law and that men are to use their God-given minds in order that they may learn more of the power and glory of God."[38]

Unnecessary conflict occurred when some oversimplified the complex and varying theories of evolution into a single phrase: "Man is descended from a monkey." McVey asserted that different forms of evolutionary thought existed and that only the atheistic or materialistic versions denied a "Creator" or "Law Giver." The scientific, theistic, and Darwinian evolutionary views, however, were not antithetical to religion. To the contrary: "The foremost thinkers everywhere, religious and scientific, have accepted the idea of evolution. The testimony of many men throughout the world is given again and again that there is no conflict between the theory of evolution and the Christian view." [39]

McVey then focused on the crucial issue of academic freedom, printing verbatim section 5 of Kentucky's Bill of Rights, which forbade giving preference to any one "sect, society, or denomination." Kentucky's constitution included provisions protecting the civil rights of an individual "on account of his belief or disbelief of any religious tenet, dogma, or teaching. No human authority shall . . . control or interfere with the rights of conscience." The issue was clear: the bills before the legislature were unwise and unconstitutional.[40]

McVey closed by arguing that the "morals, ideas, and spiritual attitudes of the students cannot be excelled anywhere." Faculty members had met voluntarily with hundreds of students in off-campus classes studying the life of Christ. Religious organizations such as the YMCA and the YWCA thrived on campus. In sum, there was "no reason for this attack upon the university."[41]

Following his letter to the citizens of the commonwealth, McVey appeared before the Senate, reading his letter in the chambers and combating those in favor of the legislation. His two calculated press releases, along with his decision to speak in the Senate, paid dividends. On 16 February, the Senate voted nineteen to seventeen for "indefinite postponement" of the Rash Bill. The *Courier-Journal* reported the following day that "the anti-evolution bill is dead, buried in the Rules Committee of the State Senate." Twenty votes would be needed to resurrect the bill, and according to the press that was highly unlikely. By indefinitely postponing the bill, the state senators could defeat it without having to cast a controversial vote and face the ire of constituents. The senators would allow the House to lead the fight and then respond accordingly, if necessary.[42]

House Bill 191, which historian William Ellis called "the nation's first ballot on legislation to suppress the teaching of evolution," came up for a vote on 9 March 1922. The packed gallery listened to five hours of impassioned debate. The bill's author argued that it was the most important bill of the session because of its impact on future generations. One member publicly lamented his own child's loss of faith during his years at the university. McVey defended the university, summarizing his public statements and arguing that the university worked to produce the best young men and women possible. Ultimately, students and professors, rather than the legislature, had the right to work out their own faith. If the legislation passed, he argued, Kentucky would "start a new form of legislation for the United States and Kentucky that will lead to disaster." It would create a system in which those in power could "say [that] men with certain religious beliefs cannot hold office. When that is done religious tolerance is gone."[43]

The antievolution forces countered with Representative Noel Gaines of Frankfort. McVey recalled years later that Gaines "put William Jennings Bryan to shame in his denunciation of those who believe in evolution, directing his remarks directly at Dr. Powell and Mr. McVey." He imitated judgment day by placing McVey, Reverend Powell, and some textbooks on one "side," with "the Bible, the Declaration of Independence, and himself on the other. . . . Finally he threw one of the textbooks to the floor and trampled it under foot." After Gaines's dramatic speech Representative G. C. Waggoner, a minister from Scott County, rose to defend the university and express his shame in the legislature, comparing its activities to the Dark Ages.[44]

Following the debate, thirty-six voted against the bill, and thirty-four voted in favor. The slim majority was irrelevant, because forty votes were needed for passage. The antievolution forces requested that those absent be called for a vote. Both sides scrambled through the capitol looking for votes. At the end of the first sweep the antievolution forces counted forty to thirty-nine in their favor. Then, "the opponents demanded a recapitulation," which resulted in a tie of forty-one votes. At that point, a Baptist from Eastern Kentucky's Breathitt County who had originally declined to vote—because he was, in his own words, "a hard-shell Baptist and believed what was would be anyhow"—decided to vote against the bill because of its encroachment on individual freedom. McVey's defense of academic freedom won by a hairsbreadth.[45]

In the days following the "monkey bill," McVey wrote thank you letters to his supporters, especially alumni and friends of the university. McVey confided, "If you had not put your whole souls in the matter, the result would have been entirely different." The president owed a great deal to the "university men" in the legislature, as well as progressive ministers throughout the state who had come to his aid. Finally, McVey received letters apologizing for Noel Gaines's vindictive tirade in the closing hours of debate. Ironically, McVey believed, Gaines actually helped turn many against the proposed legislation. Writing to one university president who was seeking advice on how to defeat a similar bill, McVey joked that he would be happy to pass along the name and address of a particular Frankfort politician who could help defeat the bill through his obnoxious support of it. In the end, without McVey's active fight the legislation more than likely would have succeeded. This fight against the antievolution forces served as a defining moment of McVey's professional career. He originally sought to modernize a campus, but his legislative battle in 1922 helped modernize an entire state, if only temporarily. Although attempts to reintroduce "monkey bills" were made in subsequent years, no serious organized effort was successful.[46]

McVey's strategic success served as a model for educational administrators throughout the South and the nation. He received congratulations from university presidents who solicited his advice as well. When University of Oklahoma president Stratton Brooks sought his counsel regarding an antievolution movement in his state, McVey suggested that he first consider remaining silent and hoping for a satisfactory resolution. This approach, however, had the potential of discrediting the university, and McVey feared that the Supreme Court "might actually declare it [an antievolution law] constitutional." The alternative option was "to fight as vigorously as possible." First one needed to "find out who is who . . . lining up the ministers as much as possible." He then encouraged Brooks to secure the assistance of the press and finally to "pick out the ground upon which the fight is to be made." McVey noted that he had "endeavored to hold it down to limitation of liberty and freedom," rather than debate the merits of science and theology. McVey responded to requests from other university presidents in a similar fashion.[47]

The entire antievolution battle provided McVey with a deeper understanding of the post–World War I fundamentalist movement. Believing at the outset of the struggle that little would come from the initial agitation, he found the ensuing legislative session disconcerting. Various northern counterparts wrote McVey after his successes, voicing the opinion that McVey had originally held. Nicholas Murray Butler predicted that the move for such legislation "will not gain headway" but would subside in the months ahead. Charles Eliot congratulated McVey and then argued that "the best way to oppose such absurd legislation is to make fun of it." McVey's response to Eliot revealed his clearer appreciation of the situation. He noted that the fundamentalist movement had gained strength and predicted, "We may look for more of the sort of thing that has happened in Kentucky rather than less." Then he suggested that the academic community "make a careful and thorough-going statement in popular language for the purpose of presenting clearly our position." Accordingly, McVey wrote the secretary of the AAUP, encouraging organized propaganda efforts to counter William Jennings Bryan's political activism.[48]

The successful push for antievolution legislation in Tennessee in 1925 validated McVey's predictions and further proved the importance of his leadership. President Harcourt Morgan of the University of Tennessee had been encouraged to take a stand against the "monkey bills" in Nashville, but he seemed more concerned with protecting the state's funding of the university in Knoxville. Professor Edwin Mims of Vanderbilt wrote Morgan, pleading with him to fight the fundamentalist forces: "I know the delicacy of your position, but my dear doctor, you and the University will suffer more than anybody else. People will inevitably contrast the fight put up by the University of Kentucky." Morgan chose instead to reject McVey's approach, opting for a passive stance. In a letter to Governor Austin Peay, Morgan explained, "The subject of Evolution so intricately involves religious beliefs, concerning which the University has no disposition to dictate, that the University declines to engage in the controversy." In the end, the legislation passed, and the state of Tennessee would be linked forever to the infamous Scopes Monkey Trial.[49]

———————

The evolution debate overshadowed McVey's efforts to ensure a landmark shift in funding for the University of Kentucky—the issue he originally thought would dominate his time and attention during the current legislative session. Despite the trip to midwestern universities and the president's own push for increased publicity, securing greater appropriations proved to be an uphill battle. McVey's struggles stemmed partially from Republican governor Edwin Morrow's insistence on paying off the state's $3 million debt without raising taxes. Morrow fervently believed that curbing expenses rather than generating revenue was the solution to Kentucky's debt problems. In addition, the governor's primary legislative goal was the passage of a $50 million bond issue for roads that would be subject to a statewide vote.[50]

Morrow's plan created an ominous tone for the upcoming months. The *Courier-Journal* editorialized, "Economy . . . will acquire a new definition at the 1922 session of the General Assembly." The paper cited a state report claiming that as much as $5 million in waste could be trimmed from expenditures on education and roads. The governor's comments emphasized his belief in the need for greater efficiency, but he faced a legislature controlled by Democrats, many of whom wanted greater support for the state's educational programs in general and the University of Kentucky in particular.[51]

Just as events surrounding the antievolution bills began heating up, the State Budget Commission offered its report and recommendations to the legislature. Governor Edwin Morrow attached a letter to the budget confirming McVey's fears. The state's chief executive called for appropriations well within the proposed state budget and sought to pay off its $3 million debt without raising taxes.[52]

McVey's vigorous public relations campaign on behalf of UK did not create the desired results. The proposed budget, which included items such as $321,000 for the Confederate Pensions Department, actually provided less money for the University of Kentucky than the previous biennium. It trimmed $80,000 annually by cutting $30,000 for engineering equipment and $50,000 in construction funds. This created a potential net loss of $160,000 in funding for UK for the upcoming biennium.[53]

McVey was disheartened by the political climate, but he expressed his opinions only privately. When speaking at a campus convocation, the president discounted a connection between the antievolution legislation and the lack of funding. He insisted that the legislature desired to support the university's plans for expansion but could not "see the way for a larger appropriation at present." However, in a letter to a friend outside Kentucky, he lamented, "We are having a lovely time in Kentucky just now. The Budget Commission cut right and left," and "we found that we had $80,000 a year less than last year." He added, "Two bills have been introduced providing fines and imprisonment for teachers or presidents of schools where evolution is being taught."[54]

McVey faced two legislative crises. The press, which emphasized the antievolution battle, still gave some attention to the university's calls for additional funding. The *Lexington Leader* called for the Budget Commission to change its recommendations and meet UK's needs. The *Louisville Evening Post* asserted that the legislature and the governor had become obsessed with the road-bond issue to the detriment of educational reform. The paper implored the Democratic majority to reject the governor's plan and develop a budget to "provide for the University of Kentucky." Under the headline "One Last Appeal" the *Post* called on the state's senate to "save the day" by providing adequate funding for UK and the state's normal schools. Finally, in March more than two hundred University of Kentucky students gathered at the state capitol to show support for the university and lobby for an increased appropriation. The legislature was willing to provide a few concessions, but McVey and his supporters were unable to overcome Governor Morrow's insistence on economy.[55]

Reporting to the Board of Trustees about the recent legislative session, McVey offered little hope or optimism. He noted that a proposed addition to the inheritance tax, which would have provided more than $100,000 annually to the university, passed the Senate but failed to make it out of committee in the House. An automobile tax to bring extra funding for UK passed both branches of the legislature but fell to the governor's veto. Although the budget was amended to increase the university's construction appropriation from $25,000 to $100,000 annually, as well as provide $90,000 to pay off the institution's indebtedness, Governor Morrow vetoed this amendment. This dismal development resulted in the loss of the extra funds and the original $25,000 as well. McVey concluded that the state had reduced the university "to practically the income of three years ago." While UK retrenched, leading universities around the nation began capital campaigns to secure matching grants from philanthropic organizations.[56]

Less than a year earlier McVey had declared that the University of Kentucky was at a turning point. The commonwealth could meet the needs of her flagship institution, or it could decide that the state could not meet the educational needs of its students. Unfortunately, the state's politicians chose the latter option. McVey became despondent: "Our outlook is gloomy for the next two years. . . . We shall have to follow a policy of retrenchment and rigid economy." In reaction, the president made a number of recommendations. The university needed to limit its enrollment to approximately fifteen hundred students rather than try to achieve goals it could not afford. A proposed upgrade of the Education Department to a full-fledged college would have to wait. The library and maintenance budgets would have to be cut substantially. Finally, faculty salaries would remain stagnant, potentially resulting in the loss of UK's best professors. As McVey planned for the academic year ahead, he told the Board of Trustees, "I want you to understand thoroughly the problem that confronts us. . . . The situation is very serious." [57]

Professionally, the first half of 1922 had proven to be difficult for McVey. The troubles in the legislature were coupled with growing challenges on campus that required his administrative acumen. However, the troubles McVey had faced in his work did not compare to the traumatic events that loomed ahead in his personal life. The time and energy McVey had exerted on behalf of the University of Kentucky infringed upon his family life, and in 1922 he faced a serious crisis at home. After struggling with health problems including high blood pressure for several months, Mabel McVey took a serious turn for the worse. Frank's wife of twenty years was hospitalized, entering Good Samaritan on 16 March. The doctors ordered her to rest and kept a close eye on her condition, hoping to see signs of improvement. McVey's daughter Virginia, then a student at the University of Michigan, wrote her mother, encouraging her to rest and get well: "You must take things much easier. I'll be home soon to see to it." Rather than becoming lower, however, Mabel's blood pressure increased, causing the doctors to fear potential "apoplexy"—a debilitating stroke or cerebral hemorrhage. The two attending physicians determined that Mabel suffered from "nephritis," an acute or chronic inflammation of the kidneys. They surmised the cause to be an infection in the appendix, the pelvis, or perhaps both. [58]

Showing no appreciable signs of improvement, Mabel consented to exploratory surgery, which was conducted on 11 April. The surgeons found signs of chronic appendicitis, as well as an inflamed ovarian cyst and a "fibroid of the uterus." After removing the appendix and cyst, her doctors were confident that her health would improve. For a week, Mabel's condition did seem less critical. Writing to a friend after the surgery, Frank reported, "Mrs. McVey came through the operation fairly well and is now feeling better." On 19 April, Dean Anderson wrote McVey, "It has been a matter of great mental satisfaction to me to know that Mrs. McVey is getting along so nicely." This letter, however, had unintentionally cruel timing. Despite general optimism, that very day Mabel's condition took a serious turn for the worse, and shortly after 7:00 p.m. she died.[59]

Three days later, on Saturday, family and friends gathered in the flower-laden parlor of Maxwell Place for the funeral. Carl Lampert directed members of the university's string quartet through their musical selections, and a vocal quartet sang "Lead Kindly Light." Benjamin Bush, pastor of the Second Presbyterian Church in Lexington, conducted the solemn service.[60]

Eulogizing Mabel McVey, Reverend Bush recalled her service to Lexington during the last five years of her life. He stressed the companionship and comfort she had provided her husband throughout the recent fight for academic freedom. He "spoke in tribute to her motherhood and home love and . . . [her] many outstanding qualities." McVey's two brothers, both ministers, spoke next: Charles McVey recited the Twenty-Third Psalm, and William offered the benediction. The University of Kentucky's ROTC battalion lined Mabel's casket and filed outside into the bright Kentucky spring day. The procession walked to the edge of campus, where automobiles awaited to carry everyone to Lexington Cemetery. Charles McVey conducted the graveside service among the budding trees and shrubs.[61]

Although hundreds attended the service, the widower could not or would not greet the flood of guests at Maxwell Place following the funeral. Rather, McVey cloistered himself in his upstairs study, asking to see only selected family members and his closest friends. The following day his sister, Kate Park, wrote their mother, Anna McVey, that "Frank is showing the strain today most of all." Confiding that he was "near the breaking point," she added, "He is very tired and his nerves are worn out but he is as sweet and gentle as anyone could possibly be." Many members of the family left the day of the funeral or soon afterward. Frank's two older children, who attended the University of Michigan, and his sister Kate were the last to leave. His youngest daughter, Janet, who was attending the University of Kentucky's Model High School, now shared the large house with her father and Mabel's mother.[62]

For several days following Mabel's funeral, Lexington newspapers offered formal resolutions and tributes to Mabel Sawyer McVey. The accolades presented Mabel as a progressive reformer. During her short time in Lexington she had served as president of the Fayette County League of Women Voters, a position from which she had resigned just weeks before her death. She had participated in Central Kentucky's Women's Club and the University Women's Club. On the national level Mabel had served as vice-president of the American Association of Collegiate Alumni. Before her death she had been slated as a delegate to the Pan-American Conference, to be held in conjunction with the National League of Women Voters.[63]

Local tributes offered their deepest sympathies to President McVey and his family. A faculty resolution offered heartfelt condolences. It noted that locals "loved and revered her for her leadership and loyalty." The resolution concluded, "Coming into this community from another, a stranger to the Commonwealth whose traditions are unique . . . imbued with the desire to serve, she became at once a commanding figure among women in her adopted community." The University Women's club wrote, "We love to recall the quiet straight forward way in which she shared with her distinguished husband his responsibilities and labors for the best good of the university." The Central Kentucky Women's Club stated, "No more shall we have her counsel; only in memory shall we hear her clear thought given in earnest, frank words."[64]

These tributes, imbued with southern gentility and discreet language, carried veiled suggestions that Mabel was an outsider who had never truly adjusted to Kentucky's culture. Only years later would frank descriptions of Mabel McVey's view of Kentucky and Kentuckians emerge. Lydia Olney, wife of longtime horticulture professor Albert (A. J.) Olney, described Mabel as rather haughty. She asserted that when Mabel arrived in Kentucky, she believed "Kentuckians needed a little bit of cleaning up. . . . She was always telling people what was proper." Mabel held numerous receptions and parties during their first years in Maxwell Place, but as time passed attendance at her functions declined steadily. According to Olney, guests disliked being "told what to do and what not to do, what was proper what wasn't proper." She noted that Kentuckians may have lacked proper midwestern social skills, but the university faculty was probably not the arena for Mabel to begin a Miss Manners class.[65]

Many who met Mabel McVey shared a common perception. J. Winston Coleman, a UK historian who had escorted Virginia McVey to several social events, remembered Mabel as "awfully cold and reserved," as was Frank McVey. Chloe Gifford, who attended the University of Kentucky from 1919 to 1923 as the sole female student in the College of Law, described Mabel as a "cold" individual who was primarily interested in Lexington's "intellectual" group. Apparently, these impressions lasted for years. Historian Thomas D. Clark, who never met Mabel, recalled that those who spoke to him about her described her similarly. Charles Talbert, another UK historian, asserted that "she just couldn't relate to Kentucky people and they couldn't relate to her." In sum, Mabel's public persona in Lexington was that of an outsider who remained aloof from her "adopted" southern state.[66]

At least a few of Mabel's comments regarding Kentucky confirmed what many suspected. When the McVey family first moved to Kentucky, Mabel did not approve of the domestic help—or lack thereof. She wrote her husband, "One thing we will have to learn and that is to have ourselves taken care of as well as some others around U.K." She added, "I am trying to let things go as easily as possible for endeavoring to do the job around here makes me so ill I fairly am frightened at results." Mabel McVey had a hard time finding and keeping help at Maxwell Place, possibly as a result of her prejudice and her discomfort around African Americans. In 1919 she wrote Frank, "My new little white maid is very nice

indeed. . . . I am advertising in the *Herald* for a cook, 'White Preferred.'"
Finally, when McVey considered the presidency at the University of Missouri, Mabel complained about Kentucky's vile weather and labeled the state "complacent."[67]

Mabel's discontent was exacerbated by her husband's demanding work schedule. In addition to his extensive travels across the commonwealth and the nation, in 1920 McVey began taking month-long trips to Michigan in order to escape his frenetic pace of work and his allergy problems. He would spend a few weeks alone on the Great Lakes at a painting school, attempting to cultivate his artistic skills. Later, his family would join him for a brief vacation. McVey had always taken trips to the Upper Midwest to go canoeing and camping when he lived in North Dakota. However, Mabel usually spent that time in the Twin Cities with her mother. After Mabel's mother moved to Lexington, both were left at home when Frank traveled. In 1921 Mabel wrote to Frank, commenting on his absence: "As far as my own happiness is concerned, complete orphanage would be preferable to which I have had for environment the past 3½ years, and if I remember I expected nothing of the sort 22 years ago," when they were married.[68]

Mabel's cosmopolitan upbringing and temperament seemed ill-suited to life in a small southern college town. When Frank attended painting school in Michigan during the summer of 1920 and expressed his liking for the place, Mabel responded, "I am glad you like that school. I was afraid New England had all of the art as well as the culture." Clearly, in her mind Lexington had none. In her letter discussing the possibility of the Missouri position, she suggested that she might find a "small + expensive" apartment in either St. Louis or Louisville, apparently depending on where Frank decided to do his work. Her outlets for progressive reform were impressive for a Kentucky woman at that time, but her condescending approach to reform clearly rubbed many the wrong way. Though she participated in formal civic efforts, she did not develop close friendships in Kentucky.[69]

McVey exhibited a stoic response to the loss of his spouse. The president, as his temperament was inclined, poured even more time and energy into his work and travel. During the summer he spent protracted periods of time with his children, who experienced difficulty adjusting to life without their mother. Janet remained in Lexington to finish high school. Virginia and Frank Jr., both students at the University of Michigan, struggled to keep up with their studies. Frank Jr. eventually transferred to Miami University in Oxford, Ohio, where he could be closer to home and under the watchful care of Miami's President Hughes, his father's personal friend.

As McVey and his family adjusted to life without Mabel, the deaths of two other individuals long affiliated with the university signaled a monumental shift. McVey was vacationing in Maine when he learned of James K. Patterson's death. Widely considered the founder of the institution, Patterson had saved it from sectarian rivalry and partisan politics during its infancy. By the time of his retirement, Kentucky's land-grant school had become a viable college. In his retirement, however, he became a liability rather than an asset. His abrasive temperament, considerable ego, and continual meddling remained a source of distraction and friction for his immediate successors. Upon learning of his death, McVey sent a short telegram offering his regards, but he chose not to return for the funeral. McVey had successfully managed to limit Patterson's influence, something his predecessor had failed to accomplish, but the pressure remained nonetheless. In many ways, Patterson's death continued the significant transition that had started when McVey arrived in Kentucky.[70]

Patterson felt that he had been treated unfairly after his retirement, but he stated in his will, "Notwithstanding the gross injustice done me by the Board of Trustees of the University of Kentucky in 1912 . . . I am unable to set aside my original intention formed many years ago of making the University my heir." He first bequeathed more than $25,000 to friends and family, institutions, and causes. He gave his personal library to UK, provided it remain intact, and he set aside enough money to draw $400 dollars a year for the library budget. He then willed the remainder of his estate to the university. These funds generated more than $11,000 annually, but Patterson stipulated that the money should go to the establishment of a school of diplomacy in honor of his late son. As with most of

Patterson's requests in his retirement, his posthumous demands failed to help McVey in the short run. The late president also required that the funds not be used until they had reached an annual income of $35,000. Given a standard rate of interest, the money would be unavailable for nearly forty years.[71]

Finally, his will added, "Should a bronze statue of myself be erected by my friends, I direct that my executors contribute Three Thousand Dollars ($3,000) for this purpose or as much thereof as its promoters may require." He gave funds for his mausoleum and for the research, writing, and publication of his biography. Patterson's will might have helped the University of Kentucky during difficult times. Instead the stipulations limited aid in the short term and served to remind future generations that Patterson, not McVey, was the founder of the University of Kentucky.[72]

Before the year's end a second longtime member of the administration also died. Judge William T. Lafferty, who had been a practicing attorney in Harrison County for many years, was asked in 1904 to serve on the Board of Trustees at State College. Three years later he was instrumental in founding the College of Law and became its first dean. He died on 9 November 1922, from what the papers called a "lesion of the brain." Lafferty had served the institution admirably and commanded respect. However, his passing signaled the end of the old-time college era. Although Lafferty had been admitted to the bar, he did not have a graduate degree in law when he became dean.[73]

Lafferty's death afforded McVey the opportunity to hire a dean with the qualifications necessary to bring standing to the College of Law. As McVey sought help in finding the right man for the job, he noted, "First, the person considered must have received a degree from a standard college; second, he must be a graduate of a first class law school; third, he must be between the ages of thirty-five and fifty and, fourth, he must have had experience in teaching law subjects under the case system." McVey wanted to be certain he was hiring the right individual, and he sought the advice of university presidents and law deans across the country. The search took more than a year. During the interim, he quietly added the position of acting dean of the law school to his long list of responsibilities.[74]

McVey could not attend the funeral services for Dean Lafferty, since he had to attend the annual meeting of the National Association of State Universities in Washington, D.C. McVey had served as secretary for the organization, but this conference held special import for him. He had been informed weeks earlier that he was going to be elected president. Though his years of service to the association were recognized, it was his fight for academic freedom that brought him great attention in the academy and served as a catalyst for the honor.[75]

The office bestowed on McVey brought recognition to the University of Kentucky, but it increased the odds that a more prestigious institution would seek his leadership. One dean at UK wrote to McVey, "I want to write the Association of Universities to congratulate *them* that *our* President is *their* President too. You would be happy to see with what pride and enthusiasm the students and faculty received the news." McVey's family, however, offered a different view. Upon hearing the news, daughter Janet wrote him, "I'm so proud of you—it is just grand you being President. . . . Kentucky will have a worse time than ever keeping you now."[76]

McVey had chosen to stay in Lexington despite the lure of more prestigious institutions, but the previous year had been such a difficult one that he began entertaining overtures from institutions more willing to implement his progressive reforms. In late April 1922, a representative from Western Reserve University approached McVey about its presidency: "Let me know when you are to be in Cleveland. . . . I have told the acting president . . . that if he would secure you as the permanent man, it would put the university strictly on the map." Later in the year he declined an offer to become director of the American Council on Education. Clearly, he still hoped to accomplish great things in Kentucky.[77]

In October McVey traveled to Oklahoma at the request of the U.S. Bureau of Education to conduct a survey of that state's system of higher education. It, too, offered McVey the opportunity to reconsider his current position. McVey wrote the dean of women, Frances Jewell, describing the advantages of Oklahoma. Jewell responded, "You are disappointed in us, and justly. You have an opportunity to objectify us and you are doing it in spite of yourself—and you are wondering if you are not going backward in purpose, accomplishments, [and] spiritual growth." Jewell pleaded with McVey to see exactly how much he had accomplished in Kentucky, especially rescuing the institution "from graft and politics that had taken place in the University since 1917."[78]

McVey's career continued on the upswing during 1922. The mood in the General Assembly and McVey's growing recognition in the academy provided him with numerous opportunities to leave the Bluegrass. His decision to stay for the 1922–1923 academic year may have been simply to afford himself the time to process the changes in his life, but the years ahead would open up greater opportunity. Two of his three children were no longer living at home, and his youngest daughter was nearing the completion of high school. The young widower would have the freedom to choose a path for the rest of his career, a road that was not necessarily in Kentucky.

Chapter 4

McVey's Era of Great Aspirations
1922–1931

Since education in a state can rise no higher than its source, a
university and normal schools must be maintained. Kentucky has all
of these; however, their financial support has not been sufficient to
permit them to do what the people and especially the children and
young people should have done for them.
—Frank LeRond McVey, 1924

The personal and professional low point McVey faced in 1922 could have
been enough to lead him away from the University of Kentucky. Having
struggled for years to pull the university forward, he had failed to capture
the imagination of the commonwealth's citizens or the legislature. Nevertheless, he remained at the University of Kentucky for both personal and
professional reasons, the former probably outweighing the latter. Most
important, the events of the 1920s would cause him to remain in Lexington for the rest of his professional career.

Fittingly, the one bright spot for McVey and the university's finances
at the close of 1922 resulted from a death. Mary F. Bingham had passed
away in 1917, willing to the University of North Carolina an endowment
that generated $75,000 annually to hire and retain promising professors.
However, a long lawsuit brought by the commonwealth ensued, concerning the taxes on her estate. Once it was resolved, Kentucky collected more
than a million dollars in inheritance taxes, and from this the university
received upward of $100,000. Once news of the decision reached McVey,

he immediately developed plans to spend it even before UK had all the funds in hand. The money would help complete an extension to the unfinished chemistry building. Although the projected expense was approximately $200,000, McVey believed the need for the facility outweighed the debt obligation, and he decided to move forward with the construction. These additional funds allowed the university, which had expected to operate at a loss, to function at approximately the same level as the previous academic year.[1]

The Bingham settlement was not the only morbid serendipity to keep the university's debt to a minimum. In 1922 a $50,000 donation from the will of the late Ernest B. Ellis provided another small boost. McVey stated in June that UK was in a "better financial situation than we have been in a number of years." This did not mean that the university had the state funding that McVey desired for long-term improvements; it simply meant that it could function fiscally without taking on greater indebtedness. McVey persisted with his mantra that UK would lose its best faculty to wealthier institutions and that the overcrowded campus could not continue to add students without expanding facilities. In short, UK needed money to be competitive with its neighboring flagship and land-grant institutions.[2]

As McVey continued looking for funds beyond operating expenses, he faced an uphill battle. The legislative debacle of 1922 offered an example of the state's lack of support for UK. At that time, McVey was three years into a stalled capital campaign to raise $300,000 for Memorial Hall "to honor the [World War I] dead and to inspire the living." In 1919, the initial phase of a highly publicized campaign garnered pledges amounting to approximately half the goal. The citizens of Lexington had pledged approximately two-thirds of the $150,000 subscribed, and alumni support was far less than McVey had originally hoped for.[3]

By the spring of 1922, the university had less than $80,000 to show for its efforts. The alumni had failed to contribute much, and most of the residents of Lexington who had subscribed refused to pay, arguing that their pledges were merely for moral support. The legislature's failure to provide extra funding led McVey and alumni secretary Herbert Graham to renew their agitation for support. In April 1922, a circular entitled "Alma Mater Is Calling" was sent to the alumni, but it had little effect on the campaign.[4]

Faced with a failed internal fund-raising campaign, McVey began corresponding with Tamblyn and Brown, a private development agency based in New York that had executed successful capital campaigns in the nascent field of university development. In September, George Tamblyn wrote to McVey, outlining the expenses involved in a drive to raise $500,000. If hired, the agency would first gather information for publicity purposes, develop campaign leaflets and other mailers, plan alumni dinners and donor meetings, and work with the state's newspapers in publicizing the campaign.[5]

The agency would also supply trained employees to come to Kentucky and work with committee chairs appointed by the Board of Trustees. The campaign would create specific committees to deal with "special gifts (of $1,000 or more), publicity, speakers for conferences and dinners, and organization of the student body. Tamblyn bragged that his agency's greatest strength lay in its ability to "organize the alumni." This included everything from a national organization to working with local chapters in small Kentucky towns. Volunteer alumni representatives would commit to donating money themselves, as well as finding a certain number of other alumni pledges, or reaching a specific quota.[6]

The entire campaign would cost $30,000. McVey told the board that he was "inclined to think that it would be well for us to consider the matter." Later in the month, two members of the board met with George Tamblyn, both in favor of increasing the campaign goal from $500,000 to $1,000,000. With much of the organization already in place for a half-million-dollar campaign, raising the other half million would only add $15,000 to the entire campaign cost, for a total bill of $45,000.[7]

During the fall of 1922, McVey received letters from numerous other development agencies. While he was not yet sure if the university should hire an outside group to conduct such work, he did seem committed to working with Tamblyn and Brown if the board decided on a formal fund-raising campaign. He wrote Clarence Hewitt, a development worker in

Spartanburg, South Carolina, that if UK decided to engage in organized development work, it would "be under the direction of a New York concern, with whom we have had some discussion of the matter." Undaunted, Hewitt responded that his southern company employed primarily southerners who were "familiar with the conditions peculiar to this section." He concluded, "We know Kentucky and I believe are better qualified to conduct a Kentucky campaign than any other organization in the country."[8]

McVey's bias for Tamblyn and Brown was due to the successful campaigns it had conducted at other universities. It had helped Colgate, Mount Holyoke, and Williams each raise in excess of one million dollars. Most intriguing to the president, however, was its success at another southern institution: the University of Georgia (UGA). Tamblyn and Brown provided a statement from the executive committee of the University of Georgia's fund drive that stated that the challenges faced by UGA seemed similar to UK's. First, they expressed difficulty in raising funds from private sources. They noted that southerners, "while they give generously to churches and hospitals—have never felt it important to support their educational institutions on the same scale." The committee stated that "the campaign was wisely planned and faithfully carried out."[9]

Despite this positive recommendation from the University of Georgia (as well as other institutions), the Board of Trustees at UK could not reach a consensus on a development drive for early 1923. At a November meeting, the board voted five to four in favor of the million-dollar campaign under the direction of Tamblyn and Brown. With such a slim majority, George Colvin asked that his vote be changed from affirmative to "nay" because he did not think it wise to begin an ambitious drive without a greater consensus. Although the proposal had not been defeated permanently, it was tabled until a later date; the board might review the issue the following year. George Tamblyn agreed that after such a close vote, it was appropriate to postpone the campaign. Tamblyn added, "There are indications that 1924 may be a better year for campaigning than this year," and he left his firm's offer on the table until 1 May 1923.[10]

In the meantime, McVey turned to others for advice. In December 1922, he wrote to Thomas Reed, the secretary, treasurer, and registrar at the University of Georgia, as well as to President George Denny at the University of Alabama, who was in the midst of a capital campaign with a different development agency. The conflicting responses did not make McVey's decision any easier. Reed affirmed the idea, noting how his university had received pledges in excess of one million dollars. He added, "The best benefit that will come from this drive will be from the new interest of the alumni in an organized manner." President Denny offered a different perspective. After asking that his comments be held in confidence, Denny revealed that the cost of the drive had been far more than he had originally anticipated. The effort had generated a number of pledges but "collected very little cash." He then opined that "in the long run a state institution does not profit by this kind of thing. I thoroughly believe that for every dollar raised in this way we shall be penalized many dollars in the matter of legislative appropriations." [11]

In a fateful decision McVey sided with Denny from Alabama. The Executive Committee of the Board of Trustees asked McVey to "consider a method of raising funds." Apparently making an executive decision, McVey never again asked the Board of Trustees to vote on hiring Tamblyn and Brown. He instead began further fund-raising efforts without the assistance of an outside agency. The president corresponded with the alumni secretary, Herbert Graham, as he tried to figure out what to do. Graham suggested that McVey either build a memorial with the existing funds or begin another fund-raising drive to procure at least another $100,000 for the facility. If McVey initiated another campaign, Graham thought it should also include a number of other projects. He suggested raising funds for a statue of the late president Patterson, the creation of a student-loan fund, a small endowment for prizes in essay- and newspaper-writing competitions, and $2,500 to aid in organizing alumni records. Most notably, Graham (who clearly understood the pulse of the alumni) thought that the university might be able to increase the total campaign amount to $200,000 if it would publicize that $60,000 of the funds raised would go toward the construction of a new football stadium. [12]

Rather than accept Graham's either/or proposition, McVey opted for a both/and approach. The president decided to construct Memorial Hall with the funds they had collected, while also beginning a new capital campaign spearheaded by the Alumni Association. As he explained to his board, there was a need "for a definite move toward the construction of Memorial Hall in the near future." The board gave McVey permission to "take such steps as [were] advisable to that end."[13]

As McVey examined the structures that could be built with the funds available, he became increasingly leery of breaking ground on the project. After the Executive Committee of the Memorial Fund, at McVey's earlier urging, recommended building an auditorium that would seat approximately 1,800, the president added, "Instead of erecting buildings such as these . . . we ought to be erecting buildings that cost half a million dollars." By the fall, McVey reported that of the $300,000 the university had originally hoped to raise, it had less than $80,000 with which to work. McVey became more ambivalent. After stating, "It is now five years since the work of the Memorial Building started, and the matter ought to come to a close as soon as possible," he added that he was "puzzled to know just what to suggest regarding the money, since it is difficult to build a building of any size with that amount." With great frustration, McVey quietly suspended efforts to construct Memorial Hall.[14]

After UK's first capital campaign failed abysmally, the Alumni Association immediately began another, this time attempting to raise around $200,000. It seemed they might have more success this time around. McVey and Graham dropped the Memorial Fund from the new drive. Instead, a football stadium became the primary focus of the campaign—something Kentuckians were likely to support. As McVey explained to George Tamblyn, "The Alumni are endeavoring to raise a quarter of a million dollars for the construction of a stadium. The University itself does not expect to enter a campaign." Eventually, the alumni drive would include money for the construction of a basketball gymnasium, a statue of the late Patterson, and a student-loan fund. Of the four projects, the latter two constituted 10 percent of the money to be spent from the campaign. Organizers hoped to raise $140,000 for a football stadium, $40,000 for a gym, and $10,000 each for the Patterson statue and the student-loan funds.[15]

Despite his letter to Tamblyn asserting that the university would not be involved, McVey immediately immersed himself in promoting the campaign. He sent a letter to university employees explaining the effort. He argued that the campaign was important because it sought to organize and ensure the loyalty of alumni, as well as develop an efficient mode of publicity for the university. Most important, if the university succeeded in its goal, it would be "a demonstration of its power and ability to do things." With that, he lauded the generosity of the students, who had already pledged thousands of dollars, and he asked the staff to make contributions in order to see the "campaign to a successful conclusion." He then endorsed the drive in the student newspaper by praising the Alumni Association's enthusiasm and stating that if all involved contributed, "June [the close of the pledge drive] will see the accomplishments of this purpose. . . . It is a challenge to the University and its alumni and it is going to be done!"[16]

Oddly, the Alumni Association hired Clarence E. Hewitt's agency (whose services McVey had earlier declined) to organize this pledge drive, paying $12,490 plus expenses for work conducted between April and June 1923. As was the case with the Memorial Hall campaign, the alumni did not even meet the fund-raising goal of $200,000 in pledges. After the Hewitt organization failed to deliver on its promise to organize the alumni effectively, the university continued to work alone toward its goal during the summer. By the opening of the 1923–1924 school year, subscriptions in the amount of $189,547.50 had been procured.[17]

The original plan for the drive allocated more than half the funds for the football stadium, and the initial announcements suggested that the stadium would be the first project completed. Events, however, quickly began to change. In March of 1923, the Athletic Council, headed by Professor W. D. Funkhouser, sought funds from the university for a new basketball gym. They argued that the current gym was unsafe, that the miniscule seating capacity resulted in a loss of funds for athletics, and that an effort to move the annual high school tournament from UK's campus to Louisville might succeed if something were not done. The council proposed borrowing money to build a structure costing between fifteen and twenty thousand dollars, which would be repaid with receipts from games. The board, while expressing its sympathy, stated that it could not loan the Athletic Council the money and that before construction could begin, the university needed to determine what to do with the stagnant Memorial Fund.[18]

After failing to convince the board to loan money for the construction of a gymnasium, the Athletic Council succeeded in luring the Alumni Association. The alumni organizing the Greater Kentucky Fund agreed to designate its first collections for the construction of the gym. After its completion, a football stadium could be built the following year. After thwarting the will of McVey and the Executive Committee of the Board of Trustees, the alumni then met with these same individuals and asked permission to build a gym on the corner of Winslow (now Euclid) and Limestone streets. The Executive Committee granted the request, and McVey reported to the board that "the basketball building will undoubtedly be built this summer."[19]

Almost immediately, the projected costs of the gym grew, and progress on construction slowed. A contract to build the foundation alone was $20,000, the amount Funkhouser had quoted earlier in the year as the cost for the entire project. Budget projections now stood at $54,000, but McVey stated, "It will be a more satisfactory building than I had anticipated." The *Kentucky Kernel* echoed his sentiment by enthusiastically reporting that the arena would provide the campus with "one of the most modern basketball plants in the South."[20]

To meet the growing expense of the gym, the Alumni Association and the Athletic Council again approached McVey and the board, seeking support for the project. This time they convinced the university to enter a contract for the completion of a gym, not to exceed $60,000. In doing so, the board advanced $20,000 to the project with the understanding that the Alumni Association would fund the remaining $40,000 with donations from the Greater Kentucky Fund drive, originally designated for the construction of a football stadium. The Athletic Council then pledged to repay the university the $20,000 over two years, using money from admissions fees, which they estimated at $10,000 a year.[21]

By the time the Board of Trustees formally agreed to include the construction of the gymnasium "under its corporate seal" (i.e., formally entering into a contract for completion of the project), the estimated price had skyrocketed to $90,000. D. H. Peak, UK's business agent, expressed concern about the cost: "In the event any large amount has to be paid on account of basket ball building, I am not at all sure we shall have sufficient funds to meet our current expenses." He suggested that "the Board today . . . make some provision for such an emergency." The board did nothing.[22]

Originally slated to be open for the 1923–1924 season, the gym continued to face construction problems. Much of the delay was due to inclement weather, and only sporadic work occurred through the winter months. The most pressing problem, however, became the financial instability of the Blanchard-Crocker Company, which had contracted to build the facility. As construction on the gym slowly came to a close, McVey reported that "the contractors had been unable to dispose of the notes executed and signed under previous agreement with the Board." Therefore, McVey reported, the university had "found it necessary to assist the contractor by endorsing notes to the amount of $20,000." McVey's archaic language essentially meant that the university had been burned by guaranteeing payment for the work of subcontractors. By March McVey reported that, despite the fact that the project had not been entirely completed, enough work had been done to play games in the gym. This allowed the university to host the state's high school basketball tournament in March and bring in some much-needed revenue.[23]

The gym was completed in 1924, but the financial problems created by the project lasted well beyond its opening. McVey informed the board that the university faced the problem of paying liens filed against it by subcontractors that had not been paid by the Blanchard-Crocker Company. University attorney J. Pelham Johnston believed that a majority of the charges would not stand in court because of the subcontractors' failure to notify UK of their intent to seek payment within the proper statute of limitations. By November the university had been sued, and Johnston stated, "We are glad this suit has been filed," holding that it would clear up the confusion concerning what the university legally owed the subcontractors.[24]

McVey did not express similar optimism. The secretary of the Alumni Association asked McVey if the home game against Washington and Lee scheduled for 30 January 1925 could be used for a dedication and dance. McVey rejected the proposal: "Until its finances are straightened out, it might not be a good idea to have the dedication." Since the university was not going to lose the facility regardless of the outcome of the lawsuits, McVey seemed to be simply protesting against the Alumni Association. The courts eventually ordered the university to pay one subcontractor upward of $9,000, and numerous other claims cost the university thousands of dollars.[25]

The frustrations faced in constructing the gymnasium did not deter those advocating a new football stadium. The Athletic Council had originally proposed the campaign to the board in January 1923. In May the *Courier-Journal* reported that UK was planning to build a "stadium which promises to be the best in the South." As noted earlier, McVey had given his enthusiastic support to the students, staff, and faculty. Students argued that if the University of Georgia or Alabama could raise $150,000 for a stadium, then Kentucky could do the same. Momentum for the grand stadium, however, slowed as the gym proved more costly and time-consuming than anyone had imagined.[26]

Timing for the revival of the stadium plans could not have been worse. The executive committee for the stadium met at the Lafayette Hotel on Friday, 6 October 1923 and decided to begin construction on the structure even though the gym had not been completed. The following day, the varsity football team traveled to Cincinnati and lost 14–0. During the game, center Price McLean was hit over his left eye. He tried to continue, but the coaches benched him because he appeared disoriented. He returned to Lexington with the team after the defeat. The next morning, his teammates could not wake him, and he was rushed into emergency surgery. The surgery was unsuccessful, and McLean died that evening. President McVey presided during his memorial service, reading psalms and reciting the Lord's Prayer.[27]

The same day that the *Kentucky Kernel* reported the death of the student, it revealed the plans to construct the stadium on Winslow Street, pending approval from the board. The horseshoe-shaped stadium would seat 21,000 fans, and extra bleachers could be added to the open end of the field. The football fatality, promoters feared, would slow progress. As the president of the Alumni Association wrote McVey, "I am deeply distressed over the death of young McLean, but hope it will not interfere seriously with the plan for University athletics."[28]

McLean's death, however, did not impede construction plans, although other developments did create problems for McVey. Herbert Graham, the able secretary-treasurer of the Alumni Association, offered McVey his resignation in order to take a job in New York City. Graham had been the organizing force of the alumni during the campaign and a trusted confidant of the president. When he had accepted his position at the university in late 1920, two alumni clubs existed. When he left, eighteen clubs operated in the state, as well as sixteen more outside the commonwealth. McVey, who desperately wanted Graham to continue his work, responded to his resignation by noting that despite Graham's good work, the campaign was still "dragging on." He added, "If you do not return to the University at this time we shall be in a very serious situation." Graham could not be convinced; the work would have to continue without his services.[29]

To add to the troubles, it was becoming clear that costs had skyrocketed to more than $90,000, and the Alumni Association found that many who had pledged money for the stadium did not approve of constructing the gym first and had decided to withhold their pledges until stadium construction commenced. The university, on the other hand, could not enter a contract without the necessary funds. In order to remedy the situation, the board agreed to borrow from the project that McVey had supported so strongly since 1919, the Memorial Fund.[30]

McVey, on behalf of the university, was now charged with borrowing $50,000 of the money collected for the World War I memorial and lending it to the Stadium Fund of the Alumni Association at 6 percent interest. This arrangement was not approved until April 1924, and by this time the university was knee-deep in the gymnasium fiasco. Many were frustrated, too, at the ways in which George Carey, treasurer of the Greater

Kentucky Fund, had been spending money. In exchange for the loan, McVey sought to gain greater control of the campaign, which had gone awry. The contract to borrow from the Memorial Fund stipulated that the managers of the Stadium Fund turn over all "cash, securities, property and pledges" to the university's business office. Thus, McVey would have direct control of the funding for the stadium.[31]

When the president took over, he made sure that construction of the football stadium would not face the same financial troubles as the gym, scaling back the stadium plans considerably. When the contract for the stadium was awarded to the Louis des Cognets Company at $100,000, it described a stadium consisting of five sections that would hold a capacity crowd of 8,500. The company agreed to the construction of a sixth section at a reduced rate of $16,500 if the university desired. The stadium was to be completed in September for the ensuing football season.[32]

Although construction proceeded slowly, it moved along more smoothly than the gymnasium's construction. By October, the stadium was not completely finished, but the stands on the south side could hold more than 5,000 fans, and games were played at the field as construction on the north side continued. The university had raised additional funds to build a sixth section, and the construction company took $1,000 off the cost as a donation. The stadium was dedicated on 1 November 1924, before the start of a game with Kentucky's intrastate rival Centre College. The homecoming game and ceremony, according to the *Kentucky Kernel,* attracted 15,000 fans. The band played "My Old Kentucky Home," and the president of the Alumni Association, C. C. Calhoun, gave the dedicatory address. Two plaques were unveiled, one honoring longtime trustee Judge Richard Stoll and the other honoring the Kentuckians who had given their lives during World War I. Apparently, it was easier to raise funds for a football stadium to honor the dead than to build an academic facility, as McVey had planned.[33]

Despite the football stadium project, it would be difficult to label the Greater Kentucky Fund a successful campaign. As late as 1927, McVey would write to the president of the Alumni Association concerning the struggles faced in raising money for the university. As he said, "I think the matter is set forth in a manner sufficiently clear for you to follow the situation without difficulty." He then went on to explain that approximately $84,000 of the $200,000 pledged had not been paid. The residents of Lexington owed $25,000, and others in the state fell short by $29,000. On campus, the students had not paid on $30,000 of their pledges, and the faculty lacked $1,600. Money was also owed on the nonathletic portions of the campaign, for the student-loan fund and the Patterson statue fund.[34]

As McVey presided over an institution that had failed in its two major fund-raising efforts, his name continued to surface as a candidate at more prestigious institutions. At the same time that the football stadium was being dedicated, for example, he was approached informally about the presidency of Ohio State University. At an earlier time McVey might have made a calculated effort to assume this post at a growing midwestern university near his childhood home. Now McVey responded that for numerous reasons he was interested in staying in Lexington. One reason in particular stood out above all the others.[35]

After the death of McVey's wife and before the commencement of the Greater Kentucky Fund campaign, the Board of Trustees passed a simple resolution stating that with the passing of Mabel Sawyer McVey, "the University loses a loyal adherent and the President himself a companion whose place cannot be filled with any other." That same month McVey sent a letter to the dean of women, Frances Jewell, its tone suggesting that another could indeed fill the place. McVey wrote that her annual report was "unusually well written and interesting. . . . You have made an excellent Dean and I much appreciate your help and cooperation during the year." Such a heartfelt response to a dean's report was unusual, and the relationship that developed so quickly transformed McVey's life and career.[36]

Frances Jewell had served only one year as dean, but her roots ran deep into the Bluegrass social, cultural, and financial world. Born in 1889 in a small town fifty miles north of Lexington, she came from a family whose success in the horse industry provided entry into the upper echelons of Bluegrass society. The Jewells moved to Lexington when she was a child. They resided on Ashland Avenue (the street where the McVeys had lived briefly as renovations on Maxwell Place were completed) and purchased a country house and farm at Pleasant View in Jessamine County, twenty miles south of Lexington, where the family spent summers and weekend retreats. Frances attended Sayre, a private girls' school in Lexington, before boarding at the Baldwin School in Bryn Mawr, Pennsylvania. She then attended Vassar College, graduating in 1913.

Returning to Lexington, Frances engaged in the social scene of the Bluegrass elite and volunteered for various reform efforts, a life common for young, progressive, upper-class southern women. After a couple of years and with no husband in sight, Frances became discontented. She wrote that her life must have been a "bitter disappointment" to her parents and expressed her uneasiness with "spending hours" getting dressed for dances and social events.[37]

Jewell found the remedy for her restlessness in education. In 1915 she began taking graduate courses in English, and within a year she moved from student to teacher when UK hired her as an instructor. In the fall of 1916 she began teaching a full load of classes for $600 a year. After two semesters she decided to complete her master's in English at Columbia. She then spent one year in New York, taking classes and writing her thesis on the literature of Kentucky's Shakers. Upon completion of her degree she returned to the University of Kentucky to continue teaching. She carried an excessive course load and engaged in numerous academic and social activities, including establishing a chapter of the American Association of University Women and serving as the chair of Kentucky's branch of the Southern Association of College Women.[38]

When Dean of Women Josephine Simmeral resigned her post in the spring of 1921 McVey appointed Frances Jewell to succeed her. The students applauded the choice. Commenting on Jewell's administrative assignment, the *Kentucky Kernel* noted that Jewell possessed "rare knowledge of student life and problems and a personality that begets confidence and elicits admiration and respect." Her acceptance of the post, the article continued, "argues well for the future of education and *culture* of women in the University of Kentucky." Frances Jewell, the intelligent, progressive, southern woman, seemed finally to have found her place in the academy.[39]

But that place was short-lived. McVey and Jewell corresponded regularly during the summer months following Mabel's passing, and initially their letters remained strictly professional. By fall the tone had shifted, as Frank began pursuing Frances romantically. Before leaving on trips, the president sent the dean flowers and wrote to her about the details of the conferences he was attending. Frances responded eagerly, and the two began sharing their ideas on education. They discussed their favorite poets, the pros and cons of short-answer tests, and the state of the University of Kentucky. Frances expressed concern about Frank's frustrations with Kentucky and then in the next breath challenged his admiration for objective, short-answer tests. Frances noted that her views were more "conservative and Victorian" than Frank's, arguing that such exams provided no room for critical thinking and the essential skill of forming a creative argument. She cited Cardinal John Henry Newman's writing on higher education. Whether or not Frank agreed with the opinions of the current dean of women did not appear to affect his determination to woo her.[40]

By the beginning of the holiday season, the relationship had evolved into a full-fledged romance. On 2 December McVey wrote a poem entitled "The Telephone Call: A Poem for Frances," expressing his desire that the dean call the president's office late in the afternoon. When he left for a conference in New Orleans, he asked Frances to begin calling him Frank rather than Dr. McVey or President McVey. Frances agreed with some trepidation, and on 4 December she wrote on official university letterhead, "Dear Frank—(How that startles me, especially when written on this paper!)" Writing of their first dates together, which had occurred in secrecy, Frances wrote, "*lovely, fine, splendid you. I shall never forget that day or any of these days.*"[41]

Frank responded from New Orleans: "What a dear, dear letter. . . . If it had begun in any other way I should have died of disappointment and you would have never seen me again." He spoke of the drudgery of the conference, which dealt with the need for clear standards and better accrediting processes, adding that he longed to have Frances there so they could walk along Canal Street and stroll into the bookstores and shops downtown. McVey then requested the pleasure of her company during the upcoming weekend before he left town again. He wrote, "The thought of not having you is just really too much. You are my dream lady . . . a personality cloaked in loveliness of mind; gentle, whimsical, gay, tender, dear and so much more; thoughtful, kindly, impulsive and yet reserved at times."[42]

McVey's soppy letters and poor poetry from New Orleans revealed the extent of his infatuation with Jewell. He wrote, "Your beautiful acceptance of these offerings that Uncle Sam carries to your door . . . drives my pen across these white deserts of paper." Noting his own giddy disposition, he wondered, "Do I not belong in the group that are just plumb crazy?" He mused rhetorically, "What . . . could do a thing like that to a hard boiled president of a state university?" As the letters continued, he expressed his desire to sing aloud to Frances from his heart. He was "crying out for companionship, for love," and he yearned "to play with you, to read with you, to talk with you, to be with you in silence, in play, in work."[43]

McVey also sought out Frances's feelings regarding marriage. He wrote to Frances sharing what he would do if he had nine lives. He desired to be a "real" painter, a great teacher, a "real" college president, an expert in international law, and an engineer, among other things. He added, "in all of them to have you as a mate." Lamenting having only one life, he offered to help Frances figure out what to do with hers. She hoped to be a great writer, an excellent teacher, and the founder of a settlement school in Eastern Kentucky, as well as dean of women until UK reached its potential. Her final wish was that she "should have" married and had nine children. She responded coolly to the possibility of marriage, comparing her stance with her objections to joining a Greek club: "Perhaps the reason I want every body to marry and do not marry is the same feeling I have about sororities." She explained, "I like for other people to be in fraternities but I *won't* belong to a privileged class—and so perhaps I gloat over not belonging to the privileged class of those who are happily married—who knows."[44]

Frank and Frances both knew that if they wed, it would end Frances's academic career. McVey attempted to assuage Jewell's fears by explaining her role as his companion. "I know you are puzzled to know what to do," he continued. "You do not want to retire to the drab life of a president's wife. That is because you don't know the many things that such a position brings." He elaborated on the numerous tasks and activities of a university's first lady. Then he reiterated his longing to be with her: "What charm you would add to living. How together we could make any presidency a radiant thing, a joy to us and others." McVey concluded that without her his job would simply be work but added that he did not want to convince Frances unless her heart was fully up to the endeavor.[45]

Despite McVey's pleadings, Frances's beautiful love letters remained noncommittal concerning marriage. Just before Christmas she confessed that Frank's gift of a "loveliness-courage-character chain" embarrassed her, and she said that the future of their relationship remained "on the knees of the gods." At the beginning of 1923 she asked Frank to pray that God would "bless us and keep us, and make us worthy of each other." She added, "My darling, I love you, my Frank, my wonderful President, my adorable goose, my very own."[46]

Frances's doting yet reserved letters spurred on McVey, and he immediately changed his style and tone of writing. He began emulating Frances, underlining words, using exclamation points, writing long descriptions of his love for her, and adopting the expression "Oh!"—an expression common in Frances's writings but noticeably absent from McVey's until that time. As his romantic writing skills emerged, he added an amorous touch by sending drawings and sketches with his notes. He attempted to persuade Frances with declarations such as, "The days we have spent together tell us we belong to each other and the days that bring separate [sic] tell us . . . the same great thing."[47]

As their romance raged, it created complex problems for them professionally. In order to protect themselves, they kept their romance clandestine. When McVey wrote from New Orleans, he placed each letter in an envelope on which he disguised his handwriting. On his first Christmas as a widower, McVey responded to a letter he had received from Frances by noting that "it was a dear, dear letter," but that since another person was present when he opened it, "all I could do was glance at the beginning." Once he was alone he "devoured" the letter "like a hungry man who didn't know what a Christmas dinner was." Even into the new year, McVey apologized for not sending letters to Frances while she spent days at her parents' home, stating that a letter could evoke "comment that might have been distressing." Occasionally, the secrecy could be fun. Commenting on the violets she wore to church, Frances wrote Frank, "Miss Liza Kinkead said, 'How lovely your violets are! I *know* who sent them to you.' I *know* she did not *know!*" [48]

The privacy did afford Frances more time to consider the relationship, and with every passing month the couple's intimacy grew more apparent. Frank spoke of himself as Frances's knight. He believed her trepidation was a result of "maidenly reserve not to say too much too soon." Frances reciprocated, noting that his self-description as a knight who would lay down all his trophies at her feet nearly brought her to tears. She stated that he was indeed a knight and that his armor was "*character*," his lance "*honesty, sincerity, truthfulness*," and his shield "*courage*." Before long she began speaking of a life together. She prayed, "*Bless us . . . give us strength* to encounter that which is to come, that we may be *brave in peril, constant in tribulation, temperate in wrath* and *in all changes of fortune and down to the gates of death loyal and loving to one another.*" [49]

By June the relative certainty of their plans allowed them to make their relationship known, spending time together in public. Frances expressed her growing confidence in their romance: "Frank you are the man for me!! I have known it for a long time—well for some time—but I am ever more and more certain." Despite her feelings, Frances spent much of the summer away from campus. The two exchanged love letters when separated, and McVey visited her in New York. By summer's end, wedding plans had been set in motion. [50]

When Frank spent time alone during the summer to rest and practice his painting, more differences between his former wife and his current fiancée surfaced. McVey no longer dealt with a companion lamenting their time spent apart. Frances expressed her longing to be with Frank but insisted that he take time to get substantial rest. And whereas Mabel had asked her husband to limit his smoking, his new love wrote that even though she thought the practice unwise, "when you sketch *you may smoke*!! Am I not a tyrant? Such a compact may result in many sketches!!!" [51]

Although Frances was free and fun-loving, she was open about her fears. As their wedding date drew closer, she questioned, "Oh! Frank, do you love me? Do you feel reasonably certain that you will continue to love me?" She worried that too many marriages were not truly loving, adding, "I want ours to be a *really* happy marriage; I shan't be satisfied even with a compensating marriage—one that is merely worth giving up being dean for—it must be joyous and fine and splendid and lovely—*Ideal*." She exclaimed, "I am risking all!! On you—gladly, willingly, not sparingly." Just weeks before their marriage Frances commented with sadness on her resignation as a professor and dean of women, adding, "I am thinking of all the things that I wish that I had done." [52]

Setting her worries and fears aside, Frances married Frank on 24 November 1923, at Pleasant View in Jessamine County. Their union, occurring the year following Mabel's death, radically changed the tone of leadership at the university. Frances Jewell's willingness to surrender her own academic career to serve as the university's first lady ushered in a new era for McVey. In many ways this era would become *the* McVey presidency. Rightly or wrongly, Frank had been viewed much like his first wife by many in Kentucky—as an extremely intelligent yet slightly cold and aloof northerner. Frances Jewell McVey was an insider—a member of the Bluegrass elite—and their marriage helped diminish his outsider status.

Frances's radiant personality and gift for hospitality radically changed the tone of Maxwell Place, but more importantly, it changed the president. D. H. Peak, the longtime business agent for the university, noted that even though McVey was a brilliant and efficient leader, "he was not a warm person." Frances helped alter this perception. For example, Levi Horlacher, a professor and associate dean of the College of Agriculture and Home Economics, had come to the university in 1918 and had witnessed both Mabel and Frances interact on campus. He later commented on the change: "It gave new direction to the way of thinking, the way of acting and the way of doing things." Concerning Frances's impact, he stated, "She was an outgoing sort of person. . . . Everybody in Lexington and the University knew her. It changed Dr. McVey's viewpoint. It made him more outgoing and . . . more friendly."[53]

These sentiments were echoed by the undergraduates. Chloe Gifford, who later served as director of the Bureau of Club and Community Service and then as president of the General Federation of Women's Clubs, said that when she was an undergraduate, "I was . . . going to avoid him [McVey]. All of the students and even the people of the state felt that way about him. They were all a little scared of him." Frances Jewell was different. She had high expectations for Gifford, but she was "warm and outgoing at the same time." Gifford recalled that the president's wife "always called me honey." She instituted Wednesday-afternoon teas to afford opportunities to develop a sense of community and at the same time help convey what Frances regularly called "the art of living," or as Gifford called it, "social diplomacy." She concluded that when Frances "became the first lady of Maxwell Place . . . she took over Dr. McVey. . . . She was the one that humanized him."[54]

Frances made the president's home more genial to those working at UK, but the differences in their native dispositions persisted. Barbara Hitchcock, Frank McVey's niece, came to the University of Kentucky after McVey's second marriage and worked as Frances's student assistant. She recalled that her uncle Frank hired her because, as he explained, "your Aunt over does these social affairs. . . . She is overworking and you are here to be her secretary." She added that McVey now spoke of his own father as a "damn Yankee soldier." When taking a group of students to the Jewells' Pleasant View farm in Wilmore, McVey lined them up and said, "Now you young Yankees, we're going to a home of southern hospitality, and this is the way you are supposed to behave." Even in imparting southern manners, McVey maintained his straitlaced tone. Frances, in contrast, helped teach Barbara Hitchcock "social graces" in a graceful manner.[55]

Frances sacrificed her professional career to marry Frank, but she had processed this issue mentally and emotionally before offering her vows. Frank's pursuit of his second bride had made it clear that he understood what she would add to his life. His letters revealed his understanding of what Frances would give up in order to join him in his endeavors. However, Frank had not yet expressed a clear understanding of what he would have to forfeit by marrying a native Kentuckian. Frances's deep roots in Kentucky would be difficult if not impossible to transplant, and this changed the trajectory of McVey's career path. From the time of his arrival in Lexington in 1917 until the time he fell in love with Frances, McVey had been courted by various universities. The lack of funding by the state legislature, the push for the antievolution bill, and McVey's growing prestige all made him a prime candidate for an established institution. The true love of his life, however, was not only married to him but committed to the state of Kentucky.

The marriage of Frank and Frances created a stronger presidency at the University of Kentucky and tied McVey to the commonwealth. After five years in Lexington, he finally began to put down roots in the Bluegrass. Although his personal life had been tumultuous, by the close of 1923 McVey had found a love that renewed his vigor. The professional landscape at the University of Kentucky, however, remained challenging. The years leading up to 1923 had provided an opportunity for McVey to lay the foundations of a university. With his lot cast in Lexington, the "Roaring Twenties" would offer McVey his best opportunity to build a modern university.

———•———

McVey's reasons for staying at the University of Kentucky were primarily personal, but professional developments also helped to minimize the lure of other institutions. Despite the shortcomings of university development in 1923–1924, other successes greatly enhanced UK's presence in the state, especially in the area of agricultural research. One notable development was what would become known as the experiment station at Quicksand, in the mountains of Eastern Kentucky. In 1922 E. O. Robinson, a businessman who had made millions in the lumber industry, created the E. O. Robinson Mountain Fund to aid in the betterment of the commonwealth and the mountain region in particular. At the close of the year, the director of the fund (C. N. Manning, president of the Security Trust Company of Lexington) contacted the university about creating an agricultural substation in Eastern Kentucky to assist in experimental activity and in demonstrations that would be beneficial to the particular topography and geography of the region. McVey's keen insight and negotiations during the discussions of the actual contract would benefit the university immeasurably in the future.[56]

The original proposal for the Robinson Mountain Fund was substantial. It entailed leasing approximately fifteen thousand acres in Breathitt, Perry, and Knott counties, land that had been deforested. The land would be used to conduct experiments and demonstrations in reforestation, soil conservation, and farming in mountainous terrain far different from the fertile bluegrass soil at the university's experiment station on campus. In May 1923 McVey and Robinson, along with members of the boards of the university and the Robinson Mountain Fund, met to survey the land and discuss the possibilities. McVey was excited, but he "pointed out the immensity of the task that was before the University in carrying out this project and in bringing about the necessary experimental, economic, and social development" that was expected.[57]

As news of the project spread through the papers, E. O. Robinson read a comment McVey had made that worried the philanthropist. McVey was quoted as saying, "These lands that the University is taking over are a liability rather than an asset." Robinson disagreed and wrote McVey to point to the good that would result, adding, "If you can convince me that it is a liability, I certainly don't want to do it. . . . I would be very glad to hear from you relative to it, and I am quite sure that you did not mean that literally it was a liability."[58]

McVey's response attempted to assuage Robinson's fears. He noted that "liability" was certainly not the proper term to describe the proposal, stating that his own view and UK's official stance was that the fund would provide the university "an opportunity of expanding its service . . . in the eastern part of Kentucky." He then praised Robinson, adding, "With the fine cooperative spirit that exists . . . there is no reason why very great good can not be done almost immediately in connection with the development of the idea thought out by you." On this specific issue, McVey was trying to show that the "liability" lay not in UK's increased activities in the area, but in the reality that the funds for such work had not been appropriated. The president, however, had another agenda as well.[59]

Ensuing correspondence between the two revealed exactly what was at issue. Robinson wrote McVey that what he continued to read in the papers led him "to think possibly you Gentlemen might be intentionally starting propaganda that would cause us to feel the necessity of deeding the land to the university." He added that since receiving McVey's letter, he "did not feel that was in your mind." McVey's next letter could not have offered Robinson any comfort: "The way of the philanthropist appears to be hard." McVey then quoted the *New York Times* as stating that Robinson had been "enriched by Ford." He added, "Yesterday I heard in Pittsburgh via some Kentuckian . . . that our gift only amounted to a tract of cut-over land which would be reforested [presumably by UK] and deeded back to your heir when the timber has grown. With best regards."[60]

McVey was indeed trying to secure the land for the university and doing a superb job of pushing the issue. Corresponding with Judge Stoll, he learned that much of the land would in fact be reforested within forty years, the new timber worth approximately fifteen to twenty million dollars. The current proposal would have the state and university provide the human resources and capital for this process, and then the land would return to the Robinson Fund, potentially leaving UK (and the commonwealth) with nothing to show for its service. Stoll concluded, "I doubt seriously whether our duty to the State would permit us to expend the State's money to do all of this work when the Robinson Foundation itself would ultimately get the benefit of the expenditure."[61]

At its July meeting in 1923, the Executive Committee of the Board of Trustees affirmed that the university would accept the tract only if it were actually deeded to the institution. Despite his earlier inclinations Robinson agreed with this stipulation. McVey immediately began addressing other problems in the contract. First, McVey wanted to make sure that the railroad, owned by the Louisville and Nashville Railroad but operated by the Mowbray and Robinson Company on the deeded land, could be used by the university. At the same time, McVey wanted to make sure that UK was not responsible for the line and that it did not have to pay fees to the L&N if it used the tracks. Finally, McVey asked Robinson to change the provision that the university "establish and maintain a school of manual training." He agreed that such a school would be beneficial, but he could not predict whether the state would provide the funding to operate it. Robinson again acquiesced to the president's demands, stating, "It will be agreeable to put a clause in there that would not bind you to do this but show that it was the intent to do so." [62]

Despite the concessions McVey managed to win, the university did not gain all it desired when the deed for the land was signed in October 1923. First, the contract stated, "There is also excepted from the foregoing conveyance the oil, gas, coal and other minerals" on the land; the owner of the mineral rights was allowed to explore the property in order to "mine, excavate, drill or otherwise develop and operate said minerals." Another clause stated that the property would revert to the E. O. Robinson Fund if UK failed "for any period of three years to carry out the terms of the trust herein defined." The university was allowed to terminate the contract if the upcoming legislature did not appropriate funds for operating the experiment station. [63]

After the contract was signed, McVey wrote Robinson, explaining why two trustees had voted against passage of the proposal. The president stated that they disagreed with the stipulation that the land would revert back to the fund if UK neglected its duties. He wondered if the university could get the property without restriction. Robinson's reply pointed to the success McVey had enjoyed in accomplishing so much. The philanthropist noted that he understood the issue but stated, "I am quite sure the Mountain Fund Board would not consider eliminating that. We have practically eliminated everything else." [64]

The sweeping changes to Robinson's original plan provided the university with clear ownership of the property, and in 1924 the legislature showed its support by appropriating $25,000 for the development and maintenance of the substation's work. As anticipated, the station conducted research in forestry and agriculture aimed at improving life in Eastern

Kentucky's distinct economic, meteorological, and topographical situation. Under the leadership of Dean Thomas Cooper and Lula Hale, a demonstration teacher, work at Quicksand flourished. Riding on horseback, Hale visited hundreds of households to advertise the work being done by the university. The station opened a modest library, and Hale taught numerous classes in home economics and family health. She also organized the annual Robinson Harvest Festival, held each September to showcase the previous year's work.[65]

The university's work so satisfied the parties involved that McVey eventually gained nearly all the concessions he had initially sought. In 1926 the L&N leased to UK, free of charge, the right-of-way on its tracks located within the experiment station. Four years later E. O. Robinson reclaimed mineral rights on the property and donated the coal rights to the university. The station's prominent role in the region virtually guaranteed annual appropriations from the legislature, removing the fear that the land would revert back to the owner. Instead, the substation at Quicksand would continue to be an integral part of the university's work into the twenty-first century.[66]

The political impact of the Quicksand development was almost as important as the substation itself. Since he had arrived in Lexington, McVey had struggled to convince the legislature to fund work that would substantially benefit the entire commonwealth. The Robinson substation did not change the collective attitude of the state, but it did play on ever-present regional allegiances, and McVey gained support for greater state funding without even lobbying. Before the work at Quicksand had begun, politically astute citizens in Western Kentucky began jockeying for a substation of their own. It was suspected that the 1924 General Assembly would grant the university funds for operations at Quicksand, but it was a political reality that the powerful politicians in Western Kentucky expected a political plum of their own in return for supporting the eastern substation.

In late 1923 Dean Cooper traveled to Paducah to discuss the placement of a station in the western part of the state. He outlined stipulations that the university would require, including the need for at least four hundred acres of land. Boosters throughout Western Kentucky explained why their town or county would make an ideal site. Early in the 1924 legislative session Senator Ben Davis, representing Fulton and Graves counties, presented a bill for a station. The problem for Senator Davis and his constituents in Mayfield, as it turned out, was the decision to proceed slowly, seeking the university's approval of the bill.[67]

In January 1924 McVey read a letter from the Mayfield Chamber of Commerce to the Executive Committee of the Board of Trustees. In it the chamber promised four hundred acres of land for an experiment station. The committee decided to "make acknowledgement of the letter" and stated that if the legislature appropriated the funding, it would be pleased to consider the offer. In February McVey read another letter submitted on behalf of Mayfield, asserting that the town did not want control of a station; it simply wanted to provide the land. After McVey read this letter, the Executive Committee decided to accept the offer of the Mayfield Chamber of Commerce, provided that the state appropriate at least $20,000 to fund the work at the substation. While individuals from Mayfield tried to work out the formalities with Cooper, McVey, and the university's board, others were pushing for action in Frankfort.[68]

Without discussing the matter with McVey or Cooper, Representative T. H. King of Caldwell County stealthily guided a bill out of committee that placed the substation near Princeton, Kentucky. The administration had been caught off guard, and Cooper now sent McVey a copy of King's bill, writing, "This was not endorsed by the Board of Trustees of the University of Kentucky and . . . no opportunity had been given for an expression upon their part." Cooper asked for McVey's opinion, while reminding him that other interested parties had been working diligently to get the university's approval before introducing such a bill. McVey, however, did nothing to stop King's bill, and King protected the legislation against proposed amendments to remove the specified location. Before the end of March the bill had become a law. King then contacted university officials to seek their help in establishing the substation. Despite the hasty passage of the bill, it proved fortuitous for UK. As highlighted by Allan Smith, the substation at Princeton was approximately fifty miles closer to Lexington than the one offered by the Mayfield Chamber, and the two types of soil on the Princeton land mirrored that in Western Kentucky.[69]

When the substation at Princeton was dedicated, a crowd of approximately six thousand showed up for the carnival-like festivities. Finally, the citizens of Western Kentucky were taking ownership in the University of Kentucky, and McVey was gaining a presence throughout the various regions of the commonwealth. The substation became the object of funding during ensuing legislative sessions, receiving state appropriations to develop houses, barns, silos, and so forth.[70]

Closer to home, the experiment station in Lexington was in dire need of land. Ambitious professors hired by McVey early in his tenure now sought to expand their research projects, and they needed acreage to afford them the opportunity. At the same time, Lexington's growth threatened to turn the farmland south of the university into neighborhoods rather than research tracts. The dramatic rise in property costs led Dean Cooper to suggest purchasing property near Versailles, but McVey and the board balked. Instead the president desired to expand the existing station. McVey sought and received permission to purchase Petit farm, just south of the university's property. UK put $13,000 down and borrowed $26,000 to buy the 130 acres, and it leased the land that lay between the experiment station and Petit farm.[71]

These agricultural holdings came at an opportune time. Kentucky's appropriations for agricultural education had remained meager, but increased state funding created greater opportunities for research. In 1925 Congress passed the Purnell Act, proving an additional boon to UK. This legislation did not require matching state funds, money granted on a project basis for research efforts related to "the production, manufacture, preparation, use, distribution, and marketing of agricultural products." The federal funding bypassed the state government and went directly to the university. As a beneficiary of this legislation, UK increased its funding of agricultural work in the second half of the 1920s from $80,000 to $140,000.[72]

The faculty hired by Cooper and McVey during McVey's first years as president wasted no time utilizing the funds. Allan Smith noted that research projects addressing sterility in mares, tobacco-disease prevention, and the production of red clover helped the commonwealth's farmers and gained international recognition. Other research focused on soil fertility, as well as the raising of cattle, hogs, and sheep. Home economics instructors studied the nutritional value of garden vegetables (such as kale and mustard greens) and animals such as hens. In all, agricultural experimentation at UK during the 1920s resulted in the publication of more than fifty research bulletins and nearly two hundred journal articles. McVey was witnessing his goal of seeing the university serve the state in tangible ways.[73]

The money appropriated in 1924 for activities at the experiment stations was both a blessing and a curse. As McVey had been preaching since assuming the presidency, research at the state university needed to aid the state itself. The institution could aid the commonwealth in many ways other than in the traditional liberal arts, which had been the late president Patterson's primary interest. The Robinson Forest and the Western Kentucky substations provided McVey with an opportunity that he had desperately desired, but it created a burden. When the legislature appropriated tens of thousands of dollars in 1924 for the university's work in Eastern and Western Kentucky, it hampered McVey's chances to secure larger appropriations for the Lexington campus.

As McVey began gearing up for the legislative session of 1924, he took an aggressive tone and an active role. This seemed to be a result of a number of factors, including his relationship with Frances Jewell, his successful defense of academic freedom, and the dire needs on campus. Beginning his preparations during the summer of 1923, he noted to the board that about $25,000 of the money from the Bingham estate tax revenue would be used for paying institutional debts and that $100,000 would be used for a chemistry building. He trusted that the legislature would help pay for the remainder of the construction. Noting that the university continued to lose professors, he returned to his plea for increased faculty salaries.[74]

McVey crafted a university budget for the General Assembly and presented it to the board for its approval in the fall of 1923. The budget for the biennium included approximately a half-million dollars for annual operating expenses, as well as $1.2 million for permanent improvements on campus, $615,000 of which would be used for construction during the 1924–1925 academic year. These funds would be used to complete the chemistry building, build a recitation hall, and erect a women's dorm. Renovations would be made on the old gymnasium to make it suitable for women's sporting activities and classes. For the 1925–1926 academic year, McVey proposed no increase to the previous year's operating budget, but he did request an additional $650,000 for an engineering building, an agricultural facility, a men's dorm, and a centralized heating plant. [75]

Faith in the success of his proposals seemed misguided, considering the historical lack of support, but McVey was justified in his request. Enrollment surpassed 1,800, and the president expected it to reach 2,000 by 1926 (and this did not include the more than 1,500 students involved in summer school, extension courses, and the university's practice school). As McVey noted frequently, the student body had increased by more than 300 percent since 1908, when enrollment was below 500. During that same time span, little had been done to the university campus. An engineering shop had been built during World War I with money from the federal government, and in 1920 the legislature had appropriated funds for a men's dorm, the old dilapidated dorms converted into recitation rooms. The politicians in Frankfort had provided nothing else to meet the demands of the growing student body. [76]

With the gubernatorial election of William "Honest Bill from Olive Hill" Fields in 1923, McVey immediately set out to court him on behalf of the university. In a congratulatory letter to the governor-elect, McVey stated that he was "very anxious" to meet with the Budget Commission to explain the needs of the university. The commission, which consisted of the governor, the state auditor, and the chair of the Tax Commission, would present a budget to the General Assembly some time during the first month of the session. McVey wanted his own requests included. [77]

In the meantime, other prominent progressive citizens of the state began a movement to propose another multimillion-dollar bond issue to the legislature. This time the bond issue would include money not only for building roads but also for state hospitals and institutions of higher learning. McVey was an ardent supporter of the bond issue, but he understood the improbability of its passing though the legislature and then being voted on favorably by the commonwealth's citizens. McVey again wrote to the governor in mid-December, tying to cover his bases. After mentioning the bond issue, he asserted that even if it passed, it "could not effect [sic] the immediate needs of the University nor provide for the expenditures during the coming two years." Hoping to discuss these issues in person, McVey again requested a meeting with the governor.[78]

As the legislative session commenced, McVey corresponded with individuals who would support his cause. For example, he continually pressed Arch Hamilton, a representative from Lexington, to urge the governor to support the university's budget. As the president said, "I think the important thing is to find out when the Budget Commission meets and present our claims as strongly as possible at that time. If you could see the governor and go over these matters I think it would be desirable." McVey found an ally in Lewis Humphrey, editor of the *Louisville Post*. McVey sent him statistics concerning the university's student growth and lack of support from the state. Contemplating ways to garner support for the university, McVey illustrated his challenge by citing a comparison: the University of Michigan had 35,000 alumni, while UK had only 2,686. Kentucky's small number of graduates made it difficult to develop a movement that could influence the legislature.[79]

McVey finally met with the Budget Commission in late January, pleading his case for expanded operating expenses, as well as for a large sum to develop the physical plant. He again discussed the university's growth despite the lack of support from the state, but his plea fell on deaf ears. In February Arch Hamilton informed the president that the governor (who, on his election, also served as president of the Board of Trustees for UK) had decided not to support McVey's requests. Hamilton suggested that the president return to Frankfort to salvage what he could for the university.[80]

By February McVey found himself clearing up other problems in the legislature. One representative had proposed a bill to abolish fraternities in the state. McVey wrote to him and explained that the fraternities housed more students than did the dorms and that unless the state was willing to build dorms, abolishing fraternities would not be possible. McVey also had to fight another bill introduced by a senator in an attempt to make himself head of the state's geological survey. This was problematic, because the legislation would make him a faculty member at UK. Of course, McVey opposed the bill on the grounds that he had no oversight in this individual's hiring or firing and did not have the budget to support the position.[81]

By late February McVey was in damage-control mode, writing the presidents of the state's teachers colleges to make sure that House Bill 536, which dealt with inheritance taxes, passed to ensure that UK and the state's other colleges would have funds for day-to-day operations. McVey knew that he would not get appropriations for the physical plant, but he was still hoping for the funds necessary to complete the chemistry building. McVey wrote to the governor in March, pleading for money. Knowing that the legislature had appropriated $50,000 for "the university" to support the experiment stations, McVey added, "Permit me to point out that the appropriations for the two new experimental stations do not help the problem on the University campus here at Lexington but add to the institution's responsibilities and labor." The legislature did actually include money for the chemistry building in the budget bill, but the governor vetoed it. He wrote McVey that he had no ill will toward the university, but that the state simply did not have the money.[82]

McVey's efforts had once again been defeated in Frankfort, but this time a glimmer of hope still existed. Despite granting virtually nothing that McVey had requested, the state government did pass a bond-issue referendum to be voted upon in November. McVey was an avid supporter of the move, writing that the voters' approval was "the only way out of the difficulties which face Kentucky. I see no other way by which Kentucky can make the necessary capital investments . . . except through the issuance of bonds." Most of the $75-million-dollar issue would go to improve roads, but UK would be the beneficiary of $5 million for permanent im-

provements. McVey finally had the transformational funding he had always wanted in sight.[83]

The Board of Trustees wanted to know exactly what McVey planned
to do with the money. Its members requested that the president develop a
pamphlet showing how UK would utilize the $5 million on the Lexing-
ton campus. McVey broke the university's needs into three categories: student care, educational facilities, and general functions. For student care,
McVey planned to spend nearly $2 million on dormitories, a student din-
ing commons, an infirmary, and updated facilities for women. Under
educational facilities, McVey hoped to build a library, various classroom
and office buildings, and a model high school for teacher training. Under
general functions, McVey placed the construction of an auditorium, a
university museum, a heating plant, and several smaller projects.[84]

To promote this program, McVey devised a plan for publicity. He
began working with the Greater Kentucky Association to find individuals
to campaign for the bond issue. The board gave him permission to start a
speakers bureau. The president reported that many university employees
would be willing to travel across the state to speak on behalf of the bond
issue if their traveling expenses could be reimbursed. McVey himself began a vigorous campaign to challenge the "pay as you go" approach that
many Kentuckians found appealing.[85]

To accomplish his goals, McVey began fund-raising efforts with the
employees under his command. In a form letter sent to university employees, McVey stated, "As you know, the Bond Issue comes before the people
at the November election. In order to have this matter voted upon intelligently, it is necessary to present it to the people in the State. This requires
money." He asked the staff to make donations. He welcomed large donations but suggested five or ten dollars a person. In the ensuing weeks
dozens of letters came back to his office with checks, pledges, and letters
of support. Few employees had the courage to write that they did not favor the issue or were unwilling to give.[86]

In the fall the *Louisville Times* questioned McVey concerning the student newspaper's editorials in favor of the bond issue. After the student
paper published an editorial entitled "Shall Kentucky Go Forward?" a

reporter from the *Times* asked McVey whether it was the "policy" of the *Kentucky Kernel* to "take sides in political matters." McVey responded, "The bond issue is not a political matter." And this he truly believed. It was not a Democratic or Republican initiative; it was a move for the entire commonwealth. However, when the reporter asked whether McVey agreed with the editorial, he said that he had not read it. The reporter asked if he could read it to McVey, but McVey declined. The *Louisville Times* then compared the president to the "publisher" of a newspaper "who has nothing to say as to what goes in his publication." McVey chose not to contest the accusation, perhaps because of lack of support from the press. As McVey recalled years later, "caustic editorials" disparaged politicians and educators alike.[87]

Other papers supported McVey's efforts for the bond issue. The *Herald* defended McVey by attacking the *Louisville Times*. The *Louisville Herald-Post* printed editorials in favor of the referendum. The *Kentucky Kernel* continued its push for the bond issue, predicting that its failure would result in "more years of poverty . . . without a chance for progress, without a hope that Kentucky can ever look another state in the face and not feel the burning of shame."[88]

President McVey, along with the governor, helped mobilize a massive campaign on behalf of the bond issue. UK's speakers bureau sent professors and students throughout the state to lobby the institution's case. The men's and women's councils at the university had been inspired by McVey's lead and volunteered to work on Election Day. McVey himself traversed Kentucky discussing the bonds, arguing that a favorable vote would help the university and benefit all the sons and daughters of the commonwealth.[89]

Despite such efforts the bond measure went down in defeat, 275,873 to 374,319. Voters in the state had made it clear that they supported the "pay as you go" approach to both roads and higher education. The loss devastated McVey. The dejected and despondent president attempted to look at other funding alternatives, but he knew that a golden opportunity had been defeated. More than a quarter century later, McVey still had not let the issue go, saying that the bond issue's failure led to "deprecating and devastating criticism" of the state's educational institutions.[90]

McVey's response to the defeat was a pivotal moment for his presidency, the university, and the commonwealth. Instead of sitting back and waiting two more years to plead his case again, the chief executive began an unannounced building program of his own, without any appropriations. McVey had already started plans for a new chemistry building when, in March, Governor Fields vetoed the appropriation that would have given the president the go-ahead. This time McVey refused to stop. Just weeks after being denied funding, he recommended that the structure be built regardless. McVey had to utilize capital from the general fund of the university, which he managed to do successfully. The president's plan was not without its trials. When bids were first let, they all exceeded what McVey was willing to spend, and he had to go back to the project's Boston architects to scale down the proposal. McVey eventually secured a bid for a smaller building, and construction began in the spring of 1925.[91]

To meet the needs of extreme overcrowding, McVey engaged in an ingenious plot that would relieve some of the crowding and eventually add to the university campus. Many women had not been able to attend the university because of lack of living space on campus or in town. In early 1925 the board asked McVey to examine possible solutions to the problem. McVey devised a plan to have the Combs Lumber Company construct a women's dormitory. When it was completed to the university's satisfaction, the Security Trust Company of Lexington purchased it, and UK agreed to lease the building from them with an option to buy the facility. The building was completed just before the 1926 legislative session began, and McVey requested that the General Assembly appropriate funds to purchase the building, which was already benefiting the university. Seeing the tangible benefit of the dormitory, Frankfort appropriated $150,000 to purchase it outright.[92]

Other than this stroke of luck, the 1926 General Assembly was in many ways a repeat of sessions past. Antievolution bills, bills to repeal the inheritance tax (which provided a substantial share of the campus budget), and attempts to add a constitutional amendment banning an inheritance tax—interesting inasmuch as the state did not yet have an income tax—were proposed. Finally, another attempt to pass a major bond issue that would give the university millions of dollars for permanent improvements surfaced. In all cases, these attempts failed to materialize during the legislative session. McVey had begun to play a more active role in opposing measures harmful to the university and exhibited growing adeptness in letter-writing campaigns to save the university from disaster. As in past sessions, however, McVey requested more than a half-million dollars for permanent improvements but was unable to get the legislature to support anything that they could not already see.[93]

Without appropriations for new construction, McVey carried on his largely unfunded building campaign. And although the legislature did not help the university take advantage of the prosperity of the 1920s though permanent improvements, McVey did announce to the board that university finances were in the best condition since he had been at the institution. Although he would have preferred to keep that money for things such as salary increases, he was forced into frugality to continue paying for buildings. After the 1926 legislative session the president continued with smaller projects, such as finishing the conversion of a small African American church into an art building and rebuilding the old stock-judging pavilion, which had been burned in a fire. McVey then began to focus his attention on larger projects.[94]

During the summer of 1926 the board requested that McVey begin planning for a library. The president had desired a new library for years but wanted to make sure that the facility would become the capstone project of the current building campaign. This required careful planning if it were to harmonize with the current growth pattern. McVey therefore consulted with James White, an architect from the University of Illinois, to help configure the campus.[95]

As the fall semester began in 1927, McVey started his second decade as president. The faculty, staff, and Board of Trustees honored him with a surprise banquet, and the *Kernel* noted the campus's growth during his tenure, but McVey was not finished. He began accepting contractors' bids for a recitation building, which the Board of Trustees would name in his honor. When construction was completed, McVey Hall became the largest classroom building on campus. It served students by including a cafeteria and relieved overcrowding by housing the math, English, and journalism departments.[96]

After construction on McVey Hall commenced, the president redoubled his efforts regarding Memorial Hall, picking up where he had left off, trusting that Kentuckians who had made pledges would actually honor them. Even after the construction of Memorial Hall in 1929, however, McVey was still writing, without much success, to individuals who had pledged support but had not followed through. The university ended up contributing part of the $125,000 price tag because of these unpaid pledges. Memorial Hall became a campus symbol, but for McVey it also served as a reminder of the state's failure to make good on what he hoped would be a $300,000 project.[97]

As McVey prepared for the 1928 legislative session, he expressed optimism, telling the board that he expected to receive considerable support. McVey lowered the amount of the university's construction budget to well under a million dollars for the biennium. He requested $800,000 for the construction of a library, a new teacher-training school, a dairy products building, and an engineering laboratory. His optimism stemmed from a number of factors. First, as the Executive Committee of the Board of Trustees noted, these requests were only "to meet the minimum needs of the university in the next biennium." More dormitories were needed, but instructional buildings were crucial. Second, the university had already spent 45 percent of its revenue on agricultural programs "for the benefit of the farmers of the state," and a dairy products building would increase that amount. Finally, McVey had requested $150,000 from the General Education Board for the construction of a teacher-training school (which would also house the College of Education), and the board had agreed, provided a matching gift of $150,000 were secured by the university.[98]

Nevertheless, the university received less than half the $800,000 requested. Still, this was enough to continue construction. The legislature appropriated matching funds for the teacher-training building, as well as $150,000 (of $200,000 requested) for a dairy products building. When library construction stalled because of the legislature's failure to provide money, McVey began planning construction of those buildings for which he had received funding. Work on both buildings began in 1929, and the facilities were occupied in 1930.

After the conclusion of the legislative session, McVey began looking for an appropriate site for a practice school. He needed a location adjacent to campus, so that students could easily and safely access the school. The president settled on a plot of land donated to the university by the city of Lexington, which the municipality had used as a dump. McVey had a study of the land conducted to make sure that building on the dump would not be dangerous, and the study revealed that minimal amounts of gases emanated from the property. When the university began construction on the facility, however, contractors ran into a number of problems with sewers on the property. They were eventually solved, and the College of Education opened the facility in the fall of 1930.[99]

In addition, McVey began preparing to build and fill unfunded dormitories. He utilized a plan similar to (but more elaborate than) the one used to build the women's dormitory. In late 1928 the university sold its own property to the Security Trust Company of Lexington, which then paid $270,000 for the construction of two men's dormitories. When they were completed in the fall of 1929, the university began buying back the buildings and land on an amortized scale, using the boarding fees paid by the students in residence. As other prominent universities utilized state funds to prepare for campus growth, Kentucky's lack of support forced McVey to mortgage part of UK's future.[100]

If navigating the treacheries of the Kentucky General Assembly was not harrowing enough for McVey during the prosperity of the 1920s, matters became even more fraught when the legislature convened for its 1930 session in the wake of the great stock market crash. In stating the university's needs, the Board of Trustees emphasized that construction had begun on a library without any state funding for that facility. It also noted "the present financial situation" and pointed out that it would be asking for "about one-half of what was requested two years ago." With this in mind, McVey hoped to get money for an engineering building, a laboratory facility, and an agricultural engineering building, as well as a service building.[101]

By this time McVey understood the political game and attempted to play it, with little success. He traveled to Frankfort regularly, usually taking one or two others with him to help argue his case. He contacted newspapers to ask them for support. He skipped a meeting in Washington, D.C., because, as he said, "the legislature is doing so many unexpected things including cutting the tax which will materially reduce the U income." When the 1930 session finally ended, McVey had successfully defended the university against large funding cuts and, despite getting less than he requested, had secured appropriations for an agricultural engineering building. At the session's conclusion, McVey revealed his attitude toward the political climate: "The legislature adjourned on Friday, and everybody breathes a sigh of relief." [102]

As work on the agricultural engineering building and the library continued, planning for further buildings subsided. McVey told the board that "the construction of these buildings completes what the University has in mind at the present time in the way of construction." He added that the growth of the student body meant that "other buildings will be required in the near future." The library had been years in the planning, and crews had already begun digging the foundation in 1929. Plans were soon formulated for the agricultural engineering building, and the two facilities were dedicated during the fall semester of 1931.[103]

The library was the culmination of McVey's building program. When the facility was dedicated on 23 October 1931, the president recorded that it was a "great day" for the university. The *Lexington Leader* lauded McVey's role in transforming the campus, stating that "under the wise and aggressive administration" of the president, "buildings of the most substantial character and the most pleasing architecture have sprung up like magic in the past few years." The library, boasted the editorial, stood as a symbol of McVey's efforts and the potential that the university had to "stand out like a beacon" and "bring out the dormant powers of the people." The library did indeed stand as a symbol of McVey's accomplishments. The facility was large enough to house hundreds of thousands of

volumes and opened the way for expanding graduate programs. Most notably, McVey had managed to complete the task with little help from the
state—a common theme during his administration. At the end of this
building program, the UK had spent more than $2 million improving the
campus. The state had provided merely $600,000 of the cost, and private
philanthropy had offered far less.[104]

Earlier in the 1920s, McVey had good reason to believe that Kentucky
would support his endeavors to literally "build" a great university campus.
Numerous endowment campaigns at other state institutions had yielded
impressive results. The University of Michigan, for example, had raised
more than $1 million for a student union. This was followed by a $5 million appropriation from the Michigan legislature for campus improvements. From 1919 to 1924 the University of Illinois raised almost $2
million, more than 90 percent of this money coming from alumni donations. During the same timeframe the University of Minnesota's development campaign had booked more than $1.5 million.[105]

The rise in support of public higher education was not limited to the
Midwest. The University of Virginia had long set the standard for state-
supported higher education in the South, but other institutions, like the
University of North Carolina and the University of Texas, also began to
benefit from increased appropriations. North Carolina's success, for example, stood in stark contrast to the bleak situation McVey faced in the
Bluegrass. The legislature in the Tar Heel state appropriated more than
$600,000 for a new library. That was more than McVey had secured for
buildings during his entire tenure as president. And while McVey struggled to raise one-third of his original $300,000 goal for Memorial Hall,
alumni from the University of North Carolina were donating hundreds of
thousands of dollars to better the campus of their alma mater.[106]

This lack of support from the state government and UK alumni hindered McVey's attempts to lure appropriations from philanthropic organizations such as the General Education Board and the Carnegie Foundation
for the Advancement of Teaching. During the 1920s philanthropists gave
more than $1 billion to higher education. While some institutions were
securing millions of dollars McVey could only secure $150,000 for a new

College of Education. This was the result of two factors. First, most foundation gifts required matching funds, and the citizens of Kentucky were simply unwilling to provide such substantial support. Second, during the second half of the 1920s the major foundations had shifted their funding efforts from endowments and physical plant growth to applied research. While McVey was still trying to convince Kentucky's legislature of the need for campus construction, the nation's leading state universities were beginning to lure grants for research projects.[107]

Kentucky's government had long been infamous for its lack of support of higher education. For example, historian James Klotter noted that in 1912 Louisville provided more support for one of its high schools than Kentucky provided for the University of Kentucky. However, this continuing neglect as the progressive movement expanded throughout the South during the 1920s requires an explanation. Much of the trouble stemmed from the legislature's mixing of politics with progressive educational reform. The growth of Kentucky's normal schools in particular seemed to inhibit McVey's efforts. In 1922 the legislature created two normal schools (eventually established at Morehead and Murray) and upgraded the two existing normal schools (Eastern and Western) to teachers colleges. It did not, however, do anything to promote a College of Education in Lexington. McVey did not oppose creating new institutions or upgrading existing ones, but these four institutions, coupled with traditional Kentucky politicking, spelled trouble for UK's future.[108]

Additional teacher-training schools, without a comprehensive plan to encompass the whole of higher education in Kentucky, inevitably led to further political jockeying for a limited supply of funds. While correspondence between McVey and the presidents of the teacher-training institutions was for the most part genial, the political maneuvering now necessary in Frankfort overwhelmed McVey. His status as an outsider, his limited political connections, and the presence of powerful political factions, along with his seemingly cold and cerebral demeanor, absolutely crippled McVey in Frankfort. While McVey struggled, seasoned booster politicians worked closely with other politically minded presidents of the regional institutions—especially Henry H. Cherry at Western State Teachers College.

The 1924 General Assembly, the first since the establishment of the new normal schools, revealed the difficulty McVey faced. McVey had requested $1.2 million for campus improvements for the biennium, essentially distributed equally over the two-year period. McVey and the university received nothing. At the same time, the legislature appropriated $200,000 for capital outlay at Western and $800,000 to be divided equally between Morehead and Murray for the development of their burgeoning normal school campuses. McVey did not protest the funding for those institutions because he knew that the appropriations were needed, but he did not understand why the state flagship institution was being neglected. As he confided in his matter-of-fact way to Lexington politician Arch Hamilton, "There seems to be some weakness in our method of presenting our case. Just what it is I am not sure."[109]

The ensuing legislative sessions continued in a similar fashion. In December 1925 McVey invited the presidents of the other state institutions to meet in order to plan a united front on legislation for the 1926 General Assembly. He wanted to discuss support for and distribution of tax revenue, proposed building programs, and matters relating to the transfer of credits and students among institutions. This provided little help. During the 1926 legislative session McVey's repeated requests were again denied as the university received only $150,000 to pay for a building that had already been constructed. The same legislature approved an additional $250,000 for Murray and Morehead, while providing Cherry at Western an additional $350,000 for construction. In 1928 UK's requests to the legislature noted that the institution consisted of seven colleges and that "the total attendance of students carrying on college work is greater than that of all other state institutions." Despite this, the regional institutions still received a larger appropriation for their campus improvements.[110]

By the close of the 1930 legislative session the teachers colleges, with their strong political ties, had clearly received far greater support for campus construction than had the University of Kentucky. Between 1924 and 1930 Morehead State Normal School and Teachers College had received appropriations of $1,220,000. The legislature provided Western State Teachers College with more than $1 million from 1922 to 1930. The University of Kentucky, on the other hand, had received only $600,000 for the physical plant since the completion of McVey's home when he arrived in 1917. This was the result of the political influence of powerful individuals. As already mentioned, H. H. Cherry held an inordinate amount of political power in Frankfort, and in Eastern Kentucky the powerful state senator Allie Young was instrumental in gaining generous support for Morehead. The faculty at Morehead understood this, and in the late 1920s that body passed a resolution commending the senator's work and publicly supported his bid for reelection.[111]

During this era only Cherry had the ambition and the political clout to attempt to duplicate work already being administered by the University of Kentucky or to create programs that would rightfully belong to a state's flagship institution. Throughout the 1920s Cherry, despite McVey's private protests in personal letters, continued to try to gain support for an agricultural experiment station at Western. Or, as Cherry originally suggested to McVey, he had "a desire to cooperate more closely with the Experiment Station [which UK was already operating in Princeton without the help of Western] in securing and disseminating scientific data." After promising not to engage in such work, Cherry reneged and sought to purchase a farm to conduct agricultural experiments.[112]

By 1930 Cherry was attempting to develop a graduate program at Western, and the 1930 legislature actually introduced a bill to create a medical school in Bowling Green. McVey wrote to Cherry, asking that he "be entirely frank with me about the bill . . . to establish a medical school at Bowling Green." McVey noted that the university had begun work in the health field and that such a move would create duplication. Asking for Cherry's opinion, UK's president reiterated, "I trust you will give it to me with full frankness." Cherry was not in Bowling Green and did not respond to McVey's letter, but the bill did not make it out of committee.[113]

During the summer of 1931 McVey tried to address the funding and duplication problems by writing a letter to all the presidents of the regional colleges, as well as the president of the University of Louisville (which was not yet state supported). In it McVey stated that he thought it was "quite apparent to all of us . . . that we need to outline rather carefully the educational program of this state." In order to begin discussing this, McVey asked each president five questions dealing with the roles of state institutions. Most importantly, he asked, "What are the functions of the state teachers college?" and "What fields should the State University occupy in coordination with these various divisions of educational organization?" Emphasizing the "unofficial" nature of the request, McVey wanted to share opinions on the subject.[114]

President Cherry apparently did not reply with answers to McVey's questions. Instead he retorted that such issues "cover a very extensive field and will require quite a great deal of time and study before I can be justified in expressing an opinion." Only Raymond Kent, president of the University of Louisville, spoke in a way that clearly contrasted the role of the state teachers colleges and UK. Kent argued that if the teachers colleges overstepped the boundaries of their specifically stated missions, it would harm the entire system of higher education. He also stated that the addition of programs other than teachers' degrees would duplicate the work at UK, limit the number of adequately trained educators, and harm the commonwealth's rural schools. McVey could not get a similar response from the other institutions, and it appeared that the struggles might continue during the years ahead.[115]

McVey's private and collegial attempts to find common ground and work for the entire system of higher education stood in marked contrast to the approach taken by the student editor of the *Kentucky Kernel*. In a far more partisan and combative tone, the *Kernel* printed an editorial in June 1931, at nearly the same time that McVey penned his questionnaire addressing UK's lack of support. Originally, this gained little attention. However, the paper decided to reprint the editorial on 25 September, and this time it created a controversy. The article reported that the state's normal schools were doing comparatively better financially because certain politicians were interested in gaining political strength at home, rather than meeting the larger needs of the state. The editorial then suggested that UK could do the work done by other institutions and that a student's education in Lexington would be "more complete" than elsewhere in the state. It called for "consolidation of functions" in order to "save money" for taxpayers. Finally, it asserted that the state's educational standards would "stand or fall by the standards maintained and the services rendered by the university" and that yet it seemed the university was last in line when it came to funding.[116]

This polemic led to protests from the presidents of the other state institutions. McVey discussed the issue at a meeting with the state presidents, and he told them he would make a statement that "would satisfy them." President Rainey Wells of Murray demanded an official retraction, but McVey refused. Instead he had an "interesting talk" with the paper's editor, the details of which he kept private. The paper did print a small statement from the president that said that the article had been unfortunate because the institutions needed to work together. In the end, however, McVey stood by his policy "to give students freedom of expression" and used the opportunity to "call to the Teachers Colleges to be fair and square with the University."[117]

UK had indeed received less for its building program than other state institutions had. The regional colleges countered by pointing to UK's larger budget for annual operations. The university, however, oversaw numerous colleges and an experiment farm in Lexington, two agricultural substations, and extension programs throughout the state. McVey knew that a state flagship university, in the larger academy, was expected to provide a wide array of programs to meet the growing demands of a changing society, and he believed that expanding the curriculum on campus would benefit the state.

The most pressing area of expansion was in the field of education. The survey commission's study, completed just before McVey's arrival in 1917, had stated that the university needed to transform its Department of Education into a full-fledged College of Education. The move was again suggested in a survey mandated by the legislature in 1920 and conducted by the General Education Board in 1921. While the study focused on primary and secondary education, it did note the poor training of Kentucky's teachers and recommended that UK create a College of Education to improve both the quality of education and the number of teachers being added to the state's schools. The state needed more teachers, and the state university in Lexington needed to help. McVey was ready for the move, and he had been eyeing his man for the dean's position. Finally, in 1923 the Board of Trustees agreed to create a College of Education at the University of Kentucky.[118]

When McVey created the College of Education, he wanted it to do more than simply expand the course offerings in the discipline. He wanted to make UK an integral part of educational policy decisions for the state and enhance the university's prestige outside the commonwealth. McVey knew firsthand that Kentucky's educational leaders had not utilized the university to any major extent, and their provincialism had resulted in McVey's outsider status. For example, when the state legislature passed a resolution in 1920 creating a commission to appoint an outside group to conduct a study of the state, McVey was not included or kept abreast of its proceedings. Even before this ostracism McVey had not been included in setting the program for the Kentucky Education Association's conferences. When he asked if he could address the gathering, he was told, "We will let you present, but you will not have much time." [119]

McVey used the state's educational survey of 1921 and the creation of the College of Education to change the status quo on campus and in the commonwealth, hiring a prominent national figure as dean of the college. William S. Taylor was a native of Kentucky who had taught in the commonwealth before pursuing his advanced degrees. He had earned his PhD at Columbia's teachers college, where he studied under the renowned progressive William H. Kilpatrick. Taylor had worked for the Federal Vocational Education Board and served in Pennsylvania's Department of Education. His educational pedigree and connections made him part of a national group of progressive educators.[120]

Along with his impressive résumé, his Kentucky roots gave Taylor a strong edge. As historian Susan Gooden noted, when McVey submitted Taylor's résumé to the board for approval, it included the president's handwritten note: "Born and raised in Kentucky." Furthermore, Taylor desired to return to the Bluegrass. Kilpatrick wrote that Taylor's "heart is in Kentucky and the work there." In order to lure him, McVey increased his original salary offer of $5,000 to $6,000 and agreed to move the educational psychology program from Arts and Sciences to the College of Education.[121]

Taylor agreed to the terms and upon his arrival began to transform the educational work at the university, as well as the institution's role in the state. Taylor replaced the model school's principal and hired Moses Ligon, a principal in Eastern Kentucky who was completing his doctorate at the University of Chicago. UK also immediately began holding annual educational conferences on campus. These meetings, which sought to examine Kentucky's educational problems within a national context, afforded McVey and Taylor the opportunity to bring in speakers from leading national universities. This marked departure had a profound impact on the state, as well as on UK's ability to secure funds from national foundations. By 1927 the college had created a Bureau of School Service, which was designed to examine the problems of the state's schools and offer policy suggestions.[122]

Far less challenging politically was McVey's creation of a College of Commerce. The president had been debating the move for some time, and after the work of the College of Education had been firmly established, he recommended that the board create a school to prepare students for business. By this time such a policy was not cutting-edge. The first business college in the United States had been formed at the University of Pennsylvania in the nineteenth century, and in 1926 there were more than a hundred business colleges or schools in the United States. McVey was simply trying to help Kentucky become current. He suggested that Edward Wiest, who had served as department chair for sociology and economics, be named dean of the new college. The board approved his recommendations, and work began in the fall of 1926.[123]

In the year following the creation of the College of Commerce, McVey helped establish a Bureau of Business Research. This was similar in nature to the bureau created in the College of Education, in that it was designed to help the commonwealth meet pressing problems in business and management. The board supported McVey's request, and in 1928 McVey had another academic division helping to satisfy the state's needs.[124]

As McVey was developing colleges and bureaus at the university, he decided that the time had come for the creation of a graduate school. A few master's degrees were being awarded when McVey arrived in Lexington, and the situation had not changed in years. When the idea for a graduate school first surfaced during his early years, McVey had opposed the move, believing that the university was not yet ready to take on such an endeavor. By 1924, however, he decided that the time had come, and the board agreed. Thinking of UK's stature in the larger academic community, McVey encouraged an increase in graduate work because, as he reasoned, "the standing of the University as a University depends on its graduate instruction."[125]

McVey's reforms were an immediate success. After just one year, the graduate school had enrolled approximately one hundred individuals, seventy-four of them as full-time, residential students. Because of this success, the president urged the board to provide more funding for graduate stipends and broached the idea of offering a doctoral program. This idea became a reality when the board adopted the president's proposal to begin conferring "the Doctor's degree" in the fall of 1926. McVey made sure that he controlled which departments would offer the terminal degree, and he moved forward cautiously. The University of Kentucky granted its first PhD in 1929 in the College of Education. During that same year more than five hundred students enrolled in graduate courses, two hundred of these in full-time study. Seven more matriculated into doctoral degree programs. Unlike the College of Commerce, the graduate school represented a monumental move on the part of President McVey, who proudly announced that until this time, the only other southern institution within five hundred miles of Lexington to offer a doctorate degree was Peabody College in Nashville (which would eventually become part of Vanderbilt).[126]

Closely related to the growth of the graduate school was McVey's continued insistence on the importance of research by the university faculty. The College of Agriculture had been the most prolific in this vein, and McVey now sought to expand on these efforts to aid the state through professional expertise. In 1924 McVey promoted the campus Research

Club, which he had been instrumental in creating for the purpose of encouraging those who had "engaged in research work and had made contributions beyond the work they did for a degree" to organize a series of
publications. He hoped to address problems in Kentucky "covering social
and economic matters, such as railroad transportation, finance, merchan-
dising methods, agriculture . . . and facts regarding the social and economic conditions of the State." He believed that the series "would be a
contribution that would be of considerable value" to the commonwealth.
The project was slow going at first, producing only three monographs in
the first year. However, it led to greater research and a streamlining of the
process to get books published through the university.[127]

As McVey sought to mobilize faculty members for research in Lexington, he also attempted to create a larger network for scholars in the South.
He and Harcourt Morgan at the University of Tennessee sought to bring
representatives from southern state universities to discuss "the problems of
the South and more specifically, those of state institutions in their own
Commonwealths." The main issue McVey wanted to address was the role
of state universities in addressing the economic and social issues of the
South.[128]

The meeting occurred as planned but did not lead to the anticipated
results. McVey called the session to order and discussed his vision for the
conference, designed to explore the "possibilities of working out a joint
program which would attempt to get at the social, educational, and industrial facts found in the different states and to draw conclusions from these
facts." McVey expressed his view that the meeting was a failure because "it
came to no conclusion and no plans for future meetings were made."
Writing the presidents of the institutions that participated, he noted that
the meeting's "purpose and viewpoint either did not impress those present, or the idea behind the call was not sufficiently analyzed to bring the
purpose before the meeting."[129]

Along with the attempts at reform, McVey sought ways to improve the
lives of the faculty and students. He proposed university-wide policies

that would help UK's matriculates and their personal needs. He created a Personnel Bureau, opening in the fall of 1931, that would offer guidance for undergraduates and "provide for more direction for the students' welfare." Imbued with the growing progressive faith in testing, the bureau tested students for language, math, and psychological aptitude and used standardized exams to place the bottom 10 percent of test takers in noncredit remedial courses so that they would have a better chance to pass collegiate work and eventually earn a degree.[130]

McVey's liberal views and policies, however, were tempered by the conservatism displayed by many of the nation's academic leaders. Like so many other progressives during the 1920s, he offered views on issues of race and gender that were not reformist. His position on race and education, for example, remained conservative, and his views concerning women students (at least in one case) proved to be reactionary. Such opinions led to policies that had a profound impact on students at UK.

In 1924 McVey, along with the dean of women, Sarah Blanding, and the director of women's physical education, Florence Stout, appeared before the University Senate and together recommended that women's basketball be banned as an intercollegiate sport at the university. Despite protests and a petition signed by more than two hundred students, the senate concurred with McVey and ended the basketball program in November 1924. This decision had been a long time in the making, as Stout had crusaded for the policy long before McVey became president of UK. With the support of Blanding (who had replaced Frances Jewell), McVey was persuaded.[131]

McVey stated his reasons for supporting the ban in the student newspaper, telling the *Kernel* that "there was no agreement as to the type of basketball to be played by girls in intercollegiate games." He then added that basketball was "a strenuous sport for boys and was, therefore, too strenuous for girls." His views and those of the female administrators at UK reflected the recommendations of at least two national athletic associations, including the National Association of Directors for Physical Education of Women. With McVey's blessing, Blanding and Stout then developed an intramural program for women's athletics that included basketball. As historian Gregory Stanley noted, in 1928 Dean Blanding happily reported to the president that UK had created an environment where there was "a game for every girl and every girl playing a game."[132]

Concerning race issues, McVey was not as reactionary, but he did not challenge the status quo. In 1926 the director of university extension, Wellington Patrick, informed McVey of the occasional requests from African Americans to enroll in correspondence courses at UK. He told the president that he usually responded that the university "would be very happy to be of service to the colored people of the state but . . . there is a law on the Statute Books of Kentucky which prohibits white and colored people from receiving instruction in the same institution." He would then refer inquiries to the "Colored Normal School at Frankfort." However, E. B. Toles, an African American from Paris, Kentucky, had persisted in asking to enroll in correspondence courses.[133]

McVey and Patrick debated the university's course of action over the next month. The president said, "The university might meet such a request," but noted one difficulty: he did not know how the institution would respond when these students presented their credits from UK to schools in the North "and the claim on the part of such students to the University of Kentucky relationship." Patrick responded that UK could allow African Americans to take correspondence courses "as special students" who were not enrolled in the university. Their transcripts could then be marked "with an explanation to this effect." Patrick noted that university registrar Ezra Gillis preferred "not to deal with them," and Patrick confessed, "I am not anxious at all to get into the job." He did conclude the policy was "rather cold, if we can legally help them."[134]

In January 1927 McVey brought Toles's application to the Executive Committee of the Board of Trustees but reported to Patrick that the committee had "passed on the matter." He then asked, "Will you please write to him and to others who make similar requests." Patrick informed Toles that the board could not legally help him and that he needed to contact the state superintendent of schools "to make some sort of provision with the Colored Institution at Frankfort to take care of colored people." McVey, not wanting to alienate anyone who might help his institution get the support it needed, refused to challenge the Jim Crow system—even if this only meant approving a correspondence course.[135]

————·————

Concerning faculty development, McVey had to deal with two sides of the career and age spectrum. The president sought to increase salaries in order to recruit promising young scholars and retain those who had made a name for themselves in the larger academy. This proved extremely challenging as he decided to transfer money from the general operating budget into construction projects. However, McVey's greatest concern during much of the decade dealt with those faculty members nearing the end of their professional careers. In 1922 McVey highlighted the growing number of professors in their sixties and stated that this was "a problem that we want to be thinking about . . . and get some sort of satisfactory solution worked out." By 1924 the president had changed his tone and now told the board that it was "incumbent upon the university to arrange a program for a retirement system." He hoped for a program through which valued faculty members who had served a "positive and long service" could step back from full-time work and still receive some income. The board, working with limited funds, was slow in moving. By 1926 it appointed a committee to consider various retirement plans. The following year the committee reported that "the University should speedily adopt a satisfactory retirement plan," but the issue still required "further investigation and study."[136]

In the meantime McVey attempted to secure help from outside agencies. He met with the Carnegie Foundation for the Advancement of Teaching, but it was not willing to subsidize McVey's plan. The university would have to conduct a program without outside help. A system was finally adopted on 13 March 1929, the board voting that upon reaching the age of seventy a faculty member would "no longer perform the duties that he has theretofore performed." Instead these individuals would serve in capacities "designated by the President of the University." In so doing, retirees would earn 20 percent of their final year's salary, as well as 1 percent "for each year of service to the University." McVey wasted no time implementing the program; during the same board meeting a number of professors were named professors emeritus as McVey explained each member's new tasks.[137]

This seemingly mundane policy so vigilantly pursued by McVey had profound implications. It relieved the classroom of individuals who were well past their professional prime. (Of course, it also discriminated against those who were still capable of teaching.) It helped older faculty members earn a living wage while moving them into research positions. At the same time it was designed to allow McVey to hire faculty members with the credentials, abilities, and outlook to transform the institution into a true university.

———•———

McVey was a university builder, and developing a nationally recognized university that would serve the commonwealth had been his goal since arriving in Lexington. The trials he faced could have forced him to accept a position elsewhere. Instead he worked tirelessly toward his end—even in the midst of hardship and defeat. Kentuckians, both politicians and alumni, seemed prone to pledge support but fail to deliver. Moreover, the alumni continually diverted the focus of fund-raising from academics to athletics.

Far more important to McVey were the troubles in the legislature, which were exacerbated by regional teachers colleges. Leaders at these institutions continued to view the University of Kentucky with suspicion. According to historian Lowell Harrison, the University of Kentucky saw the regional institutions as "unwanted siblings . . . who should certainly be satisfied with a distinctly inferior role." He added that "westerners . . . saw the university as a selfish big sister who refused to share common belongings upon an equitable basis." Eastern Kentucky University historian Bill Ellis stated that President Herman L. Donovan "felt besieged by the University of Kentucky" and that the state university "always seemed to be crippling his school's efforts."[138]

What presidents of the teachers colleges refused to recognize was that the University of Kentucky should not have been competing with them.

Instead UK needed support to rival southern institutions such as the University of North Carolina and the University of Virginia, as well as midwestern state flagship institutions. It was not a matter of snobbery, but of reality, if Kentucky desired to have an exceptional university. For example, Clyde Barrow pointed out that the Carnegie Foundation for the Advancement of Teaching chose to aid universities that had "set before themselves the ideal of a strong institution crowning the state system of education." In Kentucky, the teachers colleges clearly resented McVey's attempts to do just that. Much of McVey's trouble stemmed from President Cherry's politicking at Western. Ironically, however, Cherry's blind ambition aroused suspicion and jealousy among other teachers colleges, and these tensions precluded the regional schools from forming a united front against the university.[139]

Regardless, McVey heeded the call from Kentucky's other institutions on at least two occasions. Both the University of Louisville and Morehead State requested McVey's services in preparing surveys of their respective institutions. McVey's surveys were often critical but always professional. In both cases his reports were utilized by politically motivated individuals seeking to remove presidents (as well as other personnel) from their positions, potentially harming McVey's relationship with other educators and state institutions. Despite this, McVey did his job unselfishly and properly. McVey, more than any other president in Kentucky, failed to understand the ever-present politicking. For example, in 1931 McVey allowed the UK band to perform at the opening ceremony of the Cincinnati-Louisville Highway. What he thought would be a civic event, however, turned into a political rally led by the chair of the Highway Commission, who was "partisan in every sense, full of criticisms of the other highway commissions . . . [and] the shortcomings of Republicans." McVey, who was a pragmatist, continued to learn the nature of state politics the hard way.[140]

Despite political troubles, McVey managed to create a university with seven colleges, three bureaus existing solely to serve the state, and many new academic departments. The rapidly increasing faculty was now far more credentialed, and the campus had more than a dozen major additions in less than a decade. The student body had increased beyond three thousand full-time students, and if enrollments in the summer session, extension, and correspondence courses were included, the number of students neared seven thousand. In late 1931 McVey informed the board that, except for the University of Texas, UK had more students enrolled than any other institution in the South.[141]

In McVey's mind, however, these accomplishments were secondary to the changes in his personal life. Frances Jewell had transformed his life. From Wednesday's student teas, to graduation receptions, to dinners hosted nearly every night, Maxwell Place had evolved from the president's house to a central component of the university. As McVey commented, "Her ability to make friends and her genuine interest are real assets to the university and I rejoice in them." The impact was even greater in personal terms. Frank McVey included Frances on his annual trips to Elk Lake Lodge in Michigan, where they spent time sailing, swimming, and reading. McVey also painted during his month away from Kentucky in the summer, but after marrying Frances, he began finding time to paint in Lexington—often coaxing her into posing for his portraits. With Frances he found time for Sunday drives and visits to Pleasant View, the Jewell family farm.[142]

This dramatic shift in McVey's personal life probably served as the primary reason the president did not accept a more lucrative and prestigious presidency. On 1 January 1930 McVey penned in his diary, "Make no resolutions about New Year—what's the use." He then added that his dream was to take Frances to Europe during the fall, so that he could "see things at a distance." When McVey read about the University of Missouri, he pondered his decision to turn down its presidency. He concluded that "Kentucky has been heaven in comparison. . . . It has been an interesting ten years full of hard work. If I had gone I might have missed Frances." He seemed proud of the comments of a young guest speaker named Will Durant, who had stayed at Maxwell Place before giving a lecture entitled "Is Progress Real?" He quoted Durant as saying, "Your wife is quite a live wire, quick on the uptake and charming. It must keep you busy keeping up with her." McVey proudly added, "He is quite taken with my lady . . . for she is not only lovely and charming but intelligent & learned in every way."[143]

By the time McVey finished the library as the capstone of his building program, he was no longer able to make a smooth transition to another institution—and he did not want to. McVey was in his early sixties. Two of his three children were married, and he had two grandchildren in close proximity. The simple fact that he began keeping a journal in 1930 suggested something about his permanency. Frances had converted him, at least in part, to being a true Kentuckian, and people were taking notice. The *Kentucky Kernel* pointed to his change in demeanor in 1927, noting that McVey was "generally accused of being too reserved for Kentuckians." However, during one impassioned speech at the Kentucky Education Association in which McVey began to raise his voice, a member of the audience exclaimed, "Hurrah for him! . . . Now he's beginning to speak like a Kentuckian." [144]

McVey had also gained recognition among presidents of other southern universities. In the fall of 1931 his services were requested as part of a survey commission examining consolidation in the University of North Carolina system, and he was asked to speak at the University of North Carolina's inauguration of Frank P. Graham as the representative for institutions of higher education in the South. McVey used the time in Chapel Hill to examine the progress that had been made there, but he also hoped to gain notice for his own institution. He was rubbing shoulders with some notables, including President James R. Angell of Yale, President Robert Maynard Hutchins of Chicago, and Abraham Flexner. [145]

McVey's primary interest, as it had been a decade prior, was to have the University of Kentucky become a member of the Association of American Universities. Even before arriving in North Carolina, the president had called a meeting with Dean Funkhouser, Dean Taylor, and Ezra Gillis to discuss what needed to be done in order for UK to be invited into the AAU. McVey thus traveled to Chapel Hill with the idea that he might "learn something new" about gaining admission, adding, "When the University gains this step it is then in the role of a real university." He learned that the University of Kentucky could receive "serious consideration" for membership, but gaining admission was a dream that would require increased state support. [146]

Frank L. McVey (*front and center*), shortly after his arrival at UK. McVey oversaw the development of the ROTC, which continued after the conclusion of World War I. (KUKUARP-1998UA001-224-0006, University of Kentucky Archives)

The University Commission. McVey assembled a group of educational leaders and newspaper reporters to travel to the Midwest and report on what was being done at leading universities, hoping to use the information gathered to support his plan for increased state support. The commission recommended that the state supply $8 million for campus improvements to match the work being done at universities like Illinois and Wisconsin. (KUKUARP-2001UA025-6435, University of Kentucky Archives)

University Council, 1922. *First row (left to right):* Frances Jewell, dean of women; Robert W. Bingham, LLD; Frank McVey, president; Glanville Terrell, professor emeritus of Greek and philosophy; Paul P. Boyd, dean of arts and sciences. *Second row (left to right):* Franklin E. Tuttle, professor emeritus of chemistry; Columbus R. Melcher, dean of men; Thomas Poe Cooper, dean of agriculture and director of the agriculture experiment station; Ezra Gillis, registrar; Edwin Freeman, acting dean of engineering; George Roberts, assistant dean of agriculture. (KUKUARP-1998UA001-224, University of Kentucky Archives)

Frances Jewell, dean of women, working at her desk shortly before her marriage to McVey. At that time it was presumed that she would give up her deanship to serve as first lady of the university. (KUKUARP-1998UA001-368-0182, University of Kentucky Archives)

Constructed in 1924, Alumni Gymnasium provided ample space for crowds at basketball games. Adolph Rupp began his coaching career in Alumni Gymnasium when he came to UK in 1930. (KUKUARP-1998UA001-102-0007, University of Kentucky Archives)

The basement of Alumni Gymnasium housed the university bookstore and post office until torrential rains caused severe flooding in 1928. (KUKUARP-2001UA068-01-034, University of Kentucky Archives)

The inaugural game at McLean Stadium (Stoll Field) against intrastate rival Centre College on 1 November 1924. The field was named for longtime board member Richard Stoll, the stadium for Price McLean, a football player who died from head injuries suffered during a game in 1923. Plans for the football stadium had to be scaled back because of the skyrocketing cost of Alumni Gymnasium. (KUKUARP-1998UA002-2881A1924, University of Kentucky Archives)

Opened in 1928, McVey Hall was named to honor the work that the president had accomplished in his first decade at UK. It originally included classroom buildings and office space, along with a cafeteria and a bookstore. (KUKUARP-1998UA002-1305, University of Kentucky Archives)

The Education Building (opened in 1930) was built with a $150,000 grant from the General Education Board and matching appropriations from the state government. It would later be named in honor of William S. Taylor, who was recruited by McVey and served as dean of the College of Education for many years. (KUKUARP-1998UA002-1421B, University of Kentucky Archives)

Dedicated in 1929, Memorial Hall was built with funds from a campaign drive that McVey had started a decade earlier in order to honor the fallen soldiers of World War I. Alumni and interested citizens first desired to build facilities for UK's basketball and football teams. (KUKUARP-1998UA001-141, University of Kentucky Archives)

The University Library (later named the Margaret I. King Library in honor of King's long service as librarian to the university) was dedicated on 23 October 1931. It served as the crown jewel of McVey's first building campaign, despite the fact that it had been constructed without any state funding. (KUKUARP-1998UA001-137-0005, University of Kentucky Archives)

Frank McVey poses with Mildred and A. B. "Happy" Chandler during a luncheon at Maxwell Place after a board meeting. The McVeys also invited legislators from the surrounding counties. Chandler, who had just been elected governor at the age of thirty-seven, was very interested in supporting the athletic programs at UK, but he did not provide McVey with the budget appropriations the president had hoped for. (KUKUARP-1998UA001-247-0002, University of Kentucky Archives)

(*Left to right*) Herman Lee Donovan, president of Eastern State Teachers College; John Howard Payne, president of Morehead Normal School; President McVey; and Henry H. Cherry, president of Western Kentucky Teachers College. McVey's relationship with the leaders of the state teachers colleges, especially Cherry, was often strained, as these presidents competed for meager state appropriations. (KUKUARP-1998UA001-250-0004, University of Kentucky Archives)

First Lady Eleanor Roosevelt addresses a crowd at Memorial Hall in 1934. Seated in the first row are Mrs. Elinor Morgenthau (wife of Treasury Secretary Henry Morgenthau), Frank McVey, and Governor Ruby Laffoon. (KUKUARP-2001UA025-3036, University of Kentucky Archives)

The McVeys stand outside Maxwell Place with Eleanor Roosevelt (*center*), Governor Ruby Laffoon, and others during Mrs. Roosevelt's visit in 1934. (KUKUARP-2001UA025-3037, University of Kentucky Archives)

Built with appropriations from the federal government, the university's Law Building (later named for the late dean William T. Lafferty) and its modern architectural style became part of the controversy surrounding McVey's final building campaign in the late 1930s. (KUKUARP-1998UA001-135-0005, University of Kentucky Archives)

The Student Union Building, dedicated in 1938, provided another example of the modern architectural style that was adopted by McVey at the urging of Colonel James H. Graham, the dean of engineering, who became a polemical figure during the last years of McVey's administration at UK. (KUKUARP-1998UA001-149-0006, University of Kentucky Archives)

An aging Frank McVey works at his desk during his final months as president of the University of Kentucky in 1940. (KUKUARP-1998UA001-368-0245, University of Kentucky Archives)

Frances Jewell McVey at the time of her husband's retirement in 1940. (KUKU-ARP-2001UA028-3029, University of Kentucky Archives)

Frank and Frances entertain guests in 1940 at the annual senior brunch held outside Maxwell Place. As first lady of the university, Frances became well known for her hospitality at the president's home. (KUKUARP-1998UA001-248-0033, University of Kentucky Archives)

McVey poses for a portrait during his final year as president of UK in 1940. (KUKUARP-1998UA001-368-0246, University of Kentucky Archives)

McVey's house, built on Shady Lane in 1940, became the talk of the town due to its modern architecture. (1998UA001-267-0001, University of Kentucky Archives)

The architecture of "Flat Top House," as the McVeys named their retirement home, was matched by the modern style of its interior decorating. (KUKUARP-1998UA001-267-0002, University of Kentucky Archives)

Frank McVey's closest personal friends in Lexington were members of a small group that called themselves the "Book Thieves." They not only discussed literature but also made trips outside the state, looking for volumes to help expand the collections in the university's library. In this picture from 1942 are (*back row: left to right*) Dr. J. S. Chambers, Dr. Claude Trapp, J. Winston Coleman, Thomas D. Clark, and (*front row: left to right*) Judge Samuel Wilson, Charles Staples, Frank McVey, and William Townsend. (KUKAV-PA62W8-0020, University of Kentucky Archives)

Chapter 5

Surviving the Great Depression and Reforming the South
1932–1936

> Now the winds of adversity are blowing from the sea, stirring even
> the waters of the harbor. The tide is running out. What shall the
> captains do? Shall they stay in the harbor waiting for better weather
> and run with the tide; or caught on the seas, shall they lower the
> anchor, batten down the hatches, take in and patiently endure the
> pounding of the seas.
> —Frank LeRond McVey, 1932

As the 1932 Kentucky General Assembly neared, the nation's economic
crisis finally began to exert its full negative impact on the commonwealth's
already struggling agricultural-based economy. McVey desperately worked
to assure that his university received its share from the depleted state cof-
fers. The first day of January 1932 found McVey at Louisville's Seelbach
Hotel, not for a New Year's party but for a meeting of the state's college
presidents and Kentucky's superintendent of public instruction.

They had a simple agenda. In view of the projected revenue shortfall,
they hoped to devise a successful strategy for the legislature. McVey left
the daylong meeting thinking there had been "little constructive thought."
Yet the group at least arrived at a budgetary détente of sorts—all higher-
education institutions agreed to refrain from requesting funds for construction. McVey later reflected, "I have a great deal of anxiety about the
legislative session. I am determined not to worry about it. Of course I
will."[1]

Because the governor exerted the most control over the state budget in Kentucky, McVey met with Governor Ruby Laffoon. The nervous president left that meeting with mixed feelings. The governor seemed to grasp Kentucky's financial troubles, and McVey was pleased that Laffoon was considering both an income tax and a sales tax to meet the state's needs. Laffoon hoped to generate approximately $6 million in revenue. McVey needed the governor to succeed, but privately he worried that Laffoon's "leadership would not be energetic enough . . . [to] get the measure thru."[2]

The biennial session opened with the governor's call for efficiency in operations, as well as a 2 percent sales tax to meet the growing deficit. After conferring with his board, McVey submitted a budget request totaling $2 million for the biennium; this was $120,000 less than UK's previous annual allocation. The *Courier-Journal,* however, reported that the challenge might be worse than simple budget cuts. The paper surmised that Kentucky's funds were so depleted that state institutions, including UK, might have to close before the year's end. Nevertheless, McVey tried to accentuate the positive by announcing that despite the economic challenges, UK would meet its payroll.[3]

The Great Depression, along with Laffoon's proposed two-cent sales tax, incited the powerful conservative base of Kentucky politics. Local taxpayers' associations gained momentum by late January. The hard-line conservative activists called for the closure of the two newest teachers colleges, in Murray and Morehead, as well as an across-the-board 15 percent cut in departmental and institutional appropriations. During his frequent trips to the General Assembly, McVey tried to defend his university against draconian cuts. He lamented, "This is the day of the reactionary. Depressions bring him to the front."[4]

McVey thought he might find an ally in UK alum, Lexington lawyer, and speaker of the House John Young Brown. But after a couple of frustrating meetings with Brown, McVey could not deter Brown's support for the steep budget cuts and his opposition to the governor's proposed sales tax. McVey's progressive view of government contrasted sharply with what he considered to be Speaker Brown's "unscientific" reasoning. McVey conceded that Brown had "commendable firmness," but that did not compensate for his stubbornness and refusal to reevaluate a situation after he was committed.[5]

Even as McVey continued to maneuver through the state's political terrain for greater support, other university funds declined drastically. Two of UK's largest sources of income, the inheritance tax and the property tax, saw sharp drops in revenue. Accordingly, McVey planned for a cut in faculty and staff salaries and received board chair Richard Stoll's support. The next day he informed the university's deans that salaries in excess of $1,300 would be reduced by 10 percent, remaining salaries by 5 percent. McVey received numerous phone calls and letters from faculty supporting his decision. The beleaguered president appreciated these "expressions of gratitude."[6]

Unfortunately, the salary reductions barely met the immediate shortfall, and the future of the university hung in the balance as the state debated tax revisions.[7] The House passed the sales tax over Speaker Brown's impassioned objections. The tax bill attracted widespread interest as thousands traveled to Frankfort, attempting to influence the vote in the Senate. A smaller but rowdier group of protesters on the capitol grounds actually caused damage at the Governor's Mansion. McVey thought that the protest seemed to "have made a considerable impression on the senate," adding, "there is now talk of giving it [the sales tax] up. . . . The need for courage is greatly to be desired." McVey met with representatives of one state taxpayers' league. He emphatically disagreed with their views but came away convinced that UK's advocates needed to emulate their enthusiasm to develop "a layman's interest in government and schools." Instead he found a crowd that "expected to throw the blame on the schools. . . . In a large measure they have succeeded in doing it—Politics!"[8]

The protest at the capitol did indeed succeed in hampering the momentum on the sales tax. In the Senate, which was considered the more liberal chamber, the tax measure remained in doubt. Throughout the process, Governor Laffoon believed his tax legislation would ultimately pass. However, McVey's earlier assessment of the governor proved correct, as Laffoon was unable to convince a sufficient number of Democratic bosses in the legislature, or even Lieutenant Governor A. B. "Happy" Chandler, to support the tax. As the session wound down, it became doubtful that the legislature could pass any budget. McVey noted, "News from Frankfort is very disturbing. The bills now passed leave us with nothing. . . . We stand naked." The degree of McVey's frustration with Kentucky politics showed as he admitted taking a perverse pleasure in announcing that the university stood a chance of closing its doors for two years if nothing was done.[9]

The General Assembly eventually passed a budget that included $970,000 for university operations even without the sales tax. The 15 percent cut in state funds would still allow UK to remain open. But the situation quickly deteriorated when the governor vetoed the budget bill because the House and Senate had failed to provide revenue to fund it. The budget stalemate left McVey in a quandary. He reported to the Board of Trustees that he could not make a financial presentation without assurance that funds for the university would be allocated.[10]

One thing became clear: additional salary cuts were necessary. McVey called for a university-wide meeting on 30 March 1932 to discuss the crisis. Noting later that "self-interest" had led to "the largest number present that has ever been at an assembly meeting," McVey shared his disheartening news with the faculty and staff. Stressing that no one knew what lay ahead, he noted that salary cuts of up to 50 percent were possible and that there was a chance that no salaries would be paid in April. Despite the grim outlook, McVey remained adamant that the university stay open and continue to serve its students and the state. He pleaded for "patience and understanding" from the employees. Aware of McVey's hard work to save their jobs and the university, those present interrupted the president's remarks numerous times with enthusiastic rounds of applause.[11]

That speech in Memorial Hall became a defining moment for McVey's presidency and an important crossroads for the struggling university. McVey recalled how the rousing cheers from a crowd "hard hit by the situation" lifted his own spirits. In many ways that moment was a microcosm of his presidency. He had a loyal faculty that admired him for the work he had done, despite the state's failure to provide adequate funding. Thomas Clark, then a young history professor, later called McVey's speech the highlight of his presidency. As often happens, it took a crisis for McVey's acumen at administration and university leadership to be fully appreciated.[12]

That same day McVey met with a few local business leaders to present an ingenious plan to help UK employees weather the financial crisis. The president stressed that the university's inability to pay full salaries had resulted in a "failure of purchasing power in the community." In order to help both town and gown, he proposed the creation of a makeshift credit union that might be operated by Lexington's Board of Commerce. Wealthy citizens would be asked to contribute money to the union, and university employees could apply for small loans at low interest rates to meet their financial obligations. Since the hand-picked group appeared favorable to the plan, McVey decided to share it with others. The president then convened key faculty members and administrators who supported the plan. By day's end McVey sensed he could sleep better that night, feeling that "one big step in the solution of the matter had been taken."[13]

The following day McVey invited thirty prominent citizens to Maxwell Place, where he outlined the specifics of his entire program. Emphasizing again the importance of the university to the community, the president convinced his guests to establish a committee to carry on the work of the faculty loan fund. He secured $10,000 in pledges that evening, and the group set a goal of $40,000 for the credit union. The committee met the following week at the Phoenix Hotel, and again McVey presented his plan—this time to an even larger audience. Those present pledged $20,000 for the program. It was announced that faculty members could borrow money at 4 percent interest on fifteen-month loans. By the end of April, the credit union was accepting applications and providing small loans to help faculty members pay their bills and meet financial obligations.[14]

The credit union served as an essential relief element. On 2 April McVey held another meeting with faculty members to inform them that many of their salaries would be cut dramatically and retroactively. Staff making $1,200 or less would still receive full pay, but employees making more than that would receive only $100 for work in the month of March.

On the first Sunday of April, McVey skipped church to work on further budget cuts, coming to the sobering conclusion that "the only way out is to reduce salaries still more than has been done so far." He implemented the same strategy for April, but the $100 cap was not enough, and the faculty went without any salary for May and June. The summer provided a welcome respite, because professors worked on ten-month contracts. One citizen wrote McVey comparing him to Moses: "I realize more fully what the Hebrews were up against in the Nile delta when they were commanded to make brick without straw. But they stuck to the job, and under their incomparable leader they won out."[15]

All told, the funds lost for the 1932–1933 academic year amounted to nearly a half-million dollars, or about 40 percent of the university's operating budget. The *Lexington Herald* reported that UK's budget was comparable to what it had been shortly after McVey's arrival in Lexington as a new president, when the student body was at one-third of its current enrollment. A budget that had been in excess of $1.1 million at its height, in 1931, had now been reduced to about $650,000 for 1932–1933. McVey projected a similar cut for the following academic year as well. The president received little acknowledgment at the state level for his stewardship as politicians looked to economize and scrutinized salaries, scholarships, and programs. Political infighting kept the university from earning favor from the commonwealth's political leadership. Locally, however, McVey received the "Cup for Conspicuous Service" from the Lexington Optimist Club, symbolizing the community's high regard.[16]

If hard times showcased reactionaries within state politics, on the UK campus the Depression created a heightened sense of political activism, resulting in attacks from both the right and the left—attacks that McVey feared would harm UK's standing in Frankfort. Rumors continued to circulate that UK had been out to discredit Democrats during the past legislative session, and McVey learned that some politicians believed the university was a Republican-dominated organization. Republican stalwarts had always served on the university's board, but after years of working to remove politics from UK and to build bipartisan coalitions, McVey particularly resented these charges.[17]

Lexington Democratic boss Billie Klair continued to believe that UK faculty member J. C. Jones intended to decrease his political influence. After meeting with Klair, McVey wrote to Jones, questioning "the propriety of a professor in the University . . . organiz[ing] student groups for particular partisan purposes." McVey argued that the professor needed to avoid the specific political problems of the day and focus on teaching "the principles of government . . . [and] the study and research that he should be carrying on." McVey stated that professors who organized students "to effect a particular purpose" had overstepped their bounds. He concluded by asking Jones to use common sense in order to avoid activities that might embarrass the university. In his defense, Jones responded that he had only been encouraging reform and that he had not used his position at the university to attack Klair. McVey shared Jones's comments with Klair and left it at that.[18]

McVey was also dealing with a small but influential group of students led by radical undergraduate (and future Vanderbilt Agrarian) Richard Weaver, who organized the Liberal Club on campus. The club's student members planned to protest the working conditions of coal miners in Eastern Kentucky. Upon hearing this, McVey quipped, "Fools rush in where angels fear to tread." The situation did not subside, and as McVey continued to receive letters about the agitation, he decided to respond to one at the beginning of April, writing, "Mr. Weaver is an eccentric person who has some ability and is filled with ideas about economics and social problems." The president held that Weaver's views did not represent those of the university and believed that a formal statement in response to the protests "would do more harm than good." Less than a week later the Student Government Association passed a resolution condemning the Liberal Club. McVey feared that such a move gave extra publicity to the group, and he lamented in his diary, "Deliver us from well meaning friends."[19]

Attempting to keep in check the politics of the Board of Trustees, professors, and students proved to be a task that consumed a great deal of McVey's thoughts. At the beginning of the 1932–1933 academic year, McVey opened the convocation by addressing the "great task of the university," which he viewed as helping students "see things as they are . . . and to place the true emphasis on right action." Clearly, "right action" to McVey was not the more radical machinations of Jones and Weaver during the previous semester, but McVey was not opposed to all liberal thought emanating on campus. When the president received complaints about a Professor W. R. Sutherland promoting socialist and communist thought in the classroom, McVey invited the professor to his office to discuss the matter. The president concluded that the primary problem was the "impression freshmen students may get because they have no foundations" and suggested that the professor keep underclassmen out of his class. The Board of Trustees discussed the same professor at a meeting in March 1933, certain members criticizing him on the same charge. McVey stated that it was "the folly and foolish statements of individuals that bring the unfortunate incidents," and he successfully defended the professor's teaching.[20]

Even while appearing to be a liberal president defending academic freedom for his faculty, McVey could also seem heavy-handed to his own staff. For example, McVey appointed German professor A. E. Bigge to chair a committee to examine teaching at UK and report on problems and potential solutions. Bigge's report in the spring of 1933 noted, among other things, that many UK professors had adopted the modern teaching style of implanting "in the minds of his students his own particular notions and theories." McVey demanded that Bigge provide specific instances of indoctrination, so that he could "know the facts" and solve the problem. Bigge told McVey that he and the committee could not provide McVey with specific examples of problems. While not satisfied with this answer, McVey did not pursue the issue.[21]

This balancing of academic freedom and the need to protect the university and its standing in Kentucky continued throughout the worst years of the Depression. UK's staunchest supporter on the board, Judge Richard Stoll, had been instrumental in McVey's hiring, and he defended the president during the university's trying times. Yet Stoll seemed obsessed with finding and eliminating any Marxist teachings on the campus. In 1935 Stoll asked McVey to protect the university against communist views. McVey worried that even "liberal views might be classed as communistic" by Stoll. For example, earlier that year two professors had contributed to a short-lived paper that expressed some radical opinions. Stoll alerted McVey about their articles and laid out his own interpretation of academic freedom, arguing that professors had the right to speak their minds, but that if a professor exercised that right to the detriment of the institution, the university did not need to "interfere with his academic freedom, but should get rid of him, and should get somebody to take his place."[22]

McVey told Stoll that he disagreed with the paper's content and that he had spoken with the faculty members involved. One of the professors, Thomas D. Clark, stated that he had been misrepresented in the publication. McVey then told Stoll that the problem was convincing younger faculty members to avoid writing in "fly-by-night" papers because "the effect on the University is far more reaching than they know. I shall keep in mind what you say." McVey maintained his conciliatory tone with Stoll over the next year, even as Stoll continued to push the issue. McVey confided in his diary that Stoll's reactionary view of academic freedom meant "freedom to speak as the Board of Trustees indicated."[23]

Undoubtedly, McVey felt the pressure exerted by Stoll and other Kentucky politicians. In late 1935 McVey declined a petition from a small group of students who wanted to start a campus chapter of the League for Industrial Democracy. The *Kentucky Kernel* published an essay by one of the denied students that claimed that McVey had stopped them from organizing because the legislature was meeting soon and such a club could harm UK's ability to secure necessary funding. The student added (either naively or sarcastically), "We cannot believe that the legislature of this Commonwealth is so dominated by selfish interest as the University administration seems to think. President Frank McVey belies his every pretension to liberalism when he dictatorially refuses us what in common justice should be ours." Confronted by the students, McVey met with them and encouraged the group to meet informally without official university recognition. McVey believed that the earnest young students "confused freedom with propaganda and publicity."[24]

The 1930s also witnessed a widespread peace movement at universities across the nation. In April 1936, UK students asked McVey for permission to stage an antiwar demonstration on the campus. McVey noted that a number of colleges and universities had barred such demonstrations, but he agreed to the protest. As a part of it, the students sought to hold a parade, but McVey denied this request. At the rally numerous speakers addressed the crowd on the topic of world peace, the student paper reporting that the speeches provided a "thoughtful discussion of the problems" facing America.[25]

If political issues were difficult to deal with on campus, addressing them at the university's extension centers across the commonwealth was even more challenging. While traveling the state, McVey heard numerous complaints, some of them dealing with the extension work and correspondence courses conducted by the university. The subjects of the charges included instances of substandard work, alleged cheating, and controversy surrounding the uncut salaries of extension instructors, who earned much of their pay from federal rather than state appropriations. McVey was aware of these problems, and he attempted to correct them by reassigning the director of extension, Wellington Patrick, to a different position within the university. Nevertheless, the complaints persisted.

The episode furthered McVey's understanding of Bluegrass politics. For example, English professor George Brady told McVey about three students at an extension center in Paintsville who could never do collegiate work on campus. However, all three were candidates for the Kentucky legislature. Brady recalled that McVey put his arm around the professor and advised, "Young man, for God's sake be diplomatic. . . . We already have enough enemies in the legislature."[26]

A closely related matter was the rivalry between UK and the state's regional public colleges. These relationships had been tenuous long before McVey's arrival in Lexington, but the political atmosphere in 1932 lessened the antagonism for a time. Instead of competing for money to construct buildings, each institution simply tried to secure an appropriation large enough for survival. As the General Assembly slashed school funding, it created a commission to study the state's school system and make recommendations for the 1934 legislature. Funded largely by the General Education Board, with additional funds from the state's segregated educational associations, the State Educational Commission was to consist of educators throughout the Bluegrass and a number of concerned citizens. Shortly after the bill passed, Superintendent of Public Instruction James Richmond met with the state college presidents. In his diary, McVey simply noted that Richmond had named "President Cherry [Western] and myself among the number. We shall see."[27]

The first meeting of the commission was held in Frankfort on 16 May 1932. McVey's initial skepticism receded as he began to view the work as an opportunity for reform. Nearly all the commission's work focused on elementary and high school education. However, one of the many subcommittees created to study the state's problems addressed higher education. McVey seized the opportunity and focused his efforts on coordinating collegiate aims and programs. As he devised a strategy for organization, he sought the advice of some UK professors, as well as the opinion of President Raymond Kent at the University of Louisville, then a municipal college and not beholden to the teachers colleges.

After months of meetings it became clear to H. H. Cherry that McVey and Dean William Taylor were pushing for closer state coordination of higher education. Western's president informed Taylor that he was an "individualist" and that Western should have the right to pursue whatever program it desired. Upon hearing this, McVey privately called Cherry's views "anarchy in education" and continued to use the subcommittee to push for change, despite Cherry's "notice that Western Teachers College would fight [the creation of] a central board." At the center of the debate was Cherry's insistence on developing graduate programs at Western. McVey was opposed to this type of expansion because he knew that UK's nascent graduate school needed to be strengthened before graduate offerings were expanded elsewhere in the commonwealth.[28]

At a January commission meeting Cherry vociferously defended his institution's right to decide its own curricular initiatives, including expanding graduate programs, and McVey changed his approach to accomplishing his goals. After this meeting UK's president met with several professors in Lexington who were helping prepare the subcommittee's report on higher education and the function of the state university. They discussed the matter and decided to present their ideas as a general philosophy of higher education programming, rather than as "a statement of the University of Kentucky." The move paid dividends.[29]

At the next meeting of the commission, the subcommittee on higher education presented its report and recommended the creation of a state board of higher education. Those at the meeting, including McVey, specifically rejected the idea of a single university system like North Carolina's, but most favored some sort of council to help coordinate educational programs. Not surprisingly, McVey reported that Cherry fervently opposed the creation of a board and that Western's president hoped that no changes to the current system (which was essentially no system) would be made. Although McVey disagreed, he felt that the debate, which lasted for hours, was generally beneficial and provided good insight.[30]

McVey met with Cherry again shortly before the publication of the report of the State Education Commission. UK's president feared that Cherry would not support the recommendations. Cherry told McVey he believed that there was "a deliberate attempt being made to check the influence of the Teachers Colleges," and he was correct. Despite Cherry's misgivings, the 1934 legislature created a Council on Public Higher Education, consisting of representatives from all the state's public colleges. Although the new board had little governing authority, it stipulated that each institution was to present its budget requests before each legislative session in an attempt to avoid duplication of educational programs. A hopeful McVey reported to UK's Board of Trustees that the council could greatly enhance higher education in the state "if it takes its work seriously and brings to it a spirit of good will, tolerance and determination."[31]

————·————

McVey was thankful that the 1934 legislature created the Council for Public Higher Education, but the machinations of Kentucky politicians continued to defy his sense of logic. The president spoke with individuals on campus and around the state about holding a meeting for legislators before the 1934 session. However, he worried that this move might be seen as an "effort to coerce legislators" and could possibly backfire. If the university chose not to hold a meeting, he would need to find a number of "loyal men" willing to respond to criticisms raised against the university during the legislative session. He lamented, "To get disinterested persons who are free from entanglements is a really hard task." This revealed the extent to which McVey's progressive faith in reason or the reasonableness of Kentucky politics continued to hamper his efforts.[32]

While McVey debated the idea of a prelegislative conference, he decided to undertake a "good will tour" of Kentucky. He hoped to create greater awareness of UK's importance to the state and the need to support higher education generally. McVey gave twenty-eight speeches to more than six thousand citizens across the state, urging them to support higher education. McVey noted that UK had approximately eight hundred graduates during Patterson's tenure as president and a similar number during Barker's tenure. Since McVey's arrival nearly fifty-five hundred had earned diplomas from the university. The president believed that the growing number of graduates would eventually lead to success in the legislature, but he was not confident about the near future.[33]

In the midst of his state tour, McVey met with Governor Laffoon to discuss Kentucky's financial situation and to seek the governor's opinion of a prelegislative conference. The governor was noncommittal but shared with McVey his hope of passing a sales tax. McVey felt that Laffoon was "obsessed" with the measure and had failed to comprehend McVey's pleas for more support. In the ensuing months, McVey's concerns proved valid. Facing a $2 million deficit, the governor called a special session in August. Laffoon asked for a sales tax to cover the deficit and to provide funds for new initiatives in the 1934 General Assembly.[34]

As the special session approached, the governor asked McVey if he and others at UK could help draft legislation for the emergency session. McVey agreed and recruited director of the Bureau of Business Research James W. Martin and dean of the law school Alvin Evans to help. State newspapers contacted McVey trying to confirm rumors that he had become part of the governor's "brain trust," a popular term in use during the first months of the Roosevelt administration. McVey denied the reports, stating that he was offering informal advice to the governor. Despite UK's assistance, foes from within the governor's own party were too powerful to overcome, and his sales tax measure failed. McVey noted that the governor had made a forceful argument "for sanity of view and cooperation but partisan politics are the rule and nothing may be done. It is too bad." The following week, McVey mused that the special session had failed because the governor had sought the advice of too few and attempted to "force a program on the general assembly in which they had no part in formulating."[35]

Ultimately, McVey determined that even if a prelegislative conference somehow failed, the state's political leaders could do no worse than had been done previously. In November, therefore, McVey and other university officials held a two-day session in Lexington for all interested legislators. McVey hoped that Allie Young, a powerful state senator and partisan supporter of the normal school in Morehead, would preside. Young attended but did not take a leadership role in the meetings. McVey described Young's attitude as "mildly sarcastic."[36]

Regardless, McVey felt optimistic about the program. The issues discussed were broader than just the university's needs. The governor laid out his proposals for the next General Assembly. Then members of the House and Senate held roundtable discussions to address potential problems and solutions. McVey reported that key politicians, including Lieutenant Governor A. B. "Happy" Chandler, spoke with him about the failure to accomplish anything during the recent special session. The politicians blamed other factions but expressed a desire to do more for education. This left McVey hopeful that something could be accomplished in the coming months: "It is my impression that the University's affairs are in better shape for this session than they have been at the opening of any legislature."[37]

McVey's optimism for the 1934 General Assembly could be heard in his public comments. He told the Board of Trustees that UK had done a better job explaining its needs to the legislators, "with more definiteness of purpose than in any other legislative meeting." He was confident that the legislature would not reduce appropriations to the university. Once the session began, McVey was amazed that the governor had broken the power of the Democratic bosses by forging an alliance with Republicans. McVey wrote that Laffoon had "dethroned" Young, giving rise to the "hope that this legislature may accomplish something effective." Concerning criticisms aimed at the governor for "consorting with Republicans," McVey explained, "After all the point is to get something done."[38]

As the weeks passed, however, reality shattered McVey's optimism. The legislature "did pass some excellent laws," but it proved unwilling to deal with the financial shortfall. Without a revenue bill, McVey predicted that the already paltry university budget would be cut by another quarter of a million dollars. Saddened by the state of affairs, McVey wrote that the legislature had adjourned "with much noise, many antics, and a good deal of liquor. The net result leaves much to be done. There is now no budget and there is no revenue provided for the state to run on the next biennium."[39]

Therefore McVey began speaking publicly in a manner he had not previously. In March he told the UK board that no university budget could be created because the General Assembly had failed to pass its own budget. More important, McVey told a gathering of more than four hundred at the Phoenix Hotel in Lexington, "As I stand before you tonight, I do not know if the higher institutions of learning in the state will be able to open next year. We are faced with a complete breakdown of education in Kentucky." McVey's assessment was not an exaggeration. The governor's response was to call a second special legislative session in May.[40]

Lasting from May into July, the legislative session focused on raising taxes to produce essential revenue. The assembly considered both an income tax and a sales tax. McVey met with Lexington senator Arch Hamilton to plead for his vote and asked a number of other people to "impress upon him the wisdom of voting for the law." But the ever-stoic McVey, having lived in Kentucky for more than fifteen years, still seemed astonished at the state's governmental officials. He wrote, "Politics at Frankfort carries with it a lot of lying and deception. I am amazed at the brassness of some of it and the foolishness of a good deal of it." In the end, the assembly failed to reenact an inheritance tax (which had been repealed the session before), but it did garner enough votes for a three-cent sales tax.[41]

The governor claimed that the session had "accomplished more than any legislature in the state's history." McVey appeared less enthusiastic, but he did wonder if Kentucky was "finally at the turning of the road." Unfortunately, "contentions and difficulties that involved the University in connection with the appropriations bill" continued. Simply put, UK would not receive significant benefit from the enhanced state revenues. McVey predicted that UK would be "in about the same position . . . as it was in each of the fiscal years of the biennium just closed." With the passage of the sales tax, the state's budget woes were no longer as severe, but the university benefited little from the measure.[42]

The state's teachers colleges, however, managed to garner a larger piece of the revenue pie than the state's flagship institution. McVey speculated that UK's struggles resulted from Senator Arch Hamilton's refusal to support the sales tax. Those legislators who had voted for the bill wanted to tell their constituents what the sales tax meant for their own districts. Hamilton's staunch opposition to the sales tax meant that his district, including the university, would not see as much financial gratitude as other legislative districts.[43]

The lack of funding heightened antagonistic feelings. Some at UK asked why the teachers colleges' budget allocations increased without a similar increase for the state university. The *Lexington Leader* noted that while UK's funding remained stagnant, "all the normal schools received increases." The editorial did not suggest that the regional schools did not need the funding, but it did argue that the legislature left "the most important educational institution in the state . . . seriously crippled." Comments pitting UK against the regional schools often offended, and in this case the usually cordial Herman Lee Donovan, president of Eastern State Teachers College, expressed his frustration to McVey. McVey, on the other hand, believed that the normal schools had engaged in "collusion" against the university. While the situation annoyed both presidents, McVey said he was glad to know about Donovan's frustrations and conceded that "institutional rivalries" had become a "difficult and harassing" challenge. It seemed that the newly created Council for Public Higher Education had its work cut out for it in the years ahead.[44]

————·•·———

The interim between the 1932 and 1934 General Assemblies in Kentucky witnessed a monumental shift in American politics. Franklin Delano Roosevelt's election, along with growing Democratic strength in Congress, reconfigured the national scene, but the dominance of the Democratic Party in Kentucky resulted in intraparty fractures among conservative and liberal elements. At the national level a consensus developed into a movement that would fundamentally alter the role of the federal government in American life, and McVey hoped that UK would benefit from the change. As President Roosevelt's administration passed sweeping legislation ushering in the New Deal, McVey took note, looking for ways that he could secure federal funds from one of the many alphabet programs created by Congress.

The first New Deal programs that created an impact on the Lexington campus were those providing funds to students engaged in part-time physical labor on campus. During the 1933–1934 academic year more than 250 UK students helped pay their tuition and meet expenses by painting buildings, landscaping, and conducting artwork projects. In one noteworthy example, a student created a mural for Memorial Hall that remains a campus treasure. About this mural depicting Kentucky's history, McVey wrote that rather than a mural portraying scenes from Lexington's culture, he had hoped to have one depicting educational history. He concluded that his idea for the project "was more than a young artist could get together."[45]

McVey was pleased with the support offered to students and the help it provided in keeping undergraduates enrolled, but he was also interested in larger federal appropriations. He had long been a proponent of government and university cooperation, and FDR's policies gave McVey an opportunity beyond the borders of the commonwealth. In June 1933 the board formally authorized McVey to investigate the procurement of funds for construction and refinancing the men's dorms that had been built on an amortization plan.[46]

When Congress passed the National Recovery Act (NRA), McVey believed that it would provide the university what the state of Kentucky had denied—funds to build the institution he envisioned. McVey sought the counsel of James Stone, district chair for the NRA, and Stone reported that the university might qualify for up to $2 million in federal aid. Under the established guidelines, UK could receive a grant consisting of 30 percent down and borrow the remaining 70 percent. To secure the grant, McVey would need to argue successfully that the university could meet its obligations on the borrowed funds. This could be done through state support or by showing that the savings or earnings allowed by the structures could meet the amortized schedule. McVey expressed a desire for the state legislature to appropriate $50,000 annually to assist with the payment, and he provided the board as well as Chairman Stone with a list of seventeen projects that could be completed with federal grants and loans.[47]

By October it appeared that the board might be willing to assume the debt to secure the necessary grants. In order to improve his chances for success, McVey scaled back the projects and requested approximately $1 million. In the meantime, he instituted a series of lectures at the university entitled, "The NRA: Recovery Legislation and Its Significance." McVey then gave the first of six weekly addresses: "New Deal Legislation and Its Administration." When thanked by a federal official for instituting the lectures, McVey responded that citizens had been unable to "understand that we are entering a new period with modification of the profit purpose in business. They find it difficult to get a picture of a socialized individual and a socialized nation." Clearly, McVey had embraced that political philosophy, and he was now, through a series of speeches, trying to convince Kentuckians generally and the Board of Trustees in particular of the value of the burgeoning social order and UK's place in it.[48]

McVey met with the Executive Committee of the Board of Trustees to discuss the feasibility of constructing a central heating plant, a student union, and a home economics building with federal funds. The committee expressed concern that the state legislature would cut revenues even further than they already had. McVey described their attitude as "one of doubt." When the full board addressed the issue in December, the president noted that other institutions had applied for funds, supported by state legislation "to take care of the amortization charges." He contrasted those institutions with the University of Pittsburgh, which had not applied for funds because "it was a bad time to get into debt." For more than a decade Kentucky's politicians had refused UK's requests, leading the president and the board to "let the matter go by." McVey expressed hope that the next Congress would appropriate more money, and UK might benefit from it at a later time.[49]

Undergraduates at the university protested the decision, largely because they wanted a student union. One fraternity petitioned McVey and the board to reconsider the decision. They argued that funds raised from campus events in the building would meet the payment schedule, and they urged the university to present plans to the Public Works Administration (PWA) for a grant to construct a student union building. In late February, the board authorized McVey to present an application to the federal government for such a building, provided that it did not place the university or students under further obligation. Phrased that way, the request was impossible, and McVey was forced to wait until further plans could be developed.[50]

Even though McVey and the board decided against applying for a federal grant, the president continued to find himself drawn into the New Deal sphere. His friend and former University of Tennessee president Harcourt Morgan had been named to the governing board of the Tennessee Valley Authority (TVA). The nascent organization was outlining the strategic aims of its work in both electrification and social development, and Morgan, hoping to include McVey in the process, asked him to serve on a TVA subcommittee.[51]

McVey's role in the development of the TVA was modest at best. But his participation in the agency's programs revealed the extent to which he viewed universities as an integral part of the New Deal's push for social development in the South. In October 1933 McVey delivered an address at a land-grant college conference on the TVA's role in creating a vital social philosophy for the region. McVey knew that the agency would have to develop slowly in order to address the many social, political, and industrial factors involved. He also held the lofty vision that the TVA would help create "a new civilization or a modified one." He hoped that the federal experiment would be "an object lesson for the nation."[52]

At the conference McVey was appointed to chair a subcommittee consisting of members of land-grant colleges in the seven southern states served by the TVA. The committee's charge was to help develop plans and address potential problems for the TVA, specifically its relationship with southern universities. McVey held meetings on the topic at UK and elsewhere, and Governor Laffoon also appointed him to Kentucky's TVA planning committee. Despite these appointments, nearly a year later he wrote that little had been accomplished and that his subcommittee "appeared to have gone by the board." In the end, Dean Thomas Cooper assumed primary responsibility as liaison with the TVA, and much of the work conducted by the university was agricultural in its scope.[53]

Despite all the lofty rhetoric, by 1934 UK had not utilized New Deal programs for campus construction. Work being conducted by the TVA had little impact on improving research by UK's professors. The dams constructed in Western Kentucky had little effect on the main campus, and the expansion of agricultural programs seemed only to bolster work that had already been receiving federal support. In sum, the New Deal had not yet enhanced McVey's work in Lexington. However, another connection resulted in increased publicity for the New Deal in Kentucky and the university as well.

In May 1934 Frank McVey traveled with Frances to Washington, D.C., where he addressed the Association for Adult Education. While in the capital, the McVeys were invited to a dinner at Treasury Secretary Henry Morgenthau's home. The following morning Morgenthau's wife passed along to the McVeys an invitation from Eleanor Roosevelt to visit the White House. The McVeys accepted and had an opportunity to speak with Mrs. Roosevelt in the morning and meet the president at a formal dinner party later that evening.[54]

After the McVeys' visit to the White House, Mrs. Roosevelt wrote Frances, telling her that if she were in Lexington, she would be sure to visit the McVeys. When Frances learned that the First Lady was to speak in July in Pikeville, Kentucky, she contacted Mrs. Roosevelt and invited her to Maxwell Place. The First Lady accepted and arrived in Lexington on 7 July 1934. Frances and Frank hosted Mrs. Roosevelt for lunch before she gave a short speech to the students and assembled dignitaries. Supporters who could not get a seat waited in the rain, hoping for a chance to meet the president's wife. Inside Frank McVey rose to introduce the nation's First Lady. Nervous and wanting to make his best impression, McVey unfortunately introduced Mrs. Roosevelt as Mrs. Theodore Roosevelt. Ignoring the mistake, Mrs. Roosevelt delivered a well-received presentation about the need for an educated populace in a democracy. The following morning McVey had to endure the embarrassing newspaper reports about the most visible blunder of his career.[55]

The popularity of the First Lady during her visit with the McVeys provided evidence of growing support for the New Deal in Kentucky. Indeed, money from the Civilian Works Administration (CWA) had helped keep a number of students enrolled at the university during the past academic year. Nevertheless, McVey failed to convince the board to apply for federal funds for capital projects. After the failure of the 1934 legislative session and Mrs. Roosevelt's wildly popular visit, McVey turned his attention away from the state and became more intent on securing New Deal money for construction.

In early 1935 McVey stressed to the board that the "most important of all relations which the University has are those developing out of federal business connections, and with the departments of the United States government." The president knew the campus needed many new buildings, as well as a modernized heating plant. A steam-powered system would cut energy costs and beautify the campus. McVey met with members of the College of Engineering, and they agreed to conduct a study and submit plans for the central heating system. He also began formulating plans for buildings that he hoped would be funded by the federal government.[56]

————•————

As McVey awaited help from the New Deal, Kentucky was entering a political era of its own. In a rough-and-tumble primary and general election, one of the commonwealth's most colorful and controversial figures emerged victorious. Former lieutenant governor A. B. "Happy" Chandler won the governor's office in 1935, taking the oath of office at the age of thirty seven. With the support of the *Louisville Courier-Journal* and a coalition of powerful political insiders, Chandler ushered in "Kentucky's New Deal." Far different from Roosevelt's program, Chandler's sought to repeal the sales tax, replace the lost revenue with taxes that would be less detrimental to the state's poorer citizens, and reorganize the government to function more efficiently, all while working to solidify his political power.[57]

McVey believed that it would be wise for the university to host a second prelegislative conference to aid the new governor. However, Chandler rejected McVey's proposal on the grounds that the meeting could be detrimental to his legislative program. Once again, in his matter-of-fact way, McVey mused that Chandler "missed the point about the conference because its purpose is to get facts . . . for the information of the legislators." Apparently, it did not cross McVey's mind that the governor was more interested in maneuvering to consolidate his power than in gathering facts. Despite their initial disagreement, McVey and Chandler agreed to work together on other issues. When asked if the governor might utilize UK professors to help reorganize state government, McVey told Chandler that "he could have anything the University had."[58]

If McVey had had trouble ascertaining what to expect from Kentucky politicians in the past, the new governor created an even larger challenge. Since Chandler would become the chair of the UK Board of Trustees, McVey had to devise a strategy for dealing with the irrepressible young chief executive. At Chandler's first UK board meeting McVey presented the university's request for the next biennium. McVey hoped to secure approximately $950,000 from Frankfort. Although this included more than $800,000 for operating costs on campus, as well as extra funding for miscellaneous items such as campus repairs, loan obligations, and agricultural instruction, it remained below the amount given in 1930. After spending time with the governor, McVey noticed that the usually talkative Chandler had no reaction to McVey's report. McVey found Chandler to be "just a bit diffident" at certain times, but he still found him generally "affable and pleasant." The president added that he was impressed that Happy "had grown a good deal in the past four years."[59]

The following day, however, McVey and the rest of Kentucky learned that Chandler had called for "the resignation of all department heads, members of boards and commissions, and all assistants with executive authority that are appointed by the Governor." The maneuver, McVey realized, was intended to solidify the governor's political power, as he planned on restructuring the government. Concerning the mass firing, McVey wrote, "I am sure that the Governor has overdone the matter," and pointed out that Chandler jeopardized the control of the University of Kentucky and other state educational institutions. McVey called the governor and requested that he reappoint the same members to UK's Board of Trustees. Chandler agreed, allowing UK to continue operations with little interruption.[60]

After Chandler's state reorganization bill passed, the governor sought the help of UK in reforming the state's government. He asked that Professor J. W. Manning serve as director of the state's Personnel Bureau. McVey agreed, and Manning helped the governor with personnel changes and state departmental restructuring in order to improve efficiency. Chandler also called on economics professor James Martin, who directed the Bureau of Business Research at UK, to utilize his expertise in policy formation and tax issues. Chandler was set on repealing the sales tax, and he did. The governor needed fresh sources of revenue, and he wanted Martin, whom he appointed as director of the state's tax commission, to help devise a plan. In his post, Martin told Chandler and McVey that "he had no magic" for increasing revenue and that more taxes would be necessary. The governor called an unprecedented three special sessions in 1936 to deal with reorganization and budgetary issues. During these sessions Chandler successfully pushed through a series of taxes, including levies on alcohol and tobacco, to help meet the loss created by repealing the sales tax.[61]

While Chandler managed to balance the budget, he failed to bring the university's support anywhere close to where it had been five years earlier. The governor met with McVey in March and asked what UK needed. McVey again told him that the university needed $850,000 to $900,000 to operate effectively. McVey noted that Chandler "blinked a little" at his estimate, and once again the university ended up with less than McVey had requested. The special session allotted $660,000 for general appropriations, $19,000 less than in 1934. Extra appropriations were made for minor building repairs and summer school, but cuts were made for the agricultural substations, as well as the extension programs offered by the university. As McVey noted in 1936, "I do not see any relief short of another year when the legislature meets in 1938." Not unlike UK presidents who would follow, McVey could only hope that Governor Chandler would exhibit the same passion for academics at the university that he displayed for UK athletics.[62]

The ongoing lack of state support frustrated McVey, but he did appreciate Chandler's stance on streamlining certain elements of higher education in Kentucky. Since 1931, President Cherry and Western Teachers College had offered a master's program in Bowling Green that large numbers of students were attending. UK opposed the program, but McVey was not alone. The other teachers college presidents were also concerned about this development, as was the Southern Association of Colleges and Schools (SACS). In 1934 that accrediting agency had reported that Western's faculty credentials were "below our standards even for strictly undergraduate work." In response Cherry had noted that three of their last eight hires held doctorates. Of course, this was exactly the point McVey had been trying to make. If fewer than half of the new faculty held terminal degrees, the institution was not yet ready to offer graduate work.[63]

McVey had exercised restraint and deliberation in expanding academic offerings at UK because he wanted degree programs allowing the university to produce an extremely high level of scholarship and receive national recognition. He hoped that other institutions in the commonwealth would do the same. But Cherry blatantly rejected such a call. Despite McVey's protests, for a time it appeared that Cherry would get his way—and UK would face an in-state challenge for graduate students.

However, Governor Chandler involved himself in the work of the Council on Public Higher Education and sided with McVey. In the spring of 1936 the governor called the council to Frankfort to address statewide policy issues. On 24 March 1936, the group met to discuss focusing graduate work at UK to limit duplication of programs. Cherry protested vehemently and read a statement pleading with the council to allow Western to continue its graduate offerings. On this issue, however, Cherry stood alone among the presidents of the teachers colleges. In the end, the teachers colleges abandoned graduate work. In return, UK no longer offered the first two years of undergraduate work in education. The College of Education became a professional school, accepting students only after they had completed two years of undergraduate work.[64]

McVey's plan, with the help of the governor, allowed the university to maintain its flagship status as it worked to strengthen graduate work. As McVey told his board, "The important thing about this action is that for the first time in the history of the State, a definite policy has been adopted regarding graduate instruction." After calling the decision a "statesmanlike procedure," he argued that the responsibility needed to be met with high-quality work. This would require greater funding for the library, research, and equipment. This development also afforded McVey an opportunity to restate his claim to the board that UK needed to find funds to develop a university press for scholarly publications—a topic he would continue to raise with the board for years to come. Unfortunately, neither the state nor the council agreed to provide money to operate a press, let alone an elite university.[65]

————·————

While research, graduate work, and the academic standing of the University of Kentucky drew McVey's efforts and energy, most students, alumni, and citizens seemed far more interested in UK's standings in the Southern

Conference than in striving for membership in the prestigious American Association of Universities. McVey worked to minimize the role of big-time athletics at the university, thinking that intercollegiate sports took too much time and too many resources away from scholarly activities and a well-rounded physical education curriculum. Still, in spite of the economic crisis of the 1930s, discontented students and alumni focused on improving the poor performance of the football team, rather than on expanding academic offerings. In the decades following McVey's tenure as president, Kentucky would emerge as a "basketball school," but in the early 1930s Coach Adolph Rupp was still a young coach just beginning to make a name for himself. Football remained the marquee sport on campus.

McVey found dealing with the seemingly continual athletic problems distasteful. During the late 1920s, the Athletics Department failed to meet its obligations on the football stadium loan. As historian Gregory Kent Stanley noted, McVey requested a financial report from the department in 1930 but got no response. McVey then ordered an external audit, and he presented the findings to the board in 1931. The president found that the program's accounting procedures and record keeping had been negligent at best, and the amount of unaccounted-for petty cash suggested that the department had more than likely been financially subsidizing athletes.[66]

McVey's concerns made no impact on the fan base, but a 4–5 football record in 1932 did not go unnoticed. After the losing season, members of the Athletic Council and the Alumni Association approached McVey about the athletic situation in general and the job status of Coach Harry Gamage in particular. The president noted that Lexington's frustration with the football team was "bubbling over." McVey agreed to meet with a group of students the following week to address their concerns. More than thirty students representing different campus clubs and groups presented a petition to reorganize UK's athletics program. They explained that the current coaching staff had failed "to achieve the success with football teams which we might reasonably have expected." Their proposal included firing Coach Gamage and removing the director of the Athletics Department, S. A. "Big Daddy" Boles, from his post as well. The students said that they were "prompted only by a desire to do something constructive for our University" and hoped to help implement "a more profitable and judicious expenditure of athletic funds."[67]

McVey and Gamage discussed the agitation. The football coach informed McVey that he planned to coach through his contract and had no intention of resigning. Gamage was not without supporters, and after rumors spread that he might lose his job, many of the football players rallied behind him. They wrote McVey that student agitators and "the drugstore cowboys and gambling element of the downtown section" sought to fire their coach. The players noted that these fair-weather fans of the university had become a "howling mob" because of the team's record. They noted that Gamage had dismissed members of the team for violating rules, that the team had been hampered by injuries, and that Gamage had "carried us from one week to the next through a very tough football schedule with a display of courage and confidence seldom seen in football coaches." They concluded, "We have been defeated but we took our medicine like the men we are supposed to portray. . . . We blame no one but our lack of ability and susceptibility to injury. Our coaches are high types of men. They, too, can take it. They're OKAY."[68]

Just days later anonymous "handbills" were posted across campus railing against Gamage, stating that the coach had interfered with the election of team captains. Later that week the men's student council held a meeting and officially called for the football coach's resignation. John Ewing, president of the men's student council, actually wrote his state representative and asked him to investigate the situation. McVey listened to more student protests at the December Athletic Council meeting. The president felt that the athletic situation had evolved into a fraternity dispute, so he decided to take control and devise a plan to remedy the situation. McVey then met with members of the press to outline his plan for a thorough investigation of athletics (including finances and coaching) at the university. His plan met with the approval of the board the following day.[69]

On 15 December 1932, McVey delivered the final convocation speech to the student body before Christmas. Instead of dealing with the financial crisis facing the university, the president addressed the capacity crowd about the football controversy and his solution. He explained that the Athletic Council contained representatives of students, faculty, and alumni. McVey also noted that committees had been created to look into the charges brought against the coaches and the administration of athletics and that the situation would be addressed.[70]

During the ensuing weeks McVey received information from the investigation. Preliminary reports suggested that athletic finances were finally being handled in a relatively organized fashion, but the Athletic Council continued to spend a sizeable percentage of its funds on jobs for athletes. McVey lamented that this was "nothing less than a subsidy to members of the [football] team," but noted, "What is done here is small in comparison with the expenditures for such purposes at Tennessee, Alabama and elsewhere." Nearly fifty football players had been promised jobs and scholarships. The president believed that such scholarships would "wreck the whole athletic structure." And yet he actually hoped this would be the case: In his estimation, football and other intercollegiate sports would need to be governed by departments of physical education if there were, in his words, "to be a wider and more enduring interest in play." When the investigations were completed, McVey reported to the board that financing the athletic program had led to a situation that was "not all together a happy one" and that he wanted a committee to study and report on all athletic scholarships given at the university.[71]

Despite the precarious status of the football program and its losing record, Coach Gamage managed to keep his job. He had one year left on his contract, and McVey had no interest in paying thousands of dollars to fire someone when the university found itself financially strapped. Gamage did not help his situation by barging into Coach Rupp's office, cursing him and calling him a liar, among other things. Rupp and Boles reported the incident to McVey, who believed that the football coach was "highly jealous of Rupp" and threatened by the basketball team's success. Gamage was told to apologize to Rupp, which he did. McVey commented that Rupp had been far more "cooperative and pleasant" than the football coach during the year. As the months rolled on, McVey continued to get reports about the poor academic performance of football players. In June he conceded, "Athletics comes to wag the University."[72]

The team did not fare much better the following season, and after a 5–5 record the embattled Gamage resigned. In his place McVey wanted a football coach "who does know something of the purpose of an institution of learning." The Athletic Council found Chet Wynne, head football coach at Alabama Polytechnic Institute (Auburn). He had played for Knute Rockne at Notre Dame and had enjoyed an impressive coaching record during his short career. His 1932 team from Auburn had gone undefeated. In addition to his duties as head football coach, he was asked to serve as director of athletics and to teach in the Physical Education Department. For his work he would receive an annual salary of $7,500. While McVey did not like such large salaries for coaches, he thought Wynne understood the challenges at UK and was the right man for the job.[73]

McVey's desire to find a coach who could also teach and who understood the broader academic aims of a university resulted from his own long-standing philosophy of intercollegiate athletics, as well as from the newfound national effort to reform college sports. Although agitation to curb abuses in football had existed for decades, an impetus for reform developed in 1929 with the publication of "Bulletin Number Twenty-three," sponsored by the Carnegie Foundation for the Advancement of Teaching. Written by Howard Savage, *American College Athletics* attacked the rampant commercialism found in college football. Savage's report and its introduction, written by Henry Pritchett, placed blame on a number of converging elements in athletics. The growing influence of alumni groups, press coverage, highly paid coaches focused solely on winning, and the recruiting and subsidizing of athletes had increased at an alarming rate. These activities flourished, the report argued, because university presidents had done little to curb them.[74]

The Southern Conference, of which the University of Kentucky was a member, provided a case in point for the concerns raised by Savage. For a number of years rumors had existed that the sprawling association of more than twenty teams would be broken into two smaller conferences.

Despite repeated concerns and alleged abuses, however, the conference had failed to deal with the problems facing intercollegiate athletics. Shortly after the issuance of Savage's report, Steadman Sanford, a dean at the University of Georgia and president of the Southern Conference, wrote McVey and other executives, "We have been six years trying to define a college and we have not been able to define a scholarship nor what should be the academic requirement for eligibility after a student enters college." As he saw it, members of the Southern Conference needed to have a "full and frank" discussion of these problems and address eligibility requirements, scholarships, and employment of athletes, as well as the possibility of excluding institutions that would not comply with more stringent standards.[75]

In 1931 Savage issued a follow-up study arguing that during the previous two years "the deflation of college football" had begun. There were signs that a number of prestigious universities in the East would attempt to limit commercialism in athletics. However, as historian John Thelin argued, "a modest decline in football attendance for two years during a severe national depression did not necessarily mean that the public had lost interest in college sports." Indeed, many institutions actually experienced increased pressure for winning programs, particularly in the South. Unlike McVey, some officials at Southern Conference institutions were not bothered with the attention given to football, but they protested against influences outside the university in the recruitment and subsidizing of athletes. They reported that Savage's 1929 account had little effect in altering attitudes concerning the commercialism surrounding the game.[76]

By 1932 little had been done to change the standards of the Southern Conference, and growing budgetary problems from the Depression exacerbated the hardships faced by McVey and other university presidents. In November of that year, John J. Tigert met with McVey and a few other southern university presidents to discuss forming a smaller conference that could better regulate the growing problem of scholarships. Tigert had captained both the football and the basketball teams at Vanderbilt before earning his doctorate at Oxford. He had served briefly as president of Kentucky Wesleyan College before coming to the University of Kentucky.

As chair of the Philosophy Department, he had helped coach basketball and football. The year before McVey's arrival at UK, Tigert had taken a leave of absence to administer the athletics program. He had requested a second year's leave, but McVey had asked him to return to full-time academic work. He had done so, but then left UK and accepted the presidency of the University of Florida. Given this background, Tigert certainly understood McVey's concerns about intercollegiate sports.[77]

Tigert moved quickly, and at the annual meeting of the Southern Conference held in Knoxville, he announced the resignation of thirteen teams from the association. The group included Kentucky and Florida, as well as Alabama, Auburn, Tennessee, Vanderbilt, Sewanee, Georgia, Georgia Tech, Louisiana State, Tulane, Mississippi, and Mississippi State. The formation of the Southeastern Conference (SEC) was not contentious, and the schools were chosen on "geographical lines." The Appalachian Mountains formed the boundary for the split so that schools in the league would not have to travel across the mountains on dangerous roads for conference games. It was hoped that a smaller league would make it feasible to address the growing number of challenges developing out of the increasing popularity and pressure of college sports.[78]

McVey did not attend the meeting in Knoxville, but the group chose him to be the first president of the Southeastern Conference. Wondering whether his absence had resulted in his election, he wrote, "It may be interesting and it may be a difficult task." In less than a week he faced administrative duties for the conference, including a decision on allowing seniors to participate in a postseason bowl game in Memphis. McVey was opposed to the idea but said he did not "fancy the business" of making a decision. He requested the views of the other conference presidents, and they wired him their opinions, defeating the proposal by a narrow margin. McVey wondered if he was "to be pestered by this sort of thing thru the year I hold this office."[79]

After making the decision on the postseason game, McVey immediately faced more requests. He wrote J. F. Broussard of Louisiana State University, stating, "I am constantly being called upon for approval of conference matters, but have received no confirmation of my election or any materials or rules with which to work." He wrote a similar letter to Harcourt Morgan at the University of Tennessee, complaining, "I am floundering around in dealing with the situation," and suggesting that he might decline his election. McVey wrote President George Denny at the University of Alabama that he really did not want the job because it would "take time I haven't got."[80]

Nevertheless, McVey's peers seemed to believe that he was the right man for the job, and McVey ultimately viewed the position as a real opportunity to reform collegiate athletics. John Tigert responded to McVey, informing him that he had been chosen because of the confidence the other presidents had in his ability to accomplish a great deal. Tigert pledged, "We will not permit you to be left out on a limb trying to operate alone." Harcourt Morgan came to Lexington to discuss athletic issues with McVey and argued that the University of Tennessee needed the reform measures because the Athletic Council and boosters in Knoxville "would buy athletes and pay as much or more than anybody else." McVey later wrote that he agreed with Morgan and lamented the influence of local boosters. McVey viewed his role in the Southeastern Conference as "a golden opportunity to put the athletics in the University organization and take it out of the hands of the coach and the news writers. The down town gang that is found in every college town will be shut out and athletics conducted on a decent basis."[81]

McVey set about his work as president of the Southeastern Conference with sobriety and vigor. The first meeting of the conference coincided with the conference basketball tournament in Atlanta. Knowing the event would attract the public spotlight, McVey decided to hold a session with all the university presidents before then in order to establish a plan for the league and a strategy for implementation. He wrote each executive that it would take "serious responsibility on the administration of the educational institutions of the conference" to carry out the lofty reforms for which the conference had been created. He called a meeting in mid-February to discuss matters "carefully and seriously." He added that while he had been chosen to lead the group without consultation, he was willing to serve, provided he had the "sincere cooperation of every president of the member institutions." As a sign of their intentions he called for a meeting in Birmingham, noting, "This is not a meeting of representatives of presidents, but a meeting of the presidents themselves. I am therefore expecting you to be present."[82]

McVey used the meeting in Birmingham to learn about the aims of the conference, explain the current status of the league, and review problems that needed to be addressed. The organization was being formed out of high ideals, but the league had no formal structure and no money with which to operate. The primary issues and questions that McVey hoped to address concerned eligibility, undue influence by forces outside the university, recruiting and subsidizing athletes, scouting, and McVey's personal hope that intercollegiate athletics would be placed under the control of physical education departments.[83]

McVey later confessed that he came to the meeting "with a good deal of trepidation," because he feared little would be accomplished. He left, however, feeling that it had been a success. Of the thirteen presidents, only conference organizer John Tigert failed to attend, and that was due to serious illness. Writing Tigert to summarize the meeting, McVey stated, "The group made substantial progress in dealing with matters of eligibility, scholarship, subsidizing, and recruiting." The successes McVey alluded to included an eligibility standard requiring that athletes pass 75 percent of their classes for the academic year and 60 percent of their course work for each semester. Subsidizing, the presidents agreed, could be controlled through open records of all scholarships and aid received by the athletes. McVey predicted that general agreement on these and other issues would make the more public meeting in Atlanta a success.[84]

The meeting in Atlanta later that month was monumental, as McVey led the conference in establishing a constitution. McVey's high-minded ideals for intercollegiate athletics were officially incorporated into both the conference's statement of purpose and its by-laws. The organization was established, according to the constitution, to make athletics part of each institution's educational program and make each team "subservient to the great aims of education and place them under the same administrative control." The SEC proposed to develop "public appreciation of the educational, rather than the commercial, values in intercollegiate sports." To that end, McVey and his successors were charged with enforcing the regulations among the league's members.[85]

The reforms included a ten-week football season. The Southeastern Conference banned the use of motion pictures for scouting and limited coaches to two scouting visits a season for any opposing team. Training tables providing free meals for athletes were banned, and new matricu- lates were to be placed on freshman teams to ensure passing grades at an institution for a year before playing varsity sports. In order to encourage academics, freshman football teams were allowed to play only two games a season, excluding intramural athletic events.[86]

The Southeastern Conference stated that no university "should be permitted to engage in recruiting athletes, or in providing or inducing other persons to do so, by offering any inducements of a financial nature." The by-laws required institutions to utilize university officials to adminis- ter scholarships or loans to athletes. Complete and detailed records of fi- nancial assistance were to be made available to the conference. Student eligibility guidelines established at McVey's previous meeting were for- malized. The conference stated that no student who accepted "any gift, remuneration or pay for his services on a college team" would be allowed to participate in the league.[87]

These idealistic restrictions were coupled with naive plans for institu- tional enforcement and virtually no guidelines for discipline or punish- ment. After the meeting in Birmingham, McVey and the other presidents decided that the SEC would not hire a commissioner to conduct its work. Instead regulations would be enforced by the executives of each institu- tion. This idea was part of McVey's philosophy of institutional control of intercollegiate athletics. Unfortunately for UK's president, and those cho- sen to succeed him, many, if not most, of the institutions failed to follow the letter of the law, and virtually all appeared to ignore the spirit of the law. McVey did not see this coming and, at least for a time, remained optimistic about the future. He wrote, "Taking the work done by and large . . . it can be said that the conference did an excellent job."[88]

During the first year, McVey dealt with numerous complaints from institutions about rules violations by various teams. Presidents, athletic directors, and coaches worried that other freshman teams in the conference were playing more than two games. People wrote McVey expressing concern that conference teams were not following the by-laws put in place for recruiting and subsidizing athletes. Some letters asked for exceptions to the rules because of unique circumstances or arrangements made prior to the creation of the conference's by-laws. McVey attempted to deal with these issues as they came to him. The president maintained his stance against postseason bowl games. Furthermore, he repeated his belief that if athletics did not come under the control of universities, the whole system would fall apart, and professional teams would fill the void so desperately desired by fans. When presidents began asking McVey to serve a second year as president of the conference, he worried that during his first year he had "drifted along trying to find out . . . the situation." He wrote, "I have the very distinct impression that I am not getting anywhere in the direction of the affairs of this Conference. I feel that all that is happening now is merely holding it together. . . . Everybody is going along about as they want."[89]

Before the annual conference in 1934, McVey wrote a form letter asking each university president to report on institutional compliance with Article XVIII of the SEC constitution, which dealt with scholarships and loan funds. Specifically, McVey wanted to know whether "funds have been placed in the hands of a committee or officer of administration, and . . . [whether] full records [have] been kept of the distribution of such funds, particularly to students participating in intercollegiate athletics." All but one institution reciprocated, offering McVey a wide variety of descriptions. McVey wrote to Tigert at Florida about the different replies that he received; some of them were "evasive" and "noncommittal," while others spoke frankly about the situation. He wondered, "How are we to get at the actual facts relating to the support of students in athletics? On the other hand perhaps the only thing that can be done is to let it all go by."[90]

Traveling to New Orleans for the second annual meeting of the Southeastern Conference, McVey prepared a straightforward speech for the membership. He argued that a primary reason for the formation of the conference was to place the management of intercollegiate athletics firmly in the hands of the university presidents—a reform that had been suggested by Savage's 1929 report. If this were done, McVey argued, the league could then implement the necessary reforms. Many of the problems that developed during the first year remained unaddressed, largely because McVey had difficulty figuring out exactly what was going on at each institution. Therefore, rumors abounded, charging "violation of eligibility rules and the breaking of the requirement to report the use of funds to help students."[91]

McVey provided the members the replies he had received to his earlier query regarding scholarships, for both "information and your amusement." McVey stated that it was clear that "the institutions do not know what is being done" by different agencies and individuals interested in athletics who were not formally associated with the institutions. He urged university presidents to "really find out what is going on in the support of student athletes." He then argued that the member institutions needed to address the involvement of alumni and booster clubs in providing funds to individual players. The nearly universal bending of the rules had led to outside criticism. "The only way that such criticism can be avoided," argued McVey, "is to adhere to the regulations of the conference, not only in the letter, but in the spirit." Of course, McVey's disappointment stemmed from his seemingly naive assumption that the presidents did not know what was occurring with their respective programs and that they wished to find out about any violations and address them.[92]

McVey reiterated his mantra that operating athletics in the same way that it had been done would "result in a breakdown and the continuance of difficulties with coaches and the question of policy and procedure." University presidents needed to be "perfectly frank about the situation and place our athletic contests on a high basis, so that criticism may be reduced to a minimum." Once that step had been taken, sports could be placed under the governing control of departments of physical education, so that athletics could become part of the larger academic enterprise. Coaches interested only in wins and losses needed to be replaced by men with "larger vision and greater appreciation of the educational problems involved in athletics." If the new conference failed to be honest about the situation and earnestly seek his proposed remedies, McVey predicted that professional football would overcome the college game.[93]

Ever the optimist, McVey felt that the member institutions could address subsidizing by stating what was being done and looking the situation "squarely in the face." Athletic teams needed to be drawn naturally from the student body without recruiting high-school standouts. He asked, "Has the time come when the members of the Southeastern Conference can disarm?" He answered in the affirmative and suggested that each institution bring rumors of violations to the university presidents. McVey at least was willing to raise such difficult questions, and he felt that his work at UK and with the SEC was a step in the right direction for the necessary reforms.[94]

McVey's views were popular, at least to a point. He succeeded in convincing the conference to turn down an invitation to send teams to New Orleans for a postseason game. The members elected him to a second term as president. The week before the conference Tigert had written McVey asking him to assume a second year of leadership, arguing that under his direction the conference would be able to control athletic subsidies. Tigert felt that there were other presidents who, if elected, would not be willing to deal with the problems facing the conference. After McVey's reelection, George Denny told him, "Your administration is receiving fine comment on all hands." McVey's leadership, argued Denny, had kept before the conference the "correct principles and high ideals," which were "far more likely to secure results than any other policy."[95]

In his second year as president, McVey dealt with even more issues of player eligibility. McVey wished to minimize commercial pressure by taking power from local boosters, but little was accomplished in curbing financial aid to student athletes. McVey complained that the country was "football mad" but still believed that professional football would eventually force the game back into amateurism. Oddly, his desire to place sports within the educational program of the university was compromised by his own decision to support radio broadcasts of SEC games. A representative of the Major College Publications Company proposed to broadcast a game each week, for which the conference would receive $50,000. Every president supported this move, but no contract could be formalized for the current year. The years following McVey's term as president witnessed a rapid increase in the influence of the broadcast media in the SEC. Even McVey's close confidant George Denny requested that the conference allow the University of Alabama to participate in the Rose Bowl, despite a clear decision to decline postseason bowl offers less than a year earlier.[96]

By the conference's annual meeting in 1935, McVey was eager to relinquish the presidency. He reflected that while the executive committee claimed to be "much concerned with recruiting and subsidizing members of the conference," institutions continued to participate in activities that they said they opposed. The conference, he argued, had reached a "point of repealing all restrictions or being continued as liars," adding, "The hiring of players by scholarship has reached deplorable limits." Rather than taking decisive action and changing the constitution, the conference instead created a committee to study the situation and devise "a plan to deal with the recruiting and subsidizing" of athletes.[97]

Although lauded for his efforts, McVey had been successful only in holding the line on what he thought official policy for college athletics ought to be. In practice, SEC institutions did not change their behavior. McVey had done a better job than most presidents by regulating and reporting on the financing of football at his school. He also attempted to hire a football coach with a broader understanding of the university's mission. These decisions probably contributed to the team's continuing failures on the gridiron. At the conference level, McVey's departure as president signaled the beginning of a slow but steady move away from the SEC's founding principles.

McVey's successor as president of the conference, John Tigert, wrote McVey and other officials about the continuing problems and offered three possibilities: the SEC could continue without making any substantial changes, conference members could agree to rigid enforcement of the rules, or institutions could "openly recognize" scholarships and "the conditions upon which they may be held." McVey responded by reminding his colleagues that schools first needed to be honest about their athletic programs. Ironically, soon after McVey left the SEC presidency, the conference began legitimizing the very activities that the conference had been created to abolish.[98]

Even before McVey's term as SEC president ended in 1935, McVey confronted several agitating athletic issues in Kentucky. During the 1934 legislative session, the House of Representatives passed a resolution calling on UK to play Centre College in football. McVey had stopped this annual game years earlier because the intense rivalry resulted in on-the-field fights. McVey told the press that the Athletic Council was "glad to have suggestions from any source about the playing of games," but writing privately, he expressed dismay that the state government would involve itself in such matters, concluding, "It is this sort of thing that is so irritating."[99]

As McVey tried to sidestep a game with Centre College, he also attempted to reorganize the Athletic Council's governance and financial structure. The council agreed that it needed an athletics director, and McVey felt that football coach Chet Wynne was the person for the job. He asked Wynne to assume the extra responsibility, which he did. Despite the reorganization, McVey was displeased with the state of affairs at his university. In September 1934 the Athletic Council reported a deficit of more than $4,000 but still planned on expanding its budget the following year. He found that even at his institution "no boy plays on an intercollegiate team unless he gets support." McVey said that such news made him question "the wisdom of keeping up intercollegiate football. . . . The whole structure of intercollegiate athletics must fail if this goes on."[100]

McVey's problems were exacerbated by growing tension between Wynne and basketball coach Adolph Rupp. Emboldened by his growing popularity, in 1934 Rupp began asking for a larger salary and a multiyear contract. Wynne did not want to grant Rupp's requests, and McVey feared that the challenge would lead to Wynne's resignation. Wynne did not resign, however, and the situation intensified the following year. Shortly after McVey stepped down as president of the SEC, news spread in Lexington that Wynne sought to release Rupp from his duties as basketball coach. McVey supported his athletics director's decision, but the Athletic

Council worried about a backlash for firing the successful and popular coach.[101]

As news reports spread, McVey attempted to downplay the affair by pointing out that it was simply a disagreement over who scheduled games. Yet privately, McVey wrote that "to keep a man on because of his popularity, tho a very good coach, is to bring trouble sooner or later. Rupp wants to run his own show and not come under the director's administration." In the end, Rupp won. McVey lamented that Rupp had essentially been given permission to operate his own way, regardless of Wynne's objections, "thus subordinating the director . . . where he has responsibility but no authority." McVey added, "Wynne was asked to take the place which he didn't want and today the Council refused him the authority he needed because he did not recommend Rupp for a coach's place."[102]

By 1936 Rupp's status continued to grow as Wynne proved unable to turn things around on the football field. The *Kentucky Kernel* reported that agitation on campus concerning his coaching abilities as well as his off-the-field conduct had grown, but the paper did not believe it was enough to warrant his firing. McVey too had been receiving reports that the coach had a drinking problem. After the 1936 football season the Athletic Council discussed the matter and chose to keep the coach. McVey also requested a meeting with Wynne, the president speaking "freely and frankly" about the football team and the coach's "own shortcomings." McVey stated that the next three years were "very important ones in his life" and that he hoped Wynne would pull things together and meet the challenges.[103]

On top of personnel issues, a general push to spend more money on athletics intensified, which McVey vehemently opposed. For example, McVey refused to support the Athletic Council's call for a new field house (among other projects). Despite McVey's objections, the governor favored the proposal and noted that the state, rather than the university, could match the federal funds and build the field house. Responding to the challenge, McVey laid out a six-year plan for construction on campus, listing several facilities to be built before the field house. In fact, he slated all athletics projects for 1940 and beyond—which McVey knew would come after he had turned seventy, at which time he would be forced to retire because of the university's age-limit policy. In essence, McVey was attempting to ensure that athletics projects would not be built on his watch.[104]

These combined challenges led McVey to make rather drastic comments at the last board meeting of 1936. He noted that UK's location at the northern periphery of the Southeastern Conference had led to greater challenges. Hence, the university struggled to "keep up its status and its place" in the organization. He argued that the conference had "adopted a rather frank policy of the subsidizing of athletes" (which McVey had opposed). Moreover, UK's Athletic Council was barely managing to survive financially. He concluded by questioning "whether in the long run it is advisable to try to keep up the competition." In essence, he hoped that the board would consider dropping out of the SEC. Disappointed with the board's response, he wrote that in spite of the continual challenges they remained "emphatic in their support of such a program." McVey's high ideals for amateur athletics failed not only in the SEC but at his own university.[105]

At nearly the same time McVey presided over the SEC, he served as president of another southern agency that had gained a tremendous influence in education—the Southern Association of Colleges and Secondary Schools (SACS). While McVey's conservative approached failed with athletics, his more progressive tendencies had a greater effect on the SACS. Founded in 1895, the Association of Colleges and Preparatory Schools of the Southern States, as it was initially named, sought to hold member institutions "to a definite program of work and to definite standards." The organization attempted to accomplish this by accrediting institutions that met standards of professionalism and scholarship. As the organization grew, it created separate commissions to deal with secondary and collegiate education, and it saw an ever-increasing demand among institutions that sought its approval. By the 1930s the association's success and rapid expansion began to threaten its own long-standing internal leadership.[106]

During the 1920s a growing number of institutions, including teachers colleges and junior colleges, earned not only accreditation but representation in the association. Over time, the less wealthy and less prestigious institutions sought a greater say in the affairs and policies of the organization. Their efforts were rebuffed by the traditional power brokers, led by Vanderbilt chancellor James Kirkland and executives from smaller liberal arts colleges. As SACS historian James Miller noted, the increasing number of accredited institutions "had not been accompanied by a corresponding diffusion of power away from the founders." Instead the executive committee continued to form policies and procedures that limited the influence of the newcomers in the association. Guy Snavely, who attended the meetings as president of Birmingham-Southern College, noted that the tightening "circle of control" by the leadership had become "increasingly irksome and unjust" to the institutions not included.[107]

The tension between the older liberal arts faction and the progressive faction, which developed predominantly from the teachers colleges, began to surface. Although the liberal element had not fully infiltrated the executive committee of the association, it had gained representation on key committees such as the nominating committee. Frank McVey was thrust into the limelight just as the two groups entered into a "period of intense conflict within the Association, often acrimonious, culminating in major changes of organization and practice."[108]

McVey's first taste of the challenges that lay ahead came at the 1932 annual meeting. After giving a well-received address, McVey was selected by the nominating committee to serve as the organization's next president. When McVey's name came to the floor for a vote, members of the liberal arts faction presented William Few of Duke University as an alternative to McVey. After discussion, Few defeated McVey for the post, and the "old guard," as McVey called the conservative leaders, maintained control. McVey later wrote that he had deep respect for William Few and that he had left his name on the ballot because "the matter at issue was not one of persons but one of principle and representation. The public institutions have little to say about the affairs of the association so I let my name stand."[109]

McVey's defeat highlighted the strain between the factions, but it also paved the way for his election the following year. Events at the 1933 annual meeting in Nashville revealed the extent to which McVey stood above the partisanship that threatened the organization. Upon his arrival as president of UK, McVey had served as a "charter member of the Commission on Institutions of Higher Learning," which had been created by the "old guard" in 1917. He was respected by members of this group for the work he had accomplished in Kentucky. However, he was a proponent of change within SACS and therefore a candidate favorable to the public teachers colleges and junior colleges that were now part of the association.[110]

Having been respected by both factions yet snubbed the previous year, McVey, unsurprisingly, was elected president in December 1933. Both sides feared that the nomination of a more partisan candidate would lead the opposition to push its own representative, irreparably fracturing the organization. In this environment, McVey demanded that he be elected unanimously because he "refused to be a party to a divided and conflicting association." He criticized the growing tension between the liberals who wanted to "break up the closely held operation of the Association [and] the old guard [which] wanted to keep the same old standards and the same old crowd in. It may be now that some progress can be made toward the liberalizing of the organization."[111]

Although the association agreed on McVey, the rift in the organization remained obvious. H. M. Ivy presented a resolution arguing that the "largely self-perpetuating" representation in leadership did not serve "the best interests" of the association. His resolution called for the creation of a committee to study the constitution and by-laws in order to make changes that would be brought before the organization at the next meeting. Despite protests by the conservatives, the resolution passed. In his presidential address, William Few warned the reformers against massive change and called for moderation from the progressive element. Few lauded the "high ideals" that had guided the organization in the past and pleaded that the association "advocate nothing harsh or reactionary" as it sought reform.[112]

Clearly, McVey needed to assuage the fears of both sides as he sought to modernize the regional accrediting agency. Dean Paul Boyd understood the challenges facing McVey and wrote a journal article about his president to calm the fears of both factions. Boyd lauded McVey as "a happy combination of the conservative and the radical." He argued that McVey would preserve long-standing values while attempting to improve the organization and its mission. With McVey at the helm Boyd predicted that the group would "not be turned inside-out in a year, but it will feel a powerful urge to evolve steadily into an agency better able to . . . [meet] the demand of the South for a great educational leadership."[113]

McVey did present a combination of the old and new in education. Although he favored the more progressive group (he unsuccessfully attempted to invite John Dewey as the convention's keynote speaker), he understood his presidential role as one of tempered change. He appointed a committee of progressives, including Herman Lee Donovan of Eastern State Teachers College, to a committee charged with presenting changes to the association's constitution. The committee met with McVey before the December 1934 gathering in Atlanta, and McVey concluded that the constitution would "do much to remove the criticisms, broaden the scope, freshen the personnel, and insure progressive development in the Association."[114]

McVey noted that the committee's revisions to the constitution faced stiff opposition: "The big battle between the liberals and the conservatives in the Association was joined this morning. As president of the Association I was in the chair." McVey presided over what could have been the end of the single regional accrediting agency for higher education. As Guy Snavely recalled, "It was touch and go for a time as to whether the liberal arts institutions would not organize an association of their own." In the end, the conservatives could not stop McVey and his committee from revising the constitution. The Southern Association agreed to hold an official vote on the constitutional changes at the next annual meeting. The changes were adopted, and what some called "the revolution" of the association became the hallmark of McVey's presidency of the association.[115]

Two historians of the association disagreed with the label "revolution," arguing that the changes occurred gradually and that the alteration simply afforded a higher degree of decision making to the public institutions that had become a part of the agency—teachers colleges in particular. As historian James Miller argued, the SACS had become responsive to the changing needs of society and the role that educational institutions played in this evolving relationship. In context, McVey's success is understandable. The president viewed societal changes during the 1930s as an opportunity for higher education in the South to meet the needs of the people. His leadership meshed perfectly with the views of those who sought to bring about a fresh approach to higher education in the South. Although his reform efforts within the state of Kentucky met with opposition, he had success in the larger academy, where he functioned with greater ease.[116]

After leading the fight for change within the SACS, McVey agreed to participate in the newly created Southern University Conference. Some university presidents declined to do so, fearing that the organization would simply be an attempt by the "old guard" to form a group separate from the Southern Association. Indeed, the majority of the members of the Southern University Conference were individuals who had held prominent positions in SACS before McVey liberalized its policies and procedures. Yet McVey hoped that the Southern University Conference would help define the role of the liberal arts college, as well as take a strong stance on rigorous master's degree programs. He hoped to distinguish between a "fifth year of college work and a real thesis work for the master's degree" and was "very much in favor of holding to the standard . . . and requir[ing] in addition to the thesis at least one language requirement."[117]

McVey met with other southern university presidents such as Few of Duke, Kirkland of Vanderbilt, and Graham of the University of North Carolina in an attempt to emphasize the importance of the research university. That same month he published an article in the *Journal of Higher Education* entitled "Ways and Means: The Liberal-Arts College in the New Social Order." He tried to explicate the role and relevance of such institutions in the wake of the New Deal. But once again he struggled to reconcile different points of view. First, he argued that instead of debating curricular issues, higher education needed to "prepare youth for a new social era." He believed the role of the college (as distinct from a research university) was not to solve society's problems, but "to train and guide students to intellectual and social purposes, so that they may bring clear, unfettered minds to the problems when they take on the duties of citizens." He suggested that this required an understanding of traditional subject matter and mental development through the study of "social sciences, philosophy, and literature," as well as attention to "personal habits of courtesy and right living." He abandoned the traditional, however, for the progressive when he argued that colleges often taught "concepts that are those of a vanishing world." He suggested, for example, that texts and professors in political science were at odds with the changed role of government. He added, "No set of facts and conclusions remains unchanged; consequently, the great task of the college is to teach the student logical thought processes, where to find materials, and the need of approaching all problems in a broad social spirit."[118]

McVey worked through these issues on campus in Lexington and often wrote about them. His focus at UK had long been on useful research, but during the Depression he modified his views regarding the value of an undergraduate education. Whereas he had earlier sought to prepare undergraduates for professions, he started stressing the value of an education in terms of students developing sound philosophies as well as correct tastes in literature and history. He lamented the narrow views that students could carry with them through college, but at the same time he continued to remove himself further from student life. Thomas Clark recalled that at one point during the 1930s McVey complained to him that most students did not even know his name. Clark decided to test the president's hypothesis by asking the question in class. Among other guesses, one student responded that he was a figure from the Revolutionary War. Clark noted that "one honest scholar answered, 'I'll be damned if I know who he was.'" The anecdote had deeper implications concerning the role of a modern university president. McVey grappled with the widening chasm between the world of higher-education administration and everyday student life. He struggled to modify his own philosophy of education as he entered his late sixties, continuing to search for appropriate compromises. He was, in many ways, the epitome of historian Laurence Veysey's historiographical argument that institutions and their presidents during the university's building era found it necessary to "blend and reconcile" the varied and seemingly contradictory elements of collegiate life in America.[119]

Despite the perilous times, McVey found peace and contentment in his personal life. Every summer Frank and Frances continued their annual sojourn at the Elk Lake Lodge in Williamsburg, Michigan. During their month-long visits the McVeys read, sailed, and biked. Frank would devote himself to his oil painting. As the years passed, he increasingly noted his "considerable reluctance" to return to the work that lay ahead on campus. In 1935 the couple took a cruise to the Caribbean, and while they were gone, rumors spread in Lexington that McVey had died. The press and his family awaited news of his condition. McVey ended the rumors when he reported that he was "never better in [his] life." Unfortunately, the trip "brings out contrasts that make tedium of a desk seem more pronounced than usual." At the conclusion of his trip to Michigan in the fall of 1936, he stated, "When I think of the year ahead with its travel, banquets, lunches, conference speeches and the routine of the office it appears a bit appalling." However, he still admitted, "The job is an interesting one and I enjoy it."[120]

Throughout these challenging times the president found comfort and solace in his close relationship with Frances. She continued to serve as social hostess for the campus, as well as Frank's personal confidant. He regularly commented in his diary about his love for Frances. On their ninth anniversary he wrote, "These have been happy, glorious years with a delightful companionship that has been full of charm. We have had fun, mind contact, work and plan together. It is as near perfect as comes to one on the terrestrial globe." On his sixty-sixth birthday McVey confessed, "Every birthday is just too much of a reduction of the time with her [Frances]. So I don't like that much."[121]

During the 1930s McVey used his relative prosperity to assist his children and their young families. He worked to secure a position in a Kansas City law firm for his son-in-law, but when he was dismissed, the president helped bring them back to Lexington to find a job. McVey assisted his son in purchasing a share in a small business (Brock-McVey) in Lexington. His youngest daughter married, and McVey took delight in the frequent visits his children made to Maxwell Place. He enjoyed playing with his grandchildren, and he hoped that his family would remain close as he grew older.[122]

Over time McVey forged strong friendships in Lexington. One group of confidants became known as the "Book Thieves." Founded by Tom Clark and a few other prominent citizens, the "thieves" met regularly to drink beer, discuss books about Kentucky and other classics, and debate Kentucky politics and current events. McVey's initial participation grew out of his desire to expand the holdings of the library, but the group of about a half-dozen men grew far closer as their gatherings evolved into an informal but important regular event. During this time McVey and Clark developed what seemed to be a near father-son relationship. Clark clearly looked upon "Old Man McVey" as a mentor, and McVey relished the role.[123]

McVey's expanding personal ties brought greater recognition from across the commonwealth. In 1934 the *Lexington Leader* helped fund a project to create a bust of the president. McVey was uncomfortably humbled yet pleasantly surprised to learn that funds donated by members of the faculty had helped pay for part of the project. The bust was completed the same year that the campus dedicated a statue of former president Patterson. This seemed a fitting gesture, as many Kentuckians knew that Kentucky State College's patriarch was Patterson, but the builder of the University of Kentucky was Frank McVey. More important was McVey's election as president of the Kentucky Education Association in 1936. This agency, which had snubbed him during his early years, had come to respect his leadership in the commonwealth and beyond. Clearly, McVey had adopted Kentucky as his home, and in many ways Kentucky had come to accept him as well. It remained to be seen if he would be able to leverage this newfound acceptance into advancement for UK during the final years of his presidency.[124]

Chapter 6

Building a Legacy
1936–1940

Again I come back to the essential points of the whole matter; the attitude and spirit in the institution itself, in faculty, and in administrative officers; the breadth and wisdom and viewpoints of the teachers of all subjects; the freedom of students in discussion in the classroom and in their own organization. All these interpret and teach democratic ideals in college.
—Frank LeRond McVey, 1939

The commonwealth required that all state employees retire by age seventy, and President McVey, who would reach that milestone in the fall of 1939, was no exception. He hoped that the worst of the Depression had passed, which would allow him to reach his goal of being the true builder of the University of Kentucky. His plans included expanded academic offerings, increased pay for professors, and release time for research. He wished to enhance services to a growing student body, place additional limitations on intercollegiate sports, and—most important to McVey—expand the university's physical plant. Realizing that little time remained, he noted in his diary, "I haven't but five years in which to get the university organization in the best shape possible. It [the campus] is a good place to start."[1]

Planning the new construction projects, McVey turned to Colonel James Graham, the recently appointed dean of the College of Engineering. A World War I veteran with no previous academic experience, Graham brought his strong personality to the position. Hired to bring curricular reorganization to the College of Engineering, he would also play a key role in the 1930s building campaign at the university. McVey appreciated his no-nonsense attitude and his Washington connections. The two men worked closely and prepared an expansive proposal for the Public Works Administration to help fund the campus expansion. The plan included UK's first student union building, a new home for the College of Law, and two structures that would complete an engineering quadrangle. McVey conferred with the state director of the Public Works Administration, but it was clear that the president trusted Graham and delegated nearly all of the architectural and administrative responsibilities of the project to his new dean.[2]

Graham and McVey ultimately requested a $500,000 grant along with a loan of $600,000. Following the board's approval, an unusually dramatic McVey wrote, "I sent a telegram to President Roosevelt. . . . The matter is now on the knees of the gods." Within the week McVey learned that UK would receive only one-third of its request. The government offered a $165,000 grant along with a $201,000 loan. Disappointed, McVey rationalized that it was better than nothing. To ease the loss, UK supplemented the funds with a separate $40,000 grant to the College of Agriculture to construct an addition to the experiment station at the south end of campus.[3]

Determined to capture as much federal funding as possible, the board approved another $400,000 loan application. McVey attributed the success of that venture to "the untiring efforts" of Dean Graham. Federal rules stipulated that the university must break ground quickly, and the board directed that the building campaign's first phase focus on a central heating plant, the student union, the two engineering buildings, and the new law school building.[4]

As construction moved forward, McVey sought the advice of New York landscape architect Bryant Fleming, who visited the university in the fall of 1935 to offer his perspective on the general layout of the landscaping. In the final report Fleming provided a number of criticisms and suggestions, including moving the primary entrance of the campus. Historically, the main focal point was located at the semicircle of the administration building, but Fleming believed that it should be shifted to the corner of Euclid and South Limestone. This change would require finding a different site for the new student union.[5]

Fleming criticized the seemingly haphazard nature of UK's campus buildings. Some he characterized as "interesting," while others he considered "flagrantly bad." The architectural style of buildings constructed earlier in McVey's tenure had been abandoned. Even McVey's crown jewel, the library, did not escape comment, Fleming noting that while it was a "good building," it was "not in sufficient character and purity of design to warrant setting a precedent." To bring some semblance of planning to design and construction, Fleming recommended that UK's future buildings merge the eighteenth-century English Georgian style with southern American Colonial architecture. He suggested that UK's buildings should resemble those at the University of Virginia, which allowed for a "simpler expression, and yet . . . most dignified and less imposing." Fleming thought that the student union provided "an opportunity to start such an expression, and determine a style and feeling to follow in future work." The report suggested that the union could provide a domestic feeling by following the architectural pattern of colonial Williamsburg, Virginia.[6]

Fleming's report disturbed McVey because it took six months for him to receive it, and its observations were rather harsh. Having been burned by architects in the past, McVey retorted, "I wanted your help very much in giving us certain general ideas about the campus from a landscape point of view. . . . The delay in getting this has hampered us considerably." He noted that the locations of the new student union and science building had already been chosen and added, "Your services were not engaged for the purpose of planning the Student Union Building, but for the purpose of giving us some ideas about the general campus plan." He then requested a bill, so that "we may bring the matter to a close."[7]

Fleming responded that any valuable landscaping plans needed to incorporate architectural styles of future buildings and that UK, "like many others, has often erred in location and architectural character of its buildings and it seems too bad to continue methods which may result in still further unsatisfactory results." He offered his opinion as that of a neutral observer and apologized that his ideas "seemed to misfire and that they will be given no recognition," adding that he hoped to continue working with McVey. No explanations could placate McVey. He paid Fleming and closed the matter, choosing instead to follow the modern architectural plans of Dean Graham.[8]

While delegating the responsibilities of the building campaign to Graham, McVey nevertheless remained the focal point of criticisms surrounding the projects. He faced ongoing challenges regarding the federally funded project. Students reacted negatively to the original plans for the student union. Not having been consulted on the project, they pushed for a swimming pool as well as a larger ballroom. McVey told the students through the *Kentucky Kernel* that the plans had not been finalized and encouraged them to offer suggestions. However, the $250,000 allotted to build and furnish the structure could not "purchase luxury," and UK could not build the Waldorf-Astoria or even a union like the one at the University of Michigan. He added that the editor apparently thought that dancing "was the main purpose . . . of the student body." He reminded the students that the union primarily provided a place where students could congregate between classes and where student organizations could have offices to conduct campus business. He felt that his editorial had "cleared the air," but after meeting with students, he added, "It is amazing to learn what people think can be placed in one building." Despite these criticisms, construction on the student union began in April 1936.[9]

As work progressed on the union, McVey and Graham prepared yet another grant proposal for the federal government. As the president presented the grant to the board, he addressed what he viewed as another challenge. The Athletic Council had approached McVey about a federal grant to construct two additional sections on the football stadium. Because of the tremendous need for academic buildings, McVey told the group that he would mention their request to the board, but that he "could not recommend the construction of two sections at a cost of $40,000." McVey knew that "the University would hardly be justified in such expenditure to meet a need of that kind." In addition, students and athletic boosters were clamoring for a field house, but McVey wanted Governor

Chandler to provide the matching funds for that project. McVey actually hoped that the field house would not be constructed until after he had retired.[10]

Without McVey's support, the Athletic Council sought help elsewhere. Although unable to secure funds for expanded seating, they did secure the city of Lexington as a "project sponsor" for the construction of a press box and a running track at the football stadium. The WPA approved a grant in excess of $20,000 for construction, and Lexington paid the remaining $7,000. The state administrator of the WPA, George Goodman, asked McVey for formal acceptance of the project and used the occasion to ask the president for constructive criticism on the operations of the WPA in Kentucky. McVey expressed the board's appreciation for the funds and commented on the quality of the work. The president also sarcastically added that the funds had helped the university construct "the best running track and press box in the South." McVey wanted everyone to understand that he had different aspirations for the university.[11]

McVey hoped that athletic concerns were out of the way and that he could now turn his attention toward academic facilities. He and Dean Graham successfully petitioned the federal government for an additional $372,272 in the fall of 1936. This money, along with the federal assistance from the previous year, brought the total to more than $1 million in grants and loans from the federal government for construction on the Lexington campus. This funding helped pay off construction already under way and allowed McVey to move beyond the planning stages for the second phase of the building program, including a women's dorm, a home economics building, a biological sciences building, and renovations to Buell Armory.[12]

In June 1937 McVey told the board that the original four buildings were nearly completed and that work on the others was under way. He asked rhetorically, "Is the building program completed? This can be answered quite positively in the negative, for there are many additional buildings needed before the University can meet the demands now placed upon it." Although he did not use the occasion to restate his specific plans, the previous fall he had explained to Governor Chandler that the university needed more than $3.5 million to construct twenty new buildings to "bring the university where it ought to be." McVey clearly understood that much of the work would be completed after his retirement, but he wanted to accomplish as much as possible before he left office. He probably could not have envisioned what difficulties he faced.[13]

Actual construction first began on the engineering quad. While some expressed minor complaints about the buildings, no real opposition surfaced. Even McVey quipped in his diary that the first phase of the engineering construction was "much more intelligent than the forms we now have tho not so beautiful." Other projects proved more vulnerable to public opinion. For example, when McVey first saw the plans Graham submitted for the new law building, the president appreciated the "functional" exterior, which did away with "old adornments" that added to the cost. "On the whole," he opined, "I liked the building. . . . I felt it fitted the needs of the school." However, McVey predicted, "There will be criticism because the building does not look like a county court house."[14]

McVey could not have known the prophetic nature of his words. When he shared the plans with the law faculty, they expressed their dislike. Many hoped to delay the project in order to force changes to the building. McVey passed this along to the Board of Trustees, only to find out that some of the members agreed with the professors in the law school. Soon opposition to the structure spread beyond the campus. The local press editorialized its displeasure, requesting that the university follow its Georgian architectural pattern. The Lexington Board of Commerce took up the matter and requested that the board be made aware of its formal opposition to the program because its members believed that "a serious mistake may be made if the present plans are followed." With Dean Graham's fervent support, however, plans for the building continued, and a contract was let in December 1936.[15]

During the following year opposition to the architectural plans intensified, the law building continuing to receive the most ardent criticism. The complaints disturbed McVey, but he noted privately, "I am in favor of the new type [of architecture] for one reason if for no other . . . more building for less money." Publicly, however, McVey defended the architecture on different grounds. Instead of telling concerned citizens that elaborate architecture required greater state funding, he took a philosophical approach. While mentioning the importance of economy, he primarily argued that the latest building materials and methods required a fresh architectural style. He argued that the world had passed through both the classical Greek and Gothic architectural eras into modernism. Consequently, McVey argued, "If builders are to construct their buildings by the modern method, it follows that the architecture must be paralleled." He added that the university building program was attempting to "emphasize simplicity, precision, and reliance on basic proportions." McVey believed that "in an age of steel and concrete it was necessary to modify the style of the building to conform to the materials with which the building is erected."[16]

McVey's arguments seemed to draw from Thorstein Veblen's critique of university building programs. Veblen had contrasted modern architecture and its focus on structural framework with traditional ornate architecture, which relied heavily on masonry. Veblen concluded that wasteful spending on "architectural vagaries serve[d] no useful end in academic life." Yet in the "eyes of the unlettered" buildings needed to possess an "imposing front." This led to wasteful spending on poorly lit buildings, grand lobbies that served no academic purpose, and lecture halls with poor acoustics. All of this, according to Veblen, was designed to "conciliate the good-will of the opulent patrons of learning." McVey chose efficiency and economy rather than aesthetics, and he found himself on the defensive with individuals who, Veblen argued, found "wasteful, ornate and meretricious edifices a competent expression of their cultural hopes and ambitions."[17]

Drawing far less publicity beyond the campus, but equally challenging for McVey, was the controversy surrounding construction of the central heating plant. Even before submitting grant proposals to the federal government, McVey had requested the assistance of the College of Engineering in planning the heating plant. McVey had long favored such a project, hoping to modernize UK's inefficient and costly heating system. Professor Lester "Pat" O'Bannon, who had been at the university for more than a decade and had been involved in a similar project at Morehead State Teacher's College, agreed to help formulate the plans in 1933.

In 1935 Superintendent of Buildings and Grounds M. J. Crutcher recommended that Professor O'Bannon direct the project as well. He believed O'Bannon to be "thoroughly qualified to handle our problems from start to finish." O'Bannon began his work, but after Graham was hired as dean in May 1935, the two began to butt heads. In December O'Bannon noticed a change in plans and wrote McVey that he would be upset if his ideas were abandoned. Despite this, Graham continued to criticize the original proposal. McVey received a copy of O'Bannon's letter to Graham. Noting that the letter was simply "mean," he conceded, "I suppose there may be some reason for such opinion." As the standoff continued, O'Bannon asked to be removed from the project. McVey quipped in his diary, "There is a mess in the Engineering College and it will not be easy to straighten out." [18]

Even with O'Bannon technically out of the picture, Graham and O'Bannon continued their heated exchanges about the revised plans. At the 22 May 1936 board meeting Graham sharply criticized O'Bannon's original plans and announced that other engineers were redirecting the project. O'Bannon warned McVey, "The Colonel is the kind of man who can not have around him persons who have opinions and good ideas of their own. He is truly the kingfish type." Comparing the new dean's reaction to the "tantrum of a thwarted child," O'Bannon predicted that if McVey did not stop Graham's heavy-handed approach, the building campaign would prove to be an embarrassment to the university.[19]

O'Bannon soon found himself reassigned to the College of Agriculture with a 10 percent raise to ensure that no one interpreted the move as a demotion. McVey realized that "the engineering college is much disturbed," and worried that the problems would continue. His concerns were well founded. Soon after O'Bannon's transfer, the professor wrote McVey about his job security. Graham, who believed that the engineering faculty was too large, had started eliminating faculty positions. O'Bannon told McVey that he had requested a "temporary transfer" to the agricultural experiment station to help with air-conditioning issues related to tobacco-curing barns and could complete the work in one year. He then expected to be reinstated into the College of Engineering and hoped that he could return to his position as department chair.[20]

Dean Graham told McVey that O'Bannon was "now a full time employee of the Experiment Station by his own act." Graham added that he had not made any other plans for O'Bannon's return "during the present transition period," but he did not explain exactly what the "transition period" was or how long it would last. The following day McVey wrote O'Bannon, agreeing that the transfer was for an entire year and explaining that "other plans" had been made for O'Bannon's previous responsibilities. Using Graham's language, McVey noted that this alternate plan would continue through "the transition period." However, he added that "the matter can be taken up again in the spring."[21]

When spring arrived, O'Bannon wrote Graham to remind him that he did not wish to continue indefinitely in the College of Agriculture. He explained that he expected to return to his former position in the fall. Graham then wrote O'Bannon, "My thought that you will continue your present work with the Experiment Station is more than a mere assumption." He argued that he had worked diligently to keep O'Bannon in a post at the university (although no evidence to suggest this was provided, and O'Bannon was a full professor with tenure). Then he stated, "With all frankness . . . there exists no place for you within the plans for the future development of this College."[22]

The following month, engineering professor R. Clay Porter wrote McVey to let him know that he was resigning his job to accept a position at the University of Michigan. He clearly blamed Dean Graham for his departure. He charged that Graham had "overstepped his bounds" in denying O'Bannon's return and that a "rank injustice" had been committed against a "truly superior teacher and a gentleman of high ideals." He added that during the restructuring of the College of Engineering the dean had not met a single time with his faculty to explain his plans or procedures. Porter called Graham an incompetent leader who did not even attend the University Senate meetings to answer questions about his proposed reforms. His faculty hesitated to challenge him for fear of losing their jobs. The situation had resulted in "bewilderment and dissatisfaction" among students and faculty alike.[23]

Porter went to great lengths to let McVey know that he was thankful for the "many sacrifices" the president had made for UK, and he told McVey that he was an "ardent supporter" of his administration. Unfortunately, he felt that any critique of Graham's actions would be viewed by the board as "rebellion" against needed change. He argued, however, that he and others in engineering knew they needed change, but that they were lacking "competent leadership." He then said that he could go on listing grievances against Graham, but there was no reason to continue since "it is so evident that the die is cast." Finally, he said that he was "unable to subscribe" to Graham's practices and the conditions that they had created in the college and in the Department of Mechanical Engineering.[24]

The College of Engineering had lost one of its most notable faculty members, and the controversy had not ended. McVey responded that this was a complex matter but noted that no rule guaranteeing O'Bannon's return existed. He argued that the conflict was a matter of salary and defended Graham. However, ill feelings continued to surface. A few weeks later McVey attended a banquet for the college. He wrote in his diary that he could feel opposition to Graham in the speeches that were made and in the comments that received applause. Other student speakers praised Professor Porter and voiced their discontentment with his resignation.[25]

By early summer McVey's response to Porter had made it into the hands of faculty members. C. G. Latimer and six other professors who were members of the AAUP wrote McVey about his letter. They sought clarification regarding leaves of absence. They argued that if McVey's assertion was correct, a full professor returning from a sabbatical could be removed to a position so undesirable that it could "virtually force his resignation" and undermine the tenure system. They also asked if a faculty member was subject to transfer at any time or after a leave of absence. In a terse letter McVey responded, "No," and he suggested that if they needed further explanation they should ask him personally.[26]

The matter reached a climax of sorts in October, during a University Senate meeting. A number of faculty members decided to nominate

O'Bannon for a seat on the University Council, a rotating administrative body of administrators and faculty. When another member from the College of Agriculture was also nominated, McVey was asked to clarify the college in which O'Bannon's appointment resided. McVey paused and then replied that he was part of the College of Agriculture. As Thomas Clark asserted, "That was the wrong answer to gain any friends and influence people." The University Senate voted overwhelmingly in favor of O'Bannon. McVey noted, "It was remarkable that Professor O'Bannon received . . . the largest vote ever cast for a council member." Thomas Clark argued that the senate meeting that day was the low point of McVey's presidency and that henceforth McVey "had trouble with the faculty. . . . He was no longer the rigid Scotchman, the unflappable Scotchman." That evening McVey also lamented in his diary, "There will be more of this." [27]

There was more. O'Bannon would not give up his fight. He spoke with McVey in December 1937 asking to be returned to the College of Engineering, and he wrote the president in the spring as well. McVey responded, "You will recall that I told you that I would let you know about the situation so far as it relates to your continuance in the College of Engineering." He added that from what he understood, Graham had no position for him. McVey again discussed the issue with his dean, who argued that if the president wanted to return O'Bannon to engineering, the dean would resign his post, and "the restoration [of the college] as planned and undertaken [would] be abandoned." Three days later McVey wrote Graham that he did not think it wise for the professor to rejoin the College of Engineering, nor would his return help the building program. The president informed O'Bannon that he would recommend to the board his continuance at the experiment station. [28]

McVey remained in a terrible predicament. Not only had Dean Graham been responsible for securing more than a million dollars for university construction through grants and loans, but he was also undertaking the restructuring of the College of Engineering, which had just received a less than impressive report from a visiting accrediting committee from the American Engineering Society. This did not help McVey in the eyes of the faculty. The restructuring was not yet done, and the engineering college was about to move into two new buildings.

Harry Curtis, a member of the accrediting committee, noted that the programs in civil, metallurgical, and mining engineering had certain defects; however, they could be granted provisional approval. The programs in mechanical and electrical engineering, on the other hand, did not warrant accreditation. Curtis noted that too many "instructors" did not even have collegiate training, salaries were far too low, too many classes were at a remedial level, and teaching loads were too large. Concerning Dean Graham, Curtis concluded that he had been "preoccupied with the building program and had taken but little part in the educational activities of the University." He added that the committee had had a difficult time getting "a clear picture of the situation in respect to the engineering courses." [29]

Writing to Michigan's dean of engineering, a UK graduate, McVey listed several reasons for the committee's negative report, including having selected a dean without any academic experience. In Graham's defense, McVey added, "I think that Dean Graham has done some valuable work in the reorganization of the college." He noted the personnel changes that had taken place but said that "these considerations did not seem to enter into the thought of the Committee." [30]

Graham had harsh words for both Curtis and McVey. Concerning the accrediting committee's comments, Graham argued, "The authorities of this University were and are aware fully of the needs within this College, otherwise I would not have been chosen to take charge of it." He said he had no interest in leading any project that "was not in need of special attention." He added that he had devoted "more time and study to the details of the situation than I have expended heretofore upon much larger and more involved situations elsewhere." Concerning McVey's letter to the Michigan dean, Graham retorted to the president that he would have "preferred to have been ignored entirely in your reply rather than to have been damned by faint praise." [31]

The president stuck with Graham and trusted that he would be able to complete the reforms that the university needed. While reporting to the board regarding the failure of full accreditation, the president noted that great progress had been made. He argued that with the new facilities and changes in personnel, the college would "come into an important and impressive position." A couple of months later he reported to the board, "The plans which are under way at the present time are being slowly accepted by the staff, students, and alumni." Despite the headaches caused by the O'Bannon controversy, it appeared to McVey that the College of Engineering and the building program were finally coming together. He hoped that it would result in a cessation of the tensions which had plagued the college and the university.[32]

McVey's efforts to build a legacy at the university concerned much more than just the physical plant and the College of Engineering. As the last years of his administration wound down and the building program progressed, McVey turned his attention to other fundamental issues. In 1936 he authorized two surveys of UK. He asked his longtime friend Raymond Hughes (who had served as president at Miami University and at Iowa State College) to visit the campus and make a report. For a separate study on the state of the university, McVey requested input from more than two dozen young professors, who would gather information from their colleagues about where the university stood and where it needed to go in the future. McVey received both reports in 1937.[33]

The Committee on the State of the University of Kentucky, as it was named, kept McVey waiting for a substantial period of time. When the group finally informed McVey about its progress, he found that the issues addressed were too "narrow," but he hoped that they would eventually have something worthwhile to report. Nearly a year into the work, McVey met with members of the committee and came away feeling that they had missed the point of the survey. Instead of addressing larger problems, they were focusing on "little disturbing matters." McVey tried to guide them in the right direction, but privately he worried that the group did not have "the knowledge of educational principles" to accomplish what he desired.[34]

When the committee submitted its final report, McVey provided copies to members of the University Senate for their response. The report consisted of a letter from the chair, Neil Plummer, a "digest" of concerns submitted by faculty members, and a report making several recommendations. Plummer's letter to the faculty detailed a number of challenges that the committee had faced as it probed problems on campus. Committee members, he noted, had feared being a "rubber stamp" for the administration, a snare, the chair proudly argued, that they had avoided. Others had initially felt they were wasting their time participating in the study. Finally, Plummer contended that many of the issues raised by the university staff, such as "esprit de corps" and the quality of students, could not be solved by the committee and rested largely with each individual professor.[35]

The digest of letters provided a disorganized list of issues that bothered various faculty members. Criticisms included poor teaching, too many courses and too much course duplication, "overdepartmentalization," and lack of resources for high-quality graduate work. Some complained that professors exhibited a "reprehensible attitude of contempt" toward students. Others worried that faculty harmed the university by openly expressing their hostility toward religion in the classroom or by speaking ill of the university in the community.[36]

Some complaints dealt with the university's leadership. Others found the role of athletics "generally unsatisfactory." Some faculty believed that the "administrative machinery" was too large and cumbersome for an institution of UK's size, and some wanted rotating department chairs to bring in fresh ideas. Others sought an increased governance role for the University Senate. Faculty also wanted a clear statement on the system of tenure and promotion, readjustment for an equalized salary scale, increased funding for academic conferences, and more sabbatical leaves. In a thinly veiled reference to Dean Graham, the report noted that the student union was unsatisfactory and that "no one man should be placed in charge of a building program for the University." Apparently unaware of McVey's interaction with the board, the report suggested that a long-term building program needed to be created.[37]

The committee documented all these views and grouped them into four broad categories in its report: faculty ethics, a research program, faculty-university relations, and mimeographed material. Regarding faculty ethics, the committee called for greater participation in university events, the posting of office hours, and a cessation of criticizing other professors in class. To emphasize research, it argued that the administration needed to identify valuable projects and support them financially. The category "faculty-university relations" focused on research issues, calling for released time for writing, as well as funding for participation in the larger academy. The section on "mimeographed materials" addressed faculty members using their own unpublished work in class—work that was often unedited and poorly printed. The committee recommended the creation of a task force through which faculty members must justify using such materials. The task force also planned to make "recommendations with a view to equalizing the percentage of profit made by the authors" of such texts.[38]

During the next several months the University Senate discussed these recommendations but did not approve them, with the exception of those focused on faculty-university relations. However, the subsequent discussion did begin to reveal professors' increasing frustration with the university, as well as the growing challenge to its administration. McVey's private writing seemed to indicate that this frustration was mutual. He was disturbed by challenges from the faculty and in this instance felt that the discussions of the report's "rather unimportant" recommendations highlighted their lack of understanding. His desire for faculty input regarding the upcoming presidential transition had not been fulfilled, and McVey was left feeling frustrated.[39]

He seemed much more pleased with the Hughes survey. The president emeritus of Iowa State had spent eleven days on campus interviewing numerous individuals and now presented a different account than the one delivered by the faculty. Hughes pointed out a number of commendable developments at UK, some of which involved McVey directly, noting that the president was a nationally recognized figure whose prominence commanded respect in larger educational gatherings. He commented on the esteem in which the state's officials held him and added that McVey also commanded "unusual loyalty" from his faculty. Indirectly, Hughes's report documented Frances Jewell McVey's work at Maxwell Place, stating that the president's home had a social influence "much more notable than any other president's home of which I am acquainted."[40]

Among other positive points, Hughes noted the high caliber of UK's many deans and the programs that they operated. He praised Sarah Blanding's work in recruiting and retaining women students. W. D. Funkhouser had followed a prudent path in developing graduate programs. William Taylor's work in education was praised, and Thomas Cooper's role in the College of Agriculture, Hughes felt, was probably unsurpassed in the nation. In addition, Hughes stated that Ezra Gillis was perhaps the best-known university registrar in the country, thanks to his skills and outstanding work in that office. In short, many key leaders either recruited or promoted by McVey had brought national recognition to UK.[41]

Hughes also mentioned significant organizational and academic reforms that had helped the university. Student services were strong. The growth in the library's holdings impressed him. Hughes thought that UK's ability to secure 30 percent of its budget from the federal government surpassed that of many other notable institutions. He praised enrollment growth in the various colleges and projected that it would continue in the near future. The enlarged student body, he predicted, would be met by an increasingly impressive faculty, which was already much stronger than it had been a decade earlier. This was no small feat, considering that salaries had been stagnant since 1932. Virtually all this was a testament to McVey's leadership.[42]

Despite these accomplishments, Hughes also noted areas needing improvement. Too many department chairs were ill suited for administrative work. The survey suggested that these individuals be removed from their posts and returned to full-time teaching without a reduction in salary, so as not to foment discontent. The library needed a "first class man" at the helm, and the current librarian, Margaret King, needed to be retained to assist the new hire. Cooper needed an able assistant to handle the mundane affairs in the College of Agriculture so that the dean could continue his important endeavors. The College of Commerce was "overloaded and under staffed," a situation that could be partially addressed by giving it some of the funds currently being appropriated to the College of Engineering, which Hughes felt was making good progress but was still not totally efficient. While he felt that the graduate program had been wise to add PhD work slowly, Hughes could propose no solution to the problem of keeping graduate studies in the College of Education "from becoming a farce in the summer term in the face of the pressure on the department."

These proposed reforms required money. Hughes summarized McVey's greatest challenge as that of convincing Kentucky's legislature "to see how crucial to the welfare of the State the adequate strengthening of the University is in order to prepare her for necessary future service." This, of course, was not news to McVey, who had been fighting for increased state funding for two decades. In the meantime, Hughes offered several suggestions to bridge the gap, including consolidation. He proposed that business transactions should be consolidated in one office, that departmental libraries be merged with the main library, and that extension courses be streamlined and made financially self-supporting. Most important, the university needed to stop offering so many small classes. Hughes found that in the 1936 spring semester, 926 classes were offered. Of those, 190 had five or fewer students. Another 13 percent of classes had between six and ten students. The university, Hughes argued, needed to devise a policy under which no fewer than sixteen students would be enrolled in lower-level courses. Upper-level courses needed at least twelve students, and graduate classes should set a minimum enrollment of eight students.[43]

Hughes did not suggest any new academic endeavors that UK needed to develop. In short, he provided a plan for retrenchment and economy. Little was said in terms of expanding programs, even though the survey did suggest that the university's enrollments would expand considerably. Hughes understood that until the state offered more support, little else could be added to the offerings already in existence. McVey agreed.

———·———

Although it was given only two paragraphs in the entire survey, the issue of most concern to Hughes was sports. As he noted, "You have in this athletic situation the worst and most dangerous situation on the campus." He lauded McVey's decision to share information regarding scholarships and the boarding of athletes, but he argued that unless McVey ended this subsidization, the chief executive would face "very serious grief": "The students, the alumni, the parents, the high school authorities and the legislature, all may take a shot at you." Hughes then proudly announced that while he was president of Iowa State, the football team never posted more than six victories and that in one season it lost every game, yet "the team has a good name."[44]

McVey agreed with Hughes, but he did not have the support to do much about it. He had suggested that UK consider leaving the SEC. Rebuffed by his board, McVey then wrote Chancellor James Kirkland at Vanderbilt, arguing that if one or two important universities would take a stand and abolish their intercollegiate athletics programs, the conferences "would receive such a shock that other institutions would also withdraw and the issue would be distinctly stated and met." McVey admitted that he might be wrong, but he believed that the whole system would "break down when some one moves definitely against the kind of thing we have now." McVey hoped to convince Kirkland to do what he had been unable to do at UK.[45]

While McVey waited for the collapse of intercollegiate football, he also continued to face troubles with athletics at UK. In February 1937 a committee from the university's Athletic Council asked for a meeting to discuss a "breakdown in the athletic organization of the university." They complained that the athletic organization at UK had been divided between basketball and all the other sports. Coach Rupp did what he pleased with the basketball team without regard to other sports or the organization's financial structure. They reported that Rupp was popular, "but he does not fit into the larger athletic organization." They added, "When his teams are defeated he roars imprecations against the officials and the University reaps the hostility of other institutions." Although McVey was surprised to learn of some of these accusations, he had predicted trouble when the Athletic Council did not allow Chet Wynne, as director of athletics, to let Rupp's contract expire. In turn, Rupp's ability to go over the head of the athletic director and his astonishing success on the basketball court had emboldened the coach.[46]

Far more important to McVey than Rupp's control over basketball were football coach and athletic director Chet Wynne's personal and professional problems. McVey had spoken to Wynne about his lack of success on the gridiron, as well as his rumored drinking problem at the close of the 1936 season. Reports of his drunkenness, however, continued to surface during the off-season, so McVey met with the coach again. This time the president asked Wynne to resign if the coach felt there was any possibility of a "breakdown during the season." Wynne resisted, and McVey asked if the coach would write his resignation so the president could accept it publicly if problems arose during the next year. Wynne again refused, so McVey warned him that he would fire him during the middle of the season if he harmed the university further through his actions. Wynne then complained that the Wildcats' lack of success was not due to his personal shortcomings, but was a result of a lack of funding, scholarships, a field house in which to practice, and general support. McVey did not challenge the coach further because he did not wish to buy out the final three years of Wynne's contract.[47]

Wynne was not alone in his assertion that UK needed more resources to have a winning team. One alumnus, Wallace Muir, had tried to convince McVey and Governor Chandler, who was an avid UK sports fan, to put more money into the football team. At the end of the 1936 season he had written the governor, arguing that if the Wildcats were to compete with the premier SEC teams, they needed greater support: "You have got to have material and plenty of it to have a championship team." He added, "In this day to get that class of material you have got to be in a position to at least meet the bidding of other schools." Chandler seemed to be doing all that he could. At the request of Coach Wynne, the governor even wrote top prospects in the state who were considering attending rival institutions.[48]

Before the 1937 football season, Muir finally convinced Chandler to put more pressure on McVey. Because of Chandler's "interest in athletics," the governor finally wrote the president about a disconcerting issue he had discussed with Muir. As the governor put it, the two men were "somewhat prejudiced against one of your scholastic requirements for Freshmen."

Specifically, Chandler hoped that McVey would remove the geometry requirement for entering the university. He added, "I understand the necessity of maintaining proper standards in this direction, but you are in accord with us, I am sure, in our enthusiasm for a fine squad this coming season."[49]

McVey did not comply, and the football situation did not improve the following season. Then, during a game with Washington and Lee in October (the same week that McVey had trouble with the University Senate concerning O'Bannon), an event occurred that had little to do with football but may have been incited by frustrations on the gridiron. The UK marching band, then known as "The Best Band in Dixie" for its outstanding performances under the direction of John Lewis, asked the president for permission to travel to Massachusetts for a game against Boston College. The *Kentucky Kernel* editorially supported the trip, and students were looking for ways to raise money. McVey determined that the university did not have the funds to justify the trip and wrote Lewis to that effect, stating that he had considered "all of the phases of the matter," including the weather, time away from classes, and the cost of the trip. He determined, "I am under the necessity of refusing to give permission for the expedition to New England."[50]

Lewis apparently gave this letter to the editor of the student newspaper, who proceeded to reprint it on 15 October. The paper also included an editorial arguing once again that the band should go to Boston and discussing ways, such as a dance, that the student body could help it raise the needed funds. Enoch Grehan, a journalism professor who served as faculty sponsor for the paper, wrote McVey an apology, saying he had left the office at 4:00 P.M. on Thursday before the paper went to print, unaware that the paper had a copy of the president's letter. Grehan had himself been "dumbfounded" when he read the "editorial advocating the sending of the band to Boston, apparently, despite your executive order." Had he known, he would have not allowed the editorial to run.[51]

At a home football game against Washington and Lee the following day, Elmer Sulzer, who had formed the band in the 1920s before assuming a post as director of public relations, began making an announcement over the public address system that a dance would be held to raise money to send the band to Boston. McVey got up from his seat and, according to journalism professor Jasper Shannon, grabbed Sulzer by the coat and forced him to sit down. A correction announcement was then made, indicating that the band would not be traveling to New England. The crowd, led by the student section, began booing McVey and chanting, "Send the band to Boston." Other attendees stood up and called McVey names and cursed at him, putting the president in a very uncomfortable situation.[52]

The following week the *Kernel* ran an editorial stating that while the students had made their wishes known, many had violated the bounds of decency. The "thoughtless behavior" of the student body had been made worse by the "inebriated hoodlums" who had shouted at the president "in appalling disrespect." The paper claimed that the editorial published on the same day as McVey's letter had not been an attempt to thwart the president's decision; the editor was "sincerely sorry" if it had been interpreted as such. Instead, the editor argued that the piece "was one in a series of prepared editorials in the campaign," written before the paper received McVey's letter to Lewis.[53]

Regardless of the intentions of the student paper, the Executive Committee of the Board of Trustees met later in the week and condemned the protest at the football game, as well as the *Kernel*'s earlier editorial. After being "discussed at some length," a motion was made to put the paper under the control of the Department of Journalism, which was directed to censor the paper if necessary. The motion passed, making Professor Grehan "responsible to the Board of Trustees and to the Executive Committee of the University for everything" published in the student paper.[54]

That night McVey wrote in his diary that he had been asked his opinion at the board meeting and had stated that he thought "it was not the way to handle what appeared in the paper," but the board had voted for the measure despite his views. Grehan had learned of the order and informed the paper's staff, who, McVey said, "protested against a controlled paper." In the weeks that followed McVey met with the *Kernel* staff and with Grehan in an attempt to assuage their frustrations and fears, respectively. The students did not want to be censored, and Grehan did not want to be held responsible for what was written in the paper. The activist Student Union Association and other student groups also protested the board's move. Despite these grievances, the paper was to be watched and suppressed if necessary.[55]

Just as it seemed that the issue might pass from the spotlight, in early December journalism professor Jasper Shannon, who had recently come to UK from Transylvania University across town, presented a paper addressing censorship of student newspapers at the Kentucky Intercollegiate Press Association meeting in Morehead. Shannon condemned such censorship, stating, "The academic censor is one of the greatest menaces to the liberty of the press to be found in America, for he who accustoms youth to a tyranny invites a future tyranny." He added, "There is no college or university in the land worthy of its salt which has not long since removed all barriers from liberty of expression."[56]

Grehan wrote McVey to inform him of Shannon's presentation, noting that Shannon had not mentioned the university, but that he presumed Shannon must have been directing his comments at the board's recent action and at Grehan himself. As he said to McVey, "I take it that no one questions that the condition recently brought to notice upon this campus was the inspiration for his observation." Grehan then argued that Shannon's deliberate attempt "to bring to a faculty comrade such embarrassment as Dr. Shannon's speech invites is a gross violation of academic ethics." Grehan hoped that the board would address the speech and place a similar limit on Shannon as it had on the student newspaper.[57]

In an interview years later, Shannon stated that he had no idea the board had voted to censor the paper and that he had been researching censorship of student newspapers before the controversy erupted. He did add, however, that a student who went with him to the conference in Eastern Kentucky warned him that he would get in trouble for making the presentation. Following the speech the *Lexington Herald* and the *Courier-Journal* both mentioned Shannon's remarks but did not suggest that they related to the situation at UK. The *Lexington Leader,* however, stated that his address was aimed at the controversy surrounding the *Kentucky Kernel.* The following day, Shannon said, he met Frances McVey at the entrance of the Administration Building, and the normally jovial McVey was "just as chilly as an iceberg." In mid-December Grehan died suddenly of a heart attack, and rumors flew that it was a result of stress brought on by the censorship controversy. McVey, however, had never reprimanded Grehan. The tone for student censorship, however, had been set, and it did not help McVey's relationship with the students during his final years.[58]

That season the Wildcat football team failed to win a single conference game, and ticket sales plummeted. The football team brought in only $14,000 for the Athletics Department, less than half of the previous year's proceeds. This left the Athletic Council with a deficit it could not overcome. In addition, UK's "best coach," according to McVey, assistant coach Porter Grant, accepted a position at Auburn. When yet another assistant coach also resigned, the football team threatened to quit if the university did not rehire the coaches. The players believed that McVey was involved in firing them, even though they had left because of friction with Coach Wynne. By the close of 1937, conditions had degenerated so much that Chandler asked for a meeting with McVey to discuss the situation.[59]

McVey believed that the public controversy had already done too much damage to the university, so he decided to take action. He called a meeting with the football team and other university athletes in McVey Hall. The student athletes blamed the Athletic Council for the team's woes and called for a reorganization of that body. They wanted the assistant coaches reinstated, the Athletic Council to diversify its membership to include representatives from different parts of the commonwealth, and more state funding to support the program. Quarterback Dick Robinson requested the faculty's assistance in writing a formal petition to the Athletic Council to address these grievances.[60]

McVey then met with the captain of the football team to discuss the matter further, noting that he was "a nice chap who wants . . . the right thing. The right thing is to get a better state attitude." McVey then met with the Athletic Council to discuss the players' frustrations. The council agreed to create a committee to form a plan for reorganization. Education professor Moses Ligon chaired the committee, and McVey was one of its members. The president commented in his diary that he wished the problems had instead been addressed privately with the players and the council, rather than in a forum that gained so much public attention. He also felt that lack of money was another almost insurmountable issue for Kentucky. As he stated, the football program cost nearly $50,000 annually, "not a large sum when there are big gates; but well nigh ruinous for us." [61]

The reorganization committee met with numerous alumni groups across the state to get their advice. In Lexington, Wallace Muir restated his criticism of UK's failure to fully adopt big-time college football standards. He called for greater financial support to help the coaches and players and for the subsidization of athletic construction in order for UK to become more competitive in the SEC. He again criticized UK's admissions standards, which he believed were too strict and led some of the best athletes in the state to attend rival institutions. Historian Gregory Kent Stanley noted that many others also offered their advice to McVey. An editorial calling for more money (in direct contrast to Hughes's views on athletics) stated, "You can't build a Rose Bowl team on ethics." One individual wrote McVey to tell him that UK needed to favor southern coaches instead of midwestern ones and recruit southern players who possessed "the spirit of Lee and the fight of Jackson." [62]

McVey would just as soon have ended the football program, but as the committee gathered opinions and ideas, the president was at least glad he had the opportunity to help reform the situation. Other than finances, McVey felt that the Athletics Department's greatest problem was Chet Wynne: "There is just one element in this situation and that is the coach. How to handle it is the problem. We may be able to find a way." McVey's "problem" was his unwillingness to pay for the two remaining years on Wynne's contract when he was pinching every penny for the building program. The football team's debt had already saddled the university with responsibility for thousands of dollars it did not have, and releasing Wynne would cost $7,500 a year, along with the cost of a new coaching staff. [63]

Finally, in mid-February the members of the reorganization committee met with the governor to discuss the issue. Two days later Wynne resigned. Rumors spread that Chandler had agreed to pay the remainder of the coach's salary, and McVey's diary confirmed this speculation. As McVey noted, the governor had agreed to "help indirectly" to meet the severance obligation. During the next year, McVey wrote Chandler and asked that the "additional funds needed to take care of the salary question that we discussed the other day should be added to the repair account." The university, however, was not immediately reimbursed, and McVey again wrote Chandler, stating the problem explicitly. The university had made payments on Wynne's salary, and McVey asked that "the general appropriation for the maintenance of the University be increased by the amount of these two payments."[64]

After Wynne left, the Board of Trustees approved the reorganization committee's recommendations. All sports were to be governed by university authorities. However, the Athletic Council would become an advisory council, while the athletic director would be "charged with direct supervision and control of all athletics and . . . [be] directly responsible for their proper conduct and for the enforcement of University rules." A Department of Athletics (separate from the Physical Education Department) was created in the College of Arts and Sciences. The university would provide athletes with tuition, board, lodging, and books. However, donations to cover the costs would have to be administered through the business office and requisitioned by the athletic director.[65]

Bernie Shively, who had coached at UK under Gamage and was the current chair of the Physical Education Department, accepted the position as athletic director, as well as coach of the football team's offensive line. Ab Kirwan, a football star at UK in the 1920s and a high school coach in Louisville, accepted the head football coaching position. McVey cautiously hoped that "a very irritating matter" had been resolved; everyone he spoke with seemed to like the new arrangement. As proof, the following season the football team won only two games, but attendance and revenue improved noticeably. A puzzled McVey noted, "It is rather remarkable in view of the many lost games . . . that enthusiasm should keep up." He attributed this good feeling to the university having hired the right people for the future. He still hoped that the board would eventually give up the fight for big-time athletics but lamented, "There may be little connection between football and education but the public expects it to go on just the same." [66]

————•—•———

McVey managed to reform athletics at UK during his final years, but his efforts regarding the overall academic life of the university focused less on reform and more on retrenchment. In both his comments and his actions, McVey was resigned to the fact that he could not build the university he had initially envisioned, and expansion seemed out of the question. A case in point was the ongoing discussion regarding a medical school at UK. Years earlier McVey had requested that physician and UK employee John Chambers study the feasibility of a medical program. Chambers concluded that dozens of Kentucky counties were in dire need of additional doctors. However, a medical school already operated as part of the University of Louisville, one of the nation's first city-owned universities. In 1937, Dean Graham reported to McVey that Governor Chandler wanted to open a medical school in Lexington. McVey immediately squelched the idea, arguing that "the state was in no position to establish and finance a medical school." The president would certainly have been in favor of such an endeavor if it could have done it properly, but he knew that the legislature's appropriations would allow the university to do nothing more than "hold its own." [67]

Even if expansion was out of the question, McVey still pushed to strengthen what already existed. For example, he advocated increased library development for two reasons. First, he viewed the library as the central component of the university, and second, he hoped to bolster the research options for graduate students and faculty members alike. In the early 1930s McVey had asked Thomas Clark to canvas the state to secure primary and secondary sources, and Clark's astounding success had resulted in thousands of additions to the library. Even these treasures, however, created pressure for McVey. In 1937, after Clark secured five truckloads of state government documents dating back to the eighteenth century (documents that the state was going to pay to have destroyed), McVey stated, "This means a lot of space . . . and an expert to look after such material. The university gets bigger faster than money can be found to meet its needs." [68]

Despite his trepidation, McVey's emphasis on the library paid off. A 1936 study of southern libraries found that UK had the sixth-largest library in terms of holdings, was third in recent additions to the library, and was eighth in overall financial support. While UK lagged behind in some library categories, it compared favorably with the libraries of the flagship institutions in Texas, North Carolina, and Virginia, as well as those at private universities such as Duke and Vanderbilt. McVey worried that the increase in volumes was due not to state support, but to Clark's untiring efforts. McVey had protected the library's budget during lean economic times, but he could not keep up with the competition if the state did not provide adequate funding. This became apparent when, the following year, the same updated survey showed that UK had fallen to seventh in the number of books added during the year, ninth in the amount spent on books, and eighth in the "amount expended for library services." [69]

Closely related to McVey's efforts on behalf of the library was his desire to have a productive research faculty and an outlet for their work. Although he had always been a proponent of projects that were of direct benefit to the commonwealth, he argued that new areas needed to be explored. He told the Board of Trustees, "Research should not be confined to applied problems, but may be extended into fields of pure science." Both Hughes and the university faculty argued the same in their reports, but figuring out exactly how to promote such endeavors proved difficult. [70]

A major problem involved making research a standard for tenure and promotion when the university did not have a press. McVey had called for the creation of a press long before his final year at UK, and he spoke about it frequently during his last years as president. McVey consulted with Bill Couch at the University of North Carolina, who actually discouraged him from starting a press, but that did not deter McVey. He spoke with board members corporately and individually about how to find the money for an outlet for publications. The bottom line, however, was that money was not available, and McVey could not start such an endeavor without a means for subsidizing it. [71]

A second unresolved issue involved personnel. He argued that research required "an ability which every man does not have," but he wanted to attract such skilled individuals to campus. To secure talent, he needed to offer larger salaries. However, state appropriations had not come close to recovering the level of their highest point in 1931, and in seven years salaries had remained virtually stagnant, making it difficult to recruit or retain quality professors. As pressure built for salary increases, he told the board in June 1937, "Here again disappointment must ensue, as a consequence of the inability of the University to meet such requests. In many instances requests are justified; in the long run the University cannot hold its staff together if [it] does not pay adequate salaries." In December of the same year, McVey again brought the issue before the board, saying, "The Board is familiar with the salary situation." He quickly added that UK used the same salary scale it had used in 1932 but that the cost of living had increased, so members were actually making less than they had many years earlier. McVey believed that the problem would create "a possibly devoted, but only an average group" to conduct the university's work.[72]

Virtually all McVey's challenges were the result of inadequate funding, and he continued to emphasize this to his board. He knew that Kentucky's legislature would meet in 1938 and provide funding for McVey's final biennium as president. Rarely did a week pass when UK was "not only asked but urged to make some additional commitment. . . . All of them require money and no difference how worth-while the proposal may be, the answer is readily at hand." McVey felt he had answered "no" long enough, and the solution was that "requests should be made so that the University will do something more than hold its own." The policy of retrenchment had been in motion since 1932, but McVey said it was beginning to take its toll with a "gradual decline of prestige and effectiveness."[73]

The limited progress during the Depression years made it even more difficult for McVey to formulate a budget. Each new building constructed with federal funds required money for maintenance. While the overall size of the student body grew and UK graduated more students than ever before, incoming freshman classes actually declined in number. Funding from the National Youth Administration had dried up. McVey was frustrated that the only scholarships the university offered were for athletes or band members. Furthermore, UK had terminated its first two years of undergraduate work in education as part of a deal to become the state's sole provider of all graduate education. Graduate school enrollment had exploded, but the smaller graduate classes cost more money than undergraduate courses, and new state funding failed to materialize.[74]

Moreover, UK had assumed hundreds of thousands of dollars of debt to build needed facilities on campus. By 1937 UK owed nearly a million dollars. McVey told the board a story in which a person surveying the work on campus said that the university was going to bankrupt the state. Although the president said he "was not taking the comment seriously," it did elucidate a prevalent attitude in the commonwealth. Over the previous decade, the university had built nearly three million dollars' worth of buildings, with "little or no direct cost to the state." The last state appropriation for construction had been made in 1930. Yet many still believed that Kentucky was providing too much for its university.[75]

McVey emphasized at every board meeting the desperate need for increased state funds. The university's enrollment surpassed pre-Depression levels, and the campus continued to grow. However, state appropriations for the Lexington campus in 1937 barely reached $700,000, or a half million dollars less than in 1931, and this did not account for inflation. McVey concluded that the legislature must "be told very frankly what the situation is, and asked to remedy it by a generous appropriation for annual support."[76]

Governor Chandler, who was looking toward a race for the U.S. Senate the following year, finally seemed to agree with McVey when the two spoke during a dinner party. Chandler promised to seek $1.2 million in appropriations for the university, as well as $400,000 annually for building projects. McVey said that he was "highly gratified." In September 1937 McVey announced to the board that the governor had "shown a marked interest in the affairs of the University, and this has been of much encouragement to all considered." He then presented a tentative budget that incorporated the funding increases promised by the governor.[77]

But even before the legislature met, McVey's hopes died. Called to Frankfort in late December to meet with the governor, McVey was told that rather than the $1.2 million promised, the university would receive $815,000 per year. While this was an increase of approximately $115,000 annually, it was nowhere near what McVey had desired. The governor explained that the Legislative Council, which had met earlier, expressed hostility toward the university because of UK's unwillingness to play in-state rival Centre College in football. As McVey noted, "My position was rather difficult in that I was told what had to be done."[78]

McVey set out to change the governor's mind with his biennial report to the governor and the legislature. Ignoring athletics, he discussed other reasons members of the Legislative Council opposed UK, including the perception that UK had already spent too much money and that it was "attempting to run everything in the state." Some detractors believed either that the university did not accomplish enough or that interactions with UK employees had led to disagreements about programs or appointments throughout the state. Other families and friends were upset if students they knew did not excel at the university. Finally, McVey noted the "regional opposition to the University because of loyalty to some local institution." McVey tried to combat these feelings by arguing that UK belonged "to the whole State." It was not in competition with other institutions, but it did serve as "the guardian of the people's heritage and their guide for the future."[79]

McVey's defense in this instance was a summary argument of his position for the previous two decades. Not only did UK educate the state's future leaders, but it provided significant public service. The experiment station and agricultural extension centers assisted the state's farmers. The Department of University Extension administered the federal agricultural adjustment program, as well as conducted soil, seed, and fertilizer programs. More than three thousand Kentuckians had taken short courses through the Extension Department. The Bureau of Business Research, the Bureau of Government Research, and the Bureau of School Service all provided the state with invaluable resources. While the College of Engineering did not have an official bureau, it also conducted numerous research projects for the benefit of the commonwealth.[80]

UK's efforts had been accomplished with resources that were a fraction of what similar universities had at their disposal. McVey reported exactly where the university stood in contrast to some of its neighboring peers. Indiana appropriated more than $1.5 million each for *both* Purdue University and Indiana University. Illinois provided its flagship over $4.3 million, while Ohio appropriated in excess of $3.5 million. Even border state Missouri provided $2 million for its university. Without better state support, UK could not accomplish its mission of service to Kentucky.[81]

Ambition and politics likely played a large role in limiting UK's funds. The Kentucky Constitution forbade governors from seeking a second term, and the restless Chandler intended to stay in the political arena. In a flamboyant move even by Chandler's standards, the governor chose to oppose U.S. senator Alben Barkley. An extremely popular New Deal politician and a member of Chandler's own party, Barkley served in the important role of Senate majority leader in President Roosevelt's New Deal Congress. Central Kentucky and the area surrounding UK provided Chandler's main political strength. As a consequence, the governor decided to disperse funds to regions of the state where he had less political capital.[82]

Regardless of the reasons, any hope of expanding UK's academic programs withered. Faculty and staff salaries remained stagnant, and the university had few scholarships to offer for academically promising students. McVey's hope for a university press stalled. Even though McVey created the Department of Social Work, he did so only by moving the classes already offered in the Sociology Department into the new department. Even this was a struggle for McVey, who told the board that the department required two professors as well as an assistant. He did not have the funds for this, so the Social Work Department started with one professor, Vivian Palmer, and one graduate assistant. Reorganization of the College of Music became possible because of a $30,000 grant from the Carnegie Foundation.[83]

The budgetary setback brought about more lost opportunities for UK, some of which would have been exciting endeavors. The Lexington Chamber of Commerce, for example, had sought UK's assistance in securing a Civil Aeronautics Authority (CAA) grant for aviation training, but McVey worried that UK would be responsible for providing an airstrip as well as hangars in which the work would be conducted. When Dean Graham brought the application for a "vocational flight training program" to be submitted to the CAA, McVey convinced the board to adopt a motion to have the pilot-training proposal "indefinitely postponed."[84]

In 1939, after losing his Senate bid, Governor Chandler asked McVey to convene a meeting with representatives of the Louisville College of Pharmacy to discuss a merger with UK. The municipal college faced reaccreditation, and it would need greater funding and administrative assistance to meet the latest requirements. Affiliating with UK might provide the necessary support for the college to continue. Its administration hoped to remain in Louisville, but agreed to sell its property and move to Lexington. Even though the governor favored the merger, he was in the final year of his term and could not appropriate any funds for the reorganization. After months of correspondence with administrators in Louisville and debate among the board, McVey stated that the merger would "be an expense without adequate income, and that the University is now unable to assume burdens of added expense." UK declined the proposition.[85]

Chandler also sought McVey's assistance regarding an increasingly volatile issue. The U.S. Supreme Court had ruled in *Missouri ex rel Gaines v. Canada* (1938) that Missouri's failure to accept Lloyd Gaines into the only state law school on the basis of race violated the Equal Protection Clause of the Fourteenth Amendment. Since Kentucky was a southern border state, it seemed possible that a similar case could be filed in the Bluegrass. McVey informed the board of the Court's decision, but it was inclined to do nothing. He then wrote Chandler requesting that the state make sure it appropriated enough money to send African American students outside the commonwealth to attend law school or other graduate programs.[86]

Chandler appointed a commission to study the problem of educational opportunity for "Negroes" in Kentucky. The governor asked McVey to chair the task force, which consisted of both black and white educational leaders. McVey agreed and, despite the board's disapproval, also agreed to participate in a national conference to discuss issues pertaining to race and education. On both accounts McVey took a moderate position. He pushed for increased opportunity for African Americans but did not support judicial activism that forced educational equality and challenged the status quo in his own state.[87]

Even though McVey found himself in the middle of discussions concerning civil rights for African Americans, he did not play a prominent role in breaking down the color barrier in education. Instead, he took a centrist position, emphasizing gradualism in moving toward greater equality for black students. This position brought him criticism from both sides of the issue. In 1938 he chastised politicians who used the slogan "Keep the negro in his place" to gain political power and praised a growing trend toward equality. After attending a meeting of Phi Beta Kappa in Louisville, he felt thankful that the group "accepted the situation" of African Americans attending the conference, and he seemed pleased that "little by little a break in the color line is going on." His Board of Trustees, however, felt differently. When McVey suggested to the Executive Committee that a national meeting be held to address the subject, it disagreed, noting that "negroes wanted one thing, the right to attend state schools." McVey, however, was invited by the presidents of Atlanta University, Tuskegee, and the University of North Carolina to attend a conference in Washington, D.C., to discuss the matter.[88]

At the same time, he asked African American leaders in Kentucky to avoid litigation for integration, which he feared would backfire and result in loss of the gains that had been made in race relations. Although L. N. Taylor, the director of Negro education in Kentucky, praised McVey and his counterpart at Kentucky State for possessing a "liberal attitude and farsighted judgment," others were not as pleased. For example, W. H. Fouse, the principal of Lexington's all-black Dunbar High School, argued that if McVey's position was to equalize opportunity rather than encourage integration, the state needed to implement a dual system of highways.

As the National Association for the Advancement of Colored People (NAACP) made its first gains in the national fight for equality, McVey's role as a leading spokesman for both the state and southern state universities was noteworthy. In that role he was respected by the leaders of both races. However, the constitutional issues of segregation in Kentucky would not be fully addressed until after he left the presidency.[89]

When the "Report of the Governor's Advisory Committee on the Equalization of Higher Educational Opportunities for Negroes" was finally published, it adopted the moderate stance that McVey advocated. It argued that the spirit of the law (equality) had not been followed and that opportunities for African Americans needed to be strengthened. It called for greater funding to help Kentucky State College and the University of Louisville Municipal College and for exchanges of faculty members between black and white institutions. And most important, it stated that there might be future modification of Kentucky's Day Law, which mandated segregation of all educational institutions. This mention of challenging the system did not sit well with segregationists. On the other side, many African Americans were growing tired of the slow pace of progress. Walter White, secretary of the NAACP, criticized McVey for his failure to lead the task force in the proper direction. The report, argued White in a letter, failed to address the issue of graduate and professional training in Kentucky. And it did not even comply with the U.S. Supreme Court's position in the *Gaines* decision.[90]

In Kentucky, however, questions of racial equality were overshadowed by insufficient funding. The only financial help offered to expand the work of the university came not from the state, but from a private donation. In 1938 Margaret Voorhies Haggin, the widow of J. B. Haggin, who had owned Elmendorf farm outside of Lexington, made UK the beneficiary of a trust established in honor of her late husband. Inviting Mrs. Haggin to the university, the McVeys gave her a tour of the campus and learned that the university was to receive half of the income generated from 150 shares of the Haggin estate (which was more than $2 million).[91]

When the board met in January, McVey informed them that they had $34,000 to spend from the fund in 1939. The president announced that this was the largest single gift in the university's history. The board was free to spend it how it wished, but McVey shared his plans for the gift—and the board adopted them. The funds supported graduate fellowships, scholarships for international students, university radio programs, guest lectures, and a publication committee to promote works from the university faculty.[92]

As McVey dealt with financial issues, the building program continued to generate more criticism. The centralized heating plant had been completed in the fall of 1937, but tests revealed a number of leaks and poor heating in the buildings. McVey said that the problems "had been made into big stories," and that since Dean Graham had "gone against tradition . . . those who predicted failure are much pleased." In April 1938 McVey told the board that the heating system had been "adequate" during the winter months but that "adjustments" needed to be made before the next winter.[93]

McVey informed the board that the two initial phases of the building program would be completed during the summer of 1938. The university remained busy planning for additional construction during McVey's tenure, including an expansion of the biology building, as well as a new women's dorm and a facility for home economics. McVey's decision to construct modern buildings finally seemed justified. When the faculty of the Law School moved into its building before the 1938 spring semester, McVey basked in the news that many professors found it to be a "grand place." He added with some satisfaction that the many criticisms leveled "out of turn" during construction were now "coals of fire on the heads of the staff."[94]

In early 1938 the First Lady of the United States made a second visit to UK. Spending the day at Maxwell Place, along with her close friend Elinor Morgenthau, Mrs. Roosevelt gave speeches to enthusiastic audiences in both Memorial Hall and Alumni Gymnasium. They also took a tour of the campus to see the work that had been done with New Deal funds. After the visit Roosevelt wrote that although it was cold outside, "a warm southern welcome awaited us . . . at the University of Kentucky.

One could not feel strange for very long in the cordial and hospitable household of hosts like Dr. and Mrs. McVey." She then commented on the PWA building program, stating that UK had made "an extremely good record here on economical building." She cited McVey's approach in using the expertise of the engineering faculty, as well as the modern buildings, which required "minimum decoration."[95]

Any pleasure at the positive comments, however, was short-lived. Over the summer, a number of law professors complained to McVey that the heat in the building was unbearable. The same problem existed in the student union. Both facilities had been built with the intention of adding air-conditioning, so the windows had been sealed, but money for cooling technology was not yet available. Fans were placed in the union to try to keep the building cool, with little success, and the situation soon became so severe that extra funds had to be spent to install different windows.[96]

Then, in January 1939, a campus editorial entitled "Give Us Better Planning, Construction" confessed that the paper had ignored various problems in order to give the university's building program "a chance to succeed before being criticized." However, the problems had become so severe that the editors felt compelled to speak. Concerning the lack of air-conditioning, they asked whether it in fact took four attempts before the administration realized that either smaller buildings with cooling systems needed to be built or windows that opened should have been installed. The paper criticized the leaking roofs as well, noting, "The Engineering building leaked, the new Law Building leaked, and now the Union building leaks." The article concluded that more buildings were needed, but it begged for "careful planning of architecture and construction." The *Lexington Herald* also questioned the quality of the construction.[97]

McVey faced even greater opposition about simple curricular procedures. The University Senate initially denied Dean Graham, who did not show up at its meetings, his proposal to move lab work for engineering courses to the summer session. Graham wrote McVey on two occasions, attempting to explain that the problems in the buildings were not architectural flaws, but construction problems that could be fixed, and then offered his unsolicited advice that the growing dissent in "your senate" reflected a lack of appropriate administrative structure. He argued that the university had been governed through McVey's own "strong personality."[98]

McVey, however, trusted the administrative structure, including the senate that he had formalized upon his arrival in 1917. So the president sought advice from his dean of women, Sarah Blanding, who believed that the tensions in the senate were the result of ill feelings toward Dean Graham in the Engineering Department and Dean Paul Boyd in the College of Arts and Sciences. She suggested that McVey call a special faculty meeting to discuss "the need to pull together," but McVey did not act on her suggestion. Even if reforms were needed, McVey believed, the senate represented "the democratic way and so must be adhered to."[99]

Graham's nemesis, Lester "Pat" O'Bannon, viewed the growing displeasure with the buildings and the increased tension in the senate as his vindication. In a confidential letter to members of the board O'Bannon asserted his right to return to the College of Engineering, spelling out the reasons. He claimed that he had originally fallen out of favor because of his "discernment and foresight." He argued that the public had lost faith in McVey's administration because of the president's continued support for Graham. O'Bannon regretted the recent criticisms, but he noted that the warning he had issued had come to fruition. He said that Graham's poor work on the building campaign was coupled with his threats to the "machinery for the democratic administration of the internal affairs" of the university, which McVey had originally established.[100]

O'Bannon asserted that McVey's administration had been "spoiled" by the architecture of the new buildings. Stating that "Graham's handiwork stands for itself," the professor argued that three years ago he had "stood alone" for the right course of action. Now, however, Graham stood alone, except for McVey's "obviously self-defensive and ostentatiously innocent attempts to support him." The recent structures represented a departure from "everything good that President McVey has fostered over the past twenty years." These "incongruous monuments symbolize the disharmony from which other affairs of the University are suffering."[101]

The faculty as a whole, O'Bannon asserted, was frustrated by McVey's failure to censure Dean Graham. The president and the board had fallen prey to Graham's repeated threats to quit and had lost the opportunity to improve the university. Instead Graham's leadership had demonstrated the institution's "inferiority" and invited much-warranted criticism. O'Bannon said, "All are ready to forgive, and to forget," as long as measures were taken to "curb Colonel Graham's dictatorial powers."[102]

The board did not respond favorably to O'Bannon. At its April meeting members discussed the issue, and McVey patiently argued that O'Bannon deserved a "chance to be heard." The board established a committee to study the details of the case. However, as McVey noted in his diary, "A protesting, noisy, belligerent and none too discriminating instructor has a small chance in such protests. O'Bannon is his own worst enemy." At its June meeting the board passed a resolution expressing thanks to Dean Graham for his invaluable service to the university.[103]

In the meantime, McVey created a summary of the correspondence concerning the O'Bannon case for the committee studying the case. The president, however, selectively re-created this correspondence, chronologically citing more than twenty letters between or among himself, Graham, and O'Bannon. However, he left out one letter that he had written to O'Bannon on 6 October 1936, in which he stated that the professor's transfer was for one year and that the issue could be readdressed during the spring term. He also failed to include correspondence from Dean Thomas Cooper noting that O'Bannon's work would be for one year and that his salary would be paid for ten months by the College of Agriculture and for two months by the College of Engineering.[104]

Next McVey faced an entirely separate "insurrection of small proportions." In the midst of reorganization, the administration of the Music Department decided to discharge band director John Lewis. Several band members spoke with McVey about what they believed to be an injustice to Lewis. They threatened a protest march and McVey admitted in his diary, "Perhaps it is best for them to get the thing off their chests." The march was held the following day, and the protesters left their signs at Maxwell Place. Fifty-two members of the marching band also signed a letter of protest. In a follow-up investigation into Lewis's firing, students argued that Lewis's directorship was the reason they had become "the Best Band in Dixie." Lewis had also served as president of the Kentucky Band and Orchestra Directors Association. He had founded the *Southern Musician* and served as the publication's editor. The investigating committee concluded that the accusations of his noncooperation and his demeaning attitude toward students were false.[105]

Former band members also wrote Governor Chandler in protest. They argued that Lewis was the primary reason the band was "well known throughout the South." One asserted, "We know we haven't had a football team at UK for years, but at least we have had a band no other school in the country could shame," adding, "The UK band at present is threatening to strike, and my only regret is that I am still not in school so I might join them." Even the hard-nosed Judge Stoll conceded that the committee made a number of telling points. The decision to fire John Lewis, however, was not overturned, and the band, at Lewis's request, did not strike.[106]

A relative calm seemed to develop during the summer and fall of 1939. McVey was invited to the annual meeting of the American Association of Universities, being held at the University of Missouri. He wrote in his diary that he had decided to attend in the hope that UK would receive an invitation to join the prestigious organization. McVey had been lobbying for admission to the AAU for more than a decade, but he was again disappointed. Apparently, funding was the obstacle. So he turned his attention to the 1940 legislature and the budget that it would enact. McVey reported to the board that he was requesting $1.6 million annually for the next biennium, including increased appropriations for operations on campus, as well as $200,000 for construction. McVey recognized that the Kentucky legislature was feeling pressure to increase funding for welfare programs, but he noted, "The state will have to determine whether the youth and their education shall be sacrificed for the development of old age pensions and increased welfare provisions." He argued that ignoring funding for education would ultimately add to the welfare costs of the state.[107]

Despite his pleas, McVey's requests were denied. Governor Keen Johnson, Chandler's successor, was "friendly and interested," but determined to prevent new taxes or deficits. Hence, the budget had to remain within the $24 million in state revenue. In the end, the legislature appropriated $43,000 more annually for the Lexington campus. The university budget, as in the last session, exceeded $1 million, but this included funding for the work at the experiment stations and the extension centers, not solely for the Lexington campus. McVey would again be forced to deny salary increases and requests for more personnel. Disappointed, McVey seemed resigned to the rejection.[108]

Early in 1940 it appeared that McVey could anticipate a final semester of challenging work to keep the university on an upward trajectory. Instead the engineering controversy, which had been an internal affair, finally converged with frustrations over the building program and spilled out into the public eye. Everything seemed to unravel for McVey during his last months in office.

At the last board meeting of 1939, the committee reviewing O'Bannon's case submitted its report. The board then moved to inform O'Bannon that he had officially been transferred to the Kentucky agricultural experiment station. During that same meeting McVey reported that construction on the biological sciences building and the home economics building had been delayed. Graham submitted that the delays were the result of labor strikes both on campus and in the factories producing the materials. Later McVey learned that the grant money had run out and that the university did not have enough left to finish the two structures. He expressed frustration with Graham and with himself for not catching the error, noting that the miscalculation was "embarrassing." Further, problems with the central heating plant continued to plague the campus.[109]

Board members noted that O'Bannon had penned yet another letter protesting his permanent transfer to the College of Agriculture. This letter, which was not made public, infuriated the trustees, who then adopted a motion purporting that O'Bannon had committed "a grave offense against the proper administration of the University of Kentucky." The board added that writing such a letter proved that "Professor O'Bannon is not competent or efficient to perform the duties of his position." It then called on O'Bannon to apologize to McVey, Graham, and the Board of Trustees. Failure to do so would result in his being fired.[110]

The local press obtained a copy of the minutes of the meeting and subsequently reported the resolution calling on O'Bannon to apologize. The papers presented the issue as one of academic freedom and freedom of speech. McVey conceded that O'Bannon had a right to express his opinions, but the board believed he had exceeded that right by accusing the president and others of lying. McVey wrote that those opposed to Dean Graham had used this opportunity to criticize him and the building campaign: "So a disagreeable mess was created that looked bad and all of it fell on me to correct." The president regretted that these events were occurring "at the close of the long service I have had here," but he thought the agitation would continue as long as feelings about the dean ran high.[111]

The *Lexington Leader* editorial revealed the extent of the frustration with the problems on campus. It claimed that the issues involved were deeper than O'Bannon's apparent rebellion. "So much resentment and so much of misgiving exist generally at the University with respect to Dean Graham," the paper contended, that the situation could not be resolved easily. A number of petitions supporting O'Bannon circulated around campus. One from the College of Law stated, "It is obvious to all who wish to look that certain new buildings, notably the Student Union Building and Lafferty Hall (the law building), are already breaking into cracks and leaking badly during any extended rains." Further expenditures and attempted repairs had not succeeded. O'Bannon's criticisms seemed to predict these problems, and the eighty-nine law students signing the petition concurred that "rather than being censured, Professor O'Bannon deserves praise for daring to bring this state of affairs into the open."[112]

The *Kentucky Kernel* ran its own editorial concerning the controversy, which included excerpts from an exclusive interview with McVey. The president stated that he and O'Bannon had met to discuss the issue and that the professor had agreed it was not an issue of freedom of speech. McVey added his view that the buildings' architecture "is irrelevant to the question under discussion. Consequently many things are being said that add heat but no light to the solution of the problem." In sum, the real issue concerned O'Bannon's transfer from the College of Engineering, not the building campaign. Hence, the controversy was an internal affair and would be handled by university authorities.[113]

McVey thought the *Kentucky Kernel* editorial was "excellent." Not everyone agreed. Student Mark Harris wrote an open letter to the president, arguing that McVey's comments were "for the avowed purpose of casting light" on the situation but that they had failed to do so. Harris did not claim to understand the controversy, but he was looking for the truth and viewed McVey's comments as "the epitome of evasiveness." He challenged McVey's remark that the new architecture was irrelevant to the current controversy, insisting that it was an integral to the discussion. He cited the law protecting tenured professors unless they exhibited "incompetency, neglect of, or refusal to perform his duty, or for immoral conduct," and argued that the board might be violating this law. Responding to McVey's assertion that the O'Bannon controversy was an internal affair, Harris declared that UK was a public university, "the personalities involved are public servants; the law is public law; and the controversy is a public matter."[114]

The *Kernel* countered by denying that it was evading the issue because it was being censored. The editor suggested that the paper had not been censored but had remained quiet because it was witnessing "a juvenile squabble and declined to choose sides." The professors' attacks made "the UK campus seem more like a Punch-and-Judy show than one of the greatest educational institutions in the South." The editor added, "We have seen jealousy and pettiness and prima-donna temperament take precedence over tolerance and gentlemanly conduct."[115]

The editorial continued, "To us it doesn't matter a plugged nickel who was 'right' and who was 'wrong.'" However, "the Union clubrooms stifle and the Union plaster is cracking and the classrooms in the Biological Sciences building are so hot in April, May, and September they make one feel like an inmate of the Black Hole of Calcutta." It added that during a hard rain in April the law professors put up a sign in the flooded building reading, "Lafferty Lake—no fishing, swimming, or boating allowed." Speaking on behalf of the students, the paper's editor asserted that he no longer cared who was responsible, as long as someone would agree to help remedy the situation. Students were tired of seeing "grown men living by the kindergarten philosophy of 'If you won't play the game my way, then

I won't play at all.'" They reminded professors that "the reputation of the University of Kentucky hangs in the balance."[116]

The *Lexington Leader* then reported that an odor in the law school building had become virtually unbearable. The only comfortable rooms were the ones in which the windows had been shattered. It also printed an open letter from Stephen White Jr., a 1939 law graduate who said he considered the law school "to be the best in the South." White added, however, that the "the new law building is not one worthy to be on the Kentucky campus," and he supported the students' protests. Letters similar to White's began flooding McVey's office. One student who contended that students had planted ivy against the union to cover mistakes made by Graham was confronted by a group of engineering students who tossed him into a pond on campus.[117]

Students then planned a meeting to address the controversy and placed fliers around campus announcing it. McVey allowed roughly one thousand students to assemble, despite protests from students in the College of Engineering. The following day the *Kentucky Kernel* called on the board to create a committee to examine the complaints being made by faculty members, students, and citizens concerning O'Bannon's position and the quality of the construction on campus. The Executive Committee of the Board of Trustees held a meeting to discuss what to do and decided that the university would "issue no statement but ride out the storm."[118]

A dejected McVey wrote, "It is rather discouraging too that no one comes to help or any alumnus writes to the papers supporting the building program." As the president and the board remained silent, articles continued to appear questioning the logic of the president, the board, and Dean Graham. Graham decided to offer a press release detailing the savings his architecture had provided the university. He argued to the board that without such cost-cutting measures, the university would have been unable to build two or three of the buildings.[119]

Many wondered publicly why the president defended Dean Graham. While McVey noted the dean's arrogance and abrasive personality in his diary, he rarely failed to comment that Graham had helped UK. Thomas Clark argued that McVey needed Graham's political connections to secure federal funding. While McVey could have fired Graham for his antics, no other individual during the president's tenure had been so successful in procuring the money that McVey so badly needed. Another explanation involved the way in which Graham, a military man, addressed his superiors. In one letter to Governor Chandler, Graham opened by writing, "My dear most royal Highness." After many other accolades, he closed, "Your most obedient and loving vassal, J. H. Graham." His gallant style toward those above him did not extend to faculty members, and his caustic attitude was not fit for an academic institution. McVey's comments made years into his retirement illustrate the president's predicament. He praised Graham's ability to bring in funds, but noted that Graham's "one trouble . . . was in personal relations." Frances McVey focused on this aspect of the situation. In a private conversation with Thomas Clark, she noted that hiring Graham was the biggest mistake of Frank McVey's presidency.[120]

————•————

While McVey dealt with issues of politics and finances, the faculty began to focus on the choice of the next president. One underlying fear was that Dean Graham, who had engendered the disdain of many professors, might actually become McVey's successor. Faculty and administrators began openly discussing succession as early as 1937. O'Bannon had written to McVey, "For God's sake, Mr. President, don't spoil an outstanding successful administration and jeopardize your own reputation by bequeathing to the University a man of his personality."[121]

Other inside contenders gradually became known. To McVey's chagrin, his friend Ray Hughes intimated that Dean William Taylor in the College of Education would be the best man on campus to follow McVey. Taylor wrote McVey concerning the comment, wanting to know whether McVey had encouraged Hughes's statement and noting that he hoped he would be given the position. The president replied that Hughes's comment was "gratuitous" and that he would not recommend any individual. Instead he hoped to provide the board with a list of the personal characteristics he felt were crucial to insure the next president's success.[122]

Although the faculty continued to mull the issue, the press and the president did not give it much attention until after Happy Chandler lost his senatorial bid. Rumors then began to fly that Chandler coveted the presidential position. In January 1939, however, Chandler had said he would not take the post. McVey wrote in his diary that "the statement is timely because it will relieve a good many people of apprehension." Richard Stoll, longtime board member and confidant of the president, was not yet consoled. He told McVey that the board needed to wait until after the 1939 governor's race had been decided. Another faculty member seconded this view, stating that many professors were worried about the "danger of politics entering" the presidential search. With that in mind, McVey announced to the board in June 1939 that he would turn seventy on 10 November. The board then asked the president to serve the full 1939–1940 academic year and formed a committee to begin looking for his replacement. The committee consisted of five board members, as well as four faculty members. Judge Stoll chaired the committee, and the faculty members included deans Graham and Cooper.[123]

The following month, without any prospects in sight, Chandler changed his original stance and announced that he would consider the presidency. The governor added that he would not accept the post if it caused controversy, but almost immediately the conflict began. John Young Brown, who was running for governor against Chandler's choice, Lieutenant Governor Keen Johnson, stated that if Chandler became president and he was elected governor, he would remove Chandler from the post. Johnson, who was aligned with Chandler's camp in the Democratic Party, was put in a difficult position. He responded that he would not interfere with the Board of Trustees' choice for the next president. However, if Johnson won the governorship, he would become the chair of the board.[124]

The following week an anonymous group called "Friends of the University of Kentucky" printed a pamphlet and distributed it around campus. It begged, "SAVE U. OF K.," and argued that Chandler would "inject politics into the University of Kentucky." Citing Louisiana State University (and the influence exerted upon it by Huey Long) as an example, the pamphlet noted, "We have all seen to what low estate schools descend when politicians are put at the helm." The university had become a "source of pride to every Kentuckian," as it had been freed from politics under McVey's direction. The leaflet closed, "We ask your help to save it from the vaulting ambition of a designing politician." McVey commented on the pamphlet in his diary, stating that it was "cleverly done and made a considerable impression." He noted that many faculty members wanted to make a public statement against having a politician named UK's next president.[125]

The governor, however, was not without his supporters. One faculty member, Howell Spears, mailed a letter to Chandler expressing his support for the governor and attached the pamphlet to reveal the attitudes on campus. Chandler thanked Spears for the letter and stated that Kentuckians would have to determine who the real "friends" of the university were. Chandler accused UK professor Grant Knight of writing the pamphlet and spoke with McVey about the matter. Knight was on vacation, but when he returned, he stated that he would never attack anyone anonymously and that he had not written the pamphlet. The governor responded that if Knight indeed had not written the diatribe, he would "be glad to forget the whole thing." He did, however, want to know who had penned what he described as "the most unjustified, meanest pamphlet in my judgment that was prepared in the dirtiest campaign in the history of Kentucky."[126]

Others in Lexington also supported the governor. A letter appeared in the *Lexington Herald* in which twelve prominent businessmen encouraged the Board of Trustees to appoint Chandler as the next president. They stated that they were motivated not by politics, but by fear that a great Kentuckian might leave the commonwealth to find employment elsewhere. McVey wrote in his journal that he read the names of the signers "with some amazement because I found it difficult to understand how these men could have such a meager idea of the office of the University president." He noted that Chandler had some ability but argued that "he is not cut out for such a job."[127]

Just as it appeared that Chandler might create a serious challenge for the presidency, fate changed the governor's course and possibly the course of the university. Kentucky's junior senator, M. M. Logan, died unexpectedly on 3 October 1939, only months before the end of Chandler's term. Chandler resigned as governor, and the new governor, Keen Johnson, appointed "Happy" to the U.S. Senate. Chandler had his political post, and the controversy surrounding the presidency ended anticlimactically.[128]

With Chandler out of the picture, the search committee could begin its work in earnest. McVey, who did not want to supply just his own opinions, solicited ideas from prominent higher-education officials throughout the nation. McVey received a letter from Walter Jessup of the Carnegie Foundation, who stated, "You have been in Kentucky so long and your success has been so evident that you ought to stay there permanently. No one can fill your place or that of the 'First lady in Kentucky.'" Jessup, however, did submit names of possible candidates. McVey then wrote a short letter with two attachments. The first listed more than a dozen men who McVey thought would be strong possibilities. The second attachment, which McVey entitled "The Sort of Man Needed for a University President," included an account of what that individual would have to do in order to succeed in his post. His ideas clearly reflected his experience in Kentucky:

I

Essential Qualities

1. Integrity, honesty and trustworthiness of the highest order.
2. Unselfishness, and a real desire to serve each employee.
3. Rugged health.

II

Almost as essential as No. I

4. An understanding of a University, its objectives and ideals, of teaching, research and scholarship, sufficient to enable him to plan wisely and intelligently for the institution.
5. Sound financial judgment, not expertness or technical knowledge, but competency to prepare a budget, to keep it in balance, and understand clearly what is going on financially.

6. Ability and experience in administration.

III
Very desirable

7. A wife who will strengthen and support him.
8. Reasonable social competency.
9. Some scholarly accomplishment would help.
10. The chances of a man really succeeding who has not taught on a college faculty are not good.
11. His Board of Trustees will always be conservative and they want a man who they believe has his feet on the ground.

What the President must be able to do if at all successful.
1. He must retain the confidence of his faculty.
2. He must be able to win and retain the regard of the students and work with them without undue friction.
3. He must gain and retain the confidence of the Trustees.
4. He must win some kind of respectable standing with the alumni which will hold even if the athletic teams are not so good.
5. He should gradually gain the confidence of the people of the state.[129]

In order to seek out candidates, McVey traveled to the Northeast, stopping first in Cambridge on an unannounced visit, hoping to speak with Dumas Malone, director of the Harvard University Press, and with economist John H. Williams, among others. His trip was "futile," however, as he was unable to find anyone in their offices. The following day McVey visited the Carnegie Foundation, where he spoke with Walter Jessup and Frederick Keppel. The president narrowed the list that he hoped to present to the board. In November he attended a conference where John Tigert, who had worked at UK before accepting the presidency at Florida, told McVey that he was interested in the position.[130]

During the entire search the committee seemed to be relying heavily upon McVey, even though he was not a member of the official search team. In addition, McVey felt pressure from members of his own faculty. E. G. Trimble, writing on behalf of the UK chapter of the AAUP, wrote, "We [the faculty] are all concerned that a hasty decision not be made and that we have an opportunity to be heard." McVey wrote in his diary, "I can see [in the letter] the hand of some of our campus politicians." Dean Graham, who had created his own firestorm, told McVey that considering the situation on campus and in the state, the next president would not last two years and that Graham himself would retire when McVey left office, before the situation worsened. Finally, Dean Taylor regularly reminded the president that he wanted the job. At the University Senate meeting on 12 December 1939, many faculty members stated that they wanted the composition of the presidential search committee changed, so that the faculty could have a larger say in the matter rather than an advisory role. The vote failed 42–52, and the entire process became increasingly irritating to McVey.[131]

The president met with board members on 15 December to share his thoughts. He was asked to narrow the prospects, with the input of the faculty committee, and provide a short list to Stoll. The committee would then "go forward with the selection" in January. At that meeting the group decided on the top three candidates, each a university president: Charles Friley of Iowa State College, Harmon Caldwell of the University of Georgia, and A. A. Hauck of the University of Maine. Dean Cooper favored Tigert at the University of Florida, but apparently others had reservations, because his name did not appear on the short list.[132]

After the names had been presented, the committee did nothing for a month, and McVey grew restless. Stoll must have been unimpressed with the list, as he came by McVey's office in early February to say that he thought Dean Cooper would be the best possible candidate. The following day at a meeting of the Executive Committee of the Board of Trustees, Stoll announced his support for Cooper, but McVey said "there was no consensus of opinion." McVey did not offer an opinion, causing Stoll to say that he wished the president would "take a definite stand."[133]

The search committee then held a secret meeting that McVey knew about but did not attend. Before the meeting Stoll again asked McVey for his opinions. McVey would not name a candidate, but he did reiterate three key issues that had already been discussed. First, the candidate needed academic experience. Graduate training, research, and teaching experience were all required to understand the nature of the university. Second, the person had to be the right age (neither too young nor too old) and extremely healthy in order to meet the physical demands of the job. Finally, McVey thought the candidate should be someone from outside Kentucky. McVey did not, however, want to argue the point further, because it had already been discussed in previous meetings.[134]

The committee finally chose its leading candidate and asked McVey to write to President Friley at Iowa State. In his letter he mentioned the progress that had been made and said he hoped that the Frileys would be willing to meet Stoll in Chicago to discuss the matter. It appears that Friley declined by phone, because the following month Stoll tried to schedule a meeting in Atlanta with Caldwell of the University of Georgia. McVey told the committee chair that he did not think Caldwell would come because "he was acclimated to Georgia." Apparently, this was indeed the case; his name never surfaced again. Hauck at the University of Maine fell out of favor, and no attempt was made to contact him. Stoll continued to express his preference for Thomas Cooper, but while McVey thought he was a satisfactory choice, he feared that the dean would not be interested.[135]

McVey became increasingly frustrated with the committee and felt that many board members, Stoll chief among them, were obsessed with worries of accidentally hiring someone infected with "radicalism." In April McVey wrote in his diary that the board members had not been "handling the new presidency situation any too wisely so the newspapers are commenting on it." The *Lexington Leader* and the *Louisville Courier-Journal* both considered Taylor a frontrunner, but despite news reports, the committee had shown no interest in the dean. The committee's progress stalled. One member conceded, "There is not a chance in the world of selecting a president by June."[136]

Plagued by controversies and uncertainties, McVey found himself attempting to write his farewell speech for the June commencement. He practiced his first speech on Frances, who did not like it. She told him that this was "no time for a learned discussion of educational and administrative matters." Instead she encouraged her husband to offer "a personal and rather tender talk on the years gone by." McVey agreed and reworked his speech accordingly. The president would have to consider his long career in order to minimize the struggles of his last years, which had been particularly devastating to Frances. As her niece Chloe Gifford, who lived at Maxwell Place with them, later noted, "His last two years were pretty frightening." Gifford revealed that Frank had weakened in his last years as a result of a lack of funding, which created numerous tensions. Frances, she stated, loved two things in life: Frank and the University of Kentucky. The criticisms that he faced left her with a "great deal of distrust and feeling against some of the wives of the faculty members."[137]

McVey's public pronouncements in his last weeks as president addressed funding. He spoke to a group of alumni at the Lexington Country Club, arguing that the university needed to keep growing but that expansion demanded "alumni interest, good men in the staff and money." The following day McVey escaped Lexington and flew from Cincinnati to New York City to speak to another alumni group. He again pointed out the need for UK to keep growing and shared his fear that the university would hit a "plateau" rather than make material progress. The "spiritual growth" of the university depended upon material provisions.[138]

During McVey's final weeks in office, the papers shifted from complaints to praise for his long and successful administration. The faculty held a banquet in his honor where many faculty members spoke of the president's accomplishments. He was presented with a large leather book of letters from nearly 350 friends, congratulating him on his successes. The *Kentucky Kernel* provided a lengthy tribute to the executive, whose tenure had begun before many of the graduating seniors were born. The *Lexington Herald*, after stating that Frances had "multiplied her husband's influence a hundred-fold in the University community and in Kentucky," listed excerpts from dozens of letters from university presidents around the country.[139]

On 7 June, the same day as commencement, the board accepted L. S. "Pat" O'Bannon's formal apology to the president and received a statement from Graham defending his building program. The board approved McVey's change of work status, and as of 1 July he was no longer president, but a professor emeritus of agricultural economics. As the committee had yet to find McVey's replacement, Dean Cooper accepted the position of "acting president."[140]

During the commencement ceremony held on Stoll Field, Frank and Frances were honored for their long service to the university. As McVey gave his speech, he relived the changes that had occurred on campus and praised his true companion for her help. He predicted that there would be new frontiers to conquer but added that the great war raging in Europe was a reminder that the university needed to develop students to help the commonwealth and the country find the proper path in a world full of possibilities—good and bad. The new era required "courage, fortitude, courtesy, honesty of mind, wisdom, [and] understanding. May to each of you come opportunities and joy."[141]

Whether the crowd actually heard him was another matter. Just as McVey began his speech, a severe thunderstorm rolled across Lexington, but McVey continued. As for the graduates, faculty, and spectators, they finally had a chance to pay him unusual respect by sitting through a deluge complete with lightning and thunder. McVey said in his diary, "No event in the history of the University will be remembered as long as the Commencement of 1940 by the present generation of students and those who attended the event." McVey admitted, "The real performance was the coming of the rain, the clapping of thunder and the continuance of the performance clear to the end."[142]

In the days following graduation, McVey began transporting his belongings to his new office and to his new home. Then, on 29 June 1940, Frances met him at the president's office, and they stood together, "looking at the place while a flood of memories went thru our mind." In his stoic fashion, McVey added, "It might have been a sad time, but I have closed my mind to the emotional side of cutting ties of more than 20 years." The McVeys turned the page.[143]

Chapter 7

Turning the Page
1940–1953

Remember Kentucky, you who live elsewhere. Remember it for its beauty, its kindly living. And more than that give your voice, your interest, and your purse to its forward movement in present day industry and education.
—Frank LeRond McVey, 20 October 1928

Turning the page meant leaving Maxwell Place, McVey's home for nearly a quarter of a century. It was the home where he had raised his children; held his wife's funeral; celebrated his second marriage; and entertained intellectuals, politicians, and celebrities from around the world. Frances McVey had made Maxwell Place ground zero for Lexington intellectual and social life. As he approached retirement, Frank McVey sometimes talked with Frances about how he would spend his time as president emeritus. He yearned to write, and he entertained thoughts of moving to California or Florida. Ultimately, however, he preferred to stay closer to family and friends. In 1939 the McVeys purchased a lot on Shady Lane, in a new development just south of Lexington's limits.[1]

McVey eagerly anticipated being involved in the development of plans for his new home. Influenced by the university's building program while he was president, McVey contemplated a "modern" house with a flat roof and simple lines. In his diary he predicted that flat roofs with nontraditional floor plans would become commonplace but quickly added, "It may be a long time before there is any marked departure from the conventional style." He anticipated that his new neighbors might not look favorably on his new home and would "think us queer and I am sure they will criticize it."[2]

Nevertheless, McVey pushed ahead with his house plans and began working with an architect. When the home was built, neighbor and longtime supporter Thomas Clark recalled that Lexingtonians "could not get away from church fast enough" for their Sunday drives to see "McVey's Folly." The spectators choked both Tahoma Road and Shady Lane. The *Courier-Journal* reported that "the new home of the McVeys has Lexington in a dither. Bluegrass folks are bewildered and they describe the place, with brows uplifted, by a single word, 'Interesting.'" The paper added that the house provided "the choicest bit of controversial gossip in Lexington." The McVeys were still living at Maxwell Place, so there were traffic jams on Shady Lane as people inspected the architecture to "gape and throw up [their] collective hands in horror."[3]

After all the architectural disputes on campus, McVey was sensitive to such criticism. Upon receiving a favorable review of the house, he wrote that it "fell on grateful ears." Once in their new home, the McVeys enjoyed it immensely. McVey took pleasure in owning his own home, which gave him a greater sense of identity. After spending an evening simply sitting on the porch with Frances, he reflected, "The peace and quiet seemed to permeate one's being. I tried to recall a feeling as deep as this one, of real contentment and well being."[4]

As a fall semester began at UK for the first time in twenty-three years without McVey as president, McVey noted, "I find no difficulty in bearing up over my exclusion tho I am sure I could help if asked, but the new regime does not know how to handle the emeritus as yet." A week later McVey slipped into the back of the auditorium at the semester's first convocation. He noted, "Some people I was told were disturbed by the fact I was not on the platform. It would have been a pleasant invitation." Although interim president Thomas Cooper occasionally sought McVey's opinion, the president emeritus offered little formal assistance. Instead McVey filled his time with other activities. He taught a class in agricultural economics, and the couple began traveling. In 1940 McVey spoke at the University of Minnesota before going on to Des Moines, so that Frances could visit Frank's boyhood home. In September he traveled to the University of Pennsylvania to participate in its bicentennial celebration, featuring President Roosevelt. As the weather grew colder, the McVeys headed south, and Frank addressed the Southern Association of Colleges and Schools. Then they traveled to the University of Florida, where Frank gave three speeches in Gainesville before touring the state.[5]

When not traveling, the McVeys entertained, gardened, read, and babysat grandchildren. Both also turned their attention to writing. McVey chose a history of education in Kentucky as his first topic. At the same time Frances began organizing and editing McVey's speeches, presentations, and publications penned during his presidency. These years brought the McVeys contentment and bliss in the company of one another. Writing to Frank in 1941, Frances rejoiced in their love and in their "flat top house . . . built for us and lived in by us. I thank you for all you are to me and for all you are always doing for me to make life radiant and interesting and beautiful and useful." [6]

Finding contentment in their personal lives, the McVeys were still affected by events beyond their control. Their initial problems were with the University of Kentucky. Acting President Cooper told McVey shortly after he left office that Dean James Graham had called to ask his opinion on a matter on behalf of board member Judge Richard Stoll. McVey and Cooper agreed that it was inappropriate for Dean Graham to be a liaison to the board. While not considering Graham's motives sinister, McVey believed that Graham's involvement with the board "would wreck the administration."[7]

President Cooper's time in office, however, was short-lived and provided little opportunity for meddling by anyone. Many influential people, including Governor Keen Johnson, hoped Cooper would turn his interim presidency into a permanent one, but he declined. When he stepped down, the board named Herman Lee Donovan, then president of Eastern Kentucky State Teachers College, as Cooper's successor. However, at the meeting naming Donovan president, the Board of Trustees made several sweeping administrative changes. Most controversial was the replacement of the University Senate by a new body called "The Faculty of the University," which ironically consisted only of administrators. Although both the *Kentucky Kernel* and the University Senate formally opposed the move, the board's decision stood. The senate held its last meeting on 4 June 1941.[8]

Upon learning of the demise of the body he had helped build, McVey wrote that the new plan sounded like "Graham had set up the frame work and Judge Stoll & Hobson had provided the incentive and the feeling about tightening up the organization." He added, "The Board has acted in the most high handed way refusing to allow the faculty to have any part in making the changes." Exactly who provided the impetus for this reform remains unknown, although years later McVey attended a dinner honoring Dean Graham at which Robert Hobson, a board member, stated that Graham had worked with governors Chandler and Johnson to devise the plan. Whatever the origin, the abolition of the senate revealed the extent of McVey's administrative acumen.[9]

McVey had not been consulted about the senate's dissolution, further underscoring his distance from the university. However, these academic squabbles paled in comparison to the expanding crisis in Europe and growing concern that the United States' involvement was inevitable. Nine months before Pearl Harbor McVey commented, "We are in the midst of a war." McVey contemplated military service in an office capacity but doubted his age would allow it. Instead he pledged to "speak for our principles and the doctrine of free people."[10]

McVey traveled extensively speaking about "The American Way" and delivered four nationwide radio addresses over the Mutual Broadcasting System. He defended the nation's war production, believing that a German victory over England would result in a threat to the American way of life, as well as a diminished U.S. role in world affairs. Believing that Japan would risk too much by attacking the United States, he nevertheless speculated, "What a desperate country will do when faced with loss of prestige and believing that her future is jeopardized cannot be fully foretold." He concluded that if the Japanese were confident of a German victory against Russia, "the die will be cast for war against this country."[11]

The die was in fact cast, and after Pearl Harbor McVey wrote, "Undoubtedly our country is faced with a long war that will be won because we can out-produce the enemy." McVey desired to help, and his prestige in Kentucky created opportunities. He was asked to chair a committee to sell war bonds. However, he stated that he would "much prefer" to accept President Donovan's offer to lead a seemingly different university war effort. The job involved organizing the Key Center, which was established by the U.S. Office of Education to gather and distribute information on the war and to boost morale. McVey thus accepted Donovan's invitation, believing that the center provided a great opportunity to explain the purpose and necessary outcomes of the war. In March McVey also "succumbed" to a petition from John D. Rockefeller Jr. to serve as state chair of the United Service Organization (USO) to raise funds through the sale of war bonds, an activity at which McVey had originally balked. The work of the two committees took a considerable amount of time throughout the rest of the year, while McVey also continued his speaking engagements throughout the Midwest. In all, McVey helped raise approximately $150,000 in 1942, in addition to organizing the information at the Key Center.[12]

In 1943 McVey resigned his position with the USO in order to accept a unique international invitation. The Universidad Central de Venezuela had grown considerably during the previous decades, but buildings to accommodate the expanding student body had been purchased haphazardly, and the campus sprawled throughout Caracas. The government had decided to end this disjointed growth pattern and organize a new higher-education complex on a single campus. The Venezuelan government informed McVey that it planned to construct a massive higher-education complex and had selected a hacienda on the outskirts of the capital for the development. "In order to better adapt these plans to the purposes of the institution," McVey was asked to visit the campus site and offer his expert opinion on the educational program. He would then confer with the university architects on the educational plan and ways in which it could best be integrated into the physical plant.[13]

McVey agreed to make the trip on the condition that Frances could accompany him. The government granted the request, and the McVeys left for South America on 29 March 1943. McVey's decision to bring Frances proved to be a wise one. During his first week in Venezuela he became seriously ill. Fighting a high fever, he was draped in icy towels and given aspirin. Frances wrote in Frank's diary that she was "terror stricken," as Frank had begun "wandering in his mind." When McVey was taken to the local hospital, the culprit was determined to be McVey's gall bladder. Rather than performing surgery, McVey's doctors decided to keep a close watch on him for a week. Frank's condition slowly improved over the next two weeks, and a month after arriving, McVey was finally ready to begin his study of the university.[14]

He consulted on both academics and architectural plans. Along with a team of architects and officials, McVey visited Hacienda Ibarra, the site of the proposed campus. The group suggested a number of changes to the initial architectural plans, including shifting the center of the campus so that it would provide better views of the city. A change in the entrance along with other modifications, McVey believed, would create a more unified campus. He met with chief architect Carlos Raul Villanueva to discuss potential modifications and remarked that the architect immediately began altering his plans to incorporate McVey's ideas. During the next weeks, McVey met with officials and university administrators in order to learn more about their vision. He noted that he was addressing the types, sizes, and uses for the facilities, adding, "I am not only expected to say what their buildings should be but what should go into them." He worked closely on the administration building, library, and auditorium, which were to be the central buildings on campus.[15]

McVey worked through other stomach problems as he wrote his lengthy report. He warned, "Never come to the tropics without Pepto-Bismal [sic]." Upon completing his report, he discussed construction issues, arguing that the university needed to create a twenty-year plan. However, most of the report dealt with the intricacies of university structure and governance. Of prime importance, as McVey had experienced at Kentucky, was making sure that the university was free from political interference.[16]

McVey met again with Villanueva and discussed the cost of the project, which was estimated at $17 million over fifteen years. McVey felt that the projected costs of some buildings were too high and recommended that the estimates be lowered. He was rebuffed, however, by Villanueva, who argued that they did not know what the final amount received would be, so they needed to keep estimates high in order to get all the money they could, a practice McVey refused to adopt when he was president at UK. As he wrote in his diary, "Human nature is pretty much the same in South America as it is in the states." After a brief meeting with Venezuelan president Isaias Medina, the McVeys began their journey back to Kentucky on 12 June 1943.[17]

After returning to Lexington, McVey resumed his duties, this time as president of the USO and state chair of the State War Fund. He found that holding two posts that focused on similar activities confused people, but he continued just the same. As McVey worked to help Kentucky meet its financial quotas, he used his public position to urge the state to begin preparing for the end of the war and the return of Kentucky's soldiers. As he said in a radio address to the state, "There is much need for careful and systematic planning if we are to deal with the problems which will face us on the coming of peace." He pressed for a state planning board to put soldiers back to work on public projects, but he also urged coordination with all the state's institutions of higher education.[18]

Throughout this period, McVey's health remained a serious concern. While he was eating dinner at his daughter Virginia's house, McVey's gall bladder attack became so severe that he and Frances had to leave early and make a house call to family physician and friend John Chambers. The physician gave McVey pain medication to help him sleep, but the attacks continued, and his skin grew jaundiced. Frances was extremely worried about her husband. After a series of X-rays, the doctors decided to change Frank's diet, and slowly he began to improve.[19]

McVey began filling his schedule with work, regularly commenting in his diary about how busy he was in retirement. His war work, his committee work at UK, social events such as his "Book Thieves'" regular meetings, and his research and writing of a history of education in Kentucky took a great deal of time. Frances was working on her book project as well. Sponsored by the university's publications committee, she had been working for nearly three years to organize and edit McVey's articles and addresses into one volume. By September 1944, the page proofs of "Frances' Book" were ready for examination. Both Frank and Frances were pleased with it.[20]

As McVey worked, his health seemed fine, but Frances's health began to concern the McVeys. After months of continued coughing, Frances began coughing up blood. Dr. Chambers immediately sent Frances to the hospital. While McVey was working on a project with retired registrar Ezra Gillis, Chambers found the president emeritus and asked to speak with him privately. He stated that Frances might have lung cancer and that she needed surgery as quickly as possible. Frances had an exploratory out-patient procedure the next day in Lexington. The doctors did not find anything, but they recommended that the McVeys travel to Ann Arbor, Michigan, to consult with a specialist.[21]

Within two days the McVeys were off to Michigan, and by the week's end, Frances had agreed to a dangerous surgery to remove cancer spreading in her left lung. During the operation the surgeon came out and informed Frank that the cancer was "widespread and he might have to go farther than he at first thought." Although Frances's life would be placed at great risk, he asked for permission to remove her left lung. Failure to do so, the doctor argued, would result in a long and painful death. McVey trusted the surgeon's expert opinion, and the lung was removed.[22]

Frances survived the surgery, and the surgeons were confident that by removing the lung they had removed the source of the cancer. However, they were not sure if it had already spread to other areas of the body. As Frances spent time recovering in the hospital, Frank's gall bladder acted up again, and he found himself in a doctor's office as well. His physician believed that his relapse was the result of ignoring his diet while in Michigan. After he began eating properly again, his condition improved somewhat, but he continued to have occasional and excruciating attacks. After spending weeks in recovery, Frances improved and was cleared to leave the hospital. The McVeys returned to Lexington, and Frances slowly regained strength. Neighbor Beth Clark remembered Frances taking long, slow walks around Tahoma Road and Shady Lane, attempting to rebuild her stamina.[23]

That November McVey celebrated his seventy-fifth birthday. Later that month the couple received an advance copy of *A University Is a Place . . . A Spirit* on the day of their twenty-first wedding anniversary. They learned that the compilation would be available to the public on 18 December, and both Frank and Frances felt that it served "as a kind of symbol which summarizes a period of 23 years as president of the University of Kentucky."[24]

Medical problems continued to disturb their retirement. In March 1945, doctors determined that Frank had gall stones that needed to be removed. McVey had to leave Frances and travel to Cincinnati for his surgery. The surgery was a success, but McVey, who was anxious to return home to Frances, had to stay in the hospital two weeks to recover. When Frank arrived in Lexington, he was upset to find that Frances appeared to have had a setback in her own recovery. During April Frances's condition declined. McVey confided in his diary, "I can't believe that she is in great danger. Each day I hope and pray that she will grow stronger." A week later, when she began coughing blood, Frank worried that she was "losing ground" and prayed, "God be good to her and give her a chance." In May Frank was shaken when his wife asked him if she was dying. Frank told her that the doctors believed the cancer had spread into her right lung. Frances "smiled a beautiful smile" and told her husband that she was not afraid to die. She had spent time coming to grips with the short time she had left and felt at peace.[25]

As Frances grew weaker, the couple began talking about Frank's life without her. Frances suggested that McVey's sister Kate move from Kansas City to Lexington to live with her brother after she was gone. As the days went on, McVey cared for his wife and began to plan for the loss that lay ahead. He wrote, "Frances is such a grand person she is greatly loved for her sweet way and generous spirit. There are few like her anywhere. To me she has been a great source of happiness. God bless her now." As Frances became weaker, they began turning away visitors. On 12 June, Frank wrote, "She is losing ground fast and the end cannot be far off." The following day, Frances breathed for the last time, and just after 9:30 P.M. she died.[26]

Hundreds of individuals attended the funeral on 15 June, including both of McVey's brothers. One of the most painful moments for Frank in the days after Frances's death was learning that his wife had purchased a burial plot for herself next to her parents. Chloe Gifford was with him when he learned of the arrangements. She called it "the saddest moment I ever knew," recalling that McVey nearly "broke down." He tried to process this decision in his diary a month after her passing, saying that he was "puzzled why Frances wanted it that way." Gifford remembered that Frances reasoned that Frank needed to be buried with the mother of his children, but it offered Frank little solace.[27]

During the first weeks after Frances's death, McVey struggled with intense loneliness and grief. He grappled with unanswered questions: "I can't understand why these things should happen to her. She had so much to live for & so many plans. Both of us looked forward to a more glorious life together. It was sad, and it is sad now." Six months after Frances's death, Frank recalled her last day: "It is hard to reconcile her death to our need for her and her contributions to the happiness of those she loved." In a separate entry he commented that he missed Frances "more and more." Yet he commented regularly on how much he appreciated the efforts of his family to provide company at Flat Top House (as the McVeys called their modern home). Many different family members stayed with McVey. In September McVey's sister Kate came to live with him, just as Frances had encouraged. As he noted, the presence of others "much reduced" his sadness and isolation, yet there remained an intense "feeling of being much alone."[28]

McVey found it difficult to return to work. He thought that Frances would be upset with his inability to find motivation to return to the research he had been doing before she became ill. Consequently, he made plans to finish his manuscript on education in Kentucky and began toying with the notion of writing a biography of his late wife. McVey also began attending various meetings in Lexington. He continued working on the State War Fund even after World War II had ended. The organization feared that it would be difficult to raise its financial quotas for 1945 since the United States had dropped the atomic bomb and exacted an unconditional surrender from Japan. After attending meetings in late 1945 and early 1946, McVey commented that while the 1945 campaign had fallen short of its fund-raising goal, the state campaigns under his direction as chair had raised approximately $4 million during the previous three years.[29]

After spending New Year's Day without any visitors, McVey decided to get back to work in earnest at the beginning of 1946. He compiled a list of the various organizations, clubs, and agencies on which he had served. These amounted to seventeen, including chair of the Haggin Fund publication committee, vice-president of the Lexington Areas Planning Council, numerous war committee positions that were coming to an end, and his professorship. He said that nine of the seventeen roles required substantial time, but he felt that the work was not too burdensome.

Some of McVey's tasks were unwelcome distractions from the work he would rather be doing. One in particular had been evolving long before Frances passed away. In 1944 a couple of UK alumni had brought suit against the Board of Trustees and Colonel James Graham. Three years earlier Graham had accepted a post in the War Department, earning one dollar a year, while remaining dean of the College of Engineering. In 1943, however, Graham began earning $8,000 annually as special assistant to Under Secretary Robert Patterson. The suit argued that more than $14,000 of Dean Graham's salary should be returned to the state. In April 1944 UK's President Donovan requested that McVey elaborate on Graham's hiring. In a long letter to the president, McVey explained why he had hired Graham and the ways in which the colonel had materially improved conditions in the college. Privately, however, McVey commented that the dean, while valuable to the university, possessed "a gift of making enemies."[30]

The case took an interesting twist when, during his deposition, Graham asserted that McVey had hired him on a part-time basis. When the prosecuting attorneys met with McVey, the president emeritus maintained that while Graham had told McVey he would be working on some projects outside the university, they had never discussed his working as a half-time employee. McVey allowed Graham's work beyond campus because he believed that it helped expose students to new methods and provided them with job opportunities after graduation. The following day, McVey accompanied the lawyers to campus, where they examined personal correspondence, as well as minutes from board meetings. None of it suggested that Graham had been hired on anything but a full-time contract. Regarding the colonel's assertion, McVey stated, "I was greatly surprised to hear that the Dean had made such a statement. Certainly it was not in line with the policy or needs of the college."[31]

The following month Donovan and McVey met with Graham's attorneys. Reflecting on the meeting, McVey stated, "I made myself quite clear on the half-time employment made by Colonel Graham." Despite this, Graham's attorneys argued that the question of part-time employment was simply a "difference in interpretation." Weeks later McVey was asked to offer a formal deposition in which he stated his position again. The president had never considered Graham a part-time employee.[32]

When the lawsuit finally made it to the state circuit court in Frankfort, Judge William Ardery dismissed the case, ruling that earning salaries in two different positions did not warrant just cause to bring a suit against Graham or the university. McVey was relieved. He believed that UK had been "freed from a series of troublesome cases that have been a considerable anxiety." Despite McVey's hopes, however, the controversy had not yet come to an end.[33]

The furor of those possessing enmity toward Dean Graham would not relent. They complained to all who would listen, including members of the General Assembly. While the suit remained on appeal, four students, all of them World War II veterans attending law school, distributed formal complaints to state elected officials in Frankfort. They claimed university morale had suffered due to Graham's antics, the failed building campaign, and poor administrative decisions made during the war, among other things. Two outspoken professors, William Southerland in English and Lester "Pat" O'Bannon, supported the students' criticism. The legislature took it seriously enough to require an investigation of the university and its administration. President Donovan sought McVey's advice for handling it.[34]

On 19 February McVey, Donovan, and other university officials appeared before a House committee investigating the university and its operations. McVey addressed his hiring of Graham and the buildings constructed during his final years as president. McVey found the entire investigation "exasperating" as he listened to students and Professor O'Bannon complain about the university. McVey attended a second meeting the next day at which the university fared better. Numerous students and faculty defended McVey's building program, Donovan's presidency, and general morale at the university. McVey told Donovan that he should find comfort in the words of support.[35]

Ironically, the investigation, in the long run, may have paid dividends for the administration by solidifying support for the university. During the following week, McVey attended the second annual Founders' Day celebration on campus at a packed Memorial Hall. When Donovan asked the crowd, "How is your morale?" he was met with rousing applause. During the final meeting of the investigative committee, McVey interpreted O'Bannon's comments as an apology of sorts for his earlier diatribe.[36]

When the committee presented its opinions to the legislature in March, it expressed its full support of the university and its administration. At the close of the academic year Dean Graham requested a change of work status. The board accepted his petition, and the polarizing figure became a "consultant to the president on building and government relations." The university did not renew assistant professor of English William Southerland's contract, and O'Bannon resigned his post with a year's severance pay. The controversy that had begun a decade earlier finally came to a conclusion. As McVey reflected, the board had finally "removed some irritating situations that have disturbed the peace of the University for many years."[37]

McVey's work on behalf of the university involved more than defending it. After the war and Frances's death, McVey resumed teaching agricultural economics. However, chairing the Haggin Fund Publications Committee afforded McVey his greatest outlet to influence university policy. In that post the president emeritus lobbied to expand funding for a full-fledged university press. In September 1943, the Board of Trustees agreed in principle to McVey's dream by formally creating a university press and making him chair of the Press Committee. However, they did not provide funding for a full-time director. In the meantime Thomas Clark helped McVey by searching for the right person to start such an endeavor.[38]

In 1945 Clark successfully recruited W. H. Stephenson to serve as a history professor and editor of the University of Kentucky Press. Stephenson had taught at UK during McVey's tenure but had left to take a deanship at Louisiana State University. While in Baton Rouge, Stephenson had been involved with its press. After meeting with Stephenson, McVey believed that his experience would serve as an asset for the nascent press in Lexington. During the next months Stephenson and McVey worked to differentiate the responsibilities of the press editor from the role of the Haggin Fund Committee, which was to continue working with the press.[39]

The press served as an outlet for academic research concerning the commonwealth, including McVey's own project. His history of education in Kentucky, which McVey had begun early in his retirement, took longer to complete than he hoped, and now McVey lacked the motivation to continue. Frances Cassidy, who had been doing much of what McVey called "the spade work" on the manuscript, called McVey and offered to return to the task. McVey contemplated the offer, mentioning how difficult Frances's death had been. He was considering abandoning the project but decided that returning to work might "help in taking my mind off of the story of the past year and of starting me on a new effort."[40]

In late 1946 he was still struggling to finish his history of education and asked for an exemption from his course in the College of Agriculture the following year. On New Year's Day he resolved to complete the manuscript: "I want to do it whether I like the idea of digging on the last two chapters." He did continue, despite finding it difficult, especially his chapter on the evolution controversy. His sister Kate assisted in typing and indexing, while Tom Clark provided editorial comments. He submitted his manuscript on 11 August 1947, but it would be more than two years before the press finally published the book.[41]

Part of the problem involved editorial work and indexing, but much of the delay centered around McVey's attempts to formalize a full-fledged university press. Even as chair of the Press Committee, McVey noted that little progress was being made. The delay centered on the requirement that all printing go through the state printer even though that office did not have the capacity or mandate to print books. McVey explained that the increasing volume of university publications and the archaic laws created "confusion and overlapping in the conduct of publishing and printing. So here was a dilemma that must be met and interpreted before grants can be made by the Research Grants for publication." With inadequate financial assistance, heavy teaching responsibilities, and legal limitations, Stephenson could do little to increase the productivity of the press. Therefore, McVey continued to pressure the board to create an on-campus press with a full-time director that would be responsible for its own printing.[42]

In June 1949 McVey and other members of the Press Committee shared these goals with President Donovan. While unwilling to commit to publishing all books on campus due to funding and legal restraints, Donovan agreed to hire a full-time director. In 1950, another one of Thomas Clark's connections paid off as he recommended Bruce Denbo for the directorship. Clark convinced Denbo to leave Louisiana State University Press and come to Lexington. McVey served as chair of the new Press Board. After a board meeting at his house in July 1951, McVey reported that Denbo had accomplished much in less than a year, with seven books in publication. This level of productivity continued, and McVey's long-standing dream of a press had become a reality.[43]

Although McVey's role in medical education during the 1940s and early 1950s at UK was far less formal, he continued to influence decisions that eventually led to the creation of a medical school. McVey had long desired to see a medical college at UK, but as president he had been cautious, refusing to begin the endeavor without guaranteed support. He consulted Dr. John Chambers to establish such a school in 1930 but was unable to gain backing from Kentucky's legislature. He attempted to secure aid from leading national educational foundations without success. In the late 1930s, Governor Chandler raised the issue with McVey, but once again the money was not forthcoming.[44]

Casual discussions of a medical school continued even during the war, when such plans were unrealistic. Not until after Frances's death did Chambers approach McVey (before talking with President Donovan) about formulating a plan to develop a medical school. McVey suggested that Chambers write a formal proposal outlining the reasons for the college and share his ideas with Donovan. Chambers did so, and within weeks he and Donovan took the idea to a legislative council subcommittee. The council recommended that Donovan increase his requested appropriations by approximately $1 million for the 1946 General Assembly to cover the funds needed for a medical center. Upon learning this, McVey wrote, "This is a new slant on legislative attitudes. In my day I was always asked to cut down what the university was asking."[45]

Before the 1946 legislative session, McVey met with Donovan and Chambers to formulate a strategy for a medical program. The group determined that beyond funding from the legislature, the effort would require private financial support from wealthy Kentuckians. Dr. Chambers would write a formal proposal, and McVey would speak with Dr. Fred Rankin, a prominent Lexington physician who Donovan believed needed to be centrally involved if the medical school were to succeed. Rankin favored the proposal, but he was not as optimistic about raising private funds to subsidize the center. He was well-connected with the Bluegrass elite and believed that "they get their money from whiskey and horses, [and] they are not interested in much else."[46]

After decades in Lexington, McVey agreed with Rankin, noting that "horse people are not much interested in education." However, the Hill-Burton Bill, which became federal law in August 1946, provided $75 million annually for the construction of medical facilities across the country. If UK could secure a substantial federal grant, as well as state appropriations and philanthropic gifts, something significant could be accomplished. McVey sensed that "there is something in the air and [it] has enough basis to give hope for a realization of the University's ambition for a real medical school." [47]

McVey's optimism was bolstered by examples of public support for medical education in both North Carolina and Texas. Moreover, Kentucky's only medical school, at the University of Louisville, faced financial and administrative problems, resulting in unsubstantiated rumors that the school would close. McVey understood that having only one medical school in the state and a rapidly growing need for physicians bolstered the university's chances. As he observed, "There is money about and people are looking for a place or for a project in which to drop some of their money." [48]

These hopes never materialized during the 1948 legislative session. Rather than helping UK's efforts, the uncertain situation in Louisville hindered any progress on a medical college in Lexington. Bills were introduced in both chambers to aid the school in Louisville. McVey and Donovan protested, since this amounted to public support of a private (or municipal) institution, but their efforts failed, and the General Assembly appropriated $250,000 for medical research at the University of Louisville. President Donovan did not help the cause when he failed to lend his full support to the issue, fearing that a large appropriation for a medical school would result in decreased funding for the university generally. The issue continued to be raised during the 1950 and 1952 legislative sessions without any tangible results. McVey would not live to see the creation of the UK Medical School, but his behind-the-scenes assistance played a central role in laying the foundations for the college. [49]

———————

There were other elements of university governance over which McVey had virtually no influence, but the issues still consumed much of his thoughts, as reflected in the pages of his diary. Upon leaving the presidency, McVey believed he had placed athletics in its proper place at the university. He did what little he could to keep his policies in place during his retirement. In 1942 he continued to predict that, partially due to the war, "football will come to an end." During a meeting with football coach Ab Kirwan he encouraged an athletic program that would interest a larger section of the student body. McVey noted that after he shared his opinions, the football coach seemed "a bit dazed as tho he saw nothing to it." The former president also admitted, "I may see the possibilities without knowing the difficulties." [50]

Following World War II the pressure for big-time college athletics only grew. Having arrived as football coach with much fanfare during McVey's presidency, Coach Ab Kirwan had been unable to turn around the program. By 1945 the team was in a tailspin. After the team was crushed by Georgia, McVey asked, "Why does the Kentucky team march in the rear?" He knew that the problem was lack of financial support, adding, "If that is the case we are in a bad way because our sources of money are not equal to those possessed by our opponents." After the team lost to Alabama, McVey believed that UK would "endeavor to get money to pay a coach a higher salary and give players support enough to keep Kentucky lads from going to the University's competitors." The president emeritus thought that there would be some improvement but doubted that the university could compete with other SEC teams, adding, "Half way is better than the cellar where the team has resided thru many seasons." [51]

Not only was Donovan more optimistic about sports at UK than McVey, but he also had a different perspective of the importance of athletics within the commonwealth. As historian Charles Talbert noted, McVey's successor became convinced that the university "would never receive proper financial support until it satisfied the desire of a highly vocal portion of the population for a good football team." McVey disagreed, confiding privately that Donovan had given "hours to the matter of football for the past six weeks. Most of his time has gone to the consideration of what should be a comparatively minor matter." Instead of attempting to keep sports a minor issue, Donovan was ready to make it officially bigtime, and his view was also held by Governor Lawrence Wetherby. At the

November board meeting Donovan began his direct departure from McVey's policies by encouraging the creation of the University of Kentucky Athletics Association (UKAA), which the board approved. McVey understood the significance of the move, noting that UK had replicated Florida's approach to create "an incorporated company" whose purpose was to expand athletic fund-raising and keep it "outside of state control."[52]

Donovan immediately set about utilizing the UKAA. Holding a meeting of key boosters in Lexington, he sought to raise funds for the football program and hire a new coach. Boosters gave more than $100,000. Donovan publicly expressed his belief that "there were a million people in KY who identified the progress of the University with football prowess," and he thought that both high academic standards and big-time sports could coexist at the university. After failed attempts to bring Wallace Wade from Duke or Bo McMillan from Indiana University, Donovan and the UKAA settled on Paul Bryant, a young coach from Maryland.[53]

With Coach "Bear" Bryant at the helm and the UKAA supporting the financial side of the athletics program, the Wildcats experienced a dramatic turnaround. The team began beating Southeastern Conference foes by using a much-expanded roster. McVey noted that the coach and the team were met with "great huzzas." After continued victories during the first season, McVey concluded, "Big football is now in the Kentucky field and the public evidently likes it." As success increased, the university began plans to double the size of the football stadium. By 1950 Bryant's team had won its first SEC championship, and on New Year's Day the team defeated the Oklahoma Sooners. Bryant's contract was extended twelve years.[54]

Bryant's success was matched by Rupp's wins on the basketball court. The basketball team regularly dominated the SEC and made numerous trips to the National Invitational Tournament at Madison Square Garden. After the stadium expansion, the university undertook plans to build a coliseum in honor of those who had given their lives in World War II. (This was a marked contrast to McVey's World War I memorial chapel, which was to be used for student convocations.) The sleek, modern Memorial Coliseum also became the site of numerous student gatherings and commencement. More important, it could seat thirteen thousand, with an entire section reserved for state legislators and chairs with backs for the growing group of athletics boosters.[55]

As other state universities used the immediate postwar years to capitalize on increased student enrollment and research, UK chose to stress athletics. McVey lamented, "I am quite disturbed that the University has allowed the [basketball] team to play so many games (34) this season." He naively wondered how student athletes could complete their academic work and worried about the expanding role of sports in student life. By 1949 he complained, "I don't like the exploitation of college students in the business of athletics. It stems in part in the ambition of the coaches." Both McVey and Donovan were correct. The university exploited its athletes, but it appeared that it took big-time athletics for the state to support its ambitions for a medical school. Regardless, McVey and those who shared his views became increasingly marginalized. The growth of the sports program during McVey's retirement revealed the growing pressure on colleges to expand their sports programs and the extent to which a single president had managed to keep this trend at bay during his tenure in office.[56]

Almost as quickly as UK embraced big-time sports, athletic scandals followed. Investigations revealed that three UK basketball players had engaged in a point-shaving scheme while in New York in 1949. The SEC and the National Collegiate Athletics Association (NCAA) reported that two members of the football team had been paid by the UKAA for their services. The university accepted NCAA sanctions, and a saddened McVey noted that the penalties were imposed for infractions that "all of the members of the conference have done." Following a meeting with Donovan, McVey expressed his frustration: "To the president Rupp can do no wrong. I didn't talk much." When Donovan announced that he and the University of Kentucky would accept recruiting regulations agreed upon by all presidents of SEC schools, McVey commented, "Knowing something of the views of these men I can write down that they will hedge and do little."[57]

By the late 1940s McVey retained few formal responsibilities outside local committee memberships. As Cold War tensions mounted in 1948, McVey found himself facing a controversial role. In 1948 President Donovan called McVey to inform him that he had accepted a position on a newly created loyalty board. Donovan asked McVey if he would be interested in serving with him in investigating cases of possible disloyalty among federal employees, as suggested by the FBI.[58]

McVey accepted the position, despite his growing concern about the government's role in seeking out dissenters. As early as October 1947 he had written about the "so-called tests of loyalty." McVey saw "a good deal of insincerity in these investigations" and feared that they were being used to "smear" political opponents. He worried that the United States was headed "for uniformity of thought" where all who "disagree with the maker of a formula [were] to be branded as disloyal."[59]

After agreeing to serve, McVey received a letter from Sixth Region director Louis Lyon, explaining the role of the committee, which had been created by an executive order and was administered through the Civil Service Commission. McVey's responsibility on the six-member committee entailed "adjudicating loyalty cases involving applicants for and appointees to positions in the competitive service of the United States Government." The Sixth Region covered Indiana, Ohio, and Kentucky. President Harry Truman wanted only loyal employees, and Lyon claimed that the committee was not to engage in a "witch hunt," insisting that it was to make "fair and impartial decisions" regarding the "loyalty of government employees." The meetings were held in the Federal Building in Cincinnati, and McVey usually traveled with President Donovan to attend them. After examining twenty-four cases at the first committee session, McVey was pleased with the committee members' "ability, their consideration, and sympathy in dealing with the problems of loyalty."[60]

As the bimonthly meetings continued, McVey became sympathetic with many of the individuals accused of disloyalty or of communist affiliations. For example, McVey cited one African American who had worked with the Communist Party because its leadership had promised to "to help his race," while the Congress of Industrial Organizations (CIO) had offered little. The man under question had sought more prominent posts in his places of employment but failed. After accepting a position as a postal clerk, he abandoned the Communist Party, feeling that he had finally secured a job that would support his family. After hearing the story, McVey "felt sorry for him" and voted for a one-year probationary status, even though some other members thought three years more appropriate.[61]

As the meetings progressed, McVey privately complained that at least one-third of the cases involving federal employees concerned individuals who should have never been hired. Many had records of previous "disorderliness, drunkenness, petty theft, fighting and insubordination." McVey noted that these cases had nothing to do with "lack of loyalty," but with individual character flaws. McVey informed his friend Raymond Hughes, "If the civil service would screen persons picked for position[s] more thoroughly before they are appointed, many of these cases would not come before the committee at all." For some reason, the "slow procedure" of hiring employees with all of its "red tape" had not managed to weed out such poor applicants, whose problems had nothing to do with the Communist Party.[62]

McVey recognized that many of the targeted citizens were African Americans who sought greater equality or immigrants who had had more exposure to communists or whose relatives had been involved with the party. Believing that his loyalty board had not examined one case that "was particularly serious," McVey and the members of the board found many suspects innocent and eligible for employment. The liberal approach taken by McVey's board led University of North Carolina president Frank Graham, who was serving in a national capacity, to comment that the Sixth Region's had proven to be "the most distinguished, wisest and fairest of all the loyalty commissions in the nation."[63]

McVey appreciated such comments, especially as anticommunist fears were reaching hysterical heights with the accusations of Senator Joseph McCarthy. As these fears grew, McVey called the senator's tactics "cowardly" and felt saddened that "people of differing opinions" were "castigated by Members of Congress." He tersely added, "There are more important things to do." As the rhetoric increased and the eighty-year-old

McVey found himself tiring easily, he informed the regional director that since he was unable to attend all the meetings, he was considering resigning his post. Lyons convinced him to continue, saying that he was considering adding committee members so that individuals would not have to participate in every meeting. McVey agreed to continue.[64]

As McVey studied the cases of more individuals, he continued to sympathize with many of their situations. He noted, "I was much impressed with the struggle that these newcomers to the United States have in adjusting themselves to a new environment. This is particularly true of older people." McVey supposed that most had come into contact with communists as they attempted to find "social outlets," not realizing the extent of problems in associating with radical organizers. After meeting with communists, immigrants were placed on mailing lists for the Communist Party, and when this happened they became FBI suspects and were branded disloyal. McVey and his Regional Loyalty Board generally cleared such individuals.[65]

Throughout his service, McVey supported the loyalty boards, while considering the dangers inherent in radicalism. He was cognizant of those who questioned the justice of the boards, noting that some felt the trials created a dangerous precedent and believed, as he said, that "the cost" they imposed on America was "too high." Yet he hoped that their work would deter serious communist threats to the American system. At the same time McVey was convinced that McCarthy had become "a great disgrace to the country." Finally, in 1951, McVey was relieved from his position on the board, which had become more difficult due to health problems. However, he wrote Lyons complaining that in the previous year he had offered to step down, and his offer had been rejected. Upset that he had been "terminated," McVey wished that he would have been allowed to resign.[66]

McVey's tenure on the Sixth Region's loyalty board provided another example of his faith in democracy and reason. Suspicious of witch hunts for "disloyal" Americans, he had come to loathe the increasing influence of McCarthyism in the American psyche. For the aging progressive, however, service on the loyalty board was valuable. It provided him an opportunity to serve his country by offering impartial judgments, while sustaining the existing governmental system.

———•———

Despite having surgery on his gall bladder a few years earlier, McVey remained susceptible to excruciating attacks, even though they were not frequent. In 1948 he blamed one such episode on his diet. When he had another attack in 1949 and noticed that his skin was jaundiced, he wrote, "The attack was my old friend related to a gall bladder situation." In addition to his physical ailments, the president emeritus simply felt exhausted from his level of activity. After his spring class in 1949, McVey wrote the department chair asking that he be relieved from teaching. He did not regard the work he and the students were conducting as meeting graduate-level standards, and he added that even if changes were made, he could not continue. He said, "I find that I tire rather easily and I would hesitate to take on the work of teaching twice a week." [67]

McVey also began lightening his once-relentless public-speaking load. After giving hundreds of addresses in the first years of his retirement, he increasingly questioned the advisability of such engagements. After a speech to the Lexington Rotary Club in 1950 he complained that "the trouble, time and wear . . . was hardly worth the while." The following year, after speaking to the University Women's Club, his address entitled "Citizenship in Peace and War," he wrote, "At the end of it I felt tired and worn . . . certainly a warning not to overdo." [68]

If McVey had not made the decision to reduce his docket, it would have, in some ways, been made for him. Troubled by his enlarged prostate, his doctors recommended that he have surgery. McVey discussed the matter with his children, who would help in nursing him back to health, and they agreed that he should undertake the procedure. He went in for the surgery on 4 May 1951. However, his doctors believed he also needed a second operation, which they conducted a week later. During the second surgery McVey had a "severe hemorrhage of the stomach," caused by an ulcer. His children rushed to the hospital, and for three hours it appeared that their father might die. After several blood transfusions and the necessary procedures McVey recovered from his critical condition. In all, he spent a month in the hospital and many weeks at home recuperating.[69]

Within a few months, McVey's health improved, and he resumed his engagement in the civic life of the university and the town, albeit at a slower pace. After giving a "long anticipated" speech to the UK Arts and Sciences faculty in 1952, McVey noted, "In the past such a speech was part of the day's work, [but] now I feel the pull and the effort that goes with the task of reading a speech." Despite the challenges, McVey managed to give the commencement address and charge to the graduating class of students at University High School in 1952. It was one of his final public-speaking engagements, and he agreed to do it because his grandson Frank McVey III was graduating. McVey had given the charge at this ceremony many times during the past two decades, but in solemn awareness of his limited years, he wrote in his diary that his next grandchild would not graduate for another three years, so it was time for him to relinquish the tradition.[70]

———·•·———

Throughout his retirement McVey remained mentally sharp. He devoured books, reading many titles weekly. During a visit from longtime friend and fellow university president emeritus Raymond Hughes, the two recognized their combined fifty-plus years of presidential experience. Thinking their insights might be worth sharing with young administrators, they agreed on two dozen topics for a book in only a few minutes. When Hughes wrote McVey to formalize plans, McVey expressed trepidation: "It may be that we will . . . let the new presidents get along as best they can without suggestions from us."[71]

McVey had his doubts about the project, but he agreed to start writing. The book required little research, McVey sharing his opinions on the proper way to handle issues that would certainly challenge university executives. Less than a year after discussing the idea, the pair had more than two hundred manuscript pages. Shortly thereafter McVey's friend secured a contract with Iowa State University Press. This motivated McVey to finish his writing, and by the end of 1950, the two had completed the manuscript. As McVey reviewed the chapters, he was disturbed that his friend had reused material from a previous book he had written concerning university trustees. McVey was not pleased with the finished product, which ran to almost 350 pages. However, he felt it was too late in the process to recommend changes. By early 1952 McVey's final book was published.[72]

———·———

Throughout McVey's UK career he attempted to live a life consistent with his philosophy and worldview. Only in retirement and after Frances's death did he begin to write candidly in his diary regarding his views on faith, politics, death, and taxes. In virtually every instance he seemed to embrace his contradictions as he sought a moderate road. He became a deacon at First Presbyterian Church but expressed skepticism about an afterlife. He railed against the dogmas expressed in traditional religion, but he was saddened by his children's lack of interest in faith and church. It warmed his heart when he felt his "children had learned to let up on the dou[b]ts." His own faith was guided by science, but he believed that prayer could "have an effect on the action of nations." He was progressive in his thinking about women's role in the church, wishing his own denomination would allow them to serve as deacons and elders. At the same time he was traditional in his disdain for "so much dirt" that he encountered in the many novels he read during his retirement.[73]

Concerning political philosophy McVey had decidedly left-leaning tendencies, particularly with regard to the burgeoning push for civil rights. When in 1948 UK attempted to create an "equal" system of higher education by sending its professors to Kentucky State College, he wrote, "This is a make shift plan and will not solve the educational needs of advanced colored students," yet he hoped it would serve to help "the white majority . . . come to accept the idea of equal opportunity." He said that "providence works in wonderful ways" when Senator Theodore Bilbo of Mississippi died unexpectedly, claiming that Mississippi would be far better off with the passing of the staunch segregationist. He hoped the legislature would repeal the 1904 Day Law, banning integration, rather than fighting a legal battle. He sided with what he called "the large liberal group who are willing to go a long way in giving the Negro greater opportunities and a larger freedom." He was pleased with the lack of controversy over the entrance of African Americans at UK, and he was encouraged to witness growing tolerance in Kentucky's race relations.[74]

On other issues, McVey's liberal perspective became tempered with moderation. He had long been in favor of New Deal attempts to change the role of government in American life. In his retirement he wrote privately of the need for socialized medicine. When his children expressed their disapproval with the growing role of government, McVey explained that this was because "they can't see that such a drift is more or less sure to happen." He added, "The English are wiser than we are in this country in that they accept the trend and try to form and manage it." At the same time he worried that increased taxes and regulation harmed productivity. He thought "serious mistakes [had] been made as seen in the subsidizing of agriculture to unheard lengths."[75]

McVey took time to express other opinions as well. After a railroad strike in 1950, he recorded that unions "fail to see the larger issues involved" and that "the private management can manage the road better than the government is likely to do." On international relations he worried about American efforts in Korea. He disagreed with attempting to halt Communism through military action, because "the people of Asia do not fear it as we do. It can be met in the long run by helping the people who are so deficient in the means of living a good life." Finally, he expressed frustration at the growing role of talk radio. He called Paul Harvey "an emphatic speaker and also a[n] insinuator." He was upset with the constant negative comments being made against President Truman and England. He disliked radio personality Fulton Lewis's perspectives as well. He wrote, "What I want from a broadcaster is news, not opinions, and the special pleading that crops out in this news service."[76]

During his last years McVey's thoughts were never far from Frances. On the anniversary of her passing, the university planned a ceremony in her honor. As the day approached, McVey noted that the thought of Frances "in my mind and heart seems to grow rather than to fade out." Frank found himself continually asking why she had to die, wondering if her life could have been spared if they had sought medical advice sooner. The ceremony hosted by President Donovan was a cathartic event for McVey. Sarah Blanding, president-elect of Vassar College and a close friend of both Frances and Frank, spoke of Frances's tolerance, compassion, and firmness, all qualities that made her an amazing representative for UK.[77]

McVey's diary was still peppered with entries about Frances and his continued affection for her. He regularly wrote comments such as, "I find real pleasure in thinking of our journey together. . . . We had lots of fun and much satisfaction in what we did together." He added, "She possessed a merry heart that welcomed people and made her many friends. I feel every day that she left in this house a part of her spirit to encourage and bless us." Nearly five years after her death, Frank still wrote of Frances: "She is present in my heart and mind again and again in each twenty four hours. The memory of her is always pleasant and a source of great comfort."[78]

McVey only had memories of his wife, but he had many good times to share with his family. In addition to regular visits from his three children and six grandchildren, McVey took annual vacations to Michigan with his daughter Virginia's family. He praised his son's work ethic and business success, adding that he had two "dear daughters, very fine and growing into wise and poised women. My children have been highly satisfactory. They have had some ups and downs but they appear to be well established." At the beginning of 1952, McVey became a great-grandfather upon the birth of Deborah McVey Johnson.[79]

As McVey's energy waned, he spent more time reading books and visiting with family and friends. On his eighty-third birthday, he wrote in his diary, "I can report good health, enough activity to fill my days with pleasant things to do." Yet less than a week later his journal entries ceased as his serious gall-stone problems recurred. Admitted to Good Samaritan Hospital on 7 December, he underwent another surgery for his long-standing condition.[80]

McVey's eighty-three-year-old body could not withstand the trauma this time. He remained in critical condition throughout the rest of December. Then, on Sunday night, 4 January 1953, Frank LeRond McVey's life ended. After a funeral at the First Presbyterian Church, he was buried at Lexington Cemetery next to his first wife, Mabel Sawyer McVey. In the days that followed, the newspapers featured numerous public tributes, President Herman Lee Donovan reflecting, "His work will live on so long as the University of Kentucky survives."[81]

His work would live on because Frank McVey had not only moved to Kentucky but aspired to become a Kentuckian who helped his state. By the time of his passing, he had spent more time in Kentucky than in any other location—more than thirty-five years. During this time, he worked tirelessly on behalf of the university and the state. His "outsider" status began to change after he married a charming Kentucky native and settled into life in the Bluegrass. Most important, the toil of this Yankee progressive at the University of Kentucky was a successful attempt to remake a struggling and often provincial college. As an editorial in the *Courier-Journal* suggested, McVey could rightly be considered the true founder of the University of Kentucky.[82]

Conclusion

McVey in Retrospect

What is a university?
A university is a place;
It is a spirit:
It is men of learning,
A collection of books,
Laboratories where work in science goes forward;
It is the source of the teaching
Of the beauties of literature and the arts;
It is the center where ambitious youth gathers to learn;
It protects the traditions,
Honors the new and tests its value;
It believes in truth,
Protests against error,
And leads men by reason
Rather than by force.
—Frank LeRond McVey, 1940

Frank L. McVey was a man of exceptional vision who possessed remarkable leadership capability. Commenting on the accomplishments of leaders like McVey, Thorstein Veblen quipped, "What such a man, so placed, will do with the powers and opportunities that so devolve on him is a difficult question that can be answered only in terms of the compulsion of the circumstances in which he is placed." In a posthumous tribute UK historian Thomas Clark claimed that, despite McVey's precarious position, his vision constituted the essential component of UK's growth during the interwar years, and he argued that McVey's accomplishments were "of immeasurable importance to the world of scholars." Such a tribute from a legendary scholar was amazing, considered in light of the fact that many of McVey's contemporaries tended to lose sight of the substance of educational reform, looking only for the material trappings of success and becoming "lost to the republic of learning."[1]

Considering the challenges McVey faced while in the Bluegrass, his list of substantive achievements on campus is astounding. He set out with a goal of revolutionizing the institution, changing it from a struggling college to an outstanding university. He initially began this transformation by instituting a modern organizational structure to coordinate the efforts of the various colleges. He then established the University Senate to aid in policymaking decisions on campus and wrote new rules of governance for the institution. For the faculty he established sabbatical leaves for research, and he organized a research club to encourage publication by professors. He also implemented an insurance plan and created a retirement program for employees who had reached the mandatory retirement age of seventy.[2]

McVey helped reshape the intellectual and cultural climate of the university by lending substantial support for visiting lecturers and theater performances. He "was one of the pioneers among southern college presidents to promote art and music education." As he did so, he opened the campus to the local community and encouraged their attendance at exhibits, performances, and lectures. Academically, he helped organize Kentucky's first Phi Beta Kappa chapter. He dramatically increased the holdings of the library and made the collection's home the centerpiece of his building program. He fought for a university press, although this dream was not realized until after his retirement. Of monumental importance was McVey's "courageous" stand for academic freedom during Kentucky's antievolution controversy.[3]

All of these accomplishments led to his growing prestige among higher-education leaders across the South and the nation. Regionally, he was named the first president of the Southeastern Conference and asked to remain in the post for a second term. He was voted president of the Southern Association of Colleges and Secondary Schools and led the modernization of that organization. Nationally, he served as president of both the National Association of State Universities and the National Association of State Land Grant Institutions. His name surfaced for numerous other presidencies during his first years in Lexington, but he passed up more promising jobs in order to complete his initial mission at the University of Kentucky. National leaders such as Charles Eliot and Nicholas Murray Butler were quick to come to McVey's defense during the antievolution controversy in the early 1920s. Appreciating his administrative acumen, numerous institutions, some more prestigious than UK, requested McVey's services in conducting surveys of their institutions.[4]

In his tribute to McVey, Clark stated that Kentucky would be "indebted to him for all time to come" because of his leadership in higher education and his "public service." It praised his devotion to the commonwealth and his "sense of dignity, of progress, and of inspiration of both heart and mind." The essay concluded that personally and professionally, McVey had remained dedicated to the "enduring principles" that he set forth in his definition of a university: "It believes in truth, protests against error and leads men by reason rather than by force."[5]

One common theme of the tributes in honor of the late president was his national outlook and the successes he had enjoyed in the larger academy. When McVey accepted the presidency at UK in 1917, he was an up-and-coming progressive administrator. His work at the University of North Dakota had not gone unnoticed by national progressives, who were seeking to export their reforms outside of the Northeast across the country and into the South. This was evident in Abraham Flexner's nomination of McVey to the presidential search committee at UK and the unequivocal support he received for the post.

During his time in Kentucky, McVey's broad influence went beyond the academy. With the help of his deans, especially Thomas Cooper in agriculture and the controversial James Graham in engineering, UK secured substantial monetary assistance for agricultural experiments and publications, as well as WPA funding for campus construction. With the advent of the New Deal, McVey worked with officials of the Tennessee Valley Authority to expand the agency's work beyond electrification, supporting educational efforts and social programs. With the help of his wife Frances, he cultivated connections to the White House, and First Lady Eleanor Roosevelt's two visits to Maxwell Place on campus in Lexington helped to publicize his prominent role.

McVey's national influence was matched by his successful reform efforts on campus. At the beginning of his tenure he implemented nearly seventy reforms recommended by the survey commission that had studied the university's problems in the year before his arrival. After putting a new bureaucratic structure in place, he also removed the political appointments and nepotism that had harmed the university. At the same time he limited the destructive influence of the president emeritus James Patterson, who was attempting to exert undue influence during his retirement. In doing so, he set the foundation for developing a true university in Lexington.

After his initial reforms, McVey continually focused on improving the faculty by recruiting and retaining renowned professors. This remained difficult during his entire tenure, as his calls for increased funding to bolster salaries went unheeded. With a growing faculty McVey was able to create a full-fledged graduate school, and UK became one of the first southern universities to begin offering PhD degrees. He created new academic departments and colleges and called on the new colleges of commerce and education, along with older colleges such as engineering and agriculture, to focus on research that would help improve the quality of life for Kentuckians.

As academic programs expanded and the student body grew in kind, McVey turned his attention to building a campus that could house such endeavors. Even though he received far less funding for capital improvements than did the teachers colleges in the state, McVey managed to construct more than thirty campus structures. Experiment stations in both Eastern and Western Kentucky were established to help provide agricultural training, as well as social programs. McVey's campus construction was all the more amazing considering the fact that lack of state appropriations was coupled with minimal private support. As historian Roger Geiger noted, the era of philanthropy during which McVey served often witnessed individuals being "commemorated on college campuses by the buildings that bear their names." Of the twenty major structures that were built during McVey's tenure, however, not a single one bore the name of a benefactor who played a pivotal financial role in subsidizing construction.[6]

As McVey improved the faculty and physical plant, he did not forget about the heart of the institution—undergraduate students. In the absence of state support, he developed ingenious schemes to construct dormitories to house students on the overcrowded campus. He lobbied state politicians to provide more support, so that the commonwealth's brightest students would not leave Kentucky for more promising opportunities. Despite his pleading, he was unable to get the necessary support, and during the 1920s UK found itself turning away students for lack of housing. For the students who did decide to come to Lexington, conditions were much improved. They enjoyed new dormitories and better-trained faculty members in the classroom. McVey instituted a personnel bureau to assist students during their college career. Initially dealing with undergraduates on academic probation, the bureau eventually began testing students for class placement, offering career advice, and providing counseling for the myriad problems faced by students adjusting to collegiate life.

McVey never received his full appropriations requests from the General Assembly, which, luckily for McVey, only met biannually. Only once was the president truly pleased with the legislature's funding, and that was in 1918—one year after his arrival. This appropriation, however, was in no way excessive: it was merely an overdue attempt to bring a struggling college rife with conflict and controversy into the collegiate mainstream. When McVey accepted the presidency, UK (unlike Centre College) was not even on the approved list of colleges published by the American Association of Universities. McVey wasted no time utilizing the appropriated funds, and the following year he successfully petitioned the AAU to be added to its list of approved institutions.

Although McVey considered his early successes only the first step in implementing his grand vision for the University of Kentucky, most others in the state did not share his view. The majority seemed content with a "standard" American university, as long as the football and basketball teams proved better than average. So while many pushed McVey for increased funding and attention for athletic endeavors, he found such activities distractions from the larger aims of the university and refused to comply. Instead McVey continually sought greater state support for UK's academic endeavors, but his pleadings were met, by and large, with apathy.

Amid such struggles, it appeared likely that McVey would seek a post in a state that was more willing to adopt his own vision. As fate would have it, however, love altered such plans. Shortly after the death of his first wife, Mabel, McVey began a courtship of Kentucky native Frances Jewell. They were married the following year, and they remained madly in love for the remainder of their lives together. It is worth noting that shortly after wedding Frances, McVey, as the archives reveal, quit updating his résumé. He had married a progressive woman possessing southern charm and an acumen for hospitality. The president's home, Maxwell Place, immediately turned into a social center not only for UK but for state, national, and international figures. Frances's influence is hard to overstate, and in the years following their marriage, McVey appeared to be making great strides toward his ultimate goal of noteworthy state support.

After the state rejected a monumental bond issue that would have provided McVey with the transformational gift necessary to emerge as a leader in higher education, the president's hopes were again dashed as the nation crashed into the Great Depression. The university's operating budget was cut almost in half. During those years, McVey's greatest accomplishment was keeping the university open. Even when the state did not provide UK revenue to pay faculty salaries, McVey gave an inspirational speech that helped keep the institution at work—a sign of the staff's deep allegiance to McVey and of his leadership. At the same time he led Lexington's business leaders in creating a lending fund to help professors meet their financial obligations even when they were not receiving paychecks. Although he secured federal assistance, he never again had a legitimate opportunity to compete with the nation's leading universities. Despite numerous hardships, the professionally trained economist managed his meager budget wisely and kept UK just on the periphery of the South's leading state educational institutions. As one supporter noted, McVey's task at UK resembled the plight of the enslaved Israelites who were forced by the Egyptians to make bricks without straw.

Unlike some states, Kentucky was extremely slow to return to its pre-Depression levels of funding (which had not been overly generous to start with). McVey retired in 1940, but the operating budget for the campus never matched the level of funding he had received before the 1932 legislature, despite the fact that full-time enrollment had grown to nearly four thousand students. Under such circumstances, McVey's ability to "hold the line" and not retreat was nothing short of astounding.

While McVey remained a revered figure on campus and a renowned leader among university presidents, his greatest weakness was his inability to convince those in control of the purse strings to buy into his vision of what the university could be and the ways in which it could help the state. As Thomas Clark noted, McVey never understood Kentucky politics, and the elected officials never really understood him. This was the curse of being a Yankee progressive in a conservative southern state. McVey understood this and made his wishes clear when he told the crowd at his last university commencement address that he wanted them to view him as a Kentuckian.

Despite his many disappointments, McVey's progressive ideology remained unshakable. In a speech given at the University of Virginia during the depths of the Great Depression, McVey held fast to his philosophical vision of the role of the university in the state. He declared, "The life of the state and the continuance of civilization rest upon learning, research, and teaching. These are the very essence of a university." He argued that a state university served the state when "it gives to its students and through them to all the people a belief in the modern democratic state guided by knowledge and truth. Too often do we forget that civilization is something that must be constantly worked for." Above all, McVey maintained that universities could reveal "the errors of the past and the snares of the future." This proved a difficult task in Kentucky.[7]

In the commonwealth whose motto remained "United We Stand, Divided We Fall," it was ironic that McVey's efforts were also hampered by intense rivalries with Kentucky's other state-supported institutions. The teachers colleges, unlike UK, were led by Kentuckians, many of whom had political ties with the legislature. Although they never matched UK's annual operating expenses, the schools in Eastern and Western Kentucky continually managed to gain greater support for construction than did the state flagship. When statements concerning such facts were made public in Lexington, they were met with criticisms about UK's arrogant attitude toward its sister institutions. UK's critics assumed that the university expected privileged status among its peers in the state, apparently failing to realize that a strengthened University of Kentucky would result in stronger regional institutions as well.

The intense resistance toward UK and its leaders was evidenced by McVey's status within the Kentucky Education Association. This group of professional educators snubbed McVey early in his career as he sought to utilize the university's resources to help the state's secondary schools. Only after successful tenures in regional and national organizations did the KEA eventually choose to elect McVey as its president. As in his other posts, he served admirably and did not use the post to advance the cause of his university. Instead he focused his attention on the larger issues of Kentucky's comprehensive educational program. Only in his retirement did McVey finally secure widespread support and public recognition for his efforts at UK.

McVey came to Kentucky with a national vision that needed to be implemented in a local setting. After more than two decades of labor, he had accomplished a great deal, but he fell short of his ultimate goals. The year before retiring he had been invited to attend the annual meeting of the Association of American Universities. He went with hopes that an invitation would be extended to the University of Kentucky, an honor that would serve as a symbolic gesture recognizing all that had been accomplished during his tenure. He left disappointed and without such recognition for his university.

Such tales of shortcomings, while receiving less attention in the history of higher education, were much more common than stories of unbridled success. While the story of higher education as a whole has often been told as one of inevitable growth and irresistible change, McVey's legacy epitomized the struggles of progressive reformers in states reluctant to modernize. However, there were many state universities in the nation, especially in the South, that faced battles similar to those faced by McVey, and there were far more presidents at standard American universities than there were members of the American Association of Universities. Although there is little recognition of McVey in the historiography of higher education (because of the humble status of the state and university from which he came) his contemporaries, many of whom hailed from similar states, recognized his ability and his successes and sought his leadership.

Although personal and professional challenges may often make McVey's story seem melancholy, he maintained his faith in democracy, reason, and truth and preserved his optimistic tone. This frequently put him above the political fray rather than in it. And although it is beyond the scope of historical inquiry to answer such questions, it may be valuable for policymakers to ponder whether or not Kentucky deserved such an influential reformer. If so, was McVey the best person to lead the University of Kentucky? A central component of McVey's work at Kentucky was "removing politics" from the institution, but would the institution and the state have been better served had he become a politician-president? It is also worth wondering how far UK may have fallen behind without the continuity of McVey's long administration and his steadfast fight for the university.

While not offering complete answers to such questions, the history of the university both before and after his tenure suggests that the university and the state were fortunate to have a leader like McVey. In the years just before he accepted the presidency, leadership problems and politics had so divided the institution that the state ordered an investigation to examine the university and recommend changes. Then, in the years following his retirement, UK and its president, Herman Lee Donovan, again faced criticism, resulting in another state-initiated investigation. Not one time during McVey's tenure, however, did state politicians question his integrity or the welfare of UK, nor was an investigation required. Even though McVey faced numerous controversies, as well as the challenges of the

Great Depression, the state officials who denied his budget requests never failed to praise his integrity and leadership.

Upon his death, an editorial in the *Courier-Journal* suggested that McVey was the true founder of the University of Kentucky. This was accurate in that he had created a modern university. As such, he was the first to face certain battles that his successors for the next century would also fight. Even in the twenty-first century, nearly one hundred years after McVey took office in Lexington, current University of Kentucky president Lee Todd faced many of the same issues that Frank McVey faced, as will his successor—making the university more efficient, helping it become the service arm of the state, battling to preserve the university's budget, facing the challenges of big-time athletics, and, most important, struggling to convince the state of the importance of creating a state flagship university of national renown. After serving as UK president for twenty-three years, McVey decided to write a history of education in Kentucky. The title of the book he penned captures his own sentiments and neatly summarizes the struggles and successes of his career: *The Gates Open Slowly*. Indeed, this title not only reflects McVey's own struggles as president but reveals a theme for the University of Kentucky that continues into the twenty-first century.

Notes

Abbreviations

ARP	Annual Report of the President
BOT	Board of Trustees
Euro Journal	Frank McVey, Personal European Travel Journal
FLM Papers	Frank L. McVey Papers
GFDH	*Grand Forks Daily Herald*
KK	*Kentucky Kernel*
LCJ	*Louisville Courier-Journal*
LH	*Lexington Herald*
LL	*Lexington Leader*
McVey Diary	Frank McVey, Personal Diary
UKA	University of Kentucky Archives
UND	University of North Dakota

Introduction

Epigraph: McVey, *University Is a Place,* 35.

    1. Rudolph, *American College and University,* 417.

    2. Veblen, *Higher Learning in America,* 65–66, 161–62.

    3. Ibid., 61, 178, 78; Frank McVey, Personal Diary (hereafter McVey Diary), 20 June 1944, Frank McVey Papers (hereafter FLM Papers), University of Kentucky Archives (hereafter UKA). In this entry, written during his retirement, McVey spoke fondly of Veblen and the acquaintance they developed when McVey was a faculty member in Minnesota. McVey added, "During the years I have thought of him many times. His kindness to me as a young instructor and the vision and keen insight that he had into social and economic questions I shall always treasure."

4. Veblen, *Higher Learning in America,* 193, 178.

5. Ibid., 78.

6. Vesey, *Emergence of the American University,* 338.

7. Levine, *American College and the Culture of Aspiration,* 16–17; Roger L. Geiger, *To Advance Knowledge,* 1–2.

8. Barrow, *Universities and the Capitalist State,* 32, 201.

9. Ibid., 87.

10. Roger L. Geiger, *To Advance Knowledge,* 100.

11. Link, *Paradox of Southern Progressivism,* xi, 323; McVey, *University Is a Place,* 155.

12. Dennis, *Lessons in Progress,* 11.

13. McVey Diary, 6 Feb. 1936.

14. Robert L. Geiger, *To Advance Knowledge,* 125.

1. The Making of a Progressive President

Epigraphs: Frank L. McVey, "The University and Its Relations," speech, 29 Sept. 1910, typescript, box 82, FLM Papers; McVey, *University Is a Place,* 185–86.

1. Barbara Hitchcock, interview with Charles Talbert, 10 Aug. 1972, interview 1990OH309 A/F 409, tape, Charles T. Wethington U.K. Alumni/Faculty Oral History Project, Nunn Center for Oral History, Lexington, KY.

2. Edmund McVey, interview with Charles Talbert, 6 July 1972, interview 1990OH326 A/F 425, tape, Wethington Oral History Project; Hitchcock, interview, 10 Aug. 1972; Anna Holmes McVey, letter, n.d., box 126, FLM Papers; McVey Diary, 21 July 1904.

3. Hitchcock, interview, 10 Aug. 1972; Virginia McVey Morris (daughter of Frank McVey), interview with Charles Talbert, 29 June 1972, interview 1990OH314 A/F 414, tape, Charles T. Wethington Alumni/Faculty Project; Janet McVey Hall, interview with Charles Talbert, 16 June 1972, interview 1990OH313 A/F 413, tape, Wethington Alumni/Faculty Project.

4. Anna Holmes McVey, "Memories of a Long Life," box 126, FLM Papers; McVey Hall, interview, 16 June 1972; Edmund McVey, interview, 6 July 1972; McVey Diary, 18 Sept. 1945.

5. Hitchcock, interview, 10 Aug. 1972; Edmund McVey, interview, 6 July 1972.

6. Edmund McVey, interview, 6 July 1972; McVey Diary, 29 Aug. 1940.

7. Hitchcock, interview, 10 Aug. 1972.

8. Edmund McVey, interview, 6 July 1972; McVey Diary, 7 Mar. 1944.

9. Edmund McVey, interview, 6 July 1972; McVey Diary, 29 Apr. 1904, 27 Oct. 1928.

10. Frank McVey to Duncan McRae, 16 Jan. 1919, box 51, FLM Papers.

11. For a description of the quintessential "college man," see Horowitz, *Campus Life; Le Bijou,* 1890, 115, 190, and 1893, 178, Ohio Wesleyan University Historical Collection, Delaware; McVey Diary, 14 Jan. 1949; Frank McVey, Recollections, 1 May 1952, box 82, FLM Papers.

12. Edmund McVey, interview, 6 July 1972; McVey Hall, interview, 16 June 1972.

13. McVey Diary, 28 Aug. 1947.

14. *Kentucky Kernel* (hereafter *KK*), 8, 28 Oct. 1927.

15. McVey Diary, 23 Nov. 1948; Edmund McVey, interview, 6 July 1972.

16. J. W. Bashford to William Fowell, 15 Nov. 1895, box 127, FLM Papers.

17. Edmund McVey, interview, 6 July 1972; McVey Diary, 22–23 Nov.1948.

18. Arthur Hadley to Frank McVey, 25 July 1894, box 127, FLM Papers.

19. McVey, "Populist Movement."

20. J. Schwab, form letter, 25 May 1896, Arthur Hadley, form letter, 22 May 1892, and W. G. Sumner, form letter, 24 May 1895, all box 76, FLM Papers.

21. McVey Diary, 16 Oct. 1947.

22. Frank McVey to John DeWitt Warner, 31 July 1895, box 24, Frances Jewell McVey Papers, UKA.

23. Frank McVey to William Folwell, 14 Nov., 7 Dec. 1895, 9 Mar. 1896, box 76, FLM Papers; A. Hadley to Frank McVey, 8 Jan. 1896, box 127, FLM Papers. See also the correspondence kept in box 24, Frances Jewell McVey Papers.

24. W. G. Sumner to William Folwell, 22 Oct. 1895, and Arthur Hadley to William Folwell, 30 Oct. 1895, both box 127, FLM Papers.

25. Frank McVey to William Folwell, 28 Jan. 1896, box 76, and Frank McVey to Mabel McVey, 12 June 1898, box 127, FLM Papers.

26. Frank McVey to William Folwell, 27 Apr. 1896, box 4, William Folwell Papers, University of Minnesota Archives.

27. Frank McVey to William Folwell, 1, 25 May, 17 June, 25 July 1896, all box 4, Folwell Papers.

28. Gray, *University of Minnesota,* 142; *University of Minnesota Catalogue, 1896–1897,* University of Minnesota Archives, 90–91; *Ariel* (University of Minnesota student newspaper), 25 Aug. 1899.

29. McVey, *Government of Minnesota.*

30. Fred Rector to Frank McVey, 14 Aug. 1897, box 76, FLM Papers.

31. Frank McVey to Mabel McVey, 19, 3 Apr.1898, both box 127, FLM Papers.

32. Mabel McVey to Frank McVey, 17, 23 June 1897, and Frank McVey to Mabel McVey, 15, 19, 23 June 1897, all box 127, FLM Papers.

33. Frank McVey to Mabel McVey, 19 June 1898, box 127, FLM Papers.

34. *Ariel,* 25 Mar. 1899.

35. Frank McVey to Mabel McVey, 14 May 1906, box 126, FLM Papers; McVey Diary, 10 Mar. 1907.

36. *University of Minnesota Catalogue, 1900–1901,* University of Minnesota Archives; David Jordan to Frank McVey, 2 Sept. 1901, box 76, FLM Papers.

37. Alfred McVey to Frank McVey, 10 Apr. 1901, box 126, FLM Papers.

38. Frank McVey to Dr. George Bridgeman, 23 Feb. 1904, box 76, FLM Papers.

39. "McVey Answers Criticism from St. Paul: Not Responsible for Errors in Britannica," *Minneapolis Times,* 1 Feb. 1904; Frank McVey to G. B. Lynes, 10 Mar. 1904, and Frank McVey to Samuel Smith, 25 Apr. 1904, both box 76, FLM Papers.

40. Cyrus Northrup to Edward Sanford, 1 Mar. 1904, box 127, FLM Papers.

41. Frank McVey to Martin Hardy, 15 Feb., 23, 28 Mar. 1904, all box 76, FLM Papers.

42. Frank McVey to Charles Holt, 8 Apr. 1904, box 76, FLM Papers.

43. Frank McVey to Martin Hardy, 28 Mar. 1904, box 76, FLM Papers; McVey, *Modern Industrialism,* 290–91.

44. *Gopher,* 1908, 336 (University of Minnesota Archives).

45. McVey Diary, 12 Jan. 1907; Alfred McVey to Frank McVey, 30 Apr. 1907, box 70, FLM Papers.

46. McVey Diary, 14 Aug. 1940; *Preliminary Report of the Minnesota Tax Commission to the Governor of the State of Minnesota* (St. Paul Syndicated Printing, 1907), 56.

47. Frank McVey to Mabel McVey, 7, 8 Aug. 1907, both box 127, FLM Papers.

48. Frank McVey to Mabel McVey, 7 Aug. 1907, box 127, FLM Papers; Frank McVey to Mabel McVey, 31 July, 11 Aug. 1907, and Alfred McVey to Frank McVey, 19 Sept. 1907, all box 127, FLM Papers; Frank McVey to E. A. Nelson, 15 May 1907, and L. P. Bykre to Frank McVey, 6 Dec. 1908, both box 70, FLM Papers.

49. Frank McVey to Mabel McVey, 19 Feb. 1908, box 127, FLM Papers.

50. Frank McVey to Mabel McVey, 9 Mar. 1908, box 127, FLM Papers.

51. Mabel McVey to Frank McVey, 12 Mar. 1908, box 127, FLM Papers.

52. Frank McVey to Mabel McVey, 29 Dec. 1907, box 127, FLM Papers; John Park to Frank McVey, 3 Jan. 1908, box 70, FLM Papers.

53. Frank McVey to Mabel McVey, 23 Apr. 1908, box 127, FLM Papers.

54. *Student,* 28 Sept. 1910.

55. Frank McVey to N. C. Young, 21 Oct. 1908, 6 Jan. 1909, both box 76, FLM Papers.

56. University of North Dakota (hereafter UND), Minutes of the Board of Trustees (hereafter BOT), 11 Jan. 1909; *Grand Forks Daily Herald* (hereafter *GFDH*), 12 Jan., 17 June 1909; Frank McVey to Webster Merrifield, 13 Jan. 1909, box 76, FLM Papers.

57. *GFDH,* 14 Jan. 1909.

58. Louis G. Geiger, *University of the Northern Plains,* 139–77; Robinson, *History of North Dakota,* 309.

59. Robinson, *History of North Dakota,* 256–57.

60. Frank McVey to J. G. Gunderson, 4 Feb. 1909, box 76, FLM Papers.

61. T. A. Torgeson to Charles Talbert, 18 July 1974, box 1, Charles Gano Talbert Papers (hereafter CGT Papers), UKA; *Student,* 18 Feb. 1909.

62. Annual Report of the President (hereafter ARP) of UND to BOT, 1911–12, 14–16; ARP of UND to BOT, 1910–11, 11; Louis G. Geiger, *University of the Northern Plains,* 139–77, 197; Robinson, *History of North Dakota,* 310.

63. President's Report, in Eleventh Biennial Report, 10 Oct. 1910, 26–27; Louis G. Geiger, *University of the Northern Plains,* 200.

64. ARP of UND to BOT, 1911–12, 13.

65. ARP of UND to BOT, 1909–10, 10; Louis G. Geiger, *University of the Northern Plains,* 195, 212.

66. ARP of UND to BOT, 1909–10, 14; *Student,* 9 June 1912; Louis G. Geiger, *University of the Northern Plains,* 213.

67. *Student,* 18 Jan., 8 Feb., 26 Oct. 1911.

68. *Student,* 15, 19 May 1910, 9 Nov. 1911.

69. Clyde Duffy to Charles Talbert, 10 July 1974, box 1, CGT Papers.

70. *Student,* 12 Dec. 1912, 29 May 1913.

71. Warren Hanna to Charles Talbert, 13 July 1974, box 1, CGT Papers; Louis G. Geiger, *University of the Northern Plains,* 193; Robinson, *History of North Dakota,* 310.

72. ARP of UND to BOT, 1909–10, 11–12; ARP of UND to BOT, 1910–11, 13.

73. ARP of UND to BOT, 1909–10; *GFDH,* 26 May 1910.

74. Louis G. Geiger, *University of the Northern Plains,* 195.

75. Ibid., 196; *GFDH,* 29 Sept. 1910; *Student,* 28 Sept. 1910.

76. McVey, "University and Its Relations."

77. Ibid.

78. Ibid.

79. Ibid.

80. Ibid.

81. *Grand Forks Evening Times,* 29 Sept. 1910.

82. Thelin, *History of Higher Education,* 137–38.

83. Rudolph, *American College and University,* 362–63.

84. Louis G. Geiger, *University of the Northern Plains,* 180.

85. ARP of UND to BOT, 1909–10, 15, and 1910–11, 21.

86. ARP of UND to BOT, 1910–11, 22; Report of the Field Organizer of the Extension Division, in Twelfth Biennial Report, 1 Dec. 1912, 176–81.

87. *Student,* 10 Mar. 1910.

88. McVey, *Railroad Transportation.*

89. ARP of UND to BOT, 1909–10, 10.

90. Louis G. Geiger, *University of the Northern Plains*, 199.

91. *GFDH,* 19 Dec. 1909, 21, 26, 28 Jan. 1911.

92. Mabel McVey to Frank McVey, 31 July 1912, box 127, FLM Papers.

93. Frank McVey's European Travel Journal (hereafter Euro Journal), 2 July 1912, 26–28, box 65, FLM Papers.

94. *GFDH,* 13 Aug. 1913; Frank McVey to Editor of *GFDH,* 28 July 1912; Euro Journal, 22 Aug. 1912, 184–86, and 12 Aug. 1912, 119–21.

95. Euro Journal, 5 June 1912.

96. Mabel McVey to Frank McVey, 10 July 1912; Euro Journal, 3 Aug. 1912; Mabel McVey to Frank McVey, 7, 12 Oct. 1912, box 127, FLM Papers.

97. Mabel McVey to Frank McVey, 7, 12 Sept. 1912, B. L. Goodkind to Frank McVey, 17 Mar. 1913, Frank McVey to B. L. Goodkind, 26 Mar. 1913, and William Snell to Frank McVey, 28 Mar. 1917, all box 127, FLM Papers.

98. *Student,* 9 Oct., 13 Nov. 1913, 5 Nov. 1914.

99. *Student,* 7 May 1914; Louis G. Geiger, *University of the Northern Plains,* 218–19.

100. Louis G. Geiger, *University of the Northern Plains,* 222–23.

101. Ibid., 218.

102. Ibid., 218–19.

103. Ibid., 226–27; Frank McVey to Editor of *GFDH,* 21 Dec. 1914; *Student,* 17 Dec. 1914.

104. Joseph Lewinsohn to Frank McVey, 18 Dec. 1914, box 81, FLM Papers.

105. Ibid.

106. Frank McVey to Joseph Lewinsohn, 13 Dec. 1913, box 81, FLM Papers.

107. *GFDH,* 26 Apr. 1914; Robert Henry to Frank McVey, 17 Mar. 1914, box 81, FLM Papers.

108. *Student,* 28 Apr. 1914.

109. *GFDH,* 20 May 1914.

110. Louis G. Geiger, *University of the Northern Plains,* 279.

111. Frank McVey, "Academic Freedom and Political Activity," typescript, box 81, FLM Papers.

112. Ibid.; Louis G. Geiger, *University of the Northern Plains,* 277.

113. Lucas, *American Higher Education,* 198.

114. Barrow, *Universities and the Capitalist State,* 170.

115. Louis G. Geiger, *University of the Northern Plains,* 235.

116. Robinson, *History of North Dakota,* 315–16.

117. Ibid., 331.

118. Louis G. Geiger, *University of the Northern Plains,* 233; Frank McVey to Mabel McVey, 16 Feb. 1916, box 127, FLM Papers; Louis G. Geiger, *University of the Northern Plains,* 230–31.

119. Frank McVey to Mabel McVey, 15 Nov. 1913, box 127, FLM Papers.

120. Frank McVey to Mabel McVey, 10, 12 Nov. 1914, both box 127, FLM Papers.

121. Frank McVey to M. P. Shawkey, 15 Jan. 1915, box 65, FLM Papers; Frank McVey to Edwin Robert Seligman, 12 Jan. 1915, box 66, FLM Papers.

122. Mabel McVey to Frank McVey, 16 July 1916, box 127, FLM Papers.

123. C. A. Duniway to Frank McVey, 18 July 1917, and Frank McVey to C. A. Duniway, 1 Aug. 1917, both box 65, FLM Papers.

124. Frank McVey to Mabel McVey, 25 July 1917, box 127, FLM Papers.

125. L. Crawford to Frank McVey, Aug. 1917, box 66, FLM Papers; Louis G. Geiger, *University of the Northern Plains*, 235.

126. *Student,* 19 Oct. 1917.

127. Ibid.

128. Louis G. Geiger, *University of the Northern Plains*, 236.

129. Levine, *American College and the Culture of Aspiration*, 87.

130. Slosson, *Great American Universities*, 522–25.

2. A Southern University and a Northern Progressive

Epigraph: McVey, *University Is a Place*, 12.

1. Abraham Flexner to Frank McVey, telegram, 25 July 1917, box 76, FLM Papers.

2. Frank McVey to Mabel McVey, 25 July 1917, box 76, FLM Papers (Business Correspondence, 1914–25); Richard Stoll to Frank McVey, 1 Aug. 1917, box 3-H, FLM Papers; Thomas D. Clark, interview with the author, 21 Oct. 2004, interview 04OH182 A/F 681, tape, Wethington Oral History Project; Frank McVey Jr., interview with Charles Talbert, 10 July 1972, interview 90OH320 A/F 423, Wethington Oral History Project.

3. Richard Stoll to Frank McVey, 11 Aug. 1917, box 3-H, FLM Papers.

4. Anna McVey to Frank McVey, 6 Aug. 1917, box 126, FLM Papers; Alfred McVey to Frank McVey, 11 Aug. 1917, box 25, Frances Jewell McVey Papers.

5. Enoch Grehan to Frank McVey, 16 Aug. 1917, box 5-A, FLM Papers; McVey Morris, interview, 29 June 1972.

6. Frank McVey to Mabel McVey, 28 July 1917, box 127, FLM Papers; "Report of the Investigating Committee," *Bulletin of the University of Kentucky* 9, no. 5 (1917): 1.

7. Hopkins, *University of Kentucky* 263–65.

8. Henry Pritchett to Henry S. Barker, 26 Jan. 1910, cited in Hopkins, *University of Kentucky*, 273.

9. Gillis, *Henry Stites Barker*, 7–8.

10. Ibid., 10.

11. Ibid., 17–18.

12. "Report of Investigating Committee," 1–5.

13. Testimony Taken by Special Investigation Committee, University of Kentucky, 1917, UKA, 174.

14. Record of the Testimony Given before the Special Investigating Committee, cited in Hopkins, *University of Kentucky,* 269.

15. "Report of the Survey Commission," *Bulletin of the University of Kentucky* 9, no. 5 (1917): 18–19.

16. Ibid., 14.

17. Ibid., 11–13, 103.

18. Ibid., 103–11.

19. Ibid., 66.

20. Ibid., 106–9.

21. Ibid., 16–17.

22. Ibid., 35.

23. Ibid., 69–75.

24. Ibid., 28.

25. Talbert, *University of Kentucky,* 35–36; "Report of the Survey Commission," 41.

26. "Report of the Survey Commission," 39–40.

27. Ibid., 95–96.

28. Ibid., 36–39, 95–98.

29. Ibid., 37.

30. Ibid., 91–92.

31. Editorial, *Lexington Leader* (hereafter *LL*), 16 Aug. 1917; George Denny to Frank McVey, 7 Aug. 1917, and Frank McVey to George Denny, 17 Aug. 1917, both box 3-H, FLM Papers; Minutes of BOT, 15 Aug. 1917.

32. *LL,* 13 June 1917.

33. McVey Diary, 29 May 1947; *LL,* 15, 16 Sept. 1917; *KK,* 20 Sept. 1917; *LL,* 18 Sept. 1917.

34. Frank McVey to Mabel McVey, 16 Sept. 1917, box 127, FLM Papers; J. Winston Coleman, interview with Charles Talbert, 9 Jan. 1974, interview 1990OH335 A/F 433, tape, Wethington Oral History Project.

35. *LL,* 18 Oct. 1917.

36. President McVey's Report, 17 Oct. 1917, box 53, FLM Papers.

37. Ibid.

38. Ibid.

39. Mabel McVey to Frank McVey, 11 Oct. 1917, and Frank McVey to Mabel McVey, 23 Nov. 1917, both box 127, FLM Papers.

40. Minutes of BOT, 10 Dec. 1917.

41. Ibid.

42. Ibid.

43. *Lexington Herald* (hereafter *LH*), 6 Dec. 1917.

44. Frank McVey to Richard Stoll, 15 Jan. 1918, box 6, FLM Papers.

45. Ibid.

46. Frank McVey, "Report of the President of the University of Kentucky to the Governor and the Assembly of the Commonwealth of Kentucky," 1918, box 53, FLM Papers.

47. Ibid.; *LL*, 1 Feb. 1918.

48. Frank McVey to William Milan, 2 Mar. 1918, box 27, FLM Papers.

49. Frank McVey to Richard Stoll, 20 Mar. 1918, box 6, FLM Papers.

50. Richard Stoll to Frank McVey, 16 Aug. 1917, box 3-E, FLM Papers.

51. Frank McVey to Thomas Cooper, 21 Aug. 1917, box 1, FLM Papers.

52. Frank McVey to Mabel McVey, 30 Dec. 1917, box 127, FLM Papers; Minutes of BOT, 10 Dec. 1917, box 9, FLM Papers.

53. Frank McVey, memorandum concerning a meeting with Fred Mutchler, 24 July 1918, box 9, FLM Papers.

54. "Report of the Survey Commission," 38, 94.

55. Minutes of BOT, 4 June, 18 Sept. 1918.

56. Minutes of BOT, 10 Dec. 1918.

57. Ibid.

58. Minutes of BOT, 17 June 1919.

59. Minutes of the Executive Committee of BOT, 15 Jan.1919; Minutes of BOT, 17 June 1919.

60. *LL*, 20 June 1919; Minutes of BOT, 17 June 1919; Wellington Patrick to Frank McVey, 3 Dec. 1915, box 18, FLM Papers.

61. Minutes of Executive Committee of BOT, 26 Mar. 1919; Minutes of BOT, 1 Apr. 1919.

62. Frank McVey to Elwood Street, 25, 31 Mar. 1919, both box 14, FLM Papers.

63. Frank McVey (form letter) to J. M Davis, 9 Nov. 1917, box 30, FLM Papers, UKA.

64. Minutes of BOT, 17 June 1919.

65. Minutes of BOT, 21 Dec. 1920.

66. Minutes of BOT, 16 Sept. 1919; Minutes of Executive Committee of BOT, 23 Oct. 1919.

67. Minutes of BOT, 1 Apr., 16 Sept. 1919.

68. Arthur Calhoun to Frank McVey, 16 Aug. 1918, box 30, FLM Papers; *LH*, 21 Mar. 1919.

69. Frank McVey to M. C. Vickers, 8 May 1919, Frank McVey to President George Gross, 22 June 1919, and Wellington Patrick to the *Chicago Tribune*, telegram, 22 Aug. 1919, all box 30, FLM Papers.

70. Thomas D. Clark, interview with the author, 21 Oct. 2004; Frank McVey to Elwood Street, 25 Mar. 1919, box 14, FLM Papers.

71. Minutes of BOT, 6 June 1919.

72. Frank McVey to A. O. Whipple, 8 Nov., 13 Dec. 1917, and A. O. Whipple to Frank McVey, 14 Feb. 1918, all box 25, FLM Papers.

73. Frank McVey to Howard Ingles, 20 Aug. 1918, Frank McVey to A. O. Whipple, 1 Aug., 16 Dec. 1918, Frank McVey to "Deans and Department Heads," 10 Apr. 1918, and Frank McVey to A. O. Whipple, 11 Apr. 1918, all box 22, FLM Papers.

74. Frank McVey to A. O. Whipple, 16 Dec. 1918, 29 June 1919, both box 22, FLM Papers.

75. Frank McVey to Wellington Patrick and D. H. Peak, 12 May 1918, box 22, FLM Papers; D. H. Peak to Frank McVey, 24 Sept. 1920, B. J. Treacy to D. H. Peak, 12 Nov. 1921, and B. J. Treacy to Frank McVey, 27 Apr. 1922, all box 25, FLM Papers.

76. *LL,* 3 Mar. 1919.

77. *LL,* 14 Mar. 1919.

78. Frank McVey to Olmsted Brothers, 22 Mar. 1918, and John Olmsted to Frank McVey, 1 Apr. 1918, both box 22, FLM Papers.

79. Frank McVey to John Olmsted, 22 May 1918, box 22, FLM Papers.

80. John Olmstead to Frank McVey, 13 May 1919, and Frank McVey to John Olmsted, 27 May 1919, both box 22, FLM Papers; Groves, "Examination of Major Initiatives," 19.

81. Frank McVey to G. Moretti, 16 June 1922, box 22, FLM Papers.

82. Groves, "Examination of Major Initiatives," 21.

83. Ibid., 19, 29.

84. Minutes of BOT, 10 Dec. 1918, 17 June 1919.

85. Minutes of BOT, 10 Dec. 1918, 17 June, 16 Sept. 1919, 21 Dec. 1920.

86. Frank McVey to Lt. Col. N. H. Slaughter, 18 Jan. 1918, box 13, FLM Papers.

87. Edward Hines to Frank McVey, 18 Jan. 1918; box 13, FLM Papers; *LH,* 29 Jan. 1918; Frank McVey to Secretary of State Robert Lansing, 20 May 1918, box 126, FLM Papers; McVey Diary, 14 Mar. 1941.

88. Minutes of BOT, 10 Dec. 1918.

89. Ibid.

90. Ibid.

91. Minutes of BOT, 10 Dec. 1918, 17 June 1919.

92. Frank McVey to Captain H. M. Royden, 25 Nov. 1918, box 31, FLM Papers; Minutes of BOT, 10 Dec. 1918.

93. McVey Diary, 14 Mar. 1941; Minutes of BOT, 6 June 1919.

94. Minutes of BOT, 10 Dec. 1918.

95. McVey to H. V. Ames (dean of the Graduate School at the University of Pennsylvania), 11 Feb. 1919, box 42, FLM Papers, and box 2, CGT Papers.

96. Kendrick Babcock to Frank McVey, 17 Feb. 1919, box 42, FLM Papers, and box 2, CGT Papers.

97. Frank McVey to Kendrick Babcock, 25 Feb. 1919, box 42, FLM Papers.

98. Ibid.

99. David A. Robertson to Frank McVey, 9 Dec. 1919, box 42, FLM Papers.

100. Victor Bryant to Frank McVey, 16 May 1919, box 70, FLM Papers.

101. Frederick Koch to Frank McVey, 1 Dec. 1918, box 70, FLM Papers.

102. Wilson, *University of North Carolina,* 310–13.

103. George Denny to Frank McVey, 10 Mar. 1920, Frank McVey to George Denny, 8 Apr. 1920, and George Denny to Frank McVey, 26 Jan. 1922, all box 50, FLM Papers.

104. Klotter, *Kentucky,* 226–31; *LH,* 5 June 1918; *LL,* typescript, 4 June 1918, box 129, FLM Papers.

105. Dennis, *Lessons in Progress,* chapters 1–2.

3. McVey's Darkest Days

Epigraph: McVey, *University Is a Place,* 90.

1. Minutes of BOT, 6 Apr., 1 June 1920.

2. Minutes of BOT, 21 Dec. 1920.

3. Memorial Building circular letters, n.d., box 21, FLM Papers; Minutes of BOT, 26 Jan. 1923.

4. *LL,* 6 Feb. 1920; Frank McVey to Governor Edwin Morrow, 27 Jan. 1920, box 5, FLM Papers; Minutes of BOT, 6 Apr. 1920.

5. Minutes of BOT, 6 Apr. 1921.

6. Minutes of BOT, 13 June 1921.

7. Ibid.

8. H. Davies to Richard Stoll, 3 June 1921, box 3-E, FLM Papers.

9. Ibid.; H. Davies to Richard Stoll, 7 June 1921, box 3-E, FLM Papers.

10. Minutes of BOT, 13 June 1921.

11. Frank McVey to George Denny, 14, 22 Mar. 1921, both box 50, FLM Papers; George Denny to Frank McVey, 17 Mar. 1921, box 5-D, FLM Papers, and box 3, CGT Papers; John Park to Frank McVey, 22 Dec. 1921, box 126, FLM Papers.

12. *LH,* 12 July 1921.

13. *LH,* 13 July 1921.

14. Ibid.; *LH,* 14 July 1921.

15. *LL,* 13 July 1921.

16. Frank McVey to John Pettijohn, 13 July 1921, box 65, FLM Papers.

17. George Denny to Frank McVey, 11 Aug. 1921, box 50, FLM Papers.

18. Minutes of BOT, 5 Oct. 1921.

19. *Louisville Evening Post,* 14 July 1921.

20. *Western Recorder,* 28 July 1921, box 6, FLM Papers.

21. O. O. Green to Frank McVey, 3 Aug. 1921, box 6, FLM Papers.

22. Frank McVey to O. O. Green, 12 Sept. 1921, and Frank McVey to Victor Masters, 19 Sept. 1921, both box 6, FLM Papers.

23. Ellis, "Frank LeRond McVey," 41.

24. *LL,* 25 Dec. 1921; *LH* 26 Dec. 1921.

25. *LH,* 22 Jan. 1922.

26. Ibid.; *LL,* 23 Jan. 1922; *Louisville Evening Post,* 24 Jan. 1922.

27. Frank McVey to Richard Knott, 23 Jan. 1922, Frank McVey to Lewis Humphrey, 23 Jan. 1922, Lewis Humphrey to Frank McVey, 24 Jan. 1922 (with attached article from the *Louisville Post,* 23 Jan. 1922), and Frank McVey to Lewis Humphrey, 26 Jan. 1922, all box 6, FLM Papers.

28. Frank McVey to dozens of influential individuals, form telegram, 26 Jan. 1922, box 6, FLM Papers.

29. Responses to McVey telegram, box 6, FLM Papers (also summarized well in Ellis, "Frank LeRond McVey," 44–45); *LL,* 1 Feb. 1922; *LH,* 1 Feb. 1922.

30. Frank McVey to Woodrow Wilson, 29 Jan. 1922, box 6 and box 80, FLM Papers.

31. Charles Brown to Frank McVey, 3 Feb. 1922, and E. A. Birge to Frank McVey, 3 Mar. 1922, both box 6, FLM Papers.

32. Ellis, "Frank LeRond McVey," 46–47; *LL,* 1 Feb. 1922; Harvill, "Monkey Trial That Wasn't," 39.

33. George Colvin to Frank McVey, 2 Feb. 1922, box 6, FLM Papers.

34. Ellis, "Frank LeRond McVey," 47; *LL,* 5 Feb. 1922; *New York Times,* 6 Feb. 1922.

35. *LL,* 5 Mar. 1922; Frank McVey to E. Y. Mullins, 14 Feb. 1922, and E. Y. Mullins to Frank McVey, 2 Mar. 1922, both box 6, FLM Papers.

36. *KK,* 11 Feb. 1922.

37. McVey to "The People of Kentucky," 12 Feb. 1922, box 6, FLM Papers; McVey, *Gates Open Slowly.* appendix C.

38. McVey to "The People of Kentucky," 12 Feb. 1922, box 6, FLM Papers.

39. Ibid.

40. Ibid.

41. Ibid.

42. Harvill, "Monkey Trial That Wasn't," 40; *Louisville Courier-Journal* (*LCJ* hereafter), 17 Feb. 1922.

43. Ellis, "Recurring Crisis," 131; Klotter, *Kentucky,* 269–71; *LL,* 9 Mar. 1922.

44. McVey, *Gates Open Slowly,* 232.

45. Ibid.; Harvill, "Monkey Trial That Wasn't," 41–42.

46. Frank McVey to Emery Frazier, 11, 13 Mar. 1922, Emery Frazier to Frank McVey, 10 Mar. 1922, G. J. Jarvis to Frank McVey, 11 Mar. 1922, and Frank McVey to Stratton Brooks, 14 Mar. 1922, all box 6, FLM Papers.

47. Frank McVey to Stratton Brooks, 14 Mar. 1922, box 6, FLM Papers; Ellis, "Frank LeRond McVey," 43–45.

48. Nicholas M. Butler to Frank McVey, 27 Feb. 1922, Charles Eliot to Frank McVey, 1 Mar. 1922, and Frank McVey to Charles Eliot, 6 Mar. 1922, all box 6, FLM Papers; Harvill, "Monkey Trial That Wasn't," 14.

49. Montgomery and Gaither, "Evolution and Education in Tennessee," 148–51.

50. *LCJ,* 4 Jan. 1922.

51. *LCJ,* 1 Jan. 1922.

52. *LCJ,* 25 Jan. 1922.

53. *Louisville Evening Post,* 8 Mar. 1922; *LH,* 25 Jan. 1922.

54. *KK,* 11 Feb. 1922; Frank McVey to Frank Bachman, 26 Jan. 1922, box 42, FLM Papers.

55. *LL,* 29 Jan. 1922; *Louisville Evening Post,* 11 Feb. 1922, 1, 6 Mar. 1922.

56. Minutes of BOT, 4 Apr. 1922.

57. Ibid.

58. *LH,* 20 Apr. 1922; Virginia McVey to Mabel McVey, 20 Mar. 1922, box 127, FLM Papers; J. Hunt to Frank McVey, 28 Sept. 1923, box 65, FLM Papers.

59. J. Hunt to Frank McVey, 28 Sept. 1923, box 65, FLM Papers; Frank McVey to J. Irvine Lyle, 17 Apr. 1922, box 4, FLM Papers; F. Paul Anderson to Frank McVey, 19 Apr. 1922, box 17-B, FLM Papers.

60. *LH,* 23 Apr. 1922; Kate Park to Anna McVey, 23 Apr. 1922, box 12-B, FLM Papers.

61. *LL,* 23 Apr. 1922; Kate Park to Anna McVey, 23 Apr. 1922, box 12-B, FLM Papers.

62. Kate Park to Anna McVey, 23 Apr. 1922, box 12-B, FLM Papers.

63. *LH,* 20 Apr. 1922; *KK,* 28 Apr. 28 1922.

64. *LH,* 21 Apr. 1922; *LH,* 23 Apr. 1922.

65. Lydia Olney, interview with Charles Talbert, 28 Sept. 1977, interview 90OH310 A/F 410, tape, Wethington Oral History Project.

66. Chloe Gifford, interview with Charles Talbert, 15 Nov. 1972, interview 90OH308 A/F 408, tape, Wethington Oral History Project; Coleman, interview, 9 Jan. 1974; Olney, interview, 28 Sept. 1977.

67. Mabel McVey to Frank McVey, 28 Dec. 1918, 29 Oct. 1919, and 7 July 1921, all box 127, FLM Papers.

68. Mabel McVey to Frank McVey, 7 July 1921, box 127, FLM Papers.

69. Mabel McVey to Frank McVey, 10 Aug. 1920, and 7 July 1921, both box 127, FLM Papers.

70. *LL,* 16 Aug. 1922.

71. Dr. James K. Patterson, Last Will and Testament, copied in Minutes of BOT, 19 Sept. 1922.

72. Minutes of BOT, 19 Sept. 1922.

73. William Thorton Lafferty, Faculty/Staff Biographical Files, UKA.

74. Frank McVey to Lyman Chalkley, 5 Mar. 1923, box 15, FLM Papers.

75. *KK,* 17 Nov. 1922.

76. Frances Jewell to Frank McVey, 15 Nov. 1922, box 125, FLM Papers; Janet McVey to Frank McVey, 15 Oct. 1922, box 127, FLM Papers.

77. James Jackson to Frank McVey, 27 Apr. 1922, box 70, FLM Papers; Frank McVey to R. M. Hughes, 28 Sept. 1922, box 65, FLM Papers.

78. Minutes of BOT, 19 Sept. 1922; Frances Jewell to Frank McVey, 27 Oct. 1922, box 125, FLM Papers.

4. McVey's Era of Great Aspirations

Epigraph: McVey, *University Is a Place,* 306.

1. Minutes of BOT, 13 Apr., 12 June 1923.

2. Minutes of BOT, 12 June 1923.

3. *Kentucky Memorial Building,* pamphlet, 1919, and Frank McVey to Alumni, 17 Oct. 1919, both box 21, FLM Papers.

4. Minutes of the Memorial Building Executive Committee, 25 Apr. 1923, R. S. Webb to Frank McVey, 31 July 1923, Shelby Harbison to Frank McVey, 30 July 1923, Earl Shropshire to Frank McVey, 31 July 1923, and "Alma Mater Is Calling," pamphlet, 26 Apr. 1922, all box 21, FLM Papers.

5. George Tamblyn to Frank McVey, 29 Sept. 1922, box 21, FLM Papers.

6. "Plan and Estimate of Expense for a Half-Million Dollar Campaign for the University of Kentucky," enclosure with letter from George Tamblyn to Frank McVey, 29 Sept. 1922, box 21, FLM Papers.

7. Minutes of BOT, 19 Sept. 1922; George Tamblyn to Frank McVey, 29 Sept. 1922, box 21, FLM Papers.

8. Frank McVey to Clarence Hewitt, 12 Oct. 1922, and Clarence Hewitt to Frank McVey, 16 Oct. 1922, both box 21, FLM Papers.

9. George Tamblyn to W. H. Grady, 21 Oct. 1922, box 21, FLM Papers.

10. Minutes of BOT, 24 Nov. 1922; George Tamblyn to Frank McVey, 4 Dec. 1922, box 21, FLM Papers.

11. Frank McVey to George Denny and Thomas Reed, 9 Dec. 1922, Thomas Reed to Frank McVey, 11 Dec. 1922, George Denny to Frank McVey, 11 Dec. 1922,

and "Alumni Association Report of the Greater Kentucky Fund," n.d., all box 21, FLM Papers.

12. Minutes of BOT, 26 Jan. 1923.

13. Notes from Memorial Building Executive Committee Meeting, 25 Apr. 1923, box 21, FLM Papers.

14. Minutes of BOT, 12 June, 2 Oct. 1923.

15. McVey to George Tamblyn, 29 May 1923, and W. C. Wilson to Alumni, 24 Jan. 1924, both box 21, FLM Papers.

16. Frank McVey to Members of the University Staff, 19 Apr. 1923, box 21, FLM Papers; *KK,* 23 Apr. 1923.

17. "Alumni Association Report of the Greater Kentucky Fund."

18. Minutes of BOT, 28 Mar. 1923.

19. Minutes of BOT, 12 June, 20 July 1923.

20. Minutes of BOT, 2 Oct. 1923; *KK,* 28 Sept. 1923.

21. Minutes of BOT, 15 Oct., 19 Dec. 1923.

22. Minutes of BOT, 19 Dec. 1923; Stanley, *Before Big Blue,* 124–25.

23. C. C. Calhoun to Frank McVey, 3 Mar. 1924, box 32, FLM Papers; Minutes of BOT, 7 Mar., 4 Apr. 1924; W. C. Wilson to the Alumni Association, 16 Apr. 1924, box 32, FLM Papers.

24. Minutes of BOT, 14 Nov. 1924.

25. Frank McVey to W. C. Fields, 21 Jan. 1925, box 32, FLM Papers; Stanley, *Before Big Blue,* 135–36.

26. *LCJ,* 27 May 1923; *KK,* 23 Apr. 1923; Stanley, *Before Big Blue,* 89.

27. *KK,* 12 Oct. 1923.

28. Ibid.; C. C. Calhoun to Frank McVey, 10 Oct. 1923, box 32, FLM Papers.

29. Herbert Graham to Frank McVey, 6 Oct. 1923, box 32, FLM Papers; *KK,* 23 Nov. 1923; Frank McVey to Herbert Graham, 9 Oct. 1923, box 32, FLM Papers.

30. Minutes of BOT, 19 Dec. 1923; "Alumni Association Report of the Greater Kentucky Fund."

31. Minutes of BOT, 4 Apr. 1924.

32. Minutes of BOT, 31 May 1924.

33. *KK,* 29 Sept., 7, 21 Nov. 1924; Stanley, *Before Big Blue,* 91–92.

34. "An Analytical Statement of the Greater Kentucky Fund Activities," n.d., attachment with letter from Frank McVey to C. C. Calhoun, 21 Jan. 1927, box 21, FLM Papers.

35. Frank McVey to R. M. Hughes, 3 Oct. 1925, box 65, FLM Papers.

36. Minutes of BOT, 1 June 1922.

37. Birdwhistell, "Educated Difference," 58.

38. Ibid., 89, 98–101.

39. Ibid., 111–12.

40. Frances Jewell to Frank McVey, 19, 27 Oct., 28 Nov. 1922, all box 125, FLM Papers.

41. Frank McVey to Frances Jewell, 2 Dec. 1922, box 9, Jewell Family Papers, UKA; Frances Jewell to Frank McVey, 4 Dec. 1922, box 125, FLM Papers.

42. Frank McVey to Frances Jewell, 5 Dec. 1922, box 9, Jewell Family Papers.

43. Frank McVey to Frances Jewell, 6, 12 Dec. 1922, box 9, Jewell Family Papers.

44. Frank McVey to Frances Jewell, 6 Dec. 1912, box 9, Jewell Family Papers; Frances Jewell to Frank McVey, 13 Dec. 1922, box 125, FLM Papers.

45. Frank McVey to Frances Jewell, 12 Dec. 1922, box 9, Jewell Family Papers.

46. Frances Jewell to Frank McVey, 12 Dec., 2 Jan. 1922, and 2 Feb. 1923, all box 125, FLM Papers.

47. Frank McVey to Frances Jewell, 20 Jan. 1923, box 9, Jewell Family Papers.

48. Frank McVey to Frances Jewell, 5–12, 25 Dec., 20 Jan. 1922, all box 9, Jewell Family Papers; Frances Jewell to Frank McVey, 25 Feb. 1923, box 9, FLM Papers.

49. Frances Jewell to Frank McVey, 23 Jan., 2 Feb. 1923, both box 125, FLM Papers.

50. Frances Jewell to Frank McVey, 4 June 1923, box 125, FLM Papers.

51. Frances Jewell to Frank McVey, 8 Aug. 1923, box 125, FLM Papers.

52. Frances Jewell to Frank McVey, 2 Sept., 13 Nov. 1923, both box 125, FLM Papers.

53. Bart Peak, interview with Charles Talbert, 9 Jan. 1974, interview 90OH312 A/F 412, tape, Wethington Oral History Project; Levi Jackson Horlacher, interview with Charles Talbert, 8 Jan. 1974, interview 90OH315 A/F 415, tape, Wethington Oral History Project.

54. Gifford, interview, 15 Nov. 1972.

55. Hitchcock, interview, 10 Aug. 1972.

56. Smith, *College of Agriculture of the University of Kentucky*, 203–4.

57. Ibid.; Minutes of "A Meeting of the Joint Board of the E. O. Robinson Mountain Fund," Quicksand, KY, 6 May 1923, box 10, FLM Papers.

58. E. O. Robinson to Frank McVey, 12 May 1923, box 10, FLM Papers.

59. Frank McVey to E. O. Robinson, 14 May 1923, box 10, FLM Papers.

60. E. O Robinson to Frank McVey, 16 May 1923, and Frank McVey to E. O. Robinson, 14 May 1923, both box 10, FLM Papers.

61. Richard Stoll to Frank McVey, 21 June 1923, box 10, FLM Papers.

62. E. O. Robinson to Frank McVey, 25 Sept. 1923, box 10, FLM Papers.

63. Minutes of BOT, 2 Oct. 1923.

64. E. O. Robinson to Frank McVey, 5 Oct. 1923, box 10, FLM Papers.

65. Smith, *College of Agriculture of the University of Kentucky*, 209.

66. Ibid., 212; Minutes of BOT, 29 May 1926.

67. Smith, *College of Agriculture of the University of Kentucky*, 212–13.

68. Minutes of BOT, 21 Jan. 1924.

69. Thomas Cooper to Frank McVey, 14 Feb. 1924, box 6, FLM Papers; Smith, *College of Agriculture of the University of Kentucky*, 213–14.

70. Smith, *College of Agriculture of the University of Kentucky*, 215–18.

71. Minutes of BOT, 16 Feb., 1 May 1924; Smith, *College of Agriculture of the University of Kentucky*, 219–20.

72. Smith, *College of Agriculture of the University of Kentucky*, 222–23.

73. Ibid., 238.

74. Minutes of BOT, 12 June 1923.

75. Minutes of BOT, 26 Sept. 1923.

76. Minutes of BOT, 2 Oct. 1923.

77. Frank McVey to William Fields, 9 Nov. 1923, box 3-I, FLM Papers.

78. Frank McVey to William Fields, 14 Dec. 1923, box 3-I, FLM Papers.

79. Frank McVey to Arch Hamilton, 2, 21 Jan.1924, and Frank McVey to Lewis Humphrey, 28 Dec. 1923, 10 Jan. 1924, all box 6, FLM Papers.

80. Arch Hamilton to Frank McVey, 11 Feb. 1924, box 6, FLM Papers.

81. Frank McVey to M. E. Vaughn, 23 Feb. 1924, Frank McVey to Newton Bright, 8, 15 Feb. 1924, and Frank McVey to W. R. Jillson, 18 Feb. 1924, all box 6, FLM Papers.

82. Frank McVey to Rainey T. Wells, 8, 21 Mar. 1924, Frank McVey to President Cherry, 5 Mar. 1924, Frank McVey to Arch Hamilton, 27 Mar. 1924, Frank McVey to Governor Fields, 24 Mar. 1924, and Governor Fields to Frank McVey, 8 Apr. 1924, all box 6, FLM Papers.

83. Frank McVey to Arch Hamilton, 18 Feb. 1924, box 6, FLM Papers; McVey, *Gates Open Slowly*, 210 (see chapter 4, n. 36).

84. Minutes of BOT, 2 July 1924; *KK*, 24 Oct. 1924.

85. Minutes of BOT, 2 July 1924.

86. Frank McVey to University Employees, 16 July 1924, box 39, FLM Papers.

87. *Louisville Times*, 29 Sept. 1924; *LH*, 5 Oct. 1924; *KK*, 10 Oct. 1924; McVey, *Gates Open Slowly*, 211.

88. *Louisville Herald-Post*, 19 Oct. 1924; *KK*, 3, 24 Oct. 1924.

89. *KK*, 24 Oct. 1924.

90. McVey, *Gates Open Slowly*, 211.

91. Minutes of BOT, 4 Apr. 1924, 3 Jan., 12 May 1925.

92. Minutes of BOT, 3 Jan. 1925, 7 Apr. 1924, 11 Nov. 1925; Frank McVey to W. C. Wilson, 4 Dec. 1925, box 6, FLM Papers.

93. Frank McVey to J. B. Miner, 16 Nov. 1925, Frank McVey to W. C. Wilson, 4 Dec. 1925, Frank McVey to Lewis Humphrey, 27 Jan. 1926, and Frank McVey to E. D. Stephenson, 19 Feb. 1926, all box 6, FLM Papers.

94. Minutes of BOT, 17 Mar. 1926, 25 Apr. 1927.

95. Minutes of BOT, 21 July, 28 Sept. 1926, 12 Jan. 1927.

96. *KK,* 28 Oct. 1927.

97. Minutes of BOT, 11 Dec. 1928; Frank McVey to F. T. Justice & Company, 27 June 1929, box 21, FLM Papers.

98. "Requests of the University of Kentucky for Appropriations: Legislative Session, 1928–1930," box 6, FLM Papers; Minutes of BOT, 17 Apr. 1928.

99. Minutes of BOT, 5 Apr. 1927, 26 May, 14 June, 26 Oct. 1928, 23 Sept., 5 Nov. 1930.

100. Minutes of BOT, 6 Dec. 1928, 24 Sept. 1929.

101. "Requests of the University of Kentucky for Appropriations Legislative Session 1930–1932," box 6, FLM Papers.

102. McVey Diary, 5, 28 Feb., 13, 15, 22 Mar. 1930.

103. Minutes of BOT, 23 Sept. 1930.

104. *LL,* 20 Oct. 1931; Minutes of BOT, 31 May 1930.

105. Roger L. Geiger, *To Advance Knowledge,* 123–27.

106. Snider, *Light on the Hill,* 193–97.

107. Roger L. Geiger, *To Advance Knowledge,* 140.

108. Klotter, *Kentucky,* 164–66 (see chapter 3, n. 112).

109. Frank McVey to Arch Hamilton, 24 Mar. 1924, box 6, FLM Papers.

110. Frank McVey to Frank Button, 1 July 1925, box 38, FLM Papers; Frank McVey to E. J. Boss, 15 Mar. 1926, box 6, FLM Papers; Harrison, *Western Kentucky University,* 69; "Requests of the University of Kentucky For Appropriations, Legislative Session 1928–1930," box 6, FLM Papers.

111. Harrison, *Western Kentucky University,* 69; Minutes of BOT, 31 May 1930; Flatt, *Light to the Mountains,* 42–43.

112. H. H. Cherry to Frank McVey, 21 June, 17 July 1924, 1 Feb. 1927, and Frank McVey to H. H. Cherry, 8 Mar. 1927, all box 38, FLM Papers.

113. Frank McVey to H. H. Cherry, 28 Feb. 1930, and Frank McVey to H. H. Cherry, n.d., both box 38, FLM Papers.

114. Frank McVey to Herman Donovan, 24 June 1931, box 37, FLM Papers.

115. H. H. Cherry to Frank McVey, 29 July 1931, and Raymond Kent to Frank McVey, 7 July 1931, both box 38, FLM Papers.

116. *KK,* 25 Sept. 1931.

117. *KK,* 6 Oct. 1931.

118. Talbert, *University of Kentucky,* 43, 68, 69.

119. "Turning the Local Network to a National Channel," 312–17.

120. Ibid., 321–24.

121. Ibid., 324–25.

122. Minutes of BOT, 17 Apr. 1928.

123. Minutes of BOT, 17 Apr., 30 May 1925; Levine, *American College and the Culture of Aspiration*, 58–59.

124. Minutes of BOT, 20 Dec. 1927.

125. Minutes of BOT, 21 Jan. 1924, 30 May 1925.

126. Minutes of BOT, 15 Dec. 1931; Talbert, *University of Kentucky*, 87.

127. Minutes of BOT, 13 May 1924, 30 May 1925, 28 May, 1 June 1927, 24 Sept. 1929.

128. Frank McVey to University Presidents, 14 Feb. 1925, box 46, FLM Papers.

129. Frank McVey to University Presidents, 8 May 1925, box 46, FLM Papers.

130. *KK*, 18 Sept. 1931.

131. Stanley, *Before Big Blue*, 106; *KK*, 3, 24 Oct., 21 Nov. 1924.

132. Stanley, *Before Big Blue*, 106–8; *KK*, 3 Oct. 1924.

133. Wellington Patrick to Frank McVey, 13 Dec. 1926, box 8, FLM Papers.

134. Frank McVey to Wellington Patrick, 3 Jan. 1927, and Wellington Patrick to Frank McVey, 12 Jan. 1927, both box 18, FLM Papers.

135. Frank McVey to Wellington Patrick, 17 Jan. 1927, and Wellington Patrick to E. B. Toles, 20 Jan. 1927, both box 18, FLM Papers.

136. Minutes of BOT, 23 June 1922, 23 Sept. 1924, 13 Apr. 1926, 28 May 1927.

137. Minutes of BOT, 26 May 1928, 13 Mar. 1929.

138. Harrison, *Western Kentucky University*, 57; Ellis, *History of Eastern Kentucky University*, 76, 87.

139. Barrow, *Universities and the Capitalist State*, 90.

140. McVey Diary, 26 Oct. 1931.

141. Minutes of BOT, 15 Dec. 1931.

142. McVey Diary, 17 Nov. 1931.143. McVey Diary, 1 Jan., 21 Mar. 1930, 11 Jan. 1931.

144. *KK*, 28 Oct. 1927.

145. McVey Diary, 11–14 Nov. 1931.

146. McVey Diary, 10 Oct., 14 Nov. 1931.

5. Surviving the Great Depression and Reforming the South

Epigraph: McVey, *University Is a Place*, 222.

1. McVey Diary, 1 Jan. 1932.

2. McVey Diary, 31 Dec. 1931.

3. McVey Diary, 13, 14 Jan. 1932.

4. McVey Diary, 10 Feb. 1932.

5. McVey Diary, 5, 10, 12, 26, 27 Feb. 1932.

6. McVey Diary, 29 Feb. 1932.

7. Talbert, *University of Kentucky*, 93–94 (see chapter 5, n. 115); McVey Diary, 29 Feb. 1932.

8. Klotter, *Kentucky*, 289 (see chapter 3, n. 112); McVey Diary, 27 Feb. 1932.

9. McVey Diary, 16 Mar. 1932.

10. Minutes of BOT, 18 Apr. 1932.

11. McVey Diary, 30 Mar. 1932; *KK,* 1 Apr. 1932.

12. *KK,* 1 Apr. 1932; Clark, interview with the author, 21 Oct. 2004.

13. McVey Diary, 30, 31 Mar. 1932.

14. Minutes of BOT, 18 Apr. 1932; *KK,* 5 Apr. 1932.

15. McVey Diary, 3 Apr. 1932; Minutes of BOT, 20 Sept. 1932; *KK,* 5 Apr. 1932; Jesse Herman to Frank McVey, 1 Apr. 1932, box 7, FLM Papers.

16. McVey Diary, 10 Mar. 1933; *LH,* 11 Mar. 1933; Minutes of BOT, 4 June 1932, 14 Dec. 1933.

17. McVey Diary, 4, 7 Jan. 1932.

18. McVey Diary, 4 Jan., 3 Apr. 1932; Frank McVey to J. C. Jones, 5 Apr. 1932, box 12, FLM Papers; McVey Diary, 5 Apr. 1932.

19. Frank McVey to J. G. Bruce, 1 Apr. 1932, box 32, FLM Papers; McVey Diary, 3, 5, 6 Apr. 1932; *KK,* 8 Apr. 1932.

20. *LL,* 16 Sept. 1932; McVey Diary, 7 Dec. 1932, 20 Mar. 1933.

21. A. E. Bigge to Frank McVey, 28 Apr. 1933, Frank McVey to A. E. Bigge, 1 May 1933, and A. E. Bigge to Frank McVey, 9 May 1933, all box 29, FLM Papers.

22. Richard Stoll to Frank McVey, 18 May 1935, box 3-F, FLM Papers.

23. McVey Diary, 24 Sept. 1935; Richard Stoll to Frank McVey, 18 May 1935, and Frank McVey to Richard Stoll, 21 May 1935, both box 3-F, FLM Papers; McVey Diary, 15 Oct. 1936.

24. *KK,* 13 Dec. 1935; McVey Diary, 20 Dec. 1935.

25. Talbert, *University of Kentucky*, 112–13.

26. McVey Diary, 3, 9, 22 Mar., 8, 9 Apr. 1933; George Brady, interview with Charles Talbert, 29 June 1972, interview 90OH324 A/F 423, tape, Wethington Oral History Project.

27. McVey Diary, 7 Apr. 1932.

28. McVey Diary, 25 Nov., 22 Dec. 1932.

29. McVey Diary, 12, 30 Jan. Jan.1933.

30. McVey Diary, 11 Feb. 1933.

31. Minutes of BOT, 30 May 1935.

32. McVey Diary, 29 Nov. 1932, 23 Mar. 1933, 12 Dec. 1932.

33. McVey Diary, 27 Mar., 3, 10 Apr. 1933; Minutes of BOT, 19 Apr. 1933.

34. McVey Diary, 7 Apr. 1933; Minutes of BOT, 19 Apr. 1933.

35. McVey Diary, 17, 18, 19, 20, 24, 26 July, 1, 7 Sept., 2 Oct. 1933; Klotter, *Kentucky*, 300.

36. McVey Diary, 27 Nov. 1933.

37. McVey Diary, 12, 23 Dec. 1933.

38. Minutes of BOT, 14 Dec. 1933; McVey Diary, 2 Jan. 1934.

39. McVey Diary, 16 Mar. 1934.

40. Minutes of BOT, 27 Mar. 1934; *LL,* 27 Apr. 1934.

41. McVey Diary, 20 June 1934; Klotter, *Kentucky,* 302.

42. McVey Diary, 3 July 1934.

43. Minutes of BOT, 30 June 1934; McVey Diary, 21 June 1934.

44. McVey Diary, 27 June, 18 July 1934; *LL,* 3 July 1934.

45. Minutes of BOT, 29 May, 11 Dec. 1934; McVey Diary, 15 Mar. 1934.

46. Minutes of BOT, 1 June 1933.

47. Minutes of BOT, 19 Sept., 6 Oct. 1933.

48. Minutes of BOT, 6 Oct. 1933; *KK,* 31 Oct. 1933; Frank McVey to Louis Alber, 10 Nov. 1933, box 29, FLM Papers.

49. Minutes of BOT, 14 Dec. 1933.

50. Minutes of BOT, 21 Feb., 17 Jan. 1934.

51. McVey Diary, 2 July, 23 Oct., 15 Nov. 1933.

52. McVey Diary, 2 July, 23 Oct. 1933.

53. Talbert, *University of Kentucky,* 107; *LL,* 6 Feb. 1934; McVey Diary, 23, 31 Oct. 1933, 3 Mar., 24 Apr., 3 Nov. 1934.

54. McVey Diary, 23, 24 May 1934.

55. McVey Diary, 7, 8 July 1934.

56. Minutes of BOT, 16 Jan., 12 Feb., 2 Apr. 1935.

57. Birdwhistell, "A. B. 'Happy' Chandler," 218.

58. McVey Diary, 16 Nov., 13 Dec. 1935.

59. Minutes of BOT, 17 Dec. 1935; McVey Diary, 17 Dec. 1935.

60. Klotter, *Kentucky,* 308; Birdwhistell, "A. B. 'Happy' Chandler," 209–12.

61. McVey Diary, 18 Dec. 1935, 2, 27 Jan. 6 Mar. 1936; Birdwhistell, "A. B. 'Happy' Chandler," 210–11.

62. McVey Diary, 18 Mar. 1936; Minutes of BOT, 7 Apr. 1936; McVey Diary, 6 Sept. 1936.

63. Harrison, *Western Kentucky University,* 91 (see chapter 5, n. 107).

64. McVey Diary, 16, 24 Mar. 1936.

65. Minutes of BOT, 7 Apr. 1936.

66. Stanley, *Before Big Blue,* 136–37 (see chapter 5, n. 22).

67. McVey Diary, 4 Dec. 1932; Student Petition to Frank McVey, 5 Dec. 1932, box 11, FLM Papers; McVey Diary, 6 Dec. 1932; Minutes of BOT, 13 Dec. 1932.

68. McVey Diary, 7 Dec. 1932; Football Squad to Frank McVey, 5 Dec. 1932, box 11, FLM Papers.

69. Talbert, *University of Kentucky,* 99; Ray Moss to Frank McVey, 11 Jan. 1933,

box 25, FLM Papers; McVey Diary, 11, 12 Dec.; 1932; *KK,* 13 Dec. 1932; Minutes of BOT, 13 Dec. 1932.

70. McVey Diary, 15 Dec. 1932.

71. McVey Diary, 27 Dec. 1932, 28 Jan., 2 Mar. 1933; Minutes of BOT, 1 June 1933.

72. McVey Diary, 21 Dec. 1932, 21 Mar., 6 Apr., 20 June 1933.

73. Stanley, *Before Big Blue,* 139–40; McVey Diary, 29 Nov. 1933, 19 Jan. 1934.

74. Thelin, *Games Colleges Play,* 26–27.

75. S. V. Sanford to Frank McVey, 1 Nov. 1929, box 46, FLM Papers.

76. Thelin, *Games Colleges Play,* 39–51.

77. McVey Diary, 16 Nov. 1932; Stanley, *Before Big Blue,* 73, 78–79, 117.

78. *LCJ,* 10 Dec. 1932; Minutes of the Meeting of the Southeastern Conference, 8–9 Dec. 1932, box 46, FLM Papers.

79. McVey Diary, 10, 16 Dec. 1932.

80. Frank McVey to J. F. Broussard, 16 Dec. 1932, Frank McVey to Harcourt Morgan, 15 Dec. 1932, and Frank McVey to George Denny, 17 Dec. 1932, all box 46, FLM Papers.

81. J. J. Tigert to Frank McVey, 19 Dec. 1932, box 46, FLM Papers; McVey Diary, 7 Jan. 1933; George Denny to Frank McVey, 17 Dec. 1932, box 46, FLM Papers.

82. Frank McVey to SEC Presidents, 17 Jan. 1933, box 46, FLM Papers.

83. Minutes of the Presidents of the Southeastern Conference Institutions, 16 Feb. 1933, box 46, FLM Papers.

84. Frank McVey to John Tigert, 17 Feb. 1933, box 46, FLM Papers; McVey Diary, 16 Feb. 1933.

85. "Constitution and By-Laws of the Southeastern Conference," 1933, box 46, FLM Papers.

86. Ibid.

87. Ibid.

88. Frank McVey to A. E. Eilers, 18 Feb. 1933, box 46, FLM Papers; McVey Diary, 27 Feb. 1933.

89. Edgar Charles Jones to Frank McVey, 28 June, 8 Nov. 1933, Frank McVey to William Hemmingway, 20 July 1933, John Tigert to Frank McVey, telegram, 1 Nov. 1933, and Steadman Sanford to Frank McVey, 19 Jan. 1934, all box 46, FLM Papers.

90. Frank McVey to SEC Presidents, 4 Jan. 1934, and Frank McVey to John Tigert, 30 Jan. 1934, both box 46, FLM Papers.

91. Report of the President of the Southeastern Conference, 9 Feb. 1934, box 46, FLM Papers.

92. Ibid.

93. Ibid.

94. Ibid.

95. McVey Diary, 9 Feb. 1934; J. J. Tigert to Frank McVey, 1 Feb. 1934, and George Denny to Frank McVey, 23 Feb. 1934, both box 46, FLM Papers.

96. McVey Diary, 17 Nov. 1934; A. H. Armstrong to Frank McVey, 28 May 1934, and George Denny to Frank McVey, 4 Dec. 1934, both box 46, FLM Papers.

97. McVey Diary, 8 Feb. 1935.

98. J. J. Tigert to Frank McVey, 21 Feb. 1935, and Frank McVey to J. J. Tigert, 5 Mar. 1935, both box 46, FLM Papers.

99. McVey Diary, 13 Feb. 1934; *LL,* 27 Feb. 1934; McVey Diary, 24 Feb. 1934.

100. McVey Diary, 8, 13, 19 Mar., 24 Sept. 1934.

101. McVey Diary, 30 June 1934, 17 Apr. 1935.

102. *LH,* 19 Apr. 1935; McVey Diary, 17 Apr., 15 May 1935.

103. *KK,* 17 Nov. 1936; McVey Diary, 23 Nov., 9 Dec. 1936.

104. Stanley, *Before Big Blue,* 141–42.

105. Minutes of BOT, 8 Dec. 1936; McVey Diary, 8 Dec. 1936.

106. Miller, *Centennial History,* 14.

107. Ibid., 89; Guy Snavely, from "A Short History of the Southern Association of Colleges and Secondary Schools," reprint from the *Southern Association Quarterly* 9 (Nov. 1945): 37.

108. Miller, *Centennial History,* 86.

109. McVey Diary, 2 Dec. 1932.

110. Snavely, "Short History," 39.

111. McVey Diary, 8 Dec. 1933.

112. "Proceedings of the Thirty-Eighth Annual Meeting of the Southern Association of Colleges and Secondary Schools," Nashville, TN, 7–8 Dec. 1933, 46, 306–8.

113. *High School Quarterly* 12, no. 2 (1934): 43–45, cited in Charles G. Talbert Papers, Box 4.

114. Frank McVey to Guy Snavely, 16 Mar. 1934, and Frank McVey to C. A. Ives, 24 May 1934, both box 42, FLM Papers.

115. McVey Diary, 6 Dec. 1934; Snavely, "Short History," 42.

116. Snavely, "Short History," 43; Miller, *Centennial History,* 95–97.

117. J. R. McCain to Frank McVey, 29 Oct. 1935, box 46, FLM Papers; William Few to Frank McVey, 6 Mar. 1935, box 42, FLM Papers; James Haskins to Frank McVey, 14 Dec. 1935, box 46, FLM Papers; McVey Diary, 7 Feb. 1935.

118. McVey, "Ways and Means."

119. Clark, "Book Thieves of Lexington," 39.

120. McVey Diary, 10 Sept., 31 Aug. 1936.

121. McVey Diary, 24 Nov. 1932, 10 Nov. 1936.

122. McVey Diary, 3, 29 Dec. 1931, 21 Oct., 31 Dec. 1932, 5, 16 Dec. 1933.

123. Clark, "Book Thieves of Lexington," 30–31.

124. McVey Diary, 18, 22 Mar. 1934, 17 Apr. 1936.

6. Building a Legacy

Epigraph: McVey, *University Is a Place,* 294.

1. McVey Diary, Oct. 4, 1934.

2. Minutes of BOT, 24 Sept., 31 Oct. 1935.

3. Minutes of BOT, 31 Oct. 1935; McVey Diary, 24 Sept. 1935; Minutes of BOT, 15 Nov. 1935.

4. Minutes of BOT, 24 Sept., 31 Oct., 15 Nov., 7 Dec. 1935, 7 Apr. 1936.

5. Bryant Fleming to Frank McVey, 13 Oct., 16 Nov. 1935, and 20 Apr. 1936, all box 25, FLM Papers.

6. Bryant Fleming to Frank McVey, 20 Apr. 1936, box 25, FLM Papers.

7. Frank McVey to Bryant Fleming, 23 Apr. 1936, box 25, FLM Papers.

8. Bryant Fleming to Frank McVey, 29 Apr. 1936, box 25, FLM Papers.

9. *KK,* 2 Apr. 1936; Talbert, *University of Kentucky,* 116 (see chapter 5, no. 115); *KK,* 2 Apr. 1936; McVey Diary, 3 Apr., 7 May 1936.

10. Minutes of BOT, 4 June 1936; McVey Diary, 5, 7 Nov. 1936.

11. Minutes of BOT, 13 Sept. 1936.

12. Minutes of BOT, 7 Nov. 1936.

13. Minutes of BOT, 3 June 1937; McVey Diary, 6 Oct. 1936.

14. McVey Diary, 13 Mar., 24 Apr. 1936.

15. McVey Diary, 29 May 1936; Minutes of BOT, 4 June 1936; McVey Diary, 20 Dec. 1936; Minutes of BOT, 21 Dec. 1936.

16. McVey Diary, 5 Jan. 1937; *LL,* 4 Feb. 1937; McVey Diary, 4 Feb. 1937; McVey, *University Is a Place,* 37.

17. Veblen, *Higher Learning in America,* 104–7.

18. Frank McVey to Ezra Gillis, "Chronology and History" of the O'Bannon controversy, personal correspondence, circa Apr. 1939, box 31, FLM Papers; McVey Diary, 27 Mar. 1936. Letters concerning the controversy exist in both box 31, FLM Papers, and box 82, Chandler Papers. Typescripts of the letters in chronological order from the Chandler Papers are also cited.

19. Lester O'Bannon to Frank McVey, 9 June 1936, box 31, FLM Papers.

20. McVey Diary, 11 June 1936; Minutes of BOT, 23 July 1936; McVey Diary, 14 Aug. 1936; L. S. O'Bannon to Frank McVey, 24 Sept. 1936, box 82, Chandler Papers.

21. James Graham to Frank McVey, 5 Oct. 1937, and Frank McVey to L. S. O'Bannon, 6 Oct. 1937, both box 82, Chandler Papers.

22. L. S. O'Bannon to James Graham, 1 Apr. 1937, and James Graham to L. S. O'Bannon, 7 Apr. 1937, both box 82, Chandler Papers.

23. R. Clay Porter to Frank McVey, 17 May 1937, box 31, FLM Papers.

24. Ibid.

25. Frank McVey to R. Clay Porter, 19 May 1937, box 31, FLM Papers; McVey Diary, 1 June 1937.

26. C. G. Latimer to Frank McVey, 12 June 1937, and Frank McVey to C. G. Latimer, 15 June 1937, both box 82, Chandler Papers.

27. Thomas D. Clark, interview with Charles G. Talbert, 6 May 1974, interview 90OH346 A/F 439, tape, Wethington Alumni/Faculty Project.

28. McVey Diary, 11 Dec. 1937; Frank McVey to L. S. O'Bannon, 10 Feb. 1938, box 82, Chandler Papers; James Graham to Frank McVey, 21 Mar. 1938, and Frank McVey to L. S. O'Bannon, 24 Mar. 1938, both box 82, Chandler Papers.

29. Harry Curtis to W. E. Freeman, 26 Nov. 1937, box 17-B, FLM Papers.

30. Frank McVey to H. C. Anderson, 24 Nov. 1937, box 17-B, FLM Papers.

31. James Graham to Harry Curtis, 9 Dec. 1937, and James Graham to Frank McVey, 1 Dec. 1937, both box 17-B, FLM Papers.

32. Minutes of BOT, 5 Apr., 3 June 1938.

33. Frank McVey to R. M. Hughes, 5 Oct. 1936, box 51, FLM Papers.

34. McVey Diary, 17 Feb., 3 Apr. 1937.

35. "Report of the Special Committee on the State of the University," 1937, box 24, FLM Papers.

36. Ibid.

37. Ibid.

38. Ibid.

39. Minutes of the University Senate, 8 Nov. 1937; McVey Diary, 8 Nov. 1937.

40. R. M. Hughes, "Survey of the University of Kentucky," 1937, box 24, FLM Papers.

41. Ibid.

42. Ibid.

43. Ibid.

44. Ibid.

45. Frank McVey to J. H. Kirkland, 15 Dec. 1936, box 46, FLM Papers.

46. McVey Diary, 4 Feb. 1937.

47. Stanley, *Before Big Blue,* 144–45 (see chapter 5, n. 22); McVey Diary, 22 July 1937.

48. Wallace Muir to A. B. Chandler, 14 Dec. 1936, Chet Wynne to A. B. Chandler, 14 Jan. 1937, and A. B. Chandler to Charles Ishmael, 16 Jan. 1937, all box 81, Chandler Papers.

49. A. B. Chandler to Frank McVey, 31 Aug. 1937, box 31, FLM Papers.

50. Frank McVey to John Lewis, 13 Oct. 1937, box 13, FLM Papers.

51. Enoch Grehan to Frank McVey, 15 Oct. 1937, box 13, FLM Papers.

52. Jasper Shannon, interview with Charles Talbert, 11 July 1973, interview 90OH328 A/F 427, tape, and Neil Plummer, interview with Terry Birdwhistell and Bruce Denbo, 22 July 1981, interview 81OH84 A/F 141, tape, both Wethington Oral History Project.

53. *KK,* 19 Oct. 1937.

54. Minutes of BOT, 20 Oct. 1937.

55. McVey Diary, 20 Oct., 30 Nov. 1937.

56. Shannon, interview, 11 July 1973; Enoch Grehan to Frank McVey, 6 Dec. 1937, box 13, FLM Papers.

57. Enoch Grehan to Frank McVey, 6 Dec. 1937, box 13, FLM Papers.

58. Shannon, interview, 11 July 1973.

59. Stanley, *Before Big Blue,* 145–46; McVey Diary, 23 Dec. 1937.

60. Stanley, *Before Big Blue,* 146–47; *KK,* 11 Jan. 1938; McVey Diary, 11 Jan. 1938.

61. McVey Diary, 13 Jan. 1938.

62. Stanley, *Before Big Blue,* 148–51.

63. Frank McVey to A. B. Chandler, 23 Sept. 1939, box 31, FLM Papers.

64. McVey Diary, 3, 15 Feb. 1938.

65. Minutes of BOT, 24 Feb. 1938.

66. Minutes of BOT, 24 Feb. 1938; McVey Diary, 21 Feb., 13 Dec. 1938.

67. Talbert, *University of Kentucky,* 188 (see chapter 5, n. 115); McVey Diary, 22–23 Apr. 1937; Minutes of BOT, 6 Apr. 1937.

68. McVey Diary, 9 Nov. 1937.

69. Minutes of BOT, 7 Apr. 1936, 24 Feb. 1937.

70. Minutes of BOT, 6 Apr. 1937.

71. Minutes of BOT, 5 Apr. 1938; Thomas Clark, interview with Bruce Denbo, 27 May 1981, interview 81OH75 A/F 136, tape, Wethington Oral History Project.

72. McVey Diary, 3 Mar. 1937; Minutes of BOT, 3 June, 14 Dec. 1937.

73. Minutes of BOT, 6 Apr. 1937.

74. McVey Diary, 14 Sept. 1937; Minutes of BOT, 14 Dec. 1937.

75. Minutes of BOT, 14 Dec., 3 June 1937.

76. Minutes of BOT, 3 June, 6 Apr. 1937.

77. McVey Diary, 8 July 1937; Minutes of BOT, 21 Sept., 20 Oct. 1937.

78. McVey Diary, 24 Dec. 1937.

79. "Report of the Board of Trustees for the Biennium 1935–1937, to the Governor and the Legislature of Kentucky," *Bulletin of the University of Kentucky* 30, no. 1 (1938): 5–6, box 82, Chandler Papers.

80. Ibid., 7–14.

81. Ibid., 5.

82. McVey Diary, 17 Mar. 1938. McVey was told that Chandler was asking the legislature to open junior colleges in Paintsville and Paducah.

83. Minutes of BOT, 3 June, 20 July 1938, 19 Sept. 1939.

84. McVey Diary, 18 Apr. 1939; Minutes of BOT, 19 Sept. 1939.

85. A. B. Chandler to Frank McVey, 19 July 1939, box 31, FLM Papers; James Martin to Frank McVey, 3 July 1939, box 18, FLM Papers; McVey Diary, 19 Oct. 1939; Minutes of BOT, 19 Sept., 15 Dec. 1939.

86. Minutes of BOT, 15 Dec. 1938; Frank McVey to A. B. Chandler, 23 Jan. 1939, box 31, FLM Papers.

87. A. B. Chandler to Frank McVey, 26 Apr. 1939, box 46, FLM Papers; *LCJ,* 8 Mar. 1940.

88. McVey Diary, 17 Feb. 1939; Rufus Clement to Frank McVey, 30 Mar. 1939, box 46, FLM Papers.

89. McVey, *University Is a Place,* 350; McVey Diary, 23 Jan. 1939.

90. "Report of the Governor's Advisory Committee on the Equalization of Higher Education Opportunities for Negroes," 1940, box 46, FLM Papers; *LCJ,* 8 Mar. 1940; Walter White to Frank McVey, 20 Mar. 1940, box 46, FLM Papers.

91. Talbert, *University of Kentucky,* 126; McVey Diary, 12 Dec. 1938.

92. Minutes of BOT, 18 Jan. 1939.

93. McVey Diary, 28 Sept. 1937; Minutes of BOT, 5 Apr. 1938.

94. Minutes of BOT, 5 Apr., 3 June, 3 Aug. 1938; McVey Diary, 29 June 1938, 21 Dec. 1937.

95. *LH,* 28 Jan. 1938.

96. McVey Diary, 2 Aug. 1938; Talbert, *University of Kentucky,* 121–22.

97. *KK,* 17 Jan. 1939.

98. James Graham to Frank McVey, 20 Jan. 1939, box 18, FLM Papers; James Graham to Frank McVey, 16 Jan. 1939, box 17-B, FLM Papers.

99. McVey Diary, 9, 19 Jan. 1939.

100. L. S. O'Bannon to the Board of Trustees, 20 Mar. 1939, box 82, Chandler Papers.

101. Ibid.

102. Ibid.

103. McVey Diary, 4 Apr. 1939; Minutes of BOT, 4 Apr. 1939.

104. Frank McVey to committee members investigating the O'Bannon case, undated memo regarding L. S. O'Bannon, and James C. Humphries to Frank McVey, 16 May 1940, both box 31, FLM Papers.

105. McVey Diary, 26–27 May 1939; *LH,* 27 May 1939; Richard Stoll to Frank McVey, 31 May 1939, box 3-F, FLM Papers; "Report of Band Committee," box 31, FLM Papers.

106. Merrill Blevins to A. B. Chandler, 31 May 1939, and Reid Hoskins to

A. B. Chandler, 30 May 1939, both box 82, Chandler Papers; Richard Stoll to Frank McVey, 31 May 1939, box 3-F, FLM Papers.

107. McVey Diary, 31 Oct. 1939; Minutes of BOT, 15 Dec. 1939.

108. McVey Diary, 21, 26 Dec. 1939, 2 Jan. 1940; Minutes of BOT, 2 Apr. 1940.

109. Minutes of BOT, 15 Dec. 1939; McVey Diary, 26 Jan. 1940; Minutes of BOT, 2 Apr. 1940.

110. Minutes of BOT, 2 Apr. 1940. The minutes suggest that O'Bannon wrote another letter in addition to his letters from 1939. If this is the case, it is not included in the minutes of the Board of Trustees or in box 31 of the FLM Papers, which includes correspondence related to the "O'Bannon Controversy."

111. *LL,* 30 Apr. 1940; McVey Diary, 1 May 1940.

112. *LL,* 2 May 1940; Petition from the College of Law to Frank McVey, 2 May 1940, box 31, FLM Papers.

113. *KK,* 3 May 1940.

114. *KK,* 7 May 1940.

115. Ibid.

116. Ibid.

117. *LL,* 7 May 1940; T. T. Jones to Frank McVey, 8 May 1940, box 28, FLM Papers.

118. *KK,* 10 May 1940; McVey Diary, 10 May 1940.

119. McVey Diary, 6 May 1940; James Graham to Frank McVey, 14 May 1940, box 18, FLM Papers.

120. James Graham to A. B. Chandler, Aug. 1938, box 82, Chandler Papers; McVey Diary, 14 Jan. 1952; Clark, interview, 6 May 1974.

121. L. S. O'Bannon to McVey, 10 June 1936, box 17-B, FLM Papers.

122. McVey Diary, 15 June 1937.

123. McVey Diary, 7 Jan., 14 Feb. 1939; E. G. Tremble to Frank McVey, 27 Feb. 1939, box 12, FLM Papers; Minutes of BOT, 2 June 1939.

124. McVey Diary, 12, 15 July 1939; Keen Johnson to James Shropshire, telegram, 27 July 1939, box 3-A, FLM Papers.

125. "Happy: President, University of Kentucky," pamphlet, n.d., box 82, Chandler Papers; McVey Diary, 20 July 1939.

126. Howell Spears to A. B. Chandler, 19 July 1939, A. B. Chandler to Howell Spears, 26 July 1939, Grant C. Knight to A. B. Chandler, 4 Sept. 1939, and A. B. Chandler to Grant C. Knight, 27 Sept. 1939, all box 82, Chandler Papers.

127. *LH,* 1 Oct. 1939; McVey Diary, 1 Oct. 1939.

128. Klotter, *Kentucky,* 315.

129. Walter Jessup to Frank McVey, 29 June 1939, and Frank McVey to R. C. Stoll, 30 June 1939, both box 3-A, FLM Papers.

130. McVey Diary, 9, 10, 13 Oct., 16 Nov. 1939.

131. E. G. Trimble to Frank McVey, 27 Feb. 1939, box 12, FLM Papers; McVey Diary, 27 Feb., 10 June, 26 Oct., 12 Dec. 1939, 18 Jan., 5 Apr. 1940.

132. Frank McVey to R. C. Stoll, 5 Jan. 1940, box 3-A, FLM Papers; McVey Diary, 14 Mar. 1940.

133. McVey Diary, 24 Jan., 7 Feb., 8 Feb. 1939.

134. Frank McVey to R. C. Stoll, 14 Feb. 1940, box 5-A, FLM Papers.

135. Frank McVey to Charles Friley, 26 Feb. 1940, box 3-A, FLM Papers; McVey Diary, 29 Mar. 1940.

136. McVey Diary, 15 Dec. 1940; *LL,* 5 Mar. 1940; *LCJ,* 5 Apr. 1940.

137. McVey Diary, 21 May 1940; Gifford, interview, 15 Nov. 1972.

138. McVey Diary, 13, 14 May 1940.

139. *LL,* 27 May 1940; *LH,* 28 May 1940; *KK,* 28 May 1940.

140. Minutes of BOT, 7 June 1940.

141. McVey, *University Is a Place,* 9; *KK,* 18 June 1940.

142. McVey Diary, 7 June 1940.

143. McVey Diary, 29 June 1940.

7. Turning the Page

Epigraph: McVey, *University Is a Place,* 297.

1. McVey Diary, 27 Feb. 1938, 19 May 1939.

2. McVey Diary, 28 June 1939.

3. *LCJ,* 11 Aug. 1940.

4. McVey Diary, 1, 14 July 1940.

5. McVey Diary, 24, 27 July, 24–27 Sept. 1940.

6. Frances McVey to Frank McVey, 24 Nov. 1941, box 125, FLM Papers.

7. McVey Diary, 2 July 1940.

8. Talbert, *University of Kentucky,* 135–36 (see chapter 5, n. 115).

9. McVey Diary, 1 Apr. 1941, 28 May 1952.

10. McVey Diary, 14 Mar. 1941.

11. Radio Talks Transcripts, 4, 11, 18 Nov. 1941, box 26, FLM Papers.

12. McVey Diary, 31 Jan., 2, 13 Feb., 12, 13 Mar., 15 Oct. 1942.

13. Diogenes Escalante to Frank McVey, 25 Jan. 1943, box 31-A, FLM Papers.

14. McVey Diary, 9, 30 Apr. 1943.

15. McVey Diary, 30 Apr., 5, 10 May 1943.

16. McVey Diary, 12 May 1943; McVey's Report on Venezuela, box 31-A, FLM Papers.

17. McVey Diary, 8, 12 June 1943.

18. McVey Diary, 28 June, 30 Dec. 1943; *LCJ,* 27 Sept. 1943.

19. McVey Diary, 18, 20, 22, 23 June, 4 July 1943.

20. Minutes of BOT, 17 May 1943; McVey Diary, 8 Sept. 1944.

21. McVey Diary, 30 Sept., 1, 3, 4, 5 Oct. 1944.

22. McVey Diary, 7, 9, 11 Oct. 1944.

23. McVey Diary, 12, 13, 23, 25, 27 Oct., 28 Nov. 1944.

24. McVey Diary, 10, 24 Nov. 1944.

25. McVey Diary, 4, 6 Mar., 5–6, 29 Apr., 5 Mar., 11 May 1945.

26. McVey Diary, 13, 28 May, 12, 13 June 1945.

27. Gifford, interview, 15 Nov. 1972; McVey Diary, 15 July 1945.

28. McVey Diary, 30 July, 13 Oct., 10 Nov., 13 Dec. 1945.

29. McVey Diary, 8 Oct., 23 Nov. 1945, 18 Mar. 1946.

30. McVey Diary, 20 Jan. 1946, 18 Mar. 1944, McVey to H. L. Donovan, 28 Apr. 1944, box 17-A, FLM Papers; *Herald-Leader,* 6 Jan. 1945.

31. *Herald-Leader,* 6 Jan. 1945; McVey Diary, 16 Jan. 1945.

32. McVey Diary, 24 Feb., 3 Mar. 1945; *LH,* 8 Mar. 1945.

33. McVey Diary, 10 Apr. 1945; *LH,* 13 Apr. 1945.

34. McVey Diary, 4 Feb. 1946; *LH,* 20 Feb. 1946.

35. McVey Diary, 19, 20 Feb. 1946.

36. McVey Diary, 22, 26 Feb. 1946.

37. McVey Diary, 5 June 1946; Minutes of BOT, 4, 5 June 1946; McVey Diary, 5 June 1946.

38. McVey Diary, 4 Sept., 15 Mar. 1943; Talbert, *University of Kentucky,* 142 (see chapter 5, n. 115); Clark, *My Century in History,* 218.

39. McVey Diary, 26 Sept. 1945; Minutes of BOT, 17 Oct. 1945; McVey Diary, 14 Nov. 1945.

40. McVey Diary, 20 Oct. 1945.

41. McVey Diary, 26 Dec. 1946, 18 Jan., 11 Aug. 1947, 3 Dec. 1949.

42. McVey Diary, 18 Feb., 26 Mar. 1948; Clark, *My Century in History,* 218.

43. McVey Diary, 24 June, 6 Aug. 1949, 23 June 1950, 3 July 1951; Clark, *My Century in History,* 218.

44. Talbert, *University of Kentucky,* 190.

45. McVey Diary, 17 Oct., 5, 12 Dec. 1945.

46. McVey Diary, 27 Dec. 1945, 22 Mar. 1946.

47. McVey Diary, 6 Sept., 9 July 1946.

48. McVey Diary, 28 June, 9, 22 July, 6 Sept. 1946.

49. McVey Diary 21, 22, 29 Jan. 1948; *LCJ,* 27 Mar. 1948; McVey Diary, 29 Dec. 1946; Talbert, *University of Kentucky,* 190.

50. McVey Diary, 14, 19 Nov. 1942.

51. McVey Diary, 13 Oct., 3 Nov. 1945.

52. Talbert, *University of Kentucky,* 170; McVey Diary, 25 Nov. 1945.

53. McVey Diary, 6 Dec., 12 Jan. 1946.

54. McVey Diary, 21 Sept., 5 Oct. 1946, 11 May, 19 Sept. 1948, 12 Nov. 1950, 1, 9 Jan. 1951.

55. McVey Diary, 5, 7 Jan. 1950, 30 May 1950.

56. McVey Diary, 21 Mar. 1947, 22 Mar. 1949.

57. McVey Diary, 12 Aug., 4 May 1952, 30 Oct. 1951.

58. McVey Dairy, 30 July 1948.

59. McVey Diary, 17 Oct. 1947.

60. Louis Lyon to Frank McVey, 3 May 1950, box 81, FLM Papers; McVey Diary, 21 Sept. 1948; Minutes of the Regional Loyalty Board, 28 Sept. 1948, and Frank McVey to E. F. Ames, 1 Oct. 1948, both box 81, FLM Papers.

61. McVey Diary, 18 Oct. 1948.

62. McVey Diary, 23 Nov. 1948; Frank McVey to Raymond Hughes, 26 Nov. 1948, box 72, FLM Papers.

63. Frank McVey to Raymond Hughes, 26 Nov. 1948, box 72, FLM Papers; McVey Diary, 12, 10 May 1949.

64. Louis Lyon to Frank McVey, 3 May 1950, box 81, FLM Papers.

65. McVey Diary, 12 May 1949, 22 June 1950.

66. McVey Diary, 16 June 1950; Frank McVey to Louis Lyons, 21 Sept. 1951, box 77, FLM Papers.

67. McVey Diary, 18 Apr. 1948, 16 Apr., 8 July 1949; Frank McVey to Aubrey J. Brown, 17 Mar. 1949, box 72, FLM Papers.

68. McVey Diary, 14 Sept. 1950, 27 Feb. 1951.

69. McVey Diary, 22 Apr., 2 May, 22 June 1951.

70. McVey Diary, 27 Mar., 29 May 1952.

71. McVey Diary, 25 Apr., 6 May 1949.

72. McVey Diary, 10 May 1949, 11 Apr., 26 June, 28 Nov. 1950, 10 Oct., 6 Dec. 1951, 1 Feb. 1952.

73. McVey Diary, 25 June 1950, 10 Nov. 1947, 20 Aug. 1950, 30 Oct. 1949, 22 Jan. 1950.

74. McVey Diary, 5 Aug., 5 Nov. 1948, 22 Aug. 1947, 28 Jan. 1950, 17 May 1952.

75. McVey Diary, 20 May 1947, 22 June 1951, 9 Nov., 29 Mar., 22 May 1950.

76. McVey Diary, 17 May, 1 Dec. 1950, 3 Jan. 1952.

77. McVey Diary, 4, 14 May 1946; *LCJ,* 15 May 1946.

78. McVey Diary, 13 June 1947, 30 May 1949, 29 May 1950.

79. McVey Diary, 15 Aug. 1947, 10 Aug. 1948, 11 Aug., 22 Sept. 1950, 1 Feb. 1952.

80. McVey Diary, 10 Nov. 1952; *LL,* 26 Dec. 1952.

81. *LL,* 5 Jan. 1953; *LH,* 7 Jan. 1953.

82. *LCJ,* 6 Jan. 1953.

Conclusion

Epigraph: McVey, *University Is a Place,* 6.

1. Veblen, *Higher Learning in* America, 61; Tribute to Frank L. McVey, 1953, box 14, Thomas Clark Papers, UKA.

2. Tribute to Frank L. McVey, 1953.

3. Ibid.

4. Ibid.

5. Ibid.

6. Roger L. Geiger, *To Advance Knowledge,* 122.

7. McVey, *University Is a Place,* xiii.

Bibliography

Manuscript Collections

Archives and Special Collections. The Elmer L. Anderson Library. University of Minnesota, Minneapolis.

Manuscript Archives and Rare Book Library. Emory University, Atlanta, GA.

Nunn Center for Oral History. University of Kentucky, Lexington.

Ohio Wesleyan University Historical Collection. Delaware, OH.

Special Collections and Archives. Eastern Kentucky University Library, Richmond.

Special Collections and Archives. Margaret I. King Library. University of Kentucky, Lexington.

   Albert B. Chandler Papers

   Frances Jewell McVey Papers

   Frank L. McVey Papers

   Charles G. Talbert Papers

Newspapers

Ariel (former University of Minnesota student newspaper)

Grand Forks Daily Herald

Grand Forks Evening Times

Kentucky Kernel (University of Kentucky student newspaper)

Lexington Herald

Lexington Leader

Louisville Courier-Journal

Louisville Evening Post

Louisville Herald-Post

Louisville Times

Minneapolis Times
Student (University of North Dakota student newspaper)
Western Recorder (Kentucky Southern Baptist publication)

Books and Articles

Barrow, Clyde W. *Universities and the Capitalist State: Corporate Liberalism and the Reconstruction of American Higher Education, 1894–1928.* Madison: University of Wisconsin Press, 1990.

Birdwhistell, Terry L. "A. B. 'Happy' Chandler." In *Kentucky: Its History and Heritage,* ed. Fred J. Hood, 209–20. St. Louis: Forum Press, 1978.

———. "An Educated Difference: Women at the University of Kentucky through the Second World War." PhD dissertation, University of Kentucky, 1994.

Clark, Thomas. "The Book of Thieves of Lexington: A Reminiscence." *Kentucky Review* 5, no. 2 (1985): 39.

———. *My Century in History: Memoirs.* Lexington: University Press of Kentucky, 2006.

Dennis, Michael. *Lessons in Progress: State Universities and Progressivism in the New South, 1880–1920.* Urbana and Chicago: University of Illinois Press, 2001.

Ellis, William. "Frank LeRond McVey: His Defense of Academic Freedom." *Register of the Kentucky Historical Society* 67 (1969): 41.

———. *A History of Eastern Kentucky University: The School of Opportunity.* Lexington: University Press of Kentucky, 2005.

———. "Recurring Crisis: The Evolution/Creation Controversy in Kentucky." *Journal of Kentucky Studies* 1 (1984): 131.

Flatt, Donald F. *A Light to the Mountains: Morehead State University, 1887–1997.* Ashland: Jesse Stuart Foundation, 1997.

Geiger, Louis G. *University of the Northern Plains: A History of the University of North Dakota, 1883–1958.* Grand Forks: University of North Dakota Press, 1958.

Geiger, Roger L. *To Advance Knowledge: The Growth of American Research Universities, 1900–1940.* New York: Oxford University Press, 1986.

Gillis, Ezra, ed. *Henry Stites Barker: A Selection of Speeches and Other Writings by the Second President of the University of Kentucky.* Lexington: University of Kentucky Press, 1956.

Gray, James. *The University of Minnesota, 1851–1951.* Minneapolis: University of Minnesota Press, c. 1951.

Groves, John Russell. "An Examination of Major Initiatives in Campus Planning at the University of Kentucky, 1919–1991." PhD dissertation, University of Kentucky, 1992.

Harrison, Lowell H. *Western Kentucky University*. Lexington: University of Kentucky Press, 1987.

Harvill, James. "The Monkey Trial That Wasn't: University President Frank LeRond McVey's Role in Kentucky's Anti-Evolution Controversy, 1921–1926." Master's thesis, University of Kentucky, 1985.

Hopkins, James F. *The University of Kentucky: Origins and Early Years*. Lexington: University of Kentucky Press, 1951.

Horowitz, Helen. *Campus Life: Undergraduate Cultures from the End of the Eighteenth Century to the Present*. Chicago: University of Chicago Press, 1988.

Klotter, James. *Kentucky: Portrait in Paradox, 1900–1950*. Frankfort: Kentucky Historical Society, 1996.

Levine, David O. *The American College and the Culture of Aspiration, 1915–1940*. Ithaca: Cornell University Press, 1986.

Link, William A. *The Paradox of Southern Progressivism, 1880–1930*. Chapel Hill: University of North Carolina Press, 2001.

Lucas, Christopher. *American Higher Education: A History*. New York: St. Martin's Griffin, 1994.

McCorkle, Michael J. "Efficiency, Influence, and Leadership: The Transformation of State University, 1903–1940." EdD dissertation, University of Kentucky, 2000.

McVey, Frank L. *The Gates Open Slowly*. Lexington: University of Kentucky Press, 1951.

———. *The Government of Minnesota: Its History and Administration*. New York: MacMillan Co., 1901.

———. *Modern Industrialism*. New York: D. Appleton and Company, 1904.

———. "The Populist Movement." American Economic Association: Economic Studies, vol. 1, no. 3. New York: MacMillian Co., 1896.

———. *Railroad Transportation: Some Phases of Its History, Operation and Regulation*. Chicago: Cree Publishing Co., 1910.

———. *A University Is a Place . . . A Spirit: Addresses and Articles by Frank LeRond McVey*. Collected and arranged by Frances Jewell McVey. Lexington: University of Kentucky Press, 1944.

———. "Ways and Means: The Liberal Arts College in the New Social Order." *Journal of Higher Education* 6, no. 4 (April 1935).

Miller, James D. *A Centennial History of the Southern Association of Colleges and Schools, 1895–1995*. Decatur: Southern Association of Colleges and Schools, 1998.

Montgomery, James, and Gerald Gaither. "Evolution and Education in Tennessee: Decisions and Dilemmas." *Tennessee Historical Quarterly* (Summer 1969): 148–51.

Morelock, Kolan Thomas. *Taking the Town: Collegiate and Community Culture in the Bluegrass, 1880–1917.* Lexington: University Press of Kentucky, 2008.

Robinson, Elwyn B. *History of North Dakota.* Lincoln: University of Nebraska Press, 1966.

Rudolph, Frederick. *The American College and University: A History.* New York: A. Knopf, 1962. Reprint, Athens: University of Georgia, 1990.

Slosson, Edwin E. *Great American Universities.* New York: MacMillan Co., 1910.

Smith, J. Allen. *The College of Agriculture of the University of Kentucky: Early and Middle Years, 1865–1951.* Lexington: Agricultural Experiment Station, 1981.

Snider, William D. *Light on the Hill: A History of the University of North Carolina at Chapel Hill.* Chapel Hill: University of North Carolina Press, 1992.

Stanley, Gregory Kent. *Before Big Blue: Sports at the University of Kentucky, 1880–1940.* Lexington: University Press of Kentucky, 1996.

Talbert, Charles Gano. *The University of Kentucky: The Maturing Years.* Lexington: University of Kentucky Press, 1965.

Thelin, John R. *Games Colleges Play: Scandal and Reform in Intercollegiate Athletics.* 2nd ed. Baltimore: Johns Hopkins University Press, 1996.

———. *A History of Higher Education.* Baltimore: Johns Hopkins University Press, 2004.

"Turning the Local Network to a National Channel: Educational Leadership at the College of Education at the University of Kentucky." *Register of the Kentucky Historical Society* 93, no. 3 (1995): 312–17.

Veblen, Thorstein. *The Higher Learning in America: A Memorandum on the Conduct of Universities by Business Men.* Reprint, New York: Sagamore Press, 1957.

Veysey, Laurence R. *The Emergence of the American University.* Chicago: University of Chicago Press, 1970.

Wilson, Louis Round. *The University of North Carolina, 1900–1930: The Making of a Modern University.* Chapel Hill: University of North Carolina Press, 1957.

Index